Praise for Eri Hotta's

JAPAN 1941

"An outstanding guide to [Japan's] devastating decision [to go to war in the Pacific]. In lucid prose, Hotta meticulously examines a wide range of primary documents in Japanese . . . [and] persuasively sketches the very distinct personalities shaping the decisions that drove Japan toward war. . . . Historians will welcome Hotta's nuanced research showing the hypocrisy in Japan's position. . . . She makes it clear that there are two versions of the Asia-Pacific War in China and Japan that hardly meet at all . . . [and] concludes that after 1945, Japan's actual 'past, with its improbable story of how the war came to pass, became another country.' It is a country the policymakers in Tokyo, Beijing, and Washington should seek to understand, not least through this humane and fair-minded book."

—*The New York Review of Books*

"Superb. . . . Helps us to better fathom the mind-set of Japanese leaders at the time. . . . Hotta explains why the leaders came to take such a big chance by going to war, attributing the fateful decision to a gambler's high—and a feverish hope that the steep odds would somehow be overcome."   —*The Japan Times*

"A fascinating read for anyone interested in Japan's involvement in World War II. . . . While scholarly and thoroughly researched, it's also a highly enjoyable read. . . . A real page-turner."
—*Library Journal*

"In this focused, informed and persuasive book . . . Hotta effortlessly returns us to the moment just before the dice were so disastrously rolled. From a perspective little known to Americans, a masterful account of how and why World War II began."
—*Kirkus Reviews*

"Finely nuanced. . . . [Hotta] forcefully reframes how we should consider the Japanese with respect to their positions as emerging world powers in [an] . . . era of international turmoil.
—Asian American Literature Fans

"In this fast-moving, persuasive account of Japan's road to Pearl Harbor, Eri Hotta describes the pathetic leadership of a country who argue among themselves endlessly when the crisis across the Pacific requires decisive action to preserve the peace. It is a story of self-delusion, irresponsibility, and ignorance from which Japan is not entirely free even today."
—Akira Iriye, author of *Pearl Harbor and the Coming of the Pacific War*

"[Hotta] synergizes Western and Japanese sources, including much new material, in this nuanced analysis of a decision that was neither inevitable nor irrational. . . . Hotta painstakingly guides her readers through a convoluted mesh of personalities and principles."
—*History Book Club*

ERI HOTTA

JAPAN 1941

Eri Hotta, born in Tokyo and educated in Japan, the United States, and Britain, has taught at Oxford, in Tokyo, and in Jerusalem, specializing in international relations.

ALSO BY ERI HOTTA

Pan-Asianism and Japan's War,
1931–1945

JAPAN 1941

JAPAN 1941

Countdown to Infamy

ERI HOTTA

VINTAGE BOOKS
A Division of Random House LLC
New York

FIRST VINTAGE BOOKS EDITION, AUGUST 2014

Copyright © 2013 by Eri Hotta

All rights reserved. Published in the United States by Vintage Books,
a division of Random House LLC, New York, and in Canada by Random House
of Canada Limited, Toronto, Penguin Random House companies. Originally
published in hardcover in the United States by Alfred A. Knopf, a division of
Random House LLC, New York, in 2013.

Vintage and colophon are registered trademarks of Random House LLC.

All photographs in the text are from the archives of *Mainichi Shimbun*, with the
exception of page 5, middle, and page 6, top left, courtesy of the Naval History
and Heritage Command; page 7, top right, courtesy of Hiroko Anzai; and page 8,
top, courtesy of the Franklin D. Roosevelt Presidential Library and Museum.

The Library of Congress has cataloged the Knopf edition as follows:
Hotta, Eri.
Japan 1941 : countdown to infamy / Eri Hotta. — First Edition
Includes bibliographical references and index.
1. World War, 1939–1945—Japan.
2. Military planning—Japan—History—20th century.
3. Japan—Military policy—20th century.
4. Japan—Politics and government—1926–1945. 5. War—Decision making.
6. Pearl Harbor (Hawaii), Attack on, 1941. I. Title.
D767.2.H67 2013
940.54'0952—DC23   2013014781

Vintage Trade Paperback ISBN: 978-0-307-73974-2
eBook ISBN: 978-0-385-35051-8

Map by Mapping Specialists
Book design by Cassandra J. Pappas

www.vintagebooks.com

Printed in the United States of America
10   9   8   7   6   5

To JLH

There is a tide in the affairs of men,
Which, taken at the flood, leads on to fortune;
Omitted, all the voyage of their life
Is bound in shallows and in miseries.
On such a full sea are we now afloat;
And we must take the current when it serves,
Or lose our ventures.

—SHAKESPEARE, *Julius Caesar*

Contents

A Note on Names, Translations, and Sources   xi
Map of the Asia-Pacific Region in 1941   xii
List of Major Characters   xv
Selected Events in Japanese History Prior to April 1941   xvii
Japanese Military Leadership in 1941   xxv

PROLOGUE   What a Difference a Day Makes   3
CHAPTER 1   Rumors of War   23
CHAPTER 2   The Return of Don Quixote   58
CHAPTER 3   The Beginning of It All   76
CHAPTER 4   The Soldier's Dilemmas   89
CHAPTER 5   Good Riddance, Good Friends   108
CHAPTER 6   Japan's North-South Problem   119
CHAPTER 7   A Quiet Crisis in July   136
CHAPTER 8   "Meet Me in Juneau"   149
CHAPTER 9   An Unwinnable, Inevitable War   164
CHAPTER 10   One Last Opportunity   178
CHAPTER 11   A Soldier Takes Over   205
CHAPTER 12   Winding Back the Clock   219
CHAPTER 13   On the Brink   230

CHAPTER 14   "No Last Word Between Friends"   242

CHAPTER 15   The Hull Note   261

CHAPTER 16   Jumping Off the High Platform   269

EPILOGUE   The New Beginning   279

Acknowledgments   295

Notes   297

Index   311

A Note on Names, Translations, and Sources

All the Japanese sources cited in this book were published in Tokyo.

I have translated all Japanese sources unless otherwise indicated in the notes.

I have preserved the traditional spelling of Konoye for Konoe in contemporaneous quotations. In all other cases, Japanese names and words are Romanized in the simplified Hepburn system, without macrons to indicate long vowels.

Throughout this book, I have respected the convention of placing the family name first for Japanese men and women (e.g., Tojo Hideki rather than Hideki Tojo). That convention is reversed only when I cite English-language sources and in the acknowledgments.

Chinese names are expressed according to the standard pinyin Romanization system, but with some exceptions. For well known historical Chinese names, including Sun Yat-sen (Sun Zhongshan), Chiang Kai-shek (Jiang Jieshi), and Manchukuo (Manzhouguo), I have preserved the convention of English-language literature of the time.

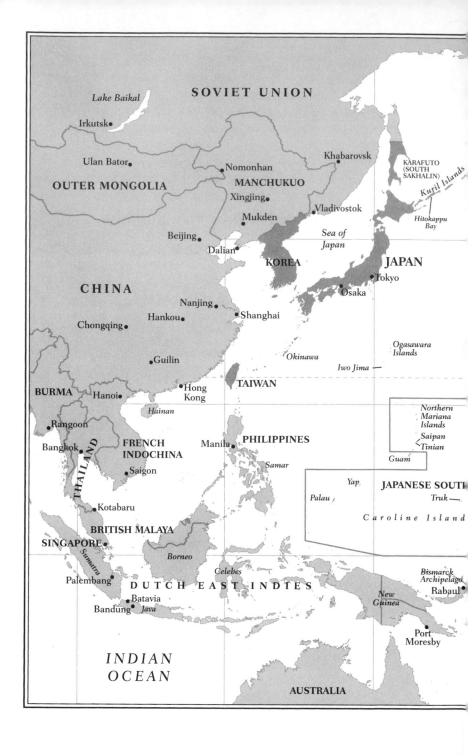

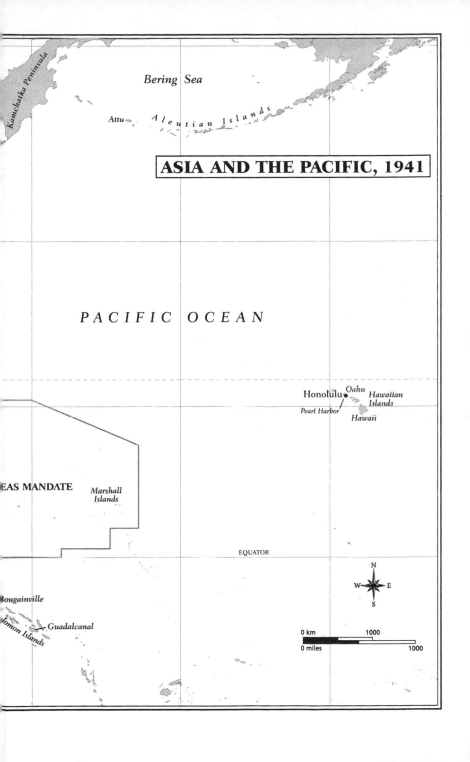

Bering Sea

Kamchatka Peninsula

Attu *Aleutian Islands*

ASIA AND THE PACIFIC, 1941

PACIFIC OCEAN

Honolulu *Oahu* *Hawaiian Islands*
Pearl Harbor *Hawaii*

EAS MANDATE *Marshall Islands*

EQUATOR

Bougainville
Solomon Islands Guadalcanal

0 km 1000
0 miles 1000

Major Characters

HIGASHIKUNI NARUHIKO Imperial prince; army general known for his liberal views; uncle by marriage of Emperor Hirohito

HIROHITO Showa emperor; ruled Japan from 1926 to 1989

KAYA OKINORI Finance minister from October 1941

KIDO KOICHI Marquis; lord keeper of the privy seal since June 1940; Hirohito's closest adviser

KONOE FUMIMARO Prince; prime minister from June 1937 to January 1939 and from July 1940 to October 1941 who led Japan during most of its period of intensifying international crisis

KURUSU SABURO Ambassador to Berlin at the time of the Konoe government's signing of the Tripartite Pact

MATSUOKA YOSUKE Konoe's foreign minister from July 1940 to July 1941; spearheaded Japan's pro-Axis diplomacy, which culminated in the signing of the Tripartite Pact in September 1940

NAGANO OSAMI Admiral; chief of the Navy General Staff from April 1941

NOMURA KICHISABURO Admiral; appointed ambassador to the United States in January 1941

OIKAWA KOSHIRO Admiral; Konoe's navy minister from September 1940

SAIONJI KINKAZU Foreign policy aide to Prime Minister Konoe; grandson of Prince Saionji Kinmochi

SAIONJI KINMOCHI Prince; the last surviving founding father of modern Japan and one of its most powerful statesmen; once regarded Konoe as his protégé

SHIMADA SHIGETARO Admiral; navy minister who succeeded Oikawa in October 1941

SUGIYAMA HAJIME General; chief of the Army General Staff from 1940; army minister in Konoe's first cabinet (1937–39), which exacerbated Japan's war with China

SUZUKI TEIICHI General director of the Cabinet Planning Board; retired army officer trusted by both Konoe and Tojo who often acted as a liaison between the two

TAKAMATSU NOBUHITO Imperial prince; member of the Navy General Staff in 1941; younger brother of Emperor Hirohito

TOGO SHIGENORI Ambassador to Berlin and Moscow in the late 1930s; became foreign minister in October 1941

TOJO HIDEKI General; army minister in the Konoe cabinet from January 1939 to October 1941; became prime minister after Konoe resigned

TOYODA TEIJIRO Admiral; Konoe's foreign minister from July 1941; vice minister of the navy at the time of the signing of the Tripartite Pact

Selected Events in Japanese History
Prior to April 1941

Here and throughout the book, the dates are indicated in local times.

1853   **July** Commodore Matthew Perry presses Japan to end its isolationist policy.

1854   **March 31** The Tokugawa shogunate signs the unfavorable Treaty of Peace and Amity with the United States, ending its isolationist policy and leading to the opening of Japanese ports to the rest of the world.

1868   **January 3** The shogunate falls and the Meiji Restoration is proclaimed.

1882   **January 4** The Imperial Rescript to Soldiers and Sailors, a code of military conduct that will form a vital part of Japanese nationalism, is issued.

1889   **February 11** The Meiji Constitution is promulgated.

1890 **July 1** Japan holds its first general elections.

November 25 The first session of the Diet, Japan's bicameral parliament, is summoned, and held four days later.

1894 **August 1** Japan declares war on Qing China, beginning the Sino-Japanese War.

1895 **April 17** Japan defeats China, concluding the war with the signing of the Treaty of Shimonoseki, placing Taiwan and the Liaodong Peninsula, strategically located to access northeastern China (Manchuria), under Japanese control.

April 23 Russia, Germany, and France pressure Japan to return the Liaodong Peninsula to China (the so-called Triple Intervention), which it does on May 5.

1898 **March 27** Russia secures a leasehold on the Liaodong Peninsula.

1902 **January 30** The Anglo-Japanese Alliance, a treaty between equals, is formed.

1904 **February 8** Japan attacks czarist Russia at Port Arthur, declaring war two days later.

1905 **May 27–28** The Japanese navy scores a major victory in the Battle of Tsushima.

September 5 The Russo-Japanese War ends with the signing of the Treaty of Portsmouth, through the mediation of U.S. president Theodore Roosevelt.

November 17 Korea becomes a Japanese protectorate.

1906 **August 1** Japan forms the Kwantung Army to protect its Manchurian possessions, newly acquired from Russia.

1910 **August 29** Japan annexes Korea.

1912 **July 30** Mutsuhito, the Meiji emperor, dies, succeeded by his son, Yoshihito.

1914 **July 28** World War I breaks out.

August 23 Japan goes to war with Germany, enabling it to take over German possessions in China and the Pacific by November.

1915 **January 18** Japan issues the Twenty-One Demands to Yuan Shikai's China, but fails to win diplomatic concessions while antagonizing the Chinese.

1918 **November 11** World War I ends, followed by the convocation of the Paris Peace Conference in 1919.

1922 **February 6** Japan ratifies the Nine-Power Treaty and the Washington Naval Treaty, commencing the era of Japan's liberal internationalist foreign policy.

1923 **September 1** The Great Kanto Earthquake and the ensuing fire destroy much of Tokyo.

1926 **December 25** Yoshihito dies and Crown Prince Hirohito becomes the emperor.

1929 **October 29** Black Tuesday marks the beginning of the Great Depression.

1930 January 21 The London Naval Conference begins.

November 4 Prime Minister Hamaguchi Osachi is gravely wounded by an ultranationalist for supporting Japan's ratification of the London Naval Treaty.

1931 September 18 The Kwantung Army launches the Manchurian Incident, a Japanese invasion of northeastern China, after blowing up a railway line near Mukden and blaming the act on the Chinese.

September 24 Prime Minister Wakatsuki Reijiro's cabinet condones the military insubordination by accepting the Kwantung Army's takeover of the Manchurian province of Jilin.

1932 March 1 The establishment of Manchukuo, a Japanese puppet state with nominal Chinese leaders, is proclaimed by the Kwantung Army.

October 2 The Lytton Commission issues its report condemning the Japanese invasion of Manchuria.

1933 January 28 The Kwantung Army occupies Rehe, a buffer province between Manchukuo and China (in today's northern Hebei Province), with a view to establishing a stronghold in North China.

February 24 Matsuoka Yosuke, Japan's ambassador plenipotentiary, announces his country's intention to withdraw from the League of Nations over its adoption of the Lytton Report.

May 31 Japan successfully pressures the Guomindang (a.k.a. Kuomintang, often referred to as the Chinese Nationalist Party) leader Chiang Kai-shek to agree to the Tanggu Truce, creating a demilitarized zone in eastern Hebei, near Manchukuo's borders.

1935   **June** Japanese pressures on Chiang Kai-shek increase, prompting him to withdraw his troops from Hebei, and Chahar, Inner Mongolia, enabling Japan to secure its sphere of influence around Manchukuo.

1936   **February 26** A coup attempt in Tokyo instigated by young army officers almost succeeds, but Hirohito's decisive intervention quells it.

December 12 Chiang Kai-shek is kidnapped by the anti-Japanese warlord Zhang Xueliang, who forces Chiang to reassess his policy, eventually making him agree to join a united front against Japan, in cooperation with Chinese Communists.

1937   **June 4** Konoe Fumimaro becomes prime minister.

July 7 The China War begins with a Sino-Japanese clash at the Marco Polo Bridge near Beijing.

December 13 Japanese forces conquer the Guomindang capital, Nanjing, followed by weeks of mass killing and rape.

1938   **January 16** Prime Minister Konoe declares that Japan will not "deal with" Chiang Kai-shek.

March 24 The National Mobilization Law is passed in the Diet, followed by a series of emergency centralization measures to carry out Japan's effective war mobilization.

July 1 The United States begins its "moral embargo" on aircraft and aircraft parts against Japan.

November 3 Konoe announces that Japan's aim in the war against China is to help create a "New East Asian Order."

1939 **January 5** Konoe's cabinet resigns.

February 10 The Japanese occupation of Hainan Island begins.

July 26 The United States announces its intention to abrogate the 1911 Treaty of Commerce and Navigation with Japan.

1940 **March 30** Wang Jingwei forms a pro-Japanese government in Japanese-occupied Nanjing.

May 7 Pearl Harbor is made the main base for the U.S. Pacific Fleet.

June 4 The United States embargoes exports of industrial equipment to Japan.

June 14 German forces begin to invade Paris, leading to the fall of France.

July 22 Konoe becomes prime minister for the second time; Matsuoka Yosuke becomes foreign minister.

From late July to early August U.S. exports of metals, aviation gasoline, and lubricating oil to Japan come under strict federal control.

August 1 Matsuoka uses the term "Greater East Asia Coprosperity Sphere" to sum up the government's ambition to build a self-sufficient regional bloc under Japan's leadership.

September 23–29 Japan occupies the northern half of French Indochina.

September 25 The United States increases its financial assistance to Chiang Kai-shek.

September 26 The United States embargoes the sale of steel and scrap iron to Japan, to go into effect on October 16.

September 27 Japan signs the Tripartite Pact with Germany and Italy.

October 12 The Imperial Rule Assistance Association is formed under Konoe's presidency, putting an end to Japan's party politics and beginning the New Order Movement.

October 31 Dance halls are closed and jazz performances become illegal in Japan.

November 10 The twenty-six-hundred-year reign of the Japanese imperial house is celebrated nationwide.

1941 **January 8** Army Minister Tojo Hideki issues "Instructions for the Battlefield," commanding soldiers to die a soldier's death rather than become captives; this code, glorifying heroic death, will form the basis of Japan's wartime credo.

February 11 The Japanese ambassador to the United States, Nomura Kichisaburo, arrives in Washington, D.C.

March 12 Matsuoka leaves for his grand tour of Europe to meet Japan's Axis partners, Hitler and Mussolini.

JAPANESE MILITARY LEADERSHIP IN 1941

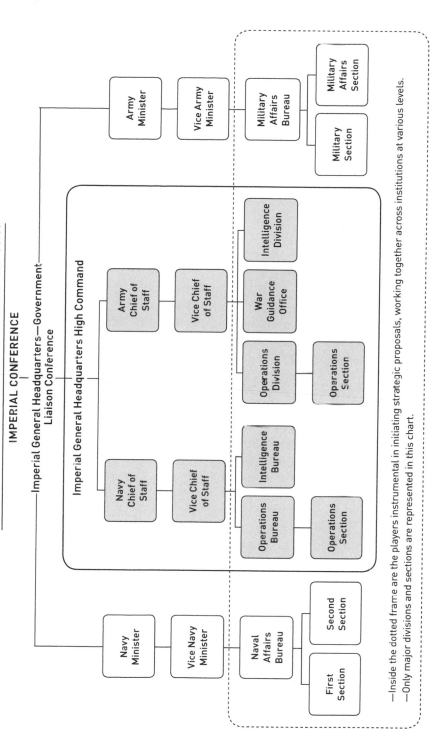

IMPERIAL CONFERENCE

—Imperial General Headquarters—Government
Liaison Conference

Imperial General Headquarters High Command

Army Minister

Vice Army Minister

Military Affairs Bureau

Military Section

Military Affairs Section

Army Chief of Staff

Vice Chief of Staff

War Guidance Office

Intelligence Division

Operations Division

Operations Section

Navy Chief of Staff

Vice Chief of Staff

Operations Bureau

Intelligence Bureau

Operations Section

Navy Minister

Vice Navy Minister

Naval Affairs Bureau

First Section

Second Section

—Inside the dotted frame are the players instrumental in initiating strategic proposals, working together across institutions at various levels.
—Only major divisions and sections are represented in this chart.

JAPAN 1941

What a Difference a Day Makes

I n the early-morning hours of a frosty day, December 8, 1941, the Japanese nation woke to astonishing news. It was announced, shortly after seven, that Japan had "entered into a situation of war with the United States and Britain in the Western Pacific before dawn." Though no specifics were given, by then the U.S. naval base at Pearl Harbor, on Oahu, had been successfully attacked—the first wave of planes was dispatched at 1:30 a.m., Japanese time, and the surprise operation was completed by 5:30 a.m. When news of the attack arrived at 11:30 a.m., the nation was electrified. This was soon followed by Japan's formal declaration of war on the Allies and the report of its further military successes in British Malaya and Hong Kong. (The Malayan operation actually preceded the Pacific offensive by almost two hours.) Throughout the day, the public broadcasting network, NHK, aired twelve special news reports in addition to six regularly scheduled ones for the millions of Japanese glued to their radios.

On what, because of the time difference, had been December 7 in Hawaii, the air force division of the Imperial Japanese Navy had sunk or damaged numerous ships, aircraft, and military facilities. About twenty-four hundred people were killed in the raid or died shortly afterward from their injuries. The devastating attack was carried out without a formal termination of diplomatic relations by Japan, let alone a declaration of war, a heavy, infamous legacy for the nation. But such tactical details did not interest ordinary Japanese citizens on December 8. The immediate public reaction was one of celebration.

When Japan sent planes to attack Pearl Harbor, it was mired in economic and political uncertainties. A sense of helplessness pervaded its population as the state took more and more control of public life. From the beginning of Japan's war with China in mid-1937, its people were led to believe a swift, decisive victory was imminent. Despite all the announcements of Japanese victories in China, however, the Guomindang (a.k.a. Kuomintang, frequently referred to as the Nationalist Party) leader Chiang Kai-shek was not about to give up. Similar to Napoleon's army in Russia, the Japanese forces were drawn far too deep into harsh, unfamiliar terrain to carry out an effective operation. The jingoistic tone of Japan's media coverage continued regardless, but people were privately beginning to question why the war had not ended. Though largely ignorant of the true state of Japanese diplomacy, they had been told that Nomura Kichisaburo, a navy admiral and former foreign minister, had been dispatched to Washington, D.C., in early 1941 to negotiate a peaceful solution to Japan's international isolation. But no good news was forthcoming, and its absence made people fearful. Many knew the United States was upset over recent Japanese initiatives—such as allying with Hitler's Germany and Mussolini's Italy and occupying first northern and then southern French Indochina—and seemed intent, unless a diplomatic settlement could be reached soon, on crippling Japan with economic sanctions.

In everyday life, luxury goods had quickly disappeared, and there was a shortage of food, most noticeably the main staple, rice. As the conflict in China went on and on, those remaining in the countryside—the best men had gone to the military and war-related industries—faced increased pressure to produce more food for the troops. Starting in the summer of 1940, even the fanciest restaurants in Tokyo resorted to serving cheaper imported rice—the drier kind some scornfully called "mouse poops"—mixed with potatoes. After April 1941, in six major metropolitan cities once replete with all the conveniences of modern life, people could obtain rice only with ration coupons. By December 1941, this system applied to 99 percent of Japan. In a country where domestically grown rice occupied an exalted, almost sacred place in the national diet, this was seen as a scandalous hardship.

Life was becoming monochromatic—or "grave yard–ish," in the words of a contemporary observer. Fashionable men and women, who until recently dressed in colorful kimonos or the latest Western-style clothes and spent their time in cinemas and dance halls, now tried to look as inconspicuous as possible. The novelist Nagai Kafu (known as Kafu), an aging bohemian chronicler of urban life who felt as much at home in the opium dens of New York's Chinatown and the cafés of Montmartre as he did in the raffish parts of old Tokyo, deplored those changes. A tall, scrawny man, Kafu did not strike one as a fussy dresser. He actually knew and cared a lot about fashion—a remnant of his high-bourgeois upbringing—though he made sure not to look too perfect in his well-tailored European suits. But he felt the recent Japanese inattention to keeping up appearances had gone too far, even for his unorthodox taste. In the autumn of 1940, the sixty-year-old complained in his diary:

> The townscape [of central Tokyo] belies its prosperity of only half a year ago. There are no activities and it is all quiet. Around 6:00 p.m., it fills with crowds of commuters just as before. But the clothes that those men and women are wearing! To say that they have become subdued is an understatement. They have become old-mannish and dowdy. Women do not seem to care what they look like anymore, not bothering to put on any makeup. The street does not get lit at night, so people hurry home. Those people who squeeze themselves into the trains, shoving one another, look like refugees.

The deglamorization of city life signified the resounding triumph of a publicity campaign to promote nationwide austerity—prompted by the prolongation of Japanese military engagement in China—that started in the summer of 1940. Fifteen hundred signs bearing slogans such as "A True Japanese Cannot Afford to Be Indulgent" and "Luxury Is the Enemy" (*Zeitaku wa Tekida*) were put up all over Tokyo (though the insertion of one syllable by a graffitist often turned the latter phrase into "Luxury Is Wonderful" [*Zeitaku wa Su-Tekida*]).

Volunteers from patriotic women's associations took to the streets, leading this campaign. These righteous women admonished those who, in their vigilant eyes, wore the kind of lavish clothes they themselves had given up, and they handed out note cards asking them to "please exercise self-restraint." Women who wore permed hairdos, rings, nail polish, lipstick, or gold-rimmed glasses were also targeted because they were seen as endorsing a "corrupt" and "individualistic" Western lifestyle. There was some angry resistance to this type of witch-hunting. One woman was spotted crying and shouting hysterically, "I can't stand this!" A young man strutted down the street wearing makeup, daring the patriotic fashion police: "Well, aren't you going to say something?" But these were very small acts of defiance in the larger scheme of things.

Department stores, once places where dreams were sold, came under strict surveillance, too. Every store was told to enforce a one-item-per-customer policy to discourage excessive spending, which was deemed disrespectful of the general austerity efforts. In 1935, the cosmetics company Shiseido began having beautifully presented "service girls" give free makeup lessons to customers at its department store counters, increasing sales of its beauty lotion twenty-three-fold within two years. But as the China War dragged on, "wartime care packages" replaced cosmetics as top-selling products. These packages, filled with little snacks, handkerchiefs, pencils, and notepads, were sent to soldiers at the front as a show of moral support from home.

On the evening of October 31, 1940, the night before dance halls and jazz performances were to become illegal (they, too, were thought to undermine people's sense of morality and public order), every hall was packed with men and women having one last, desperate fling. They crowded the dance floors like "new potatoes being boiled up in a pot, constantly bumping into one another," as the metropolitan newspaper *Asahi* reported the following day. In fact, only women who were professional dancers had been allowed in dance halls since mid-1938, and their numbers had declined by half, having been pressured to join women's associations, which competed with one another for recruits and urged new members to take up more "respectable" (but much less profitable) jobs as typists and factory workers. But that evening, even after the bands had finished playing the farewell song of "Auld Lang Syne," the men and women refused to leave the dance floors, as if to defy—again, in a very small, too small, way—the coming of Japan's long journey into night.

But December 8, 1941, changed everything. The gloom of the national impasse that had arisen over the past couple of years turned almost instantly into euphoria as most Japanese cheered the successful attack. A man who was a second grader at the time of the attack, whose father owned a radio shop in Tokyo, recalled his surprise at the sight of a long line forming in front of his father's store. People were waiting to get their radio sets repaired, in anticipation of more special government announcements. He never saw his father do so much business in one day before or after.

There was very little of the famous Japanese reserve. Strangers congratulated each other on the street. Others gathered at the public square outside the Imperial Palace in the heart of Tokyo, falling to the ground and thanking the emperor for his divine guidance of their nation. Aboard an overcrowded train that evening, the diarist Kafu detachedly observed "a fellow making speeches in shrill voice," apparently unable to contain his excitement over the day's news. This outpouring of emotion stood in stark contrast to the many contrived victory celebrations orchestrated by the government over the previous few years in an effort to rouse support for its lingering war in China.

Men of letters were not immune to the Pearl Harbor spell. One of the most distinguished poets of twentieth-century Japan, Saito Mokichi, fifty-nine at the time, recorded in his diary: "The red blood of my old age is now bursting with life! . . . Hawaii has been attacked!" The thirty-six-year-old novelist Ito Sei wrote in his journal: "A fine deed. The Japanese tactic wonderfully resembles the one employed in the Russo-Japanese War." Indeed, that war started with Japan's surprise attack on Russian ships in Port Arthur on February 8, 1904, two days before Japan's formal declaration of war. Japan won that war.

Even those Japanese who had previously disapproved of their country's expansionism in Asia were excited by Japan's war with the West. In an instant, the official claim, gradually adopted by the Japanese government over the preceding decade, of liberating Asia from Western encroachment gained legitimacy in their eyes. Until then, the innately self-contradictory nature of fighting an anti-imperialist war for Asia against fellow Asians in China had tormented them. Takeuchi Yoshimi, a thirty-one-year-old Sinologist, now said he and his friends had been mistaken in doubting their leaders' true intentions:

Until this very moment, we feared that Japan, hiding behind the beautiful slogan of "Building East Asia," was bullying the weak. [But now we realize that] our Japan was not afraid of the powerful after all. . . . Let us together fight this difficult war.

Despite the celebratory mood that dominated the country on December 8, there were still people with cool minds and hearts who were doubtful about, if not dismayed by, Japan's new war. Private sentiments also often differed substantially from the public outbursts of joy. Many were simply tired of war and its restrictions on daily life. Others seriously worried about their loved ones having to fight.

A nine-year-old in a rice-growing village forty-five miles (seventy-two kilometers) northeast of Tokyo learned of the Pearl Harbor attack when he came home from school. His mother had been waiting for him outside their house. She cried and said, "We're at war." Those were no tears of joy; rather, she was anxious for the lives of her six older sons. If this war was to be anything like the China War, who knew how long it would go on, and the new war might even take her youngest away. The boy was struck by the vivid contrast between the deep sadness of families all over his village and the upbeat voice coming out of the radio.

The small number of Japanese with substantial knowledge of the West could not celebrate, either. They were too aware of Japan's limited resources and were convinced that the country would be annihilated in the end. A young man working for Mitsubishi Heavy Industries in Nagoya recalled a strange combination of exhilaration and fear upon hearing the radio announcement at work. Though he felt a certain satisfaction over the successful attack on Pearl Harbor, he was afraid of what awaited Japan in the long term. His workplace, dedicated to the manufacturing of the Zero fighter plane, would become a prime target of U.S. bombing in a few years' time. Many of his colleagues perished, and he would barely escape death himself.

But to voice such concerns in the midst of post–Pearl Harbor excitement was to risk arrest for insufficient patriotism. A great tidal wave of enthusiasm following victories in the Pacific and Southeast Asia was felt by most Japanese. They were able to forget, at least for the moment, the immensity of the task that lay ahead.

ON THE OTHER SIDE of the Pacific, Pearl Harbor had stimulated an equally pervasive and patriotic response. President Franklin Delano Roosevelt delivered a speech to a joint session of Congress in a measured but determined voice: "Yesterday, December 7, 1941—a date which will live in infamy—the United States of America was suddenly and deliberately attacked by naval and air forces of the Empire of Japan." Roosevelt's cabinet, led by Secretary of State Cordell Hull, initially urged the president to present to Congress a comprehensive history of Japan's international misconduct. Roosevelt decided instead on an accessible five-hundred-word speech so that his message would get through to as many people as possible: The Japanese attack was treacherous, and the United States had to defeat this cowardly enemy, no matter what it took.

The presidential tactic to stir his nation's deepest emotions against Japan succeeded. The isolationist opposition with which Roosevelt had been struggling over his desire to take the United States into the European theater of war was nowhere to be seen, and his request for a declaration of war was immediately approved, with just one dissenting vote, cast by Jeannette Rankin, a pacifist Republican from Montana. From that historic moment on, Pearl Harbor was etched in the American psyche, reinforced by the powerful battle cry memorialized in the hit song "Remember Pearl Harbor." Recorded within ten days of the attack, it urged Americans: "Let's remember Pearl Harbor as we go to meet the foe. Let's remember Pearl Harbor as we did the Alamo. . . . Let's remember Pearl Harbor and go on to victory!"

Hawaii must have seemed almost like an exotic foreign country to the majority of Americans before the Japanese attack. Ironically, Japanese and Americans of Japanese ancestry accounted for nearly 40 percent of its population. Now this unique island territory in the peaceful Pacific Ocean suddenly found itself forever ensconced at the heart of the U.S. patriotic narrative.

The Pearl Harbor attack also changed the fate of those already at war. Chiang Kai-shek was jubilant when he heard the news. He reportedly played "Ave Maria" on his gramophone (he was a converted Methodist) and danced. Many months of lonely fighting were finally over for Britain, too. Winston Churchill was dining with the U.S. envoy Averell Harriman and the U.S. ambassador, John Gilbert Winant, when he received a call from Roosevelt, informing him of the attack. That night, Churchill said, he "went to bed and slept the sleep of the saved and thankful." Hitler's declaration of war on the United States four days later reaffirmed Churchill's feeling of relief.

ON DECEMBER 8, 1941, cinemas and theaters in Japan were made to temporarily suspend their evening performances and broadcast a speech recorded by Prime Minister Tojo Hideki earlier that day. U.S. films—films such as *Mr. Smith Goes to Washington*, which the Japanese relished in easier times—were now officially banned. That night, audiences were confronted with the voice of a leader who hardly resembled Jimmy Stewart.

Tojo was a bald and bespectacled man of middle age with no remarkable features other than his mustache. His exaggerated buckteeth existed only in Western caricatures, but he did not look like a senior statesman who had just taken his country to war against a most formidable enemy, and his voice was memorable only for its dullness. He recited the speech, "On Accepting the Great Imperial Command," with the affected diction of a second-rate stage actor.

> Our elite Imperial Army and Navy are now fighting a desperate battle. Despite the empire's every possible effort to salvage it, the peace of the whole of East Asia has collapsed. In the past, the government employed every possible means to normalize U.S.-Japan diplomatic relations. But the United States would not yield an inch on its demands. Quite the opposite. The United States has strengthened its ties with Britain, the Netherlands, and China, demanding unilateral concessions from our Empire, including the complete and unconditional withdrawal of the imperial forces from China, the rejection of the [Japanese puppet] Nanjing government, and the annulment of the Tripartite Pact with Germany and Italy. Even in the face of such demands, the Empire persistently strove for a peaceful settlement. But the United States to this day refused to reconsider its position. Should the Empire give in to all its demands, not only would Japan lose its prestige and fail to see the China Incident to its completion, but its very existence would be in peril.

Tojo, in his selective explanation of the events leading to Pearl Harbor, insisted that the war Japan had just initiated was a "defensive" war. He faithfully echoed Japan's deep-seated feelings of persecution, wounded national pride, and yearning for greater recognition, which together might be called, for the want of a better phrase, anti-Westernism. It was a sentimental speech, and it was notable for what was left unsaid.

There had been no clear-cut, overwhelming consensus among the Japanese leaders to take preemptive actions in the Pacific and Southeast Asia. Many remained hopelessly uncertain and ambivalent about their decision. True, Tojo is famous for having said, "Occasionally, one must conjure up enough courage, close one's eyes, and jump off the platform of the Kiyomizu," and these words, referencing a Buddhist temple in Kyoto known for a veranda that juts out over a cliff, are often cited as a sign of his rash adventurism. But even Tojo, vilified as a military dictator who blindly pushed Japan into war, felt torn, especially in the two months preceding the attack. Throughout the course of the government's final discussions over going to war, Tojo was acutely aware of the small possibility of Japanese victory. As a result, at the last minute, he tried to conciliate those who argued for immediate war. When he became prime minister on October 18, 1941, the first task he set himself was to attempt to resurrect diplomatic options with the United States.

Some leaders were misguidedly hopeful, but *none* were confident of Japan's eventual victory. Tojo's predecessor, Prince Konoe Fumimaro, a civilian politician, was prime minister on and off for nearly three of the four years immediately prior to Pearl Harbor. His flirtations with a totalitarian style of leadership did incalculable damage to Japan's international standing and helped to maximize the military voice in the government. But at the same time, Konoe was unmistakably against a war with the West. According to his aide and son-in-law, Hosokawa Morisada, upon hearing the news of Japan's entry into war, Konoe barely managed to say, "What on earth! I really feel a miserable defeat coming. This [favorable situation for Japan] will only last two or three months."

Unlike Prince Konoe, the novelist Ito Sei did not have access to political or strategic information. But that very absence of information led him to intuit correctly. On December 22, just two weeks after he joyfully compared Pearl Harbor to the Russo-Japanese War, he expressed his rising suspicions in his diary:

> They've so far only announced that a couple of [Japanese] steamships were damaged upon landing on Malaya and the Philippines. Nothing has been damaged after that? Or is it their policy not to announce any loss on our part? If it is the latter, I would be worried.

Whatever their fears about the war's resolution, most Japanese were inclined to see it as a war of liberation not only for Japan but for the whole of Asia. This was understandable, especially for soldiers. Who would not prefer to believe that one was dying for a meaningful cause, rather than a misguided one?

Sure enough, the so-called Greater East Asia Coprosperity Sphere began with great fanfare as the Western colonial possessions fell one by one to Japanese military advances from late 1941 to early 1942. Almost all the nations in the sphere—including Burma (now Myanmar), British Malaya (Malaysia and Singapore), the Dutch East Indies (Indonesia),

French Indochina (Vietnam, Cambodia, and Laos), and the Philippines—had been part of Western colonial empires (though the last was no longer a colony at the time of Japanese invasion). So the Japanese occupiers could conveniently claim that they were finally freeing their oppressed Asian brothers and sisters in order to help them reorganize their societies into a viable cultural, economic, and political bloc under Japan's leadership. Though cloaked by a veneer of a civilizing mission, however, the sphere was first and foremost about Japanese economic imperialism, meant to strengthen its hold over much of the Southesast and East Asian resources needed for Japan to continue fighting. That need would grow all the more pressing with time.

The Imperial Navy would lose its winning momentum soon, owing to a major defeat at Midway in June 1942. The tactical planning for that battle had been carried out by the same team that devised the Pearl Harbor attack. This time, Japan lost more than three thousand lives, 289 aircraft, and four aircraft carriers. Midway also revealed that the Japanese had left many jobs unfinished at Pearl Harbor.

On December 7, 1941, the pilots under the command of Vice Admiral Nagumo Chuichi did accomplish their most immediate goal of hitting all eight U.S. battleships, sinking four and damaging four others. But Nagumo's team missed other vital targets that proved to be of more critical importance. Oil tanks and ammunition sites were spared from Japanese strikes. Repair facilities were not struck, either, and this allowed for the majority of the damaged battleships to be quickly repaired or even improved. Of the eight battleships hit by the Japanese, only the *Arizona* and the *Oklahoma* could not be salvaged. Most important, no American aircraft carriers were present during the attack, which allowed the United States to win at Midway.

From then on, almost everything went badly for Japan. As a result of the strict censorship that Ito had already suspected in his diary in December 1941, the Japanese long remained officially ignorant about their country's losses. But as the months and years passed, they came to sense Japan's slipping control over the war situation, and their acute hunger was proof. The rationing system wasn't working because there was too little to be distributed to begin with. Longer and longer lines formed, and fresh products such as vegetables and seafood became impossible to find. One doctor's wife in her forties, who had lived in the United States for many years before the war, noted in her diary: "Rationed goods don't actually mean that you don't pay for them. You pay for every bit, but you still get treated like beggars. It's so infuriating!"

The caloric consequences were undeniable by the second and third year of the war. The rationed diet alone provided only about fourteen hundred calories a day. (A 140-pound adult male requires twenty-four hundred calories daily.) The government told individuals to be "inventive" in the way they procured food. This meant, for instance, buying on the black market, growing their own vegetables, and using straw, sawdust, or rice husks as fillers when baking "bread."

By late 1944, life on the home front had become even more desperate, with Japan's major cities, including Tokyo, Osaka, Kobe, Sendai, Nagoya, and Yokohama, burned to ashes by U.S. carpet bombing. In the wee hours of March 10, 1945, much of old Tokyo was engulfed in fire in one of the most devastating air raids carried out by B-29 bombers. Kafu, awakened by the neighbors' shouting, hastily gathered his diary and manuscripts and fled with his briefcase. He made a dash through billowing smoke, helping others on the way. But when he finally reached a vacant plot on a hill, an irrepressible urge to witness the fate of his home of twenty-six years made him turn around. His house had been miraculously spared from the devastating fire that followed the Great Kanto Earthquake of 1923, and so perhaps he hoped for another miracle. He hid himself behind trees and telegraph poles in order to escape the eyes of a policeman who was directing people from harm's way. Kafu managed to get back to his neighborhood, where he was halted by black smoke. He looked to the sky as flames suddenly blazed up, a result, he was convinced, of his upstairs library catching fire. Kafu, who claimed to have no profound attachments to people, "regretted deeply having to part with those books."

Kafu and his diary survived. Many did not. More than a hundred thousand people are thought to have died in just one night, though the exact figure remains unknown. By then, unless one was seriously deluded, it was clear that Pearl Harbor and the invigorating sense of liberation it brought had merely been the start of a catastrophic war.

SUPERFICIAL OBSERVERS ARE QUICK to label as an apologist anyone who tries to explain the unsavory past of his or her country to the outside world. It should be clear in the following pages that justifying Japan's behavior is the least of my aims in recounting the eight months leading up to the decision to attack Pearl Harbor. To the contrary, Japan's leaders must be charged with the ultimate responsibility of initiating a war that was preventable and unwinnable. War should have been resisted with much greater vigor and much more patience.

To be sure, it is all too easy to adopt an air of moral superiority when indicting those who lived many years ago. Still, that should not stand in the way of a critical evaluation of how and why such an irresponsible war was started. If anything, it is a great historical puzzle begging to be solved. And with the emotional distance that only time can accord, one should be able to look back on this highly emotive period of history with a clearer vision.

Unfortunately, clarity does not come easily; so many complexities and paradoxes surrounded the fateful Japanese decision. There is no question that most Japanese leaders, out of either institutional or individual preferences, avoided open conflict among themselves. Their circuitous speech makes the interpretation of records particularly difficult. For most military leaders, any hint of weakness was to be avoided, so speaking decisively and publicly against war was unthinkable, even if they had serious doubts. That is why the same people, depending on the time, place, and occasion, can be seen arguing both for and against the war option. Some supported war at a liaison conference of top government and military leaders, for example, while making their desire to avoid it known to others in private. Many hoped somebody else would express their opinions for them.

The scarcity of conference records also presents a major difficulty. The Sugiyama Memo, an official name given to a collection of notes kept by Army Chief of Staff Sugiyama Hajime, provides a rare glimpse into what was discussed in top-level conferences. The papers survived by chance, thanks to the sheer ingenuity of a junior officer who, near the end of the war, defied the order to destroy them and instead kept them in a steel oil drum in the basement of his home, convinced of their historical value. And yet these "memos" are far from sufficient. For a start, the manner in which they were kept was inconsistent. After each conference, Sugiyama gathered his senior staff officers to report what was discussed, relying primarily on his notes and memory; one of the officers would then jot down what Sugiyama said. Clearly, not every word was recorded, and the memos lack descriptions that could help us imagine the general atmosphere and mood inside the conference room, adding to the eerie sense that Japan's most critical decisions were made in some symbolic void. The language often switches between stilted and flowing, with varying degrees of formality, making it even more difficult to determine the true tone, let alone the nuances, of the recorded words. Even a precise, immaculate translation would not fully convey what was at stake in those conferences.

However, these surviving records do provide a sufficient testament that the leaders, after numerous official conferences, made a conscious and collaborative decision to go to war with the West. Having talked themselves into believing that they were victims of circumstances rather than aggressors, they discarded less heroic but more rational options and hesitantly yet defiantly propelled the country on a war course. Manifest in Tojo's December 8 speech was the self-pitying perception that Japan was somehow pushed and bullied into war by unrelenting external forces—be they U.S. economic sanctions, the willful U.S. misreading of Japan's peaceful intentions, or, more broadly, Western arrogance and prejudice.

One should not, of course, underestimate the enormous pressure these leaders faced on the eve of Pearl Harbor. They felt they had to choose between waging a reckless war and giving up all of Japan's imperialistic conquests of many years in order to stave off war. They tended to ignore that such extreme choices grew directly out of their own recent decisions and actions. As they made more diplomatic missteps and committed themselves to an impracticable war, claiming all the while to be more prepared than they ever were, their range of policy options both at home and with the outside world narrowed considerably. It was as if Tokyo had gotten stuck in the thin end of a funnel. The war option, it must have seemed to those leaders, provided the quickest and surest way of breaking free of that constricting situation. That they didn't think about what would happen afterward was a tragic act of negligence.

Why didn't they? Mainly for reasons having to do with Japan itself, as this book will show. Still, Japan and its immediate surroundings in 1941 were undeniably a product of the tumultuous experiences of the 1920s and 1930s, when the world at large underwent a significant transformation. In the aftermath of World War I, which many saw as a clash of imperialist ambitions, various attempts were made to create a new kind of international order to prevent the outbreak of another devastating war. The League of Nations, the Washington Conference (1921–22) on disarmament, and the Kellogg-Briand Pact (1928) outlawing wars were all manifestations of such efforts to regulate and facilitate international affairs so that all nations, great and small, could work together toward the goal of bringing about a more peaceful world. But many nations felt cheated by this newly emerging, highly idealistic, and more democratic order.

Germany, the vanquished power, was the primary example. Its desire to fulfill an imperialist dream—of achieving greater territorial expansion, glory, military buildup, and self-sufficiency through conquest—had led it to start World War I, lose it, and be disarmed. Perceiving postwar settlements and their offshoot internationalist movements as a conspiracy of the victors to emasculate Germany, it was even more anxious to resurrect those ambitions, eventually enabling the rise of National Socialism. From 1933 to 1938, in a cleverly incremental fashion, Hitler's Germany left the League of Nations, rearmed the country, reoccupied the Rhineland, and moved into Austria. Liberal Western powers, preferring to keep peace at any cost, sacrificed Czechoslovakia—Central Europe's only viable democracy. When they realized that Hitler would never be satisfied and would always up his demands, it was too late, and the greater part of Western Europe had succumbed to Nazi invasion by the middle of 1940. This disheartening experience would have repercussions on how the West perceived Japan, a Nazi ally, in 1941.

Japan fought on the winning side in World War I, and the League of Nations duly rewarded it with territorial and mandate rights. For a while, many Japanese subscribed to the principle of liberal internationalism with gusto, though some remained dissatisfied. The dissenters believed that the so-called status quo, or "have," powers, especially Britain and the United States, were bent on keeping Japan from achieving true greatness because they were either selfish or racist. In the late 1920s and early 1930s, when Japan faced severe social problems stemming from a deepening economic depression, such a claim gained currency.

Of course, similar socioeconomic problems were confronted worldwide, and people sought remedies in diverse ideologies, ranging from the extreme right to the extreme left, which divided the world as well as nations (as was the case in Spain and France). In the 1930s, a considerable number of Japanese fell to the easy temptation of blaming their social ills on foreign powers while attaching excessive, metaphysical significance to Japan's nationalism, notching it up to the level of ultranationalism. The veneration of the emperor, who was regarded as a living god and the benevolent patriarch of Japan's family-state, played a central role in this intensification of Japanese nationalism. Many Japanese claimed that an incomplete nation could be completed by imperialist expansion abroad and militarization at home. And not unlike in Nazi Germany, the fulfillment of old imperialist goals—some no longer viable—became an integral part of the ultranationalist agenda.

Young officers in the low to middle echelons of the armed forces were especially susceptible to this brand of aggressive nationalism because it gave them a key role. They loudly accused the "have" powers of creating after the Great Depression bloc economies, which put high tariffs on imported Japanese goods, and declared it a Western conspiracy. The ultranationalists also saw the rise of Bolshevism in the Soviet Union, modern Chinese nationalism, and U.S. economic and military assertiveness in Japan's backyard as threatening the country's regional dominance. They had specific domestic enemies as well. Westernized conglomerate capitalists and their client party politicians, sympathetic to democratic liberalism, were blamed for pretty much everything and became targets of ultranationalist violence, including assassinations. Though those ultranationalist terrorists never succeeded in taking over Japan, they did succeed in creating a fearful atmosphere that would partly compromise the outspokenness of Japanese leaders in 1941.

MANY OF THE REAL or imagined constraints that Japan's leaders faced in 1941 had historical roots going back to Japan's opening of its doors to the wider, often hostile world in the second half of the nineteenth century. The end of Japan's self-imposed isolation, the fall of the Tokugawa shogunate, and the subsequent founding of a modern Japanese state coincided with a large-scale realignment in the power configuration of the world itself. The predatory nature of Western colonialism, as well as the collapse of the old Chinese, Spanish, and Ottoman empires, impressed on Japan that power was the very basic requirement for survival. It was also the age of uncritical belief in linear progress, New Imperialism, Social Darwinism, and white supremacy, all of which in turn confirmed the racialist view of the world. Like a model student, Japan went about becoming a proper power, feeding, educating, and industrializing its society to catch up with the West, though the Japanese could not, of course, change the color of their skin.

It is important to note that throughout its fledgling years, modern Japan understood extremely well that becoming a great power was not simply about becoming industrialized and militarized. It was also about playing by the rules and gaining international respectability—hence the need to secure favorable world opinion. After the victory over Qing China in 1895, Japan's emperor cautioned his subjects against becoming "arrogant by being puffed up with triumph and despising others rashly, which would result in losing the respect of foreign Powers. . . . We are particularly against insulting others, and falling into idle pride through elation over victories, and thus losing the confidence of friendly States." By the 1930s, however, such modesty and humility had been willfully forgotten by most Japanese. Its success as a modern nation-state, coupled with historical resentment over having been treated unfairly by the West, fueled the irrational conviction that Japan could somehow pull through times of internal and international crises with sheer force of determination (and good luck, which it had usually had). Such conviction would eventually push Japan to conquer Manchuria, to expand its sphere of influence farther in North China, to escalate its conflict with China, and to seek resources in Southeast Asia, so that it could continue fighting the China War to a favorable conclusion while breaking free of economic dependence on the outside world, taking the first of the series of wrong steps toward the war in the Pacific. Colonial Asia's overall weakness caused by Hitler's war in Europe would make it doubly tempting for Japan to be daring.

Japan's self-righteous calls for expansion on the eve of the Pacific War prevented an accurate assessment of its more recent policy mistakes and a reassessment of its aggressive imperialism carried out over the previous decades in China, Korea, and Taiwan. Still, its belief that it was a nation destined for greatness, despite all the disadvantages of not having enough natural resources of its own, died hard. Self-confidence bordering on hubris had become very much a part of the mind-set of Japan's policymakers as they contemplated the nation's options in 1941.

Japan's official line that the war with the West was forced upon it reflected a state of mind based on a long historical memory. In part, it explains why the suicidal war could readily be sold to the public, which embraced it in December 1941. But in the end, pent-up negative feelings alone do not explain why Japan launched a war despite the real and pervasive reservations of its leaders.

One of postwar Japan's leading political scientists, Maruyama Masao, reflected on this very issue in 1949:

> Trembling at the possibility of failure, [the leaders] still thrust their way forward with their hands over their eyes. If we ask, "Did they want

war?" the answer is yes; and if we ask, "Did they want to avoid war?" the answer is still yes. Though wanting war, they tried to avoid it; though wanting to avoid it, they deliberately chose the path that led to it.

It is especially difficult to assess blame when individual responsibilities were vague and diluted, as they were in this case. Unlike its fascist partners, Japan was never a dictatorship, even though its parliamentary politics had formally ceased to exist in the fall of 1940. Its decision-making process was drawn out and often baffling. It involved a complicated structure and a political culture that straddled different institutions, including the military, government ministries, and the Imperial Palace.

Most of all, it did not help that the government was formally divided. Under the constitution, the military was allowed to "advise" the emperor independently of the civilian government, a prerogative commonly referred to as "the independence of the supreme command." This meant that Japan could have two governments with completely contradictory foreign policies. And to complicate matters further, there were deep political and ideological divisions within those two "governments." The army and the navy were constantly at odds, and each service itself was divided in its political sympathies, worldviews, cliques, and strategic preferences and had different primary enemies. In light of such disagreements, it is surprising that the Japanese leaders were able to agree to embark on a war that no one really knew how to win.

Japanese culture, with its intrinsic preference for consensus and harmony—even if of a most superficial kind—could not have helped to encourage honest discussion about the country's future at various crucial junctures over the course of 1941. The Japanese language itself, brilliant in negotiating intricate social relations, preserving nuances, and saving face, is not known for its strength in clarifying thoughts or fostering open debate. Nonetheless, though these structural, cultural, social, and even linguistic considerations might help to explain what happened, they are no excuse for the calamitous political misjudgments.

Japan's fateful decision to go to war can best be understood as a huge national gamble. Social factors made the gamble harder for the leaders to resist, but their final decision to take the plunge was a conscious one. Believing that Europeans fighting Hitler had left their colonial possessions relatively unguarded, some bellicose strategists in the military planning bodies effectively pushed their aggressive proposals forward, convincing their superiors that the more time they took, the fewer resources they would have left to fight with and the more time the United States would gain to prepare for what was in their minds an "inevitable" clash—a geopolitical necessity to determine the leader of the Asia-Pacific region. If it had to happen anyway, why not dictate the timing? Objectively speaking, it was a reckless strategy of enabling a war by acquiring new territories to feed and fund that war, tersely expressed in the ancient Roman saying *Bellum se ipsum alet* (The war feeds itself). To be sure, many of Japan's leaders did not see a Pacific clash as a historical certainty. Not everyone gave up completely on a diplomatic settlement with the United States until fairly late. But nobody was ready to assume responsibility for Japan's "missing the bus," in a popular expression of the time, to gain a strategic advantage.

The law of risk taking commands that the slimmer the chance, the sweeter the victory. Encouraged by the memory of Japan's modern wars, both of which were successful (the Sino-Japanese War of 1894–95 and the Russo-Japanese War of 1904–5), the leaders felt there was always a chance this reckless war could turn out well, too, though they didn't dwell on how that might be accomplished. Their state of mind might have been one of desperation, but it was also one quickened—bizarrely—by a gambler's high. Especially when they concentrated only on the short-term prospects, that high grew even headier. No matter what the leaders' psychological state, however, the war was completely reckless. An unlikely Japanese victory was predicated entirely on external conditions (aside from Japanese willpower, that is) that were beyond Japan's control, such as the wishful scenarios of the United States quickly suing for peace or of Nazi Germany conquering Europe. Just as the Japanese leaders claimed that they were pushed into war, they seemed to think that they would somehow be pushed into peace. Japan on the eve of Pearl Harbor could be described as being led by men like Hermann, Pushkin's impoverished antihero in "The Queen of Spades," who quietly prepares himself for a maximum win in a game of cards and loses his mind.

The great irony in Japan's decision to go to war is that its leaders could not have even conceived of taking such a grand gamble had it not been for Admiral Yamamoto Isoroku, who was fundamentally against war. As a coolheaded political analyst, Yamamoto warned the naval general staff in Tokyo in late September 1941 that "a war with so little chance of success should not be fought." But at the same time, as an operational planner, Yamamoto, Japan's most informed commander and its biggest gambler, could adamantly insist on the adoption of his Pearl Harbor strategy even though he knew the United States would not give up the fight easily.

People are entitled to waste their own money at casino tables. But Japan's national gamble risked the lives of its own people, as well as of those in the countries it attacked and invaded. To explain a decision of that magnitude simply by saying that the war was "inevitable" is utterly inadequate. So exactly who and what brought Japan to attack Pearl Harbor?

CHAPTER 1

Rumors of War

Prince Konoe Fumimaro, a lanky, mustached aesthete who once translated Oscar Wilde's "The Soul of Man Under Socialism" and was now the prime minister of Japan, was in a melancholy mood. He was rarely seen smiling in official photographs and was often lost in thought, but in the spring of 1941 there were powerful reasons that he should be especially heavyhearted.

Since the previous fall, Japan's relations with the United States had entered a new, much tenser phase. The arrival of Japanese occupation forces in northern French Indochina on September 23, 1940, alarmed the Roosevelt administration. From the Japanese perspective, the occupation was partly a measure taken in response to the U.S. "moral embargo" on the export of all aircraft to Japan since mid-1938 and to the termination by the United States in January 1940 of the thirty-year-old Treaty of Commerce and Navigation, which resulted in stricter control of the exportation of American industrial materials. The designation of Pearl Harbor as the base for the U.S. Pacific Fleet in May 1940 also added to Japanese alarm. The United States was reacting to what it felt were provocative actions by Japan, beginning with its war in China.

Additionally, the growing Nazi preponderance in Europe was giving Japanese expansionism in Asia more fuel. After Paris fell to Germany in June 1940, the timing seemed propitious for the Japanese to gain access to strategic materials they now lacked because of U.S. policy. By occupying northern French Indochina, Japan also hoped to ensure the closing of one of the main routes for the British and Americans to transport aid to Chiang Kai-shek, and thereby end the China War.

The policy backfired. Although the occupation was ostensibly carried out in accordance with a defense treaty with the French colonial government (in both French Indochina and the Dutch East Indies, the European colonialists remained in power despite the Nazi invasion of their home countries), Japan's action was deemed a clear manifestation of its ambition to take over greater parts of Southeast Asia. That was why the United States responded with retaliatory economic measures. It immediately boosted its support for Chiang, with the Export-Import Bank extending $50 million in financial assistance to his regime. It also placed an embargo on all scrap metal shipments to Japan, which would greatly hamper its metal production.

The day after that U.S. response, on September 27, 1940, Japan signed the Tripartite Pact in Berlin, forming a military alliance with Germany and Italy. Germany had dispatched a special envoy to Tokyo to negotiate directly with Konoe's government, completely bypassing the discontented Japanese ambassador in Berlin, who was vehemently opposed to the alliance. Germany was keen to get closer to Japan because it was becoming increasingly anxious about its declining prospect of conquering Britain. The Luftwaffe's defeat in the Battle of Britain, fought from July to October 1940, undermined Nazi plans to invade the British Isles. By allying with Japan and Italy, Germany hoped to deter the United States and minimize the chance of U.S. participation in a European war. The Japanese, in a similar way, saw the fascist alliance as a way of balancing power. Foreign Minister Matsuoka Yosuke embraced a speedy signing of the alliance, believing that this would drastically improve Japan's negotiating position with the United States.

In a Japanese propaganda postcard promoting the triple alliance, captioned "The Three Are Good Friends," jubilant children from Germany, Japan, and Italy wave their national flags. Across the top of the card is a row of small photographs of Hitler, Konoe, and Mussolini, with Prince Konoe, in the middle, managing to look elegant and foolish at the same time. The white boa ornament on his hat, presumably an official Western-style court uniform from the previous century, was doubtless unfortunate. With his weak chin and dreamy eyes, he could not help looking a bit weedy and unreal.

This postcard had actually been created a few years earlier to commemorate the Anti-Comintern Pact, which was reached between Germany and Japan in late 1936 and was joined by Italy a year later. Though it is tempting to think that the new Axis alliance of 1940 was a natural outgrowth of this older liaison, that was simply not the case. The Anti-Comintern Pact was not meant to be a fascist alliance only; the Japanese Foreign Ministry had failed to convince other powers, including Poland and Britain, to join, while Oshima Hiroshi, ambassador to Germany from 1938 to 1939 and again in late 1940 and at the time an army attaché at the Japanese embassy in Berlin, had skillfully obtained Nazi participation in the agreement. (Oshima, educated from an early age in German, was extremely intimate with the Nazis.) Afterward, whenever a proposal for an Axis military alliance came up in the top circles in Tokyo, the Navy Ministry, worried about risking war with the United States and Britain, firmly rejected it. Besides, Tokyo was greatly alarmed by the news of the Molotov-Ribbentrop Pact, the nonaggression treaty between Germany and the Soviet Union signed on August 23, 1939 (at the height of Japanese-Soviet battles over the border between Mongolia and Manchuria), with a secret protocol for dividing Poland and giving the Soviet Union predominance in the Baltic region. This shook the basic foundation of Japan's earlier anti-Soviet, anti-Communist agreement with Germany. Prime Minister Hiranuma Kiichiro, who had succeeded Konoe after the latter's first term running the government, was flabbergasted; he resigned, saying, "The European state of affairs is too complicated and bizarre."

With the German military successes in Europe since the spring of 1940, the call for solidifying Japan's ties with Germany resurfaced. Still believing that a fascist alliance would be a mistake, Navy Minister Yoshida Zengo, in the autumn of 1940, opposed the signing of an Axis pact with such vehemence that a heart condition (but some also speculate a failed suicide attempt) landed him in the hospital, forcing him to resign right before the German negotiators arrived in Tokyo. Without Yoshida, and with more and more admirers of Germany in their midst (owing in no small part to the initial blitzkrieg successes), the navy agreed to support the pact, as long as it was explicit that Japan would not automatically be required to participate in a German war with the United States. (For falling in line with the government and army preferences, the navy was promised a bigger budget.) A new era of Japanese diplomacy had begun.

In early 1941, rumors of war began to circulate within Tokyo's diplomatic community. The deteriorating relations with Japan prompted the United

States to start bringing back home family members of the U.S. embassy personnel stationed in Japan. An American school in Tokyo was forced to announce its closure in February, just as a major publisher released a book predicting and analyzing a hypothetical Japanese-American war (won by Japan, naturally), which sold fifty-three thousand copies in one month.

Japan's relations with Britain, too, had been strained of late. Traditionally, the British attitude toward Japan had been one of pragmatism and conciliation. In July 1939, the two countries had reached the Arita-Craigie Agreement, signed by Foreign Minister Arita Hachiro and British ambassador Sir Robert Craigie: Britain had agreed to neither actively resist nor legally recognize Japanese conduct in China. One year after that agreement, in July 1940, Britain conceded to Japan's request to close the Burma Road, a vital supply route for the transportation of materials to Chiang Kai-shek. But Japan's occupation of northern Indochina finally prompted Britain to abandon its appeasement policy. In December 1940, Britain agreed to lend £10 million to the Guomindang and to reopen the Burma Road. And in the north, one shouldn't forget, lurked the Soviet Union, with its threat of Bolshevism. Japan started 1941 facing more enemies than it was ever prepared to handle.

For the Japanese people, 1941 was a year of less and less food and fuel. The struggling epicurean Kafu, who had developed an overwhelmingly carnivorous appetite during his long stays in the United States and France, was always ready to pay a good price for a good meal. But even he had tremendous problems. "Compared to half a year ago," he complained that spring, "the quality of meat and vegetables has declined drastically." This was only the beginning. Within a few months, he would write: "I have not seen any vegetables or fruit for the past few days. Tofu isn't sold, either. People are feeling distressed." Even a gourmet grocer in the fashionable Ginza district, famous for its pampered fruits (the shiniest apples wrapped in delicate washi paper, fragrant melons sold in individual wooden boxes, and the like), did not have anything to sell, except for a few measly peaches. As for the meat that Kafu so craved: "No beef to be seen anywhere." And for cooking and heating, citizens had to make do with charcoal, since petroleum and coal were reserved for military use. Public buses ran on charcoal, and those resources were beginning to get scarce.

Like vehicles running on ersatz fuel, Japan's diplomacy was stalling, too. In a letter addressed "Dear Frank" to President Roosevelt, dated December 14, 1940, Joseph Grew, the U.S. ambassador to Japan, despaired:

No doubt you have seen some of my telegrams which have tried to paint the picture as clearly as has been possible at this post where we have to fumble and grope for accurate information, simply because among the Japanese themselves the right hand often doesn't know what the left hand is doing. Their so-called "New Structure" [Konoe's centralization program, more commonly known as the New Order Movement, which had recently ended Japan's party politics] is in an awful mess and the bickering and controversy that go on within the Government itself are past belief. Every new totalitarian step is clothed in some righteous-sounding slogan. This, indeed, is not the Japan that we have known and loved.

In Grew's analysis, the United States had to "call a halt to the Japanese program." The only questions were when and how?

Meanwhile, U.S. involvement in the European war was becoming more and more likely. Planners from Britain and the United States gathered in Washington, D.C., from January 29 to March 29, 1941 (the so-called American-British Conversations, or ABC), to discuss future joint strategies, while the signing of the Lend-Lease Act in March put a decisive end to the pretense of U.S. noninterventionism. The latter arrangement enabled the United States to supply war matériel to the Allies and act as the "arsenal of democracy," despite the Neutrality Acts and the staunch isolationist opposition President Roosevelt faced.

Washington's increasing support for the Allies in turn helped to intensify U.S.-Japan relations. Even as the Japanese government was feeling its way into colonial Southeast Asia, while acquiring disreputable friends in Europe and making enemies of the United States and its allies, Konoe had no desire for Japan to go to war with the West. Japan under his leadership was still struggling to extricate itself from the China War—euphemistically referred to in Japanese as the "China Incident" partly because it was never officially declared a war, but also because it was not meant to last for years. The country was in no position to start another. This feeling was shared by many in the highest positions of military and civilian power. After all, they recognized that the United States, the provider of 93 percent of Japan's petroleum in 1940, had far greater war-making powers than Japan could ever hope to muster in the foreseeable future.

In January 1941, Konoe dispatched a seasoned diplomat, Yoshizawa Kenkichi, to recommence negotiations with Dutch authorities in Batavia

(Jakarta) so that Japan could secure an alternative source of petroleum without resorting to force. In February, another veteran, Admiral Nomura Kichisaburo, arrived as ambassador in Washington. A big teddy-bear-like man of sixty-two with a disarming smile, Nomura had to be talked out of his semiretirement for this momentous task. He was known as an Anglo-American sympathizer—as was the case with most navy men of his generation who came of age in the heyday of the Anglo-Japanese Alliance (1902–23)—and an opponent of war. He was deemed the best candidate for the job since he and Roosevelt were old acquaintances.

All the leaders knew that the root causes of Prince Konoe's problems, however, lay not in the Dutch East Indies or the United States but in China. From the Guomindang's powerbase of Chongqing, Generalissimo Chiang Kai-shek had been putting up a dogged fight against Japan since the fall of his former capital, Nanjing, in late 1937. To avoid international sanctions on war matériel, neither side officially called it a war, but it was, in fact, a savage conflict, one that confirmed the reputation as a rogue state that Japan had earned after its invasion of Manchuria in 1931. When Konoe became prime minister for the second time in July 1940, he hoped to end the conflict, especially since he had frittered away the opportunity to do so during his first tenure.

Konoe's initial premiership began on a buoyant note in 1937. He was not popularly elected. (Japanese premiers were traditionally appointed by the emperor on the recommendation of powerful oligarchs who had founded modern Japan and acted as kingmakers. Later, they were nominated by a group of senior statesmen assisting Prince Saionji, the last surviving oligarch, to be approved by the emperor. Saionji, in this instance, had nominated Konoe.) Yet it seemed as though the entire nation wanted the forty-five-year-old prince to be its leader. His pedigree and relative youth burnished his public image in a country that had adopted emperor worship as a matter of national policy since the second half of the nineteenth century. He held one of the noblest titles, with a lineage going back to the powerful Fujiwara family, which originated in the seventh century and whose members once ruled Japan as imperial regents and provided their daughters as brides to the imperial house.

Konoe was not your ordinary politician. Though he was said to have a common touch (he was once heard humming a cheesy popular love song, "I Pine for You," while taking a stroll in the country), he was accustomed to a coddled life. At the time of his first appointment, his extreme pickiness in food was discussed with great curiosity. The prince was known to decline even the freshest and most carefully prepared sashimi at lavish political dinners. (People assumed he regarded raw fish as too primitive for his refined taste.) A geisha attending to him would put the sliced fish into a bowl of boiling water, fondue-style, and spoon-feed—or, rather, chopstick-feed—it to the prince.

A newspaper profile, published on the eve of his becoming prime minister, reported in half jest that Konoe ate his favorite fruit, strawberries, in a similar fashion. (In reality, the prince merely had them washed in sterilized water.) He confessed to his foibles in a magazine interview and explained that he did not eat raw food because of his delicate stomach. But rather than make him seem too soft to lead a country, such quirks somehow added to his aristocratic mystique and political charisma. Konoe could do no wrong in the eyes of the awestruck public.

Konoe's popularity might have been based on surface impressions, but the public expectation that his appointment heralded change was genuine. On June 4, 1937, Konoe was literally cheered into Japan's top political office by a nation that had been suffering from economic depression, natural disasters, agricultural failures, and a threat of army rebellion in the name of radical reform. Konoe's choice of cabinet members immediately disappointed some astute observers, however. One columnist said his selection did not live up to the fanfare for change, as Konoe opted to retain the army, navy, and law ministers from the previous cabinet. "One should be greatly alarmed," the columnist declared, "that we are reminded of the accommodationism [of the preceding governments]." Despite the sweeping victory of major political parties the previous spring, which prompted the last government's fall, Konoe refused to include major party politicians in his own cabinet. The only two ministers with any party affiliations belonged to a new party with proarmy, totalitarian sympathies. There was no hint that Konoe wanted to resuscitate Japan's ailing parliamentary system, which enjoyed its heyday in the second half of the 1920s. The nation was too enthralled by Konoe to see the latent danger of his apparent distaste for multiparty politics.

After just one month in office, Konoe was prompted by the outbreak of Japan's war with China to further toughen his political stance. On the night of July 7, 1937, a skirmish between Chinese and Japanese forces transpired, though its exact origin is still highly contested. What is commonly told is that a small group of Japanese soldiers were engaging in exercises on the banks of the Yongding River, firing blank cartridges. (The Japanese forces were stationed there under the 1901 international treaty signed after a multinational expedition—which included the United States and European powers—quelled the antiforeign Boxer Rebellion.) To their consternation, the Japanese heard their fake shots being answered by live rounds, presumably by Chinese forces. Adding to their alarm was the roll call immediately afterward that revealed one of their soldiers to be missing. The Japanese request to search the nearby town that was normally out of bounds was rejected by Chinese guards, and an altercation followed, causing both sides to mobilize. That the stray soldier came back in one piece, after having gone off supposedly to relieve himself, made no difference. The small fight between local Chinese and Japanese forces quickly spiraled into serious hostilities. Because the night's event took place near the Marco Polo Bridge, just outside Beijing, whose beauty was memorialized by the thirteenth-century Venetian merchant traveler, it came to be known in the West as the Marco Polo Bridge Incident.

Initially, Konoe was too engaged with his domestic agenda to be distracted by a small clash abroad. He was especially preoccupied with obtaining pardons for the ultranationalist officers who had been court-martialed the previous year for an almost successful military coup d'état. His efforts showed not only the extent to which he would go to support the extreme right but his fundamental obliviousness, despite his international travels, to the world beyond his own. Now the events in China demanded his attention.

Ishiwara Kanji, the charismatic mastermind of Japan's invasion of Manchuria in 1931, argued that a military engagement with China should be avoided while a greater enemy, the Soviet Union, threatened from the north. However, some officers in Tokyo and in China believed that Japan was missing a God-sent opportunity to deal Chiang Kai-shek a decisive blow, especially now that the Soviets were caught up in the domestic chaos of a Stalinist purge and would not likely intervene if Japan attempted to expand its reach in China. In the end, the opinion that Japan was nowhere near prepared for a full-blown war in China prevailed, and a truce with China was reached on the night of July 11. Hostilities seemed to be contained to the level of a local conflict, as had been a number of other similar skirmishes in the previous year.

On the same day the local truce was being signed, Konoe nonetheless forced through a plan to send more troops to northern China, ostensibly to protect Japanese residents in conflict zones, making a great show of his eagerness to placate and impress hard-liners in the military, who were dissatisfied with the conciliatory policy of war avoidance that the truce represented. The reinforcements could readily be perceived as war mobilization, as Konoe signaled to China that despite the cease-fire, Japan was not backing out of the country and entertained expansionist aims.

Konoe took it upon himself to garner support for his China policy by launching a charm offensive in Tokyo. On the evening of July 11, he summoned members of the parliament, the financial world, and the media to his official residence. He announced the troop reinforcement and asked for help in mobilizing Japan behind this patriotic enterprise in the name of national emergency. The following day's newspapers depicted the additional dispatch of troops to northern China as "intended to facilitate due repentance" from the Chinese, and the news of the truce was either pushed aside or summarily ignored.

Trying to appear tough in the eyes of others—including Chiang Kai-shek, his colleagues in the government, the military, and the general public—Konoe had taken the lead in rallying the nation around the flag, acutely conscious that his popularity was his greatest weapon. He did not want, and likely did not anticipate, a prolonged war with China. He thought that mere posturing and strong language would suffice to strengthen Japan. He often broadcast his speeches on NHK (he had become president of the network the year before and would retain that position until his suicide in December 1945). But Konoe was, in the words of a shrewd contemporaneous observer, "the man who ordered the nation to cross the Rubicon when the first shots were fired."

The truce had become a dead letter by July 20, with Chiang taking his time to give it his official approval. As the war spread and intensified—Japan bombed Nanjing, Shanghai, Hangzhou, and other major Chinese cities—Konoe blamed it on others, especially the army's bellicose elements, who were, conveniently, nameless and faceless. In the summer of 1937, he told Lieutenant Colonel Ikeda Sumihisa, a staff officer who had just been sent back from China because of his opposition to the fledgling war, that the conflict was "the making of young army officers." Ikeda responded:

Prince, I am afraid it's not the army, but you, the prime minister, who made this war. . . . Look at what the newspapers are saying, despite your government's earlier profession of a nonescalation policy. It would be surprising if we didn't have a war [after all you have said and done to encourage and empower those war-hungry officers].

Konoe's self-servingly short memory and his tendency to carry out contradictory policies as a way of political mediation, purely for the sake of dodging potential conflicts at home, continued. Tellingly, in January 1938, in the wake of the fall of the Guomindang's capital of Nanjing and the ensuing mass killing, looting, and rape, Konoe, falsely confident that the end of the war was in sight, gave one of the most patronizing and jingoistic statements of his political career. Konoe charged that the Guomindang's acts of aggression have not ceased despite its defeat, "subjecting its people to great misery." Having run out of patience, Japan was not going to "deal with" Chiang Kai-shek. Six days later, Konoe followed up this arrogant statement with a radio speech. In dramatic contrast to its forceful contents, however, the voice reading it was high-pitched and unnervingly feminine. He reiterated that Japan was not to blame and the Guomindang was disrupting East Asia's peace.

Japanese atrocities and bombings in various parts of China after August 1937 were not only inhumane but also self-destructive. They did not prompt China to sue for peace—on the contrary, they hardened Chinese determination—and at the same time crystallized the already hostile world opinion against Japan. The German bombing of Guernica that spring, and the international recrimination that followed, were still fresh in Western memory. The China War was becoming a quagmire. Successive Japanese victories had allowed Japan to occupy certain "dots" (cities) and "lines" (railways and transportation routes). But the farther the Guomindang forces retreated, the more difficult it became for the Japanese to acquire and maintain those dots and lines. Human resources were limited, as was familiarity with the terrain. Chiang Kai-shek's temporary ally, the Chinese Communists, fighting from their strongholds in the north, would allow the Japanese to occupy towns and villages by quickly disappearing from their sight, only to reemerge after the Japanese had left. (The Guomindang would have preferred for them to stand up and fight. The Communists' wartime preservation of strength would later contribute to their victory over the Guomindang.)

Konoe did not know how to end the conflict. The result was a disastrously inconsistent policy toward China. While approving the dispatch of ever more troops to the continent, increasing the military budget without any prodding from the armed services, and endorsing laws that would allow for a more concentrated war mobilization at home, Konoe pursued direct contact with Chiang, despite his tough talk, to negotiate an end to hostilities. But whenever there was a possibility for peace, the prince gave in to hard-line military expectations, took too long to decide how to respond, or simply exercised bad judgment. For example, in early December 1937, when Chiang—through the German ambassador in China—showed willingness to negotiate with Japan, the fall of Nanjing was imminent, and Konoe rejected the Chinese overture.

Foreign affairs, clearly, were never Konoe's strong suit. He was exceptionally good, though, at making those around him feel they were being listened to with flattering attention. His distinct brand of lip service enabled him to deal effectively with those of various political persuasions and to navigate his career deftly through the most tumultuous years of Japanese politics, perhaps in much the same way that his forefathers had perpetuated the family's intrigue-driven courtly existence over many centuries. But this had obvious drawbacks. "I have neither obvious enemies nor allies," he once remarked. "Even if one had five enemies, one could manage to engage in politics with five true allies. But ten allies [of the kind I have] could very well become ten enemies at any given time."

The prince's sense of isolation might have been the result of his complicated upbringing. He was the only child from his father's first marriage, his mother dying just a week after she gave birth. His father soon remarried. The bride was his deceased wife's younger sister, with whom he fathered several children, making Fumimaro's siblings something more than half siblings. The family patriarch died at forty-one, leaving the Konoes as perhaps the noblest but hardly the wealthiest of the old families. Twelve-year-old Fumimaro inherited the family seat, as well as the enormous debts incurred through his father's political activities. The young prince felt abandoned and was prone to melancholy. It was Marquis Saionji Kinmochi (he was made a prince later), a descendant of the same ancient Fujiwara family as the Konoes, who discreetly ensured that the family did not suffer from any financial embarrassment.

Konoe was at the university when he first met Saionji, and he did not warm to him immediately. Much influenced by Marxist philosophy at the time, the young prince was offended by Saionji's insistence on addressing him as "my lord." In fact, the two had a lot in common. On a surface level, they had slender physiques on which expensive clothes, be they Western suits or Japanese kimonos, hung well. More important, both had a combination of brains and ambition that was uncommon in men of their social background. They became close as Konoe was drawn to a political career after graduation. Saionji was thrilled to have such a bright protégé.

Saionji, a practical man, opposed the deification of the emperor but felt the emperor was important in unifying modern Japan. In his view, the unnecessarily elaborate court rituals were created either by old aristocrats who had nothing better to do or by new ones with poor taste (during the modernization of Japan in the late nineteenth century). But while dismissing the excessive importance attached to the class system, Saionji knew very well the benefit of having an aristocratic title in rank-conscious Japan. The key was to have the title work to one's advantage. He judged Konoe, forty years his junior, intelligent enough to play in this precarious game.

Saionji, unfortunately, did not impart his values to his younger disciple. Born in 1849, Saionji was a classic liberal, a product of nineteenth-century Europe who came of age as a student in Paris under the Commune and was a friend of his fellow lodger Georges Clemenceau, who would become a celebrated statesman. Saionji's political consciousness had been awakened in his teens when the imperial court in Kyoto suddenly found itself in the midst of a political transformation that culminated in the Meiji Restoration of 1868. His life would subsequently be about surviving radical political changes without compromising his principles.

Konoe, who had never lived outside Japan and had been raised in an overprotective environment, had quite a different take on life. An avid student of political philosophy, his intellectual interests included Marxism and fascism (liberalism never seems to have attracted him). Konoe was convinced that Japan should seek greatness in the wider world, obsessed as he was with the notion that Japan should not appear weak in the political competition of nation-states. Himself the embodiment of privilege, he wanted Japan to occupy a similar position on the international stage. His first trip abroad confirmed his rigid view. In 1919, as a twenty-seven-year-old political novice, he accompanied Saionji to the Paris Peace Conference, where post–World War I settlements were discussed. He had begged Saionji to take him along, sensing that the event would be of great historical importance.

Konoe found the timing convenient for personal reasons, too. The prince was dismayed that his geisha mistress from his student years, Kiku, whom he had brought from Kyoto to Tokyo some years earlier, had become pregnant with their child. He had originally sought her companionship as a break from his fast-growing family. Producing offspring bearing the Konoe name was his wife's job, and she did it very well. He knew that the baby would take his place in Kiku's affections, and there would be no point in keeping her as a mistress. She was sent home. And with money he had collected by auctioning off some of the family treasures, he set off for Paris.

Konoe's emotional investment in the peace conference was considerable. On the eve of the armistice, he had written an article entitled "I Call to Reject the Anglo-American Peace," which was published in a nationalistic magazine. Though not entirely opposed to Woodrow Wilson's idea of establishing an intergovernmental organization, he was deeply suspicious of the moralizing and ambitious claims attached to the League of Nations. He asserted that the new postwar order, as conceived by Britain and the United States, had nothing to do with the promotion of democracy or peace claimed by those powers. Rather, he saw it as a reflection of the Anglo-American desire to continue exercising economic imperialism to their advantage, enhancing their international standings. That the two aims—preservation of the status quo and peaceful coexistence—could be mutually reinforcing certainly would have been a more sophisticated reading.

Konoe believed that those of his countrymen who favored the liberal internationalist proposal did so simply because they were sentimental and too easily impressed by its flowery language of justice and humanity. He told his Japanese readers to wake up to the hard realities of international inequality and injustice, citing racial prejudice against yellow-skinned people in the United States, Australia, and Canada. He said that those countries

> welcome white immigrants but persecute yellow ones, including, of course, us Japanese. This fact is nothing new and remains a persistent source of our anger and frustration. By judging us by the color of our skin, white people prevent us from obtaining employment and renting houses or land. We are sometimes even refused one night's rest in a hotel, unless we have a white guarantor. This is a deplorable problem from a humanitarian point of view.

Konoe intended this polemical article for domestic readers only, but it reached the outside world. The piece was translated into English and criticized in the Shanghai-based *Millard's Review of the Far East,* winning Konoe some notoriety as a radical. Saionji, who regarded the article as thoughtless, provocative, undiplomatic, and inappropriate for someone about to attend the Paris Peace Conference with the official delegation, voiced his displeasure. But Sun Yat-sen, the leader of modern Chinese nationalism and a Pan-Asianist, invited Konoe to dine with him in Shanghai, where they agreed on the importance of Asian nationalism.

In Paris, Konoe witnessed the most significant intergovernmental conclave ever to take place. From some distance, he observed Clemenceau and Wilson. The range he noted in skin color among the participants astonished him. Because there were only so many official places given to each delegation, which did not include Konoe, he arranged for a journalist's pass to listen in on a major session one day. Saionji scolded him afterward for not acting with enough dignity. Saionji also reproached him for plucking a flower in a public park: "You don't have the proper manners of a member of a great nation," he said. Saionji was even more aghast when he overheard Konoe taking part in lighthearted banter about how to talk one's way out of trouble with customs officers.

For Konoe, a new member of the House of Peers—one of the houses of Japan's bicameral parliament, the Diet—the trip served as a great introduction to the bigger world. He was able to gain, or so he believed, a more global perspective on how diplomacy was conducted. When he left the delegation to tour Europe on his own, he was enthralled most notably by the loveliness of English gardens. He then visited the United States. But his first great adventure abroad in the end did not alter his fundamental conviction that the post–World War I settlements were a Carthaginian peace, imposed on the vanquished to keep the status quo in place. Even though the Japanese were on the winning side, he felt they were losers, too. To him, the Japanese attempt to include racial equality and religious freedom clauses in the League of Nations' covenant failed because of white prejudice.

Shortly after his return to Japan, Konoe published a booklet recording his impressions of his Western travels. He pondered how Japan could go about achieving higher international status without having to beg for it. Commenting on the rising anti-Japanese sentiments in the United States due to immigration, Konoe wrote:

That the white people—and the Anglo-Saxon race in particular—generally abhor colored people is an apparent fact, so blatantly observable in the U.S. treatment of its black people. I for one felt a sort of racial oppression more in London than in Paris, and that sense was heightened even further upon my arrival in New York.

It is truly ironic that two decades later Japan, under a man who had always despised Anglo-American racism, would ally itself with the most fanatically racist of all European regimes, Nazi Germany.

The young Konoe went on to discuss, admiringly, the success of Chinese public relations in the United States and to deplore Japan's relative failure to promote its national cause. He explained how Chinese students studying in the United States were far more effective than their Japanese counterparts in enlightening their American peers about their country and, more important, in eliciting their sympathy for it. Oddly, he did not see China as a fellow Asian power in Japan's worthy struggle against discriminatory treatment by the Anglo-Americans. Rather, China, in Konoe's mind, was a threatening rival vying for Western respect and recognition as a top Asian country. Fearing that China might outdo Japan, he called for Japan to adopt a more self-assertive diplomatic approach. In the end, he was far more of a Japanese chauvinist than an Asian nationalist. And like with many chauvinists, his claim to national greatness went hand in hand with a great measure of insecurity and fear of rejection.

Accordingly, Konoe, who was grooming his eldest son, Fumitaka, for a career in politics, sent him to Lawrenceville, an exclusive American prep school, and then to Princeton, so that someday he could become an effective proponent of Japanese interests among American elites. Prince Konoe liked to tell his more right-wing friends, who wondered why on earth he had sent his son to America, that it was easier to nurture a true Japanese spirit abroad, that universities at home tended to take the Japanese spirit out of their students. On the other hand, he said, living abroad made it easier for people to love their country. The more convincing reason for Konoe's sending his son to America was that most of his closest aides and friends, from a similar aristocratic background, were products of top Anglo-American educational institutions. They all had the social and linguistic facility to be citizens of the greater and privileged world. Konoe, owing to his father's untimely death, did not benefit from such a formative experience, and most likely he had a certain inferiority complex as a result. Konoe's professed anti-Anglo-American views should be seen in this light. Needless to say, he was conflicted about China, too. He admired its ancient civilization but felt threatened by its rising nationalism.

Konoe's pet claim of Japan having suffered from predatory Western imperialism and racism was by no means original in the context of his time. But he managed to profess his feelings without appearing overtly reactionary or dangerous (at least most of the time), so observers at home and abroad too often failed to see his true colors. Because of his seemingly close connection to Prince Saionji, Konoe was sometimes even mislabeled a liberal.

Toward the end of Saionji's life, he would be increasingly disappointed and alarmed by his onetime protégé's provocative pronouncements on foreign policy. Konoe's appearance as Hitler in a Nazi uniform at the costume banquet on the eve of his daughter's wedding in the spring of 1937 did not help their often strained relationship. A charitable interpretation would be that this was no more than an aristocratic diversion. But news of the event infuriated Saionji, and Konoe became more cautious about professing his admiration for Nazism. Still, Konoe's subsequent policies would more often than not suggest an attraction to at least some aspects of fascist ideology, particularly the idea of a "New European Order," celebrated by Mussolini and Hitler. The idea that superior nations were destined to lead others in the revival of a larger civilization meshed well with his Japan-centric view of Asia. That was why in late 1938 he announced his intention to build a "New East Asian Order," a vain attempt to reverse the damage done by his earlier policy and to give some ideological coherence to Japan's war aims in China.

But the harm could not be undone so easily. Konoe's declaration in January 1938 that he would not "deal with" Chiang Kai-shek had alienated the Guomindang leader and would obstruct all future Japanese attempts at a diplomatic settlement. As Saionji remarked to his grandson in private, Japan had to make Chiang Kai-shek

> into a legitimate negotiating partner. . . . The Chinese negotiator for the settlement of the Sino-Japanese War [of 1894–95], Li Hongzhang, also had a terrible reputation in Japan. But then there was only him to be dealt with in China. So one makes do with what one has. There is nothing else to do other than to identify who is at the top and negotiate with that person.

Konoe's impatience with Chiang put him temperamentally in line with those who believed they could quickly defeat China. In the meantime, the prolongation of the China War under Konoe's leadership had increasingly constricting effects on Japanese life. In order to ensure that home-front mobilization would be carried out efficiently, the government in the fall of 1937 established the Cabinet Planning Board for resource allocation. This paved the way for the passage of the National Mobilization Law, which took effect in April 1938. Invoking a state of national emergency, the law represented an attempt to regulate all aspects of professional, economic, and social endeavors by giving the state ultimate control over them. It put in motion the conversion of Japan's semiwar economy into a war economy, drastically reducing the flow of raw materials into the market and preparing the nation, eventually, for total war.

The National Mobilization Law defeated its purposes when enforced on a microlevel, however. The diarist Kafu noted that a hefty fine was imposed on a well-meaning pastry shop owner who had paid his employees a bonus. "Why should anyone be punished for giving too much? What a strange world we live in!" Kafu lamented. It was a sure sign that every little move was being watched by the state and one could readily be punished for the wrong reasons.

Because of the China War, the fundamental power structure at the center was also changing quickly, which would prove critical later. In November 1937, Konoe instituted a system of joint conferences between the government and the military. They were called liaison meetings, or liaison conferences, and were meant to help leaders overcome the civil-military divide and unify policy at a time of heightened international crises. These gatherings became more frequent during Konoe's second premiership and took place in the prime minister's official residence until July 1941 and at the Imperial Palace after Konoe became prime minister for the third time. Regularly in attendance were the prime minister, the foreign minister, the army minister, the navy minister, and the chiefs of the Army and Navy General Staffs, all of whom were deemed to have an equal say. Contrary to the original intention, however, the conferences would become a theater for advancing strategic agendas, rather than for debate. As four of the six key attendees of the conferences were affiliated with the military (even though the duties of army and navy ministers were technically within the civilian cabinet), their preferences tended to dominate. This would prove a major structural flaw in prewar Japanese decision making.

Under Konoe's leadership, an ambitious program to create another Guomindang regime sympathetic to Japan headed by Wang Jingwei, a direct disciple of Sun Yat-sen and Chiang's biggest rival, was set in motion. Wang, unlike the hard and pragmatic Chiang, was a naïve and romantic idealist. He had escaped from the new Guomindang capital, Chongqing, in December 1938, but his government was not formed in Nanjing until the spring of 1940, after numerous setbacks, including an assassination attempt that he barely escaped. Wang's acts were driven by patriotism as well as personal ambition. Japan, for its part, needed a more pliable negotiating partner. In late November 1940, two months after Japan's signing of the Tripartite Pact with Germany and Italy, Konoe's second government would recognize Wang as the new leader of China. Konoe might have felt morally obligated to recognize the regime whose birth he had connived in. But the timing could not have been worse. By then the Wang government had lost all its credibility in China. (And besides, Japan never conceded the entire control of China to Wang, having maintained a handful of occupational, colonial, and client regimes, including Manchukuo, Taiwan, northern China, and Inner Mongolia, thus undermining Wang's domestic prestige.) Once again, Konoe had demonstrated his ineptitude in foreign affairs.

The official line was always that the Japanese forces continued to make great progress in China. In reality, Japan was acting much like the delusional protagonist of the classic black comedy *Eternal March Forward* (*Kagirinaki Zenshin*), a film based on Ozu Yasujiro's story and released shortly after the outbreak of the conflict in 1937. Fifty-two-year-old Tokumaru is laid off from a company for which he has worked most of his life. Right before his dismissal, he had started building a house beyond his means, counting on a promotion. Now depression pushes him to the edge of reason. He is no longer able to distinguish wishful thinking from reality. Convincing himself that he has been promoted, he begins to show up at work behaving like an important man, much to the embarrassment of his family and former colleagues. Tokumaru "eternally marches forward" in his unhinged state.

JAPAN'S CHINA PROBLEM, which would complicate Tokyo's political choices in 1941, had roots far beyond Prince Konoe. Over the course of its national existence, Japan had imported (often through Korea) and synthesized many aspects of Chinese civilization, including its writing system, Confucian thought, and Buddhism. Japan historically looked up to China with awe, albeit with a certain detachment that came easily to a geographically isolated island society. But by the 1840s, in the face of the Western imperialist threat, the once-glorious Middle Kingdom seemed thoroughly helpless and decadent, opium addicted and suddenly decrepit, no longer a model for Japan.

After two and a half centuries of relative tranquillity under the Tokugawa shogunate, Japan was forced to shake itself out of a self-imposed isolation that had limited the country's contact with the outside world. China's weakness in the mid-nineteenth century meant that it could no longer be a buffer—Japan had to face the Western powers on its own. Equally worrying was that, immediately to the north of Japan and China, czarist Russia appeared eager to extend its already overextended empire.

Completely new to the great-power game, Japan had to learn its rules quickly. That it was able to do so owed a great deal to a group of remarkably talented young visionaries who gave birth to modern Japan. By the early twentieth century, Japan, amazingly for an Asian power, had attained a certain standing in the elite club of Western imperialists, though it never felt entirely at home in such company. Theodore Roosevelt's reported comment, meant as a compliment, that the Japanese were an "honorary white race" explains why. Japan was often overwhelmed with feelings of inadequacy and suspicion and by the conflicting senses of being superior and a loner.

Japan's touchiness was sometimes simply a paranoid response. But at other times, the country had good reason to feel slighted and even excluded. The diplomatic efforts in the first few decades of Japan's new Meiji regime, formed in 1868, concentrated on the reversal of the unequal treaties Japan had been forced to sign with Western powers, including the United States (expiring only in 1911). Those treaties, imposed by gunboat diplomacy, deprived Japan of its commercial and legal sovereignty, prompting the opening of various ports to foreign trade, fixed low tariffs, and the extraterritoriality of foreign residents.

Even victory in the Sino-Japanese War of 1894–95, fought over Korea, was tainted by Western intervention. The Treaty of Shimonoseki, which ended the war, accorded Japan the island of Formosa (now Taiwan) and the Liaodong Peninsula. With its strategically located seaports of Dalian and Port Arthur serving as the gateway to Manchuria and Northeast China, the peninsula had become the target of a power scramble for concession-ary rights among the powers, particularly Russia and Japan because of their proximity. Once the settlement in favor of Japan became public, how-ever, Russia, France, and Germany, with Britain and the United States turning a blind eye, successfully pressured Japan to return the peninsula in the so-called Triple Intervention. Such were the hard realities of inter-national politics. Three years later, Russia would acquire leasehold rights in the coveted peninsula.

Japan was undeterred. It carried on in its determined quest for a more respectable status, greater territorial expansion, and a stronger army. In 1904–5, it fought Russia and won—an imperialist fantasy come true—and was much applauded abroad, especially in Britain and the United States. Japan now possessed protectorate rights in Korea, which it would annex in 1910. It also acquired the former Russian railway and mining rights in southern Manchuria. Japan claimed or reclaimed some territories in the Russian empire, such as the leasehold over the old sore spot of Liaodong and southern Sakhalin, an island north of Japan where Japan's indigenous Ainu population had long settled. There still lingered the big question of what to do about China.

In the aftermath of their country's defeat in the Sino-Japanese War, reform-minded Chinese, impressed by Japan's quick ascent, flocked to Japan, often as students of Western science and political thought. The Jap-anese had acquired those tools to protect their independence, and many Chinese, including the first Guomindong leader, Sun Yat-sen, admired them for it, as they considered Japan a successful model of modernization. Some Japanese in turn embraced Sun and his colleagues' cause. One of them, the movie studio tycoon Umeya Shokichi, drew on his fortune to help finance Sun's nationalist movement, as did others who believed that a stronger China would enhance the future of Asia as a whole.

Konoe's father, Prince Konoe Atsumaro, advocated a strong Sino-Japanese alliance. In his capacity as a member of the House of Peers, he helped found in 1898 a cultural organization called the Same Character Society, whose members believed that the two countries were bound to help one another because Chinese and Japanese, racial kin, shared the same writing system. Its most notable project was the founding of an acad-emy in Shanghai whose graduates became Japan's top China specialists in politics, diplomacy, journalism, and economics.

Despite such attempts to strengthen Sino-Japanese relations on various civic levels, Japan, as a state, consistently pursued a hard-nosed, classically imperialist approach in dealing with China. The Qing dynasty's collapse in 1912 prompted an ultimate competition among domestic Chinese, as well as between outside powers, to gain further control of the vast country and its seemingly limitless resources; Japan acquired various concessionary rights through bargaining and coercion, as well as threats of force.

In 1915, Japan revealed its more ambitious designs regarding China. Wanting to take advantage of a severe internal crisis in the newly established Republic of China and the war in Europe, Japan presented the so-called Twenty-One Demands to President Yuan Shikai, the one who would soon try to crown himself emperor, Napoleon-style. Japan demanded, among other things, German concessions in Shandong, where Japan had just defeated Germany; the extension into the twenty-first century of Japanese leasehold on the South Manchurian Railway zone, which had been acquired from Russia and was scheduled to expire in 1923; and the placement of Japanese advisers in the Chinese government. The Chinese resisted, and the last demand, which would have turned China virtually into Japan's puppet regime, was dropped. In the end, the episode proved a public relations disaster, with Japan managing only to consolidate more or less the rights it had already possessed while decisively antagonizing the United States, now the self-appointed watchdog of the Open Door policy in China. To some Japanese, this smacked of a self-serving U.S. rejection of its own Monroe Doctrine, enabling American intervention in Japan's backyard and preventing Japan from claiming regional leadership in Asia.

Japan's demands had of course also upset China, where nationalism was further galvanized when Japan won its claim to Shandong Province at the Paris Peace Conference, a reward for having joined the right side of the war against Germany. This sparked powerful and broad-based Chinese nationalism, culminating in the anti-Japanese, anti-imperialist May Fourth Movement of 1919. Japan's interests in China grew more exposed and vulnerable as a result. (Japan would eventually agree to return Shandong to Chinese control through U.S. mediation, at the Washington Naval Conference in 1922, a humiliating concession in the eyes of Japanese nationalists.) Still, these were by and large diplomatic episodes.

The Manchurian Incident, staged by Colonel Ishiwara Kanji, changed everything. On September 18, 1931, some soldiers of the Kwantung Army stationed in the Japanese-leased railway zone to protect Japan's interests in southern Manchuria exploded a small bomb on the railway and claimed that anti-Japanese Chinese elements were responsible. Using the incident as a pretext to launch a full-scale assault on local Chinese troops, Japanese troops occupied the entire northeastern area over the next five months.

Ishiwara was a magnetic and eccentric officer who had formulated an apocalyptic war theory some years before. His pivotal role in the Manchurian takeover would make him a key figure in Japan's military buildup for war in China (though he personally opposed the China War) and eventually in the Pacific. He had long regarded a titanic clash between East and West—most likely between Japan and the United States but also possibly the Soviet Union—as a matter of historical inevitability. This type of rhetoric, glorifying Japan's heroic destiny, would influence many a middle-ranking strategist in the army and the navy.

On the eve of the Manchurian Incident, Ishiwara believed that Chiang Kai-shek's brand of assertive Chinese nationalism, supported by many industrialists, and the increasing Western recognition of Chiang's power had become major problems for Japan. In 1925, Chiang attained leadership of the Guomindang, following Sun Yat-sen's death. Shortly afterward, he launched a Northern Expedition, with the help of the Communists, in order to bring the parts of China torn by warlord factionalism under his control. During the expedition he fell out with the Communists, massacring them in April 1927 in Shanghai, which caused a temporary rift between "right" and "left" factions of the Guomindang, the latter led by Wang Jingwei. Despite a series of setbacks, however, the Northern Expedition continued through 1928, when Guomindang troops clashed for the first time with Japanese forces—dispatched to protect Japanese nationals. By 1931, Chiang had succeeded in establishing himself as the nominal leader of a unified China, although he would repeatedly be challenged by his warlord allies as well as by the Communists. From the Japanese perspective, one thing was sure, that Chiang was increasingly leaning toward cooperation with Western powers (primarily the United States), while distancing himself from Japan and adopting strong anti-Japanese rhetoric.

To many in Japan, the Western support Chiang garnered in a relatively short time represented a betrayal, a turning back from the tacit and time-honored imperialist method of keeping China divided so that foreign powers could benefit from its weakness. By the end of the 1920s, Japan was equally obsessed with the rise of Bolshevism, as the Soviet Union launched its Five-Year Plans to strengthen its economy while building up its Far Eastern military presence immediately to Japan's north. All these factors compelled Ishiwara and his followers to go far beyond the call of duty and invade Manchuria. Their reckless initiative came as a surprise to most leaders in Tokyo, though the plotters may well have had supporters in the higher ranks of the Army General Staff. At the beginning of the Manchurian campaign, Prime Minister Wakatsuki Reijiro and Foreign Minister Shidehara Kijuro, among others, wanted to contain hostilities. Japanese public opinion, however, fueled by the jingoistic media, keenly supported Ishiwara's adventures. The public was fed reports commending the courage of the field army, swelling national pride. Major newspapers competed with one another, issuing extras with exclusive photos of Japan's every strategic move, profiting greatly from their suddenly booming circulation. Correspondents were sent to war zones to report under such dramatic headlines as "Our Army Heroically Marches from Changchun to Jilin" and "Our Imperial Army Charges into Qiqihar, Its Great Spirit Piercing Through the Sky!"

The papers at this time made a conscious political choice that would haunt them in the coming decade: self-censorship. Despite their knowledge, passed on to them in private by some army officers, that the supposedly Chinese-orchestrated bombing was a sham, all the major newspapers chose to withhold this information. They never divulged to the reading public the false pretext of a Chinese plot, and they fully backed the Kwantung Army's claim, successively featuring bogus reports that professed to reveal "the truth of the [Manchurian] incident." These reports were illustrated with photographs of the damaged rail beds and the corpse of a Chinese soldier allegedly responsible for the act. (He was actually killed and placed near the railway by the Japanese.)

Cornered by what seemed like unequivocal public endorsement, forged in no small part by such newspaper coverage, Wakatsuki's government, on September 24, grudgingly approved the military operations. A pattern had been set: a hopelessly passive government accepting military aggression that it had neither initiated nor endorsed. Wakatsuki, unable to rein in the military, resigned in December and was succeeded by the leader of the opposition party, Inukai Tsuyoshi.

By February 1932, the three Manchurian provinces of Liaoning, Heilongjiang, and Jilin were all under the control of the Japanese army. That garrison forces could occupy portions of China without formal approval sent a dangerous signal. Young and frustrated soldiers, willing to blame those in power for various social and economic difficulties facing Japan, had been wanting to force radical change for some time. Now inaction in Tokyo and the absence of clear instructions from the top invited further violent actions. The ancient samurai would have called this a retainer supplanting his lord. In modern military terms, it was simple insubordination. Yet no army leader was willing to put his foot down.

Japan's actions in Manchuria marked a major step toward political isolation, even though very few Japanese recognized it as such. The Kwantung Army's establishment of the puppet state of Manchukuo—comprising the captured provinces—was proclaimed on March 1, 1932. International condemnation followed. On May 15, a group of young naval officers and army cadets burst into the prime minister's official residence and shot Inukai; he died that evening. The killers were alarmed that Inukai was becoming soft on China, possibly yielding Japanese control of Manchukuo. Japan had been an exemplary member of the League of Nations throughout most of its existence, but the country renounced its membership in March 1933 on account of Manchukuo.

Sino-Japanese relations did not break down entirely, however, because of the confluence of pragmatic interests on both sides. Through the mid-1930s Tokyo oscillated between a more cautious, even friendly, China policy and a hardline approach backed by military pressure. Chiang, preoccupied by the problem of consolidating his control over the rest of China, and especially by fighting the Communists who had established independent "Soviet Republics" in the hinterland of southern and central China, seemed willing to overlook the sticky question of Manchukuo for the time being. He certainly did his best to avoid major clashes with Japan in the north. Recognizing a window of opportunity, the Kwantung Army expanded Japan's sphere of influence first toward Rehe (Jehol) Province, west of Manchuria, which became part of Manchukuo in 1933, and then toward the nearby areas of Hebei and Chahar (Inner Mongolia). In a series of Sino-Japanese agreements reached in 1933 and 1935, the Guomindang accepted humiliating terms that included partial demilitarization of North China, the withdrawal of the Guomindang organizations from Manchukuo's vicinity, and the establishment of autonomous, pro-Japanese governments in East Hebei and Chahar.

At home, as Japanese society struggled to recover from the economic slump caused by, among other things, the worldwide depression, fear and unrest were growing. In this dismal atmosphere, on February 26, 1936, a nearly successful coup was launched in Tokyo by young army officers. The officers assassinated several key government figures before surrendering. Prince Saionji, the principal target of the assassins, escaped. Prime Minister Hirota Koki's cabinet was formed on March 9, but only after Prince Konoe had declined to assume the post, claiming poor health. (He may well have not wanted to purge elements sympathetic to the rebel officers, as he himself wished to remain on good terms with them. His later attempt to pardon the indicted officers only corroborates this view.)

Hirota's government now adopted a tougher foreign policy as a way to divert domestic discontent. It called for a military buildup in preparation for a possible war with China, the Soviet Union, and the Western powers, all the while making plans for advancing into Southeast Asia. The Japanese policy shift was immediately felt in China, which explains the volatile atmosphere at the Marco Polo Bridge. The number of Japanese troops had tripled in 1936, to almost six thousand, without prior consultation with the Chinese.

China's domestic situation had substantially changed by then. Japanese expansionism and Chiang's ambition of leading a strong, unified China could only cohabit for so long. Because of his earlier concessions to Japan, Chiang had become increasingly vulnerable to Communist propaganda, which painted him as a traitor to the nation who gave into Japanese imperialist pressure and who was willing to sacrifice fellow Chinese. The decisive turning point happened in December 1936, when Chiang was kidnapped by the Young Marshal, Zhang Xueliang, the son of Zhang Zuolin, a Manchurian warlord assassinated by the Japanese in 1928; Zhang wanted Chiang to join a united front against Japan together with the Communists. To preserve his legitimacy as China's national leader, Chiang decided he could no longer afford to look conciliatory toward Japan. This meant that he and the Japanese army stopped sharing the same priority of defeating the Communists, be they Chinese or Soviet. This development, in turn, persuaded the Japanese military hardliners to push for a more aggressive policy, especially in the north, to sustain and maximize its existing interests.

KONOE, who had just taken office at the time of the Marco Polo Bridge Incident, managed to escalate it, as we have seen, even though he would disclaim any such intention. He formulated and encouraged policies that more often than not compromised one another, never quite seeing any of them to their completion, and the cumulative effect was disastrous.

More and more men, including those in their late thirties, were removed from the workforce and dispatched to war zones. The compulsory Conscription Ordinance of 1873 had been replaced by an even more extensive and universal Military Service Law in 1927, which would continue until 1945. Under the new system, a draftee for the army was expected to serve two years on active duty and remain on reservist duty for approximately fifteen years. In the case of the navy, the active service was three years and the reservist duty lasted nine. In order to mass-produce soldiers as the China War escalated, the military came to adopt looser health and physical fitness requirements (for example, the minimum height was lowered from five feet one to four feet eleven). Desperate to avoid serving, many men faked physical disabilities and illnesses. Some drank a supersize bottle of soy sauce before a physical in the hope of inducing temporary liver or heart failure. Others lost a massive amount of weight through the use of laxatives. The march toward mobilization continued anyway. The number of men qualified for military service climbed from approximately 20 percent in 1935 to 23 percent in 1937 and to 47 percent in 1939.

One soldier, Ushiotsu Kichijiro—let us call him Soldier U, as he could have been any of tens of thousands of others—was drafted in August 1937 to serve in the army right after the outbreak of the China War. Until his unit landed near the mouth of the Yangtze River, this shop owner from Kyoto had never heard a gunshot. Nor had he smelled anything as indescribably malodorous as the decomposing body of a Chinese soldier he stumbled over, which emitted a powerful stench of death and was being attacked by thousands of ravenous flies. The flies made such a loud, almost booming sound that he could not believe they were mere insects. At the ripe old age of thirty-one, Soldier U felt utterly unprepared for his new incarnation.

On patrol duty in one of the cities that the Japanese had just overtaken, Soldier U was checking houses to see if anybody was still inside when he was approached by a pretty young girl of about twelve. To his astonishment, she voluntarily led him to her bed. He was aghast and saddened by the girl's desperate gesture, fully conceding that some others would have easily taken advantage of the situation. (The eventual Japanese decision to institute the system of "comfort women," virtual sex slaves who were often forcibly recruited from the Korean Peninsula and elsewhere, was prompted by the overwhelming need to keep the urges of its soldiers under some kind of control.)

On another occasion, Soldier U witnessed a young Chinese woman who had just given birth stumble out of her house to escape a shoot-out. She was killed by stray bullets as she held her newborn, whose umbilical cord was still attached. Just as haunting, Soldier U helplessly looked on as Japanese soldiers threw Chinese captives into a creek and gunned them down as they struggled for their lives, their blood turning the water scarlet.

At the end of October 1937, when Soldier U heard the rumor that Tokyo's talks with the Guomindang were stalled, he was dismayed and fearful that what was supposed to have been a quick and easy war might last for some time. On his perilous way to Nanjing, Chiang Kai-shek's capital, he was delighted but surprised to cross paths with his older brother, who had been drafted after Soldier U's departure. He could not believe that a thirty-six-year-old was expected to serve, confirmation that things were not going so splendidly for Japan.

Soldier U had not yet seen the worst. As his unit made its way through the already fallen capital of Nanjing, the familiar odor of corpses overwhelmed him. Bodies were piled up at the Yijiang Gate, which served as the only escape route for the panicked Chinese soldiers and Nanjing citizens fleeing the Japanese advance on December 12, 1937. His unit had to slowly navigate the mountains of dead bodies, some of which had been completely flattened, like sheets of paper, by stampedes. He said his Buddhist prayers as he struggled on.

The sudden expansion of Japan's armed forces with people like Soldier U meant that the China War provided a major opportunity for speedy promotion for professional soldiers. They were expected to oversee those often unwilling and unfit recruits. This added to the professionals' perceived importance and ensured the further militarization of Japanese society, one manifestation of which was the emergence of patriotic women's associations. They petitioned volunteers to contribute to "thousand-stitch belts"—sashes with decorative embroidery sewn by a thousand different women in order to make them, purportedly, bulletproof—which were sent to the Chinese battlefields as a show of support. The belts became ideal homes for bedbugs (pejoratively called Nanjing bugs) to the dismay of many a wretched wearer.

The China War cost Japan the chance to recover the international respectability it had lost with its incursion into Manchuria. In July 1936, exactly one year before the outbreak of the war, Tokyo had won its bid to host the Olympic Games in 1940. The Japanese had lobbied tirelessly for the honor. It was to be one of the most important national projects for modern Japan, the first non-Western country to host the games. Construction of stadiums began swiftly. By 1938, though, international pressure on Japan to give up the games had been mounting. Some countries, including the United States, hinted at a boycott.

With no end to the China War in sight, the military, worried about its resource requirements, suggested that only lumber and stone be used for projects related to the games. Major newspapers that had been the biggest cheerleaders for the Tokyo Olympics became conspicuously silent on the issue. In late June 1938, Konoe's cabinet placed quotas on the use of industrial materials meant for projects other than war. This effectively put an end to Japan's Olympic dream. Tokyo would have to wait another two dozen years for its moment of Olympic glory.

Ironically, the hardening of international opinion against Japan took place just as the country was experiencing a surge in self-confidence apart from its military might. At the 1937 Paris Exposition, the thirty-six-year-old architect Sakakura Junzo, a disciple of Le Corbusier, won the top prize for his Japanese Pavilion. In August, Tokyo proudly hosted the World Federation of Education Associations' seventh biennial conference, the first to be held in Asia, which was attended by three thousand participants from forty-eight countries. And then there was the flight of the *Kamikaze*. When the two-seater left Tokyo on April 6, 1937, nobody in Europe seemed to have taken any notice of the great challenge that its twenty-four-year-old pilot, Iinuma Masaaki, and thirty-six-year-old flight engineer, Tsukagoshi Kenji, had undertaken. Japan was a completely unknown quantity in the glamorous but highly dangerous world of record-setting long-distance air races dominated by European and North American pilots. The Japanese flight was ostensibly planned to celebrate the coronation of King George VI, to be held on May 12, and to make goodwill visits to various European capitals. It was, in fact, a great publicity stunt for the *Asahi,* which followed in the footsteps of European newspapers by employing its own pilots to promote itself (and to gather news, of course).

The *Kamikaze* vogue became much more than a corporate advertisement as the whole nation became engrossed in the exploits of the two fliers. The aircraft, a test plane manufactured by Mitsubishi in Nagoya for military reconnaissance, was touted as "purely" Japanese-made, adding to the patriotic fervor. (Actually, the metals to construct it had come from somewhere else, as did the gasoline to fly it. And Tsukagoshi was half English.) The name of the plane was chosen from approximately five hundred thousand entries from *Asahi* readers. The naming ceremony on April 1 was presided over by Imperial Prince Higashikuni Naruhiko, the emperor's uncle by marriage, making the flight's success all the more a matter of national pride.

The Western media, indifferent at first, became enthralled. By the time the plane left Karachi and entered Mediterranean airspace on April 8, Europe began to hold its breath. On April 9, the plane appeared in the sky over the southern London neighborhood of Croydon. The aircraft circled around a few times, as if to please the cheering crowd of four thousand, including three hundred Japanese filled with joy and pride. The plane made an impeccable landing at half past three. The two aviators had established a long-distance world record, flying between Tokyo and London in fifty-one hours, nineteen minutes, and twenty-three seconds, with an average speed of 185.9 miles (299.2 kilometers) per hour. *The Times* of London reported: "As the airmen struggled to the ground from Divine Wind, they were greeted with cheers and cries of 'Banzai' ('live forever'), were decked with garlands of flowers and were submitted to an ordeal of handshaking and congratulation." The two continued to receive an enthusiastic welcome, winning great accolades, including the Legion of Honor accorded by the French government. In Brussels, on April 16, they were presented with flowers by Suwa Nejiko, a former child prodigy about to launch her career as a concert violinist in Europe, along with the family of the Japanese ambassador to Belgium, Kurusu Saburo.

Not unlike the *Kamikaze* aviators, the violinist Suwa had known something of the weight of enormous national expectations. Her success on the international stage had been a great source of Japanese pride for most of her young life. Still, she was like any other awestruck seventeen-year-old when she met the pilots. "How dreamy they are, both of them! Mr. Iinuma particularly is so very handsome . . . and I could just stare and admire him as much as I liked! Such a happy day it's been!" she recorded in her diary. This brief encounter in a Brussels airport presented a snapshot of the youthful beauty and exuberance that would soon elude Japan, like an ever-fleeting mirage. It was an image of Japan that could have been.

To celebrate the success of the *Kamikaze* flight, the proud sponsor published a message to the British nation in the pages of *The Times* on April 10, 1937. The flight, it said, would foster "an atmosphere of peace and cordiality in the midst of the storms and thunder which rage over international relations today and threaten the world peace of tomorrow." If only that had been true. Alas, Konoe's leadership did not live up to the feats of the *Kamikaze.*

Konoe felt his failures acutely. By the spring of 1938, he began to let his aides know that he was ready to resign. It took him until January 1939. Always believing himself to be on the right side, without quite knowing which side it was, and torn between conflicting interests, beliefs, and obligations, Konoe abandoned his country when it was caught in the China quagmire. People were still being told that Japan was leaping from victory to victory (from "dot" to "dot") in China, so the prince's exit was a source of bewilderment to many Japanese. Doubts about the success of the China War crept in.

None of the three short-lived cabinets before Konoe's comeback in July 1940 resolved the war in China. At the same time, Germany's military successes since September 1939 muddled Japan's strategic thinking. With the Netherlands and a large part of France now under Nazi occupation, and with the British having retreated from Dunkirk, their East Indian, Indochinese, and Malayan colonial possessions seemed ripe for the plucking. This tempted some strategists to conclude that Japan would probably be able to gather enough resources from Southeast Asia to settle the conflict with China to its advantage. In their minds, if Germany prevailed, the Western-backed Chiang Kai-shek regime would have to sue for peace. It therefore seemed imperative for Japan to secure the friendship of Germany.

On July 22, 1940, Konoe became prime minister for the second time when his predecessor, Admiral Yonai Mitsumasa, would not align Japan with the Nazis. The increasingly frail Prince Saionji declined to endorse Konoe's appointment. Their relationship had become irreparable, and would remain that way until Saionji's death in November of that year.

Encouraged by the strength of Germany—a fellow "have-not" country in Konoe's mind—he began his second premiership, as we have seen, hoping to end the war with China and carry out large-scale political reform. He envisioned a strong centralized political institution that would supersede parliamentary politics, and he counted on his supporters on both the right and left to launch his New Order Movement. How he thought he would avoid ideological conflict is anyone's guess. Originally, Konoe's adviser Ozaki Hotsumi, who was a secret communist, called for the creation of completely new local associations and assemblies to anchor the government. But bureaucrats succeeded in preserving the existing structure of the government, thus avoiding their own power bases being demolished.

Konoe's personnel choices reflected his tendency to try to please everyone, and he failed to stick to a specific political agenda. The country was stuck with a heavily compromised political entity called the Imperial Rule Assistance Association, some of whose programs followed fascist ideas of controlling every aspect of human endeavor, including reproduction.

One of the dubious projects that the new association embraced was the "redefining of IRAA-type beauty." Shortly after its formation, the association convoked a conference of physicians, dancers, artists, and ethnologists to consider the subject. It concluded that the ideal beauty was a sturdy, big-boned woman with wide hips. Unlike the willowy types preferred in the past, these wide-hipped beauties were thought more likely to bear many strong children, and so they were to be celebrated.

The establishment of mandatory neighborhood associations in the fall of 1940 would transform everyday life in Japan for years to come. Groups of about a dozen households were formed by the Home Ministry as the smallest and most basic building blocks of national mobilization. These associations were expected to fulfill many patriotic duties, such as organizing firefighting units (with a view to defending the nation under aerial attack), participating in patriotic rallies, and, increasingly, distributing rationed goods.

Representatives from neighborhood associations took turns waiting in long lines to buy rationed materials. They would then divide the purchases carefully according to the number of people in each household. Whenever a notice from the distribution center came (the frequency was random), those on duty were expected to "stop everything, leaving our half-cooked rice or precious hot water for washing made from the precious rationed fuel, and run to the distribution center," complained a doctor's wife in her diary. The vigilant and jealous eyes of one's neighbors made the task of equitable distribution a nightmare. Wilted lettuce leaves were taken with great offense even when they were the only kind available.

The possibility of being informed on by one's neighbors meant the associations were anything but neighborly in many cases. The system of mutual surveillance was too often based on mutual suspicion and fear. It was understood that the Special Higher Police, notorious for the brutal persecution of ideological crimes, had informers in every association. The force was founded in 1911 and gained power during the 1920s, when its primary enemies were Marxists, Communists, pacifists, and anarchists, who were all regarded as threats to the preservation of Japan's imperial polity.

In the state of national emergency caused by the China War, the Special Higher Police hugely expanded its target, prompting the very nature of social relations to change at the most fundamental level.

Those social changes notwithstanding, Konoe's foreign policy in his second government turned out to be rather like in his first: indecisive and impulsive. He usually took too much time when swiftness was called for and acted impulsively when caution was essential, and he had an alarming penchant for catering to the loudest voices around. In an attempt to counter increasing restrictions on imported industrial materials from the United States, his 1940 cabinet approved a proposal for the Japanese military to secure a firmer base in Southeast Asia. It was predicated on an army guideline that had been drawn up before Konoe's comeback. The Japanese occupation of northern Indochina that began on September 23, which initiated the U.S.-Japanese tit for tat, was a direct consequence of this policy shift.

Japan's signing of the Tripartite Pact with Germany and Italy on September 27 only added to the existing tensions. Konoe believed, along with his new foreign minister, that Japan's fascist alliance would deter the United States and lead to more advantageous diplomatic negotiations for Japan. The former ambassador to the United States, Viscount Ishii Kikujiro, and other members of the emperor's council were skeptical about Konoe's alliance making. In a meeting the day before the pact was signed, Ishii, in front of the emperor and other advisers, expressed his grave concern. He referred to Bismarck's remark that "alliances in international relations require a donkey and a rider, and that Germany should always strive to be a rider." Italy too could not be trusted because it was after all a "country that begot Machiavelli." But Ishii could not dissuade Konoe, who had earlier that day declared to the imperial advisers: "It is necessary to act defiantly with the United States so that it would not underestimate Japan. . . . But if the worst-case scenario happens, my government is resolved to deal with it."

Konoe followed up on his swaggering posture more publicly in a press conference on October 4: "I believe it is better for the United States if it tries to understand Japan's intention and actively participate in the building of the world's new order. If the United States deliberately misunderstands the true intentions of Japan, Germany, and Italy . . . and continues its provocative acts, there won't be any other options left to us but to go to war." His bluffing never worked. The following six months saw no diplomatic breakthroughs. Konoe faced his "worst-case scenario": a head-on collision with the United States.

The prince's melancholy mood in the spring of 1941 was therefore understandable. His government was confronted by increasing U.S. economic pressures and the dim prospect of winning the China War, or even of "exiting China honorably," as Richard Nixon might have said in Konoe's place. Konoe regretted his decision to ally Japan with the fascist powers but could still see a glimmer of hope. While military hotheads and ultranationalists urged war with the United States, leaders around Konoe recognized the utter impracticability of such a war.

The unspoken problem for many military leaders was keeping up appearances—that is, eliminating the war option without losing soldierly credibility. They were hesitant to concede to Chiang Kai-shek, or the United States, partly because their own restless officers had to be appeased. The Imperial Navy and Army were always vying with each other for more glory and more money, and neither could afford to appear weaker than the other. (Securing a bigger budget, remember, was one of the major reasons that the navy finally agreed to the signing of the Tripartite Pact.)

The military was not the only institution being pulled by different forces within it. The Foreign Ministry was divided primarily into pro-German and pro-Anglo-American factions. In the summer of 1940, Konoe's foreign minister had relieved many of the pro-Anglo-American diplomats from prominent posts and appointed Shiratori Toshio, the pro-Axis former Italian ambassador, as a special adviser to the Foreign Ministry. This had decisively undermined the ministry's liberal factions, with grave implications for the near future.

The vague constitutional position of the emperor also complicated matters. Although Hirohito had retreated more and more into a symbolic role as the godly patriarch of the family-state, he remained the supreme commander of Japan's armed forces. In these troubling times, Hirohito became even more sanctified in the eyes of the Japanese (those in power made sure of it). On November 10, 1940, almost fifty thousand people gathered in front of the Imperial Palace for the commemoration ceremony, presided over by Prime Minister Konoe, of the putative twenty-six-hundred-year existence of the Japanese imperial house. The ceremony was broadcast over the radio, and similar events were held throughout Japan; the people, who had been told for some time to give up any vacation plans, were encouraged to make pilgrimages to famous Shinto shrines. Many gladly acted on this recommendation, if only to break free of the drudgery of everyday life. Lavish entertainment was categorically discouraged, another signal of hard times.

The imperial anniversary succeeded in further elevating the status of the emperor, but at the same time, by stressing the role of the imperial household as a venerable, quasi-religious institution, it reduced the heavenly sovereign's *worldly* authority. This meant that Konoe could not expect much overt help from the emperor in steering Japan out of harm's way. As the highest of highborn Japanese who could stand on an equal social footing with the emperor, Konoe should have been able to candidly discuss political matters with Hirohito. But Marquis Kido Koichi, lord keeper of the privy seal since June 1940, made direct communications with the palace difficult. Konoe's government required an inordinate amount of patience and skill to lead. That is why the prince felt so anxious and often succumbed to the temptation to slip out of his office and into the arms of his favorite geisha mistress. Good news finally arrived from the United States in the early morning of April 18, 1941. Ambassador Nomura, in Washington, D.C., since the middle of February, had sent a telegram to the Foreign Ministry summarizing the so-called Draft Understanding between the United States and Japan. The hazy plan included a proposed U.S.-Japanese agreement on the recognition of Manchukuo, the merger of Chiang Kai-shek's and Wang Jingwei's governments to conclude the China War, and the normalization of trade relations. At the very least, the proposal could bring the estranged parties to the negotiating table.

The U.S. overture was enough to make Vice Foreign Minister Ohashi Chuichi rejoice. Apparently flustered upon reading the telegram, he reportedly cried out, "If this plan were to come true, the fate of the world will be changed for the better!" Hirohito welcomed the news, too. According to Kido's journal entry for April 21, the emperor remarked to the privy seal: "It was quite unexpected that the U.S. president came to us so willing to talk things over. I suppose one can say that all this happened as a result of Japan's making an alliance with Germany and Italy. In the end, it's all about being patient and persistent, wouldn't you say?" He spoke as if peace were at hand. At the liaison conference of key decision makers later that evening, the military leaders, including Army Minister Tojo, were for the most part delighted. The possibility of a U.S.-Japan rapprochement was especially welcome, as it came soon after the joint decision by the army and navy to tone down the previous year's ambitious plan to expand south. Resources in the Dutch East Indies had to be gained "in principle, only through diplomatic means," the joint decision said, and Japan should refrain from a military advance into Singapore and other parts of Southeast Asia.

Contrary to Hirohito's speculation that Roosevelt was "so willing to talk things over," the Draft Understanding was, in fact, the work of several amateur diplomats on both sides of the Pacific who wished to avoid war between the two countries. Bishop James Edward Walsh and Father James M. Drought, two American Catholic priests who belonged to Maryknoll, a foreign mission society based in upstate New York, launched the initiative when they arrived in Japan on November 25, 1940. During their monthlong stay, armed with letters of introduction from some powerful Wall Street figures, they requested interviews with Japan's key political, business, and military players, including Matsuoka Yosuke, Konoe's foreign minister. In these meetings, the priests expounded on the importance of improving U.S.-Japan relations. When asked about the exact nature of their relationship to the U.S. government, they gave enigmatic responses and discouraged further inquiries.

Upon their return to America, the priests contacted President Roosevelt's postmaster general, Frank C. Walker. A devout Catholic, Walker arranged their January 1941 visit to the White House, where they reported to Roosevelt that the Japanese leaders they had met desired better relations with the United States. The president continued seeking contacts with the Japanese through Walker and the priests, who eventually came up with the Draft Understanding, which would be revised by their Japanese friends (about whom we will hear more later).

At the April 18 liaison meeting, most Japanese leaders expressed a wish to respond to the U.S. overture immediately. Vice Foreign Minister Ohashi, however, felt that the dispatch of an affirmative reply had to wait until his superior, Foreign Minister Matsuoka, returned from Europe in four days. Ohashi's view prevailed. Little did they know that they were waiting for the arrival of a great storm.

CHAPTER 2

The Return of Don Quixote

On an early spring evening in 1941, with a sharpness in the air on the Russian steppes, the Japanese foreign minister was ecstatic. Traveling the Trans-Siberian Railway, nestled in the splendor of the Red Arrow's luxurious first-class car, one equipped with a salon and a private bathroom, Matsuoka Yosuke was basking in his greatest diplomatic achievement. He had just signed, on April 13, 1941, a neutrality pact with the Soviet Union. Courtesy of Joseph Stalin, there had been no shortage of vodka and caviar on this leg of his grand tour. Matsuoka's face grew redder and redder as he drank glass after glass.

When the foreign minister embarked for Europe on March 12, he was criticized by other government leaders. The stated goal of the trip was to celebrate the signing of the Tripartite Pact, despite the fact that no diplomatic benefits had been reaped from it. Many colleagues complained that the insufferably vain and flamboyant foreign minister was acting to promote his own interests and not those of his country. It was neither necessary nor useful, they thought, for Matsuoka to make a long international tour when, traditionally, the job of a Japanese foreign minister had been to instruct diplomats stationed around the globe from his base in Tokyo.

Matsuoka visited Hitler in Berlin, where he received a sumptuous welcome. There was a stiff, regimented kind of beauty in the Teutonic reception that overwhelmed his retinue, which included members of the Foreign Ministry, military officers, and journalists. All railway stations in Berlin had been adorned with the swastika and Rising Sun flags. When Matsuoka's train arrived, it was greeted with drumrolls and calls of *"Heil*

Hitler! Heil Matsuoka!" Matsuoka had the train windows opened and answered the impeccably uniformed Hitler Youth, raising his right arm in the Nazi salute. The gesture seemed to come instinctively, as if he were a Kabuki actor trained from birth to perfect the most unnatural theatrical effects. Only the reddening of his cheeks betrayed his true excitement at the sight of this Nazi welcome. Later, he was received cordially in Rome by Mussolini and the pope, but the Italian reception was nothing like this.

Matsuoka believed that his pact with Stalin was the greatest souvenir he could bring home. It would augment the Tripartite Pact, making it a quadripartite entente (or a "Eurasian Continental Alliance," in his words) pitted against the liberal Anglo-American alliance. He had envisaged this alliance for some time. "To shake hands with Germany is a temporary excuse to shake hands with the Soviet Union," he explained to his secretary before their departure for Europe. "But that hand shaking with the Soviet Union is also nothing more than an excuse to shake hands with the United States." He maintained that the sheer strength of this coming together of "have-not" powers would pressure the United States, an arrogant "have" power, into making conciliatory diplomatic gestures. Japan would then be able to live in a peaceful world—or the world according to Matsuoka—without having to fire even one bullet!

Matsuoka loved to shock, and he adored the limelight. If Konoe was the melancholic Hamlet, Matsuoka was Don Quixote, afflicted with a severe case of megalomania. Or, to use a Japanese theatrical metaphor once again, Matsuoka was a Kabuki actor, overstating his every move and line to thrill the audience, while Konoe was a Noh actor, moving very little and concealing his sentiments behind a silent, expressionless mask, leaving it to others to interpret him.

Physically, there was nothing remarkable about the bespectacled, mustached Matsuoka, a man of average height. Yet he was one of the most influential foreign ministers in the history of modern Japan. What set him apart was his extraordinary energy and belief in himself. Nothing pleased him more than to expound on his foreign policy philosophy for hours on end, ideally over some strong drink. He relished every opportunity to hold forth for anyone who was willing, or polite enough, to listen. He was one of the rare people bold enough to have what resembled a freewheeling discussion between equals with Hitler, a German interpreter noted.

Unlike many Japanese, Matsuoka did not try to hide his lack of modesty. In the summer of 1940, he lobbied tirelessly to become foreign minister in the second Konoe cabinet. Konoe was impressed, seeing in Matsuoka a self-made man with a genius for self-promotion that could be put to use for the benefit of Japan. Matsuoka was the kind of spokesman the prince felt the country desperately needed. Matsuoka's large-scale reorganization of the Foreign Ministry shortly after his appointment was unheard of, though, and hardly made him a popular figure there. He didn't care.

In a government where leaders were rarely willing to take individual responsibility for a policy outcome, and in a decision-making process that was prone to reduce decisions to the lowest common denominator, there was something to be said for Matsuoka's strong personality. It meant that he could get things done quickly. But his excessive nervous energy often put those around him off balance, as Konoe would soon realize. Matsuoka was so hyperactive that some thought he was addicted to cocaine, a substance to which he was rumored to have been introduced as a student in the United States. Unlike Konoe, who had led a sheltered life and had been handed everything, including the premiership, Matsuoka had to fight every step of the way to get where he was. He was born in 1880—eleven years before Konoe—in the prefecture of Yamaguchi, at the southwestern tip of the main Japanese island, into a once-wealthy family of wholesale maritime merchants. Because of debts arising from his father's speculative investments and his elder brothers' fast living, the family fortune had declined precipitously. That was why the thirteen-year-old Matsuoka set sail for the West Coast of the United States, where a relative had started a business.

Over the course of his New World adventures, Matsuoka lived with American families in Portland, Oregon, and Oakland, California. An ambitious boy, now known as Frank, he continued his studies while taking on various odd jobs—as a busboy, a farmhand, a janitor, a railroad worker, and even a substitute pastor presiding over weddings. The United States was to Matsuoka a haven from family destitution and a land of opportunities, no matter the hardships. He grew to love it, though he was deeply affected by the racial and social prejudices that were a blatant and undeniable part of his everyday existence. It was also in the United States that he first encountered Christianity, becoming a Methodist (he converted to Catholicism a few hours before his death). He obtained a law degree from the University of Oregon, graduating second in his class, all the while teaching himself Japanese law. He was not a mere bookworm. His Oregon classmates were impressed by his poker skills, which no doubt aided him in his diplomatic career.

Because of his mother's ill health, Matsuoka returned to Japan in 1902, at the age of twenty-two, having spent nine formative years in the United States. Despite his aggressive posture with the United States as foreign minister, he regarded the country as his second home. In his fifties, he would revisit the place of his adolescence and young adulthood to erect a marker and plant a tree at the grave of "my American mother," Isabelle Dunbar Beveridge, a devout Christian who had guided him in the Methodist faith.

In 1904, the young Matsuoka passed the Foreign Ministry exam at the top of his class (only seven passed out of an already select group of 130) and began his career as a diplomat. By choosing this professional path, he narrowly escaped being enlisted as a soldier in the Russo-Japanese War. He spent many years in China and had a short stint in Russia, where he was seduced, he later liked to boast, by beautiful women. In reality, he seemed to prefer alcohol to womanizing.

Since Matsuoka had a knack for making memorable speeches, a definite asset in multilateral conferences, he was dispatched as a Japanese spokesman to the Paris Peace Conference in 1919. It was there that he first met Konoe and got a whiff of what it was like at the top of the world. He yearned to be more than a bureaucrat. That was why in 1921, at the age of forty-one, he quit the Foreign Ministry. He was recruited for the board of the South Manchurian Railway, a semiprivate Japanese company with numerous subsidiary enterprises dealing with the development of northeastern China. His career flourished, and he became the vice president of the company in 1927. Three years later, he ran successfully for the Diet's lower house, the House of Representatives, as a member of the conservative political party Friends of Constitutional Government.

The Manchurian Incident of September 1931, when young Japanese officers laid the groundwork for the annexation of Northeast China, was of tremendous importance to Matsuoka's fledgling political career. Though he had not advocated the military occupation of Manchuria per se, he welcomed the takeover. He had been urging Japan to adopt a strong China policy on the basis of regional security, fearing a possible advance from the Soviet north. As a "Manchurian specialist," one who insisted that Manchuria was "Japan's lifeline," he saw his public career take off.

A LITTLE OVER a year after the Manchurian Incident, on February 24, 1933, in an auditorium of Switzerland's elegant Palais Wilson, a former luxury hotel on the western side of Lake Geneva, Matsuoka was the center of attention. The grand room was lit by five Bohemian glass chandeliers hanging from the arabesque ceilings painted in gold leaf. The delegates from some forty League of Nations member countries listened in silence as Matsuoka solemnly began to read aloud a prepared statement. It announced that Japan, one of the Big Five framers of the Covenant of the League of Nations, intended to withdraw from the league. This was a decisive first step that put Japan on the road to international isolation.

The league had just voted 42–1, Japan's the lone negative vote, to adopt the Lytton Commission's report. The document, submitted to the league in September 1932, was compiled by an independent commission, led by Lord Lytton of Britain, dispatched to the Far East to take stock of what had happened in Manchuria. It recommended that Japan should withdraw its troops and restore the country to Chinese sovereignty. Matsuoka, acting in close and often strained consultation with Tokyo, refused to accept the verdict.

Personally, Matsuoka was opposed to Japan's withdrawal from the league and doubted the integrity of Tokyo's last-minute decision, one based on its unwillingness to face the public humiliation of the league's final decision. As long as it remained in the league, the leaders in Tokyo argued, Japan would most likely be the victim of punitive economic sanctions (as would be the case with Italy over its invasion of Ethiopia). Such sanctions, they felt, would be hard to stomach. In the end, the government dodged the possibility of sanctions by leaving the intergovernmental arbitration forum altogether. For a country that had been preoccupied with international opinion throughout its modern existence, this was a drastic and shortsighted stopgap measure indeed.

The best Matsuoka could do was to minimize the damage of leaving the league by thoroughly explaining Japan's situation. On the podium, Matsuoka abandoned his prepared text, and his voice rose to a shout: "Read your history! We recovered Manchuria from Russia. We made it what it is today. . . . Japan has been and will always be the mainstay of peace, order, and progress in the Far East." He opposed international control of Manchuria: "Would the American people agree to such control of the Panama Canal Zone? Would the British permit it over Egypt?" After finishing the speech, he waved his arm at his delegation, and they all walked out.

This was without a doubt the most dramatic meeting in the league's history. Reporting from Geneva, the United Press correspondent described "the delegation, led by the dapper Yosuke Matsuoka" as looking "grim and determined." When the delegation departed, he wrote, "the crowded galleries broke into mingled hisses and applause."

Although the Lytton Report condemned the Japanese military action, it tried to recognize Japan's existing interests in and past contributions to the development of the region. After all, many of the leading powers, despite paying lip service to the importance of sovereignty, self-determination, equality, peace, and international understanding for all nations of the world, still enjoyed substantial colonial possessions. To single out Japan would have compromised their own empires. So the assembly was genuinely taken by surprise when Matsuoka's delegation left the hall in such a dramatic manner.

Matsuoka had been chosen to lead the Japanese delegation to the league's special session in part because of his knowledge of Manchuria. He was to convince the international assembly of the legitimacy of Manchukuo—a creation of the Japanese field army, as we've seen—with claims of Asiatic racial harmony, hypermodern urban planning, and vast agricultural frontiers the size of France and Germany combined and to turn international opinion in Japan's favor. Soon after Matsuoka arrived in Geneva on December 8, 1932, he made a memorably eccentric speech off the cuff, as he always preferred to do. "Currently, no one sees the significance of it," he said in defending Manchukuo, "[but] the world will eventually recognize that Japan was right." He continued in his typical dramatic fashion: "Japan is about to be put on a cross like Christ, and just as he was later redeemed in European societies, Japan will be redeemed." The address lasted for nearly ninety minutes. Matsuoka was then given a standing ovation by the audience, which was more likely applauding the conclusion of his long-winded speech than its content.

Ironically, Japan had been an exemplary member of the League of Nations since the organization's formation in 1920, sending its ablest bureaucrats and contributing substantial financial resources, largely because it judged that multilateralism and international cooperation were fast becoming the accepted norms of twentieth-century diplomacy. To its dismay and despite its best efforts, Japan quickly earned the nickname Silent Partner, as its representatives were often conspicuously reticent. Amused by the loquacious ambassador plenipotentiary, many in Geneva flattered Matsuoka, saying that Japan had finally moved on from a silent motion picture to a talkie.

The final vote on the Lytton Report came as a great disappointment to

Matsuoka, his intensive public relations work of the previous two months having proved utterly ineffective. He and his team had worked day and night, installing themselves in the Hotel Metropole on Lake Geneva and engaging in all sorts of lobbying activities, including screening a propagandistic documentary film on Manchukuo. Matsuoka's assistant at the time reminisced that even though his boss was stubborn and craved attention like a willful child, he was, by and large, kind to his junior staff throughout the stressful deliberations. The same assistant also revealed that Matsuoka rehearsed his "improvised" speeches for hours in his hotel room.

On that fateful day when Matsuoka announced Japan's intention to withdraw from the league, he remarked to those who'd gathered:

> The Japanese government now finds itself compelled to conclude that Japan and other members of the League entertain different views on the manner to achieve peace in the Far East, and the Japanese government feels it has now reached the limit of its endeavors to cooperate with the League with regard to Sino-Japanese differences. The Japanese government will, however, make the utmost efforts for the establishment of peace in the Far East and the maintenance and strengthening of cordial relations with other powers.

Matsuoka's defiant exit from the international conclave made him one of the country's most recognizable faces. Major Japanese newspapers, erring on the side of excessive jingoism to boost circulation, took the lead in portraying him as a man who stood up to the arrogant Western bullies and their pathetic client states. The enthusiastic reaction at home flabbergasted Matsuoka, but he was soon relishing the role of returning hero. He was now a full-fledged populist and a popular politician. Determined to capitalize on his newly acquired fame, in December 1933 he resigned from the House of Representatives and quit the Friends of Constitutional Government. For about a year afterward, he traveled across Japan on a lecture tour, giving 184 speeches to a total of seventy thousand people, promoting his so-called League for the Elimination of Political Parties. During the tour, he started putting up a huge Rising Sun flag behind the podium, which would become a customary practice to show one's patriotic allegiance.

In a December 1933 speech to a packed house at Japan Youth Center in Tokyo, he talked of the evils of both capitalism and communism and announced the death of Japan's parliamentary system: "I don't think that party politics is the only way to achieve a constitutional government. . . . Party politics is just one way of doing it."

By this time, his political credo had tilted toward fascism. But like Konoe's, his fascination with fascism was qualified and superficial. Matsuoka was certainly impressed with the rise of Nazi Germany, though obviously he could not embrace the racialist backbone of German National Socialism, which placed Asians in a subordinate position. That Matsuoka could not foresee the Nazi genocide is not to his credit. But he had, in fact, shown himself to be critical of Nazi policy. As the president of the South Manchurian Railway, where he worked again from August 1935 to February 1939, he was asked a favor by Major General Higuchi Kiichiro, stationed in Harbin. Higuchi had experienced and witnessed discrimination while on assignment in Poland and Germany, which led him to take an interest in Zionism and the plight of European Jews. After Japan's signing of the Anti-Comintern Pact with Germany in 1936, Higuchi said publicly that Jews should be given a homeland before being driven out of Europe. In March 1938, when Higuchi heard that a group of Jews escaping Germany was being kept out of Manchukuo, he turned to Matsuoka for help. Matsuoka had his company's trains safely carry the refugees to Shanghai, where they escaped persecution.

So Matsuoka's craving to be a strong and charismatic leader who could captivate and mobilize a nation like a fascist dictator in part explains his fascination with the Axis powers, though the primary reason for his alliance making, in his mind, remained first and foremost to gain relative power advantage in diplomatic negotiations with the United States. The superficiality of his grasp of Axis ambitions also explains why he utterly failed to appreciate the profound Anglo-American aversion both to the Nazis and to Japan's alliance with them.

"DIPLOMACY IS POWER, my dear young man. The Axis diplomacy is a lever used to gain power. Nobody has to tell me that. I know as much," an inebriated Matsuoka said as the Red Arrow roared through Russia on April 13, 1941. He was simply repeating to Saionji Kinkazu, a Foreign Ministry adviser in his thirties, what he'd said earlier on the trip. Matsuoka lectured Saionji in a state of drunken bliss: "The Tripartite Pact is not about an alliance made to wage war. It is made to keep peace!"

Matsuoka insisted that he was guided by power. He worshiped Metternich, the Austrian statesman celebrated for his skills in creating a sustainable balance of power between states and for successfully concluding the Napoleonic Wars at the Congress of Vienna. But times had changed. Fascism, liberalism, communism, and all their varieties competed with one another. Saionji believed Matsuoka was dangerously wrong to make light of the vast ideological differences among regimes.

Saionji, who received his higher education entirely in Britain, had always been close with his liberal grandfather Prince Saionji Kinmochi. He did not believe President Roosevelt or Secretary of State Hull could be intimidated into making a deal with Japan because Japan had signed a neutrality pact with the Soviet Union. In drinking sessions, Saionji told Matsuoka that Japan should not get too close to the Axis powers. Knowing that Konoe now regretted the Tripartite Pact, he wished that somehow Matsuoka, too, could see it as a diplomatic liability. "You must really support Prince Konoe," Saionji would tell Matsuoka, who would reply, "Yes, yes, I am supporting the prince. I even said that I would serve him as a secretary once he formed the cabinet. . . . But, Kinkazu-san, diplomacy requires expertise. And I know better what to do next."

As the train traveled on, Matsuoka felt increasingly sure that Japan's premiership was easily within his reach. Alcohol surely had something to do with it. But he was equally intoxicated by his memory of Stalin's recent largesse. A few hours earlier, just as Matsuoka's train was about to depart the station, Stalin emerged out of a deep Moscow fog with Foreign Minister Vyacheslav Molotov in tow. The Soviet leader had come to see Matsuoka off personally—a rare gesture, since Stalin was almost never seen in public, even with foreign dignitaries. "You see, I am an Asian," Stalin said. "I am from Georgia! We are brothers, so we must work together!"

Stalin had not taken his customary time to agree to the pact with Matsuoka. Just as the Japanese delegation had returned to Moscow from Berlin, Germany had attacked Yugoslavia, increasing Stalin's anxiety and perhaps leading him to overvalue Japan's involvement with the Nazis. To Stalin, the neutrality pact was a great bargain, one that ensured the safety of the Soviet eastern front without requiring any transfer of territory to Japan. Because Matsuoka had suggested the neutrality pact after visiting Berlin, Stalin believed that the Soviet Union was also safe from German attacks on its western front, at least for the time being. Stalin betrayed his anxiousness in his own understated way. When Japanese and Soviet delegates took turns signing diplomatic documents in Molotov's large spartan office in the Kremlin that day, Stalin, dressed in his signature charcoal-gray stand-collar suit unadorned by medals or other insignia, paced slowly, a cigarette in his hand. He then walked over to the buffet table that had been set up along one wall and started to inspect and rearrange glasses and cutlery as if he were the head butler of a stately mansion. Everything went smoothly afterward.

By the time Stalin and Matsuoka parted with a tight embrace at the station, they were equally cheerful and drunk. Long after the alcohol wore off, Matsuoka still felt the heady glow of invincibility. The growing tension between him and Konoe appeared to ease somewhat as a result of the good news Matsuoka was bringing home. "Matsuoka is an able man!" Konoe said upon hearing the news from Moscow.

The Japanese nation, accepting as usual the general tone set by uncritical radio and newspaper coverage, was thrilled to hear the news. The *Asahi* on April 23 praised Matsuoka for "breathing new life into the Tripartite Pact," suggesting that he had secured peace for Japan when it was on the verge of war with the West. Neither the United States nor Britain would dare provoke Japan now that the Soviet Union had made it clear it was not an Allied pawn. At the height of Matsuoka's popularity, his photographic portraits outsold those of most popular movie stars, even of Li Xianglan, a Manchukuo propaganda film star. (She was actually a Chinese-born Japanese called Yamaguchi Yoshiko and was secretly dating Matsuoka's eldest son.)

Matsuoka triumphantly returned to Japan on April 22, four days after Ambassador Nomura telegraphed the summary of the Draft Understanding to Tokyo. Though this news from Washington was a surprise, Matsuoka was initially pleased, as he wrongly surmised that he had been responsible for the sudden U.S. overture to begin diplomatic negotiations, that his balance-of-power approach with the Soviet Union had borne instantaneous fruit.

During his time in Moscow, Matsuoka had met with U.S. ambassador Laurence Steinhardt three times to see if Roosevelt could be persuaded to talk to him in light of "the new situation." According to a journalist who accompanied Matsuoka on the grand tour, he had a plan for winning the president's attention: Matsuoka would request a meeting with Chiang Kai-shek, and Chiang would agree. After their successful meeting, they would fly to Washington to meet Roosevelt. Roosevelt, Chiang, and Matsuoka would agree to the neutralization of the areas to the north of the

Great Wall of China, to Japan's withdrawal of troops from China, and to Manchukuo's recognition as an independent state. Then China-Japan and U.S.-Japan nonaggression treaties would be signed. When he first heard about the Draft Understanding from Konoe on the phone, while waiting in Dalian for a plane home, Matsuoka said to his secretary in high spirits: "Next we'll fly to America!" Such was the extent of Matsuoka's megalomania. When Matsuoka learned about the true origins of the Draft Understanding, he felt he was being upstaged. He had not authorized any of those involved on the Japanese side—or Ambassador Nomura, for that matter—to carry on critical diplomacy, and he was furious that the Draft Understanding proposed a meeting between Konoe and Roosevelt, not Matsuoka and Roosevelt, in Hawaii. He saw the news as threatening his authority, and it certainly shifted the limelight.

On the night of Matsuoka's return to Tokyo, a liaison conference of the cabinet and the general staffs was held to coordinate a Japanese response to Washington. In attendance were the key cabinet ministers, the army and navy chiefs of staff, and Vice Foreign Minister Ohashi, who had first received the news of the Draft Understanding. Matsuoka was determined to sabotage the discussion. This was supposed to be *his* moment. He opened the conference by boasting of his accomplishments on his European trip. When the discussion moved to the "U.S." proposal, Matsuoka barked at the attendees that Nomura had no idea what he was doing and that it was important to remain loyal and truthful to Germany as an ally. For that reason, he insisted that the content of the Draft Understanding had to be reported to the Germans. He was convinced that the proposal "was a product of 70 percent malicious intent and only 30 percent goodwill." He delayed a decision on what action to take and, citing exhaustion and ill health, left the room.

Following Matsuoka's exit, Ohashi said Matsuoka had made it clear to him, on his way back from the airport, that he was not going to reply to the United States anytime soon. But most of those in the room, including the military men, were in favor of engaging with the United States as soon as possible. In a typical display of disengagement and indecision, Konoe, who said he had a high fever, retreated to his villa.

Impatient for instructions, the Japanese negotiators in Washington telephoned Matsuoka on April 29, to no effect. Nomura was upset and disappointed; he had believed Matsuoka would jump at the opportunity to start negotiations, especially since the Draft Understanding conformed to Matsuoka's core diplomatic aim of settling matters through talk. Nomura kept apologizing for the delay during his frequent visits to the secretary of state's apartment at the Carlton Hotel, asking Hull not to "become impatient," as "there was politics in the situation back in Japan."

ROOSEVELT AND HULL HAD NOT ACCEPTED the Catholic priests' claim that the majority of Japan's leaders wished to avoid war. Washington simply regarded the document as a way of initiating official communication with the country. The fact that the document had no direct association with the White House and had been initiated by diplomatic amateurs on both sides eluded most in Tokyo, however.

The foremost member of such aspiring peacemakers on the Japanese side, Ikawa Tadao, was a forty-seven-year-old banker. Ikawa had gone to school with Konoe and had helped to establish a brain trust for the prince some years earlier. Once married to an American woman, he served as treasurer for the Japanese consulate in New York for most of the 1920s and had many contacts in the United States. He had arranged for the two American priests to gain access to the Japanese leaders during their visit to Tokyo the previous winter. Over the course of their stay, he decided he, too, would like to have a role in the peacemaking project.

Suave and good-looking, Ikawa seemed at such ease with the world that he gave off an almost frivolous, supercilious air, which many, including Matsuoka, distrusted. But he possessed an equal amount of energy and ambition. Upon receiving the news from the priests that Roosevelt had agreed to engage in finding a diplomatic solution, Ikawa went to New York in a purely private capacity, ostensibly to settle matters with his American ex-wife. He arrived on February 27, 1941.

Because he lacked official institutional affiliation with the Foreign Ministry, he was treated frostily by the staff of the Japanese embassy in Washington. Still, he managed to win the trust of the most senior appointee there. Newly stationed and also something of an outsider, Ambassador Nomura was at first skeptical of Ikawa. Though he had been told by Matsuoka to steer clear of him, Nomura took Ikawa more seriously after the banker set up a surreptitious meeting on March 8 at the secretary of state's apartment to introduce the ambassador to Hull. With the arrival of Colonel Iwakuro Hideo, a forty-two-year-old elite staff officer with detailed knowledge of the China-Japan conflict, the American-Japanese "informal conversations"—as the talks would be called by the Americans—soon began.

The proposal originally drafted by the priests was heavily revised by Iwakuro in consultation with Nomura, the embassy's military attachés, and a treaty specialist. The Japanese team gathered in a basement room of the embassy, long after other staff members had gone home, to prepare a lengthy document whose important points can be paraphrased as follows:

1. The United States and Japan would recognize that they were powerful neighboring countries in the Pacific and, through mutual effort, would strive to achieve peace in the region and a friendly understanding.

2. Japan would affirm that the aim of the Tripartite Pact was to prevent the expansion of the European war. Japan's military obligation would be called for only if Germany were to be aggressively attacked by a third party not yet part of the war. The United States would determine its response to the European war solely on the basis of protecting its own welfare and security.

3. The U.S. president would advise Chiang Kai-shek's government to make peace with Japan if the president approved of, and the Japanese government agreed to, the following conditions: (a) China's independence, (b) withdrawal of Japanese troops based on Sino-Japanese treaties, (c) nonannexation of Chinese territory, (d) no indemnities, (e) China's resumption of the Open Door policy, (f) the merger of the Chiang Kai-shek and the Japanese-backed Wang Jingwei governments, (g) Japanese self-restraint on massive immigration to China, and (h) recognition of Manchukuo.

4. Both the United States and Japan would refrain from placing aerial and naval power on duty in the Pacific for intimidation purposes.

5. The governments would resume the U.S.-Japan Treaty of Commerce and Navigation.

6. Japan would not resort to force and would rely only on peaceful means for its advantage in the Southwest Pacific (including Southeast Asia). In return, the United States would help Japan secure resources, including oil, rubber, tin, and nickel.

7. For the political stabilization of the Pacific, neither the United States nor Japan would accept European advancement into the Pacific region, both would guarantee the independence of the Philippines, and the United States would guarantee that Japanese immigrants were treated like all others, without discrimination.

Twenty-year-old Crown Prince Hirohito (center) visiting British prime minister David Lloyd George (to his right) in May 1921

Emperor Hirohito, supreme commander of the armed forces, 1941

Lord Keeper of the Privy Seal Kido Koichi, the emperor's closest aide, acted as the gatekeeper of the palace.

A rare glimpse of an imperial conference attended by top military and civilian leaders in January 1938

Jubilant actors and their audience at the Kabukiza Theater cheer the fall of Nanjing in December 1937.

Rice rationing began in major cities in April 1941. The sign at this distribution center reads INCREASED DISTRIBUTION FROM TODAY.

Well before the de facto total U.S. oil embargo in August 1941, the dearth of petroleum in Japan led to the invention of cars that ran on charcoal.

Prince Konoe Fumimaro impersonates Adolf Hitler at the costume banquet held on the eve of his daughter's wedding in the spring of 1937, shortly before he was named Japan's prime minister.

Konoe moderated his hawkish stance in this radio address on November 3, 1938, announcing that Japan was fighting China to build a "New East Asian Order" for the good of the whole of Asia.

At the signing of the Tripartite Pact in Berlin in September 1940 are Ambassador Kurusu Saburo (left), Foreign Minister Galeazzo Ciano of Italy (center), and Hitler.

Konoe leads banzai cheers at the founding ceremony of the Imperial Rule Assistance Association, formed in October 1940.

Early in 1941, Konoe's government dispatched Admiral Nomura Kichisaburo to Washington, D.C., in the hope of averting hostilities. Joseph Grew, the U.S. ambassador to Japan, sees him off at Tokyo Station.

The Konoe government's pro-Axis policy was led by Foreign Minister Matsuoka Yosuke (middle), a U.S.-educated eccentric with a flair for publicity. In the spring of 1941, he is welcomed at Anhalter Station in Berlin. Joachim von Ribbentrop, the Nazi foreign minister, is to his left.

Matsuoka negotiated a neutrality agreement with Stalin, signed on April 13, 1941. The two bid farewell at Moscow's Yaroslavsky Station.

On July 18, 1941, Konoe (first row, right) formed a new cabinet without Matsuoka, including Navy Minister Oikawa Koshiro (second row, far left), Foreign Minister Toyoda Teijiro (third row, far left), Army Minister Tojo Hideki (next to Oikawa), and the general director of the Cabinet Planning Board, Suzuki Teiichi (in the light-colored suit a few steps behind Konoe)

In early August 1941, Japanese forces start arriving in Cambodia, part of French Indochina.

The August 1941 meeting between U.S. president Franklin D. Roosevelt and British prime minister Winston Churchill in Newfoundland to discuss the future of their alliance and the war in Europe culminated in the Atlantic Charter

Admiral Yamamoto Isoroku was opposed to Japan's Axis alliance. This photograph was taken in November 1940, shortly before he started devising his Pearl Harbor strategy.

The chief of the Navy General Staff, Nagano Osami (above), and the chief of the Army General Staff, Sugiyama Hajime (right), strongly pushed for war preparations in the summer and fall of 1941.

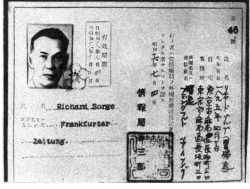

The German newspaper reporter Richard Sorge was a Soviet spy operating in Tokyo on the eve of the war in the Pacific. Shown here is his foreign correspondent ID.

Ozaki Hotsumi, a secret Communist and a well-known journalist, helped Sorge infiltrate Japan's political elite.

Ozaki profited greatly from his close friendship with Saionji Kinkazu, who, as Konoe's aide, had access to government information.

Togo Shigenori, a veteran diplomat, became foreign minister in the Tojo government following Konoe's resignation on October 18, 1941.

In Washington, Ambassador Nomura (left) and the recently arrived diplomat Kurusu are led by Secretary of State Cordell Hull from the State Department to the White House to meet Roosevelt in November 1941.

Pearl Harbor in the aftermath of the Japanese attacks, December 7, 1941

An Osaka crowd reads handwritten reports of the Japanese attacks on the United States and its allies.

Imperial Prince Higashikuni Naruhiko addresses the first postwar session of the Diet, Japan's parliament, on September 5, 1945.

On April 16, Hull asked Nomura whether Japan would be willing to start negotiations on the basis of this Japanese-revised document, one that "contained numerous proposals with which my Government could readily agree." Hull also said that the document would "require modification, expansion, or entire elimination" of some sections, in addition to "some new and separate suggestions." Nomura's telegram reporting on his meeting with Hull failed to make clear that the Draft Understanding was not an official U.S. government proposal. This was, according to a later admission by Iwakuro, a deliberate choice in wording made by an aide to Nomura; Minister-Counselor Wakasugi Kaname thought it more effective to emphasize the U.S. eagerness and to deemphasize the Japanese hand in the document. Nomura's telegram to Tokyo was nonetheless clear on the U.S. government's wish to revise it further. It is possible that Vice Foreign Minister Ohashi, in his initial excitement over receiving Nomura's telegram, failed to stress this U.S. qualification, so the leaders in Tokyo may therefore have been left with the impression that Washington was suggesting a proposal far more accommodating of Japanese demands than the Americans were probably ever inclined to be.

Matsuoka, to his credit, realized that his colleagues in the government had celebrated too soon. He discarded the distorted version of the Draft Understanding in Nomura's dispatch and demanded to consult the original English text. In early May, he complained to a Foreign Ministry official in private that "the Draft Understanding that came from America is appalling" because

> clearly, that's not a U.S. document. That thing has been written by Japanese. Everyone, including Prince Konoe, seems to think that the hardest part is over, that we just need to give the United States a positive reply. What fools! . . . I guarantee you, once we start negotiating, all sorts of problems are bound to emerge. . . . With the China Incident still going on, we cannot negotiate [with Washington] properly. . . . And if the negotiation fails, that will have given the military an excuse to start a war. I know I am right.

Matsuoka was right that things weren't as rosy as they'd first looked. But rather than seeing the proposal for what it was—a chance to signal Japan's readiness to talk—he overreacted partially out of personal pettiness and spite. At a liaison conference of key government ministers and military leaders on May 3, having finally emerged from his self-imposed seclusion (though in the middle of his absence he felt well enough to criticize Konoe in a public speech), Matsuoka presented what came to be called the May 12 Plan. (It would be delivered by Nomura to Hull on that date.) It could have been called the Matsuoka Plan. It claimed to be an elaboration of the Draft Understanding, but the content differed greatly. One of the more conspicuous changes involved the future of the European war:

> The Governments of the United States and Japan make it their common aim to bring about the [sic] world peace; they shall therefore jointly endeavor not only to prevent further extension of the European War but also speedily to restore peace in Europe.

Matsuoka's aspiration—propelled by his unquenchable thirst for "greatness"—to broker peace in Europe may have been well meant, but he completely misread the situation: The Roosevelt administration wasn't in any way inclined to negotiate with the Nazi regime. Besides, how could a country that was unable to end its own war with China be of help to others? Japan's new proposal eliminated all the conditions for peace talks in China, presumably because Matsuoka did not want to be bound by specific terms. He insisted that if Chiang Kai-shek would not agree to make peace with Japan, the United States should abandon its support for his regime. Japan wanted to be left alone and to be helped at the same time. Matsuoka offered to guarantee the independence of the Philippines on the condition that the islands would "maintain a status of permanent neutrality" and that "Japanese immigration to the United States shall receive amicable consideration—on a basis of equality with other nationals and freedom from discrimination." The Draft Understanding had pledged that "Japanese activities in the Southwestern Pacific area shall be carried on by peaceful means, without resorting to arms." This language was struck from the new proposal because it was deemed "inappropriate and unnecessarily critical" and because "the peaceful policy of the Japanese Government has been made clear on many occasions in various statements made both by the Premier and the Foreign Minister." This deletion meant that Japan would not give up military options in Southeast Asia. The Roosevelt administration was alarmed by that.

Matsuoka surprised even the Japanese military with his uncompromising posture. He wanted everyone to know he would negotiate only from a position of power—or, rather, a semblance of power. He was acting on his conviction that defiance and assertiveness were the most valued currencies in dealing with the United States.

In their desire to see a tougher Japan, Matsuoka and Konoe were remarkably alike, despite their great differences in personality. When he had just returned from the United States, the twenty-two-year-old Matsuoka reportedly told his old schoolteacher that "the important thing to remember is never be underestimated by the Americans." He then went on to describe a hypothetical scenario in which a Japanese and an American came across one another on a narrow path:

> The American would not thank you if you bowed to him and politely gave way. He would actually look down on you, thinking that you were a total pushover. If you give him a punch in the face, that's when he will start respecting you, seeing you as his equal. Japanese diplomats should take note of this [American character] from now on.

The "Matsuoka Plan" only solidified Hull's utter dislike of the Japanese foreign minister. (Hull and Nomura had been forming a curious bond over this of late. When Hull complained to Nomura on May 11, the day before he received Matsuoka's new plan, of the difficulty in trusting the foreign minister's "acts and utterances," Hull noted that "not only did [the ambassador] not take issue with anything I said, but I felt that he was really in harmony with the statements I made about Matsuoka.") Upon receiving the document from Nomura and discovering the deletion of the "without resorting to arms" passage, Hull murmured to himself, "So this means that there is no guarantee that they won't go south," a reference to Japan's forays into Southeast Asia to strategically strengthen itself.

Washington had suggested at the outset that the unofficial Draft Understanding should be the starting point for a new thrust of U.S.-Japanese dialogue. But Matsuoka insisted that Japan could not start talks unless certain demands were accepted by the United States first. By being difficult, he believed, Japan was earning Washington's respect. In reality, Japan was squandering an opportunity for a practicable settlement.

At this point, Washington was still prepared to make some substantial accommodations for Japan. For instance, Hull had said he could negotiate with Japan only if it accepted his Four Principles: (1) respect for the territorial integrity and the sovereignty of each and all nations, (2) support of the principle of noninterference in the internal affairs of other countries, (3) support of the principle of equality, including equality of commercial opportunity, and (4) continuation of the status quo in the Pacific, though the status quo might be changed by peaceful means. But in a personal exchange with Nomura, Hull said the fourth principle "would not . . . affect 'Manchukuo,' but was intended to apply to the future from the time of the adoption of a general settlement." Matsuoka's response had set an irreversible premise for the Japanese negotiators, as well as for the military. By insisting on Japan's right to use force in the south, he unnecessarily made an issue out of something that the military itself had been willing to forgo. The army in particular wanted to arrest further adventures after it had fought, from May to September 1939, a series of disastrous border battles with the Soviet Union at Nomonhan near Manchukuo. Matsuoka, a civilian who had avoided military service, was coaxing the military to adopt a tougher attitude.

Konoe said he had gone to the airport to personally welcome Matsuoka home after the European trip and so that they could discuss the background of the Draft Understanding. He didn't want the hypersensitive Matsuoka to be offended by having been left out of this new development. But according to Konoe, Matsuoka would not ride back with him, insisting that the foreign minister's first duty was to make a formal ceremonial bow to the Imperial Palace. Taken aback by Matsuoka's frostiness, Konoe gave up on sharing a ride. Because of this, Konoe later said, the rift between them deepened.

In spite of his growing dissatisfaction with Matsuoka, Konoe let him take charge of his government's diplomacy, even at the risk of alienating Washington. Konoe simply refused to confront his foreign minister. Matsuoka kept telling other leaders that he knew so much more than they did about the big and hostile world beyond Japanese shores. No one could refute him. As one army officer on the general staff later recalled, "Matsuoka's customary method was to bring in his proposal directly to a liaison meeting and force it through no matter what. The way he managed it was actually quite admirable." In a political culture where surprises were wholly unwelcome and prior consultations remained the norm, Matsuoka was one of a kind. The Japanese expression "digging around a tree's root before transplanting it" did not apply to his methods.

Konoe, on the contrary, preferred behind-the-scenes deal making and was slowly starting to lay the groundwork for the ouster of his foreign minister. Matsuoka was no ordinary foe, and the prince felt his fall had to be carefully orchestrated in the time-honored tradition of political intrigue, at which the prince innately excelled. But for that to happen, Konoe needed some time, a lot more time than Japan could really afford.

CHAPTER 3

The Beginning of It All

The year 1882 was key in Japanese military history because of an official document issued by Japan's fledgling modern government.

Mutsuhito, twenty-nine years old and the first modern emperor of Japan, held that document in his hands on the fourth day of the new year, in a red-carpeted hall of the Imperial Palace. As with so many other things in the nascent state, the palace in which the emperor and his select audience gathered was makeshift. The official residence—the previous one had burned down some years before—was still under construction. Dressed in a black military uniform and wearing a pair of ceremonial white gloves, Mutsuhito, like a well-trained gymnast, stood bolt upright behind a podium covered in heavy gold-threaded fabric fit only for such pageantry. Conspicuous in the mostly Western-style setting was the traditional hibachi charcoal burner placed behind him to warm His Majesty's imperial backside.

By the standards of his time, Mutsuhito was tall, five feet six. (The Japanese would experience a growth spurt due to a Westernized diet that included meat and dairy introduced under his rule.) He had a stern expression, glaring eyes, and a thick black beard. On the other side of the podium stood Army Minister Oyama Iwao. A pudgy man ten years older than Mutsuhito, Oyama shared with the emperor a weakness for Western epicurean pleasures, especially beefsteak and fine French wines. Affectionately known among his peers as Toadie, Oyama was also clad in a dark Prussian-style uniform (copied, along with other institutional arrangements, from the Prussian army at the height of its power). When the moment came for him to accept the imperial document, Oyama extended his arms with all the ceremonious solemnity he could muster. He then bowed deeply to the emperor. With great pomp, the Imperial Rescript to Soldiers and Sailors, the emperor's decree on how to become a good soldier, descended from the hands of the heavenly sovereign into those of his humble subject. The ceremony was meant as much for the outside world as for the domestic audience, to drive home the message that Japan took the business of modernizing seriously and that it would not be satisfied with the unequal treaties that had been forced upon it by the great powers of the West.

Some Western witnesses scorned Japan's initial efforts at state pageantry. Most famously, the French sailor and novelist Pierre Loti lampooned the Japanese in his *Madame Chrysanthème,* an autobiographical story of a brief marriage of convenience between a French naval officer and a Japanese woman that would inspire Puccini's opera *Madama Butterfly.* His lesser-known *Un Bal à Yeddo* (*A Ball in Edo*) describes a night at the Rokumeikan, a two-story building in Tokyo with a ballroom that opened in late 1883 to entertain foreign guests. This is how Loti depicts Japan's newly modernizing gentlemen and their ill-fitting Western clothes: "The suit of tails, so ugly even on us, how strangely they wear them! . . . It is impossible to say why exactly, but it seems to me they all somehow resemble monkeys."

A ladies' man, Loti is a little more charitable to the opposite sex:

Oh! and these women! . . . young unmarried girls stuck on chairs, or their mothers lining the walls like tapestries, on close observation they are remarkable creatures. What is it that is wrong with them? Search as I may, I cannot define it precisely: it is probably that the hoops are too much or insufficient, their position too high or too low, or that the curve-inducing corset is unknown. But their appearance is neither vulgar nor common, with their tiny hands and their costumes imported directly from Paris. . . . No, they really are strange, in spite of everything—they remain unconvincing, smiling, with their narrow eyes, pigeon-toed, and flat nosed.

The self-consciously lavish soirées at the Rokumeikan, which began after the promulgation of the Imperial Rescript to Soldiers and Sailors, were part of Japan's national project, a demonstration of the newly modernizing state. Designed by the young British architect Josiah Conder, the Rokumeikan, which looked neither completely Western nor Eastern, was meant to be the site of impressive bashes. But it was not only the condescending Loti who was taken aback by the strangeness of it all. The uneasiness extended to the Japanese themselves. Many women were reluctant to dance, out of either decorum or embarrassment, which was why men far outnumbered women at these balls. But nothing kept some patriotic Japanese from literally dancing for modern Japan. Okura Kihachiro, an eccentric and fun-loving hotelier who cofounded the Imperial Hotel in Tokyo as well as the Rokumeikan, described an odd couple he witnessed on the dance floor one evening:

> The partners were both men, one with the huge build of a sumo wrestler, the other an especially skinny fellow; the couple was dancing in all seriousness but since their contrast was peculiar it created a commotion among the spectators, who were trying to determine their identity. On closer observation, the huge man turned out to be Oyama, Japan's minister of war, and the skinny man was the then governor of Tokyo. . . . Now on this occasion Oyama was in formal Western military attire while his companion was in Japanese kimono and *hakama,* and they were earnestly engaged in dancing, at which neither was very good.

For Japan, the so-called Rokumeikan epoch represented an era of profound transformation. The Imperial Rescript to Soldiers and Sailors was a critical initial step in this. Together with the Imperial Rescript on Education, issued in 1890, it would come to define the very character of modern Japanese nationalism and the Meiji state. (Meiji, meaning "enlightened rule," was the name given to Mutsuhito's reign after his death.) It constituted not simply a code of military conduct but also an imperial order to military men, who were expected to nurture and retain an essential Japanese spirit even in the fast-modernizing world. The preamble of the rescript stated that the emperor was the supreme commander of the armed forces, made up of military professionals as well as draftees serving compulsory three-year terms of military service, which were instituted in 1873. The men were to cherish five virtues—loyalty, courtesy, bravery, honor, and frugality—as their guiding principles. The most significant virtue of all was loyalty, which stressed the military man's absolute deference to the emperor (rather than to any elected government). "We are your Supreme Commander-in-Chief," the rescript began, and continued:

Our relations with you will be most intimate when We rely upon you as Our limbs and you look up to Us as your head. Whether We are able to guard the Empire, and so prove Ourself worthy of Heaven's blessings and repay the benevolence of Our Ancestors, depends upon the faithful discharge of your duties as soldiers and sailors. . . . The soldier and sailor should consider loyalty their essential duty. . . . Remember that, as the protection of the state and the maintenance of its power depend upon the strength of its arms, the growth or decline of this strength must affect the nation's destiny for good or for evil; therefore neither be led astray by current opinions nor meddle in politics, but with single heart fulfil your essential duty of loyalty, and bear in mind that duty is weightier than a mountain, while death is lighter than a feather. Never by failing in moral principle fall into disgrace and bring dishonor upon your name.

Despite the wording, the exact relationship between the government and the armed services would prove highly difficult to define.

The Meiji Constitution, which went into effect approximately eight years afterward, did not clarify the matter, failing to mandate that the military was answerable to the government. This left far too much room for right-wing politicians and radicalized officers half a century later to claim that they were free to pursue separate policies by "advising" the emperor and to invoke the notion of the independence of the supreme command. That is why the 1882 imperial decree could be considered one of the latent underlying causes of Japan's militarization of the 1930s and, eventually, its attack on Pearl Harbor.

In the beginning, the rescript served the immediate purpose of consolidating the new regime's fledgling armed forces. It was drafted by the leading military and intellectual figures of the time, most notably the architect of the Imperial Army, Yamagata Aritomo. It was meant, above all, to assuage feelings of discontent brewing in certain segments of the new and open Japan. In 1882, many disenfranchised samurai remained dissatisfied with the regime that had replaced the Tokugawa shogunate in 1868. Having lost their social privileges as a warrior caste, they bore a grudge against the Meiji state and yearned for the old order.

Beyond such mundane resentment, there were very good reasons to be unhappy with the new government. Progressive-minded people, typically idealistic young men from the educated samurai class, felt that the Meiji reforms did not go deep enough. In the 1870s, such sentiments gave rise to Japan's first mass freedom and popular rights movement, which spread to all social and economic classes. Inspired by the writings of Western liberal philosophers such as John Stuart Mill and Jean-Jacques Rousseau, democratic activists attacked the oligarchic tendencies of the new regime and called for the establishment of a constitution and an elected representative legislature. They also made pioneering efforts in promoting general social welfare and individual rights, including those of women and social outcasts historically discriminated against for their hereditary association with "tainted" professions, such as tanning and butchery.

By 1880, this had become a powerful, sometimes subversive mass movement. As would any government whose newly attained power was anchored in force, the new regime reacted at first by resorting to repressive measures. This approach had limited success. With surprising flexibility, the government then switched course, acknowledging the extent of the movement's success by promising in 1881 that there would be a national assembly in ten years' time.

When the Imperial Rescript to Soldiers and Sailors was issued soon after that, the democratic activists were less than happy with the emperor demanding categorical loyalty and obedience. But the 1882 decree was tenuous. Japanese emperors could boast the longest continuous monarchical line in the world, but they had not exercised much earthly power for centuries. Certainly, on the eve of the birth of modern Japan, the Tokugawa shogun was a much more obvious leader of Japan than was Mutsuhito.

For a long time, the task of centralizing and reigning over Japan, in a political sense, had been left to samurais, with emperors relegated to supporting roles, giving the warrior rulers their blessing. In 1603, the warlord Tokugawa Ieyasu emerged as the victor in the bloodiest power struggle to unite Japan, and rulers from his family governed Japan for more than 250 years. A sophisticated system of hierarchy and patronage was installed to prevent internal rebellions. The Tokugawa rulers took precautions against the influx of disruptive foreign ideas and influences, the most threatening of which, they believed, was Christianity. Although Chinese and Koreans could still enter Japan, the Tokugawas allowed only a handful of Dutch merchants (the least proselytizing of all Westerners) to establish a tiny trading post on Nagasaki Bay.

To its credit, the imperial institution had proved its resilience by repeatedly adapting to changing times. In the age of competing warlords, the emperors barely preserved their position as the guardians of Shintoism, an animistic and syncretic religion based on nature and ancestral worship. But thanks to the Tokugawa rulers, who looked to emperors to legitimize their claim to temporal power, the court went through something of a renaissance. By according imperial sanction to the Tokugawa family to rule Japan, the emperors revived their legitimacy as ultimate and inviolable kingmakers endowed with heavenly power. The symbiotic relationship was not unlike that of some European monarchs and the Vatican.

When young reformers replaced the Tokugawa government in the Meiji Restoration, they, too, looked to the emperor for his blessing. But they went even further. They made the fifteen-year-old Mutsuhito the public rallying point for Japan's rebirth as a modern power. A year after the restoration of "direct" imperial rule over the country was declared in January 1868, the imperial family completed its move from Kyoto, where it had traditionally been housed, to the old Edo Castle in Tokyo, which the last Tokugawa shogun had only recently vacated. For the first fifteen years of his life, the boy-emperor had been hidden from the view of his subjects. Now his portrait was displayed in public spaces and private homes.

In the early years, Mutsuhito was paraded across the country—271 times in the first decade of his reign—in order to connect him with his subjects, who did not even know that they had an emperor. Erwin von Bälz, a German physician who came to Japan to teach Western medicine, noted in his diary in 1880 that it was distressing to see "how little interest the populace take in their ruler." People had to be coerced to celebrate Mutsuhito's birthday: "Only when the police insist on it are houses decorated with flags. In default of this, houseowners do the minimum."

The Mutsuhito who ceremoniously issued the Imperial Rescript to Soldiers and Sailors was a modern emperor, one who looked, behaved, and spoke like the antithesis of the kimono-clad adolescent he had been in the ancient capital. The emperor's Western clothes and full facial hair were now admired as signs of civilization, modernity, and enlightenment and emulated by common men. Proving their appetite for new things, Japanese soon started embracing the meat-based diet that Mutsuhito endorsed, and sukiyaki, a soy-sauce-based hot pot of sliced beef, quickly became a popular national dish.

Mutsuhito took to his new role with ease, though being Japan's first modern emperor was fraught with contradictions from the start. The emperor was meant to represent the ancient and sacred imperial institution, yet he also embodied a new Westernized monarchy. The Meiji Constitution of 1889 made Shinto into a quasi state religion, and Mutsuhito was its high priest. Having studied European powers, the founding fathers of Meiji Japan knew that Christianity provided those nations with a spiritual linchpin, and they thought Shinto could serve that purpose for their country. They also understood that secular governments are an important aspect of successful parliamentary systems and that Japan should stick to the modern European concept of separating church and state. As a result, Mutsuhito's position had to become more symbolic, the constitution establishing that the throne was sacred and sacrosanct and above politics, even though the emperor remained the supreme military commander. The glorification of the emperor as the essence of Japan's national polity proved to be a highly efficient way of inventing a modern Japanese identity. By the 1930s, Japanese society consisted of people who grew up steeped in the cult of emperor worship. In 1882, however, many things about the new Meiji state and the role of the emperor were unclear. It was a government without a solid foundation, either spiritual or practical. The Meiji Restoration had left fresh emotional wounds to be healed and institutional deficiencies to be worked on.

The Meiji Restoration came about because of an 1866 military alliance between the two southern feudal domains of Satsuma and Choshu. Traditionally anti-Tokugawa and therefore second-tier domains, both Satsuma and Choshu had long been dissatisfied with the shogunate. In the late 1860s, a series of political missteps by the Tokugawas allowed idealistic and ambitious samurai from those two domains to finally seize the day. Thanks to its connection with Britain, Satsuma possessed modern war technologies (though the Tokugawa shogunate, too, started quickly modernizing its army under the auspices of French military advisers after 1867). After securing the imperial blessing, the forces of Satsuma and Choshu gradually worked their way north to topple the shogunate supporters. The Boshin War of 1868–69 was a civil war that consolidated their seizure of power.

The lower-ranking young samurai from those victorious domains came to dominate the new government and were later given aristocratic titles. Some were corrupted by the spoils of their hard-won power. But many more were exceptionally driven, talented, disciplined, and imaginative men who longed for Japan to become a powerful nation-state.

Army Minister Oyama was one of them. A Satsuma man, he was the first cousin of the so-called last samurai, Saigo Takamori, the famous

Boshin War hero noted for his enormous physique and simple yet magnetic personality. Oyama himself was very much a part of that revolutionary war and of Japan's search for a modern identity. He was impressed with the display of British arms technology in the Anglo-Satsuma War of 1863 (which was more of a skirmish than a full-fledged war). As a result, he became an avid student of Western firearms. (Satsuma, looking ahead to the future, had then decided to cultivate contacts with Britain.)

Oyama's professional career was closely intertwined with the growth of the Imperial Army itself. After helping to suppress rebellions against the new regime during the early years of the Meiji government, he set out for Europe to deepen his knowledge of Western arms technologies. He witnessed the Franco-Prussian War and attended a course in strategic studies in Geneva in the early 1870s. Celebrated as an able commander in the Sino-Japanese War of 1894–95 and the Russo-Japanese War of 1904–5, he successively held the posts of army minister and home minister, acquiring the noble title of prince along the way.

THE UNITED STATES HAD no part in Japan's wars of the Meiji era. But some of the tight and important links, often of a personal nature, that had developed made a future confrontation between the two countries seem inconceivable. The pioneering ethos of the new Japanese state was actually rather American.

In the summer of 1882, the year the Imperial Rescript to Soldiers and Sailors was issued, a tall and slender beauty with a perfectly oval face stood on a college auditorium platform in Poughkeepsie, New York. She was one of the select few in the graduating class asked to deliver a valedictory address based on her dissertation. Yamakawa Sutematsu stood out among her classmates at Vassar. She was class president, graduated magna cum laude, and was a member of several prestigious societies. She behaved like a perfect Western woman, but beneath her soft, elegant appearance and impeccable manners lay a will of steel. She was the first Japanese woman to be awarded a bachelor of arts degree.

Having lived in the United States since the age of eleven, Stematz (as she spelled her name for the benefit of her American peers) was a product of the successful social engineering undertaken by the young Meiji government, with help from goodwilled Americans. She was one of five girls sent to the United States on government stipends to become prototypes of the modern Japanese woman, an idea originally conceived by the samurai-turned-statesman Kuroda Kiyotaka, who was in charge of developing Hokkaido, the northernmost island of Japan. The minister was impressed with the American women he saw on a trip to the United States in 1871. He was especially impressed with the sturdy ladies he saw tilling the soil of the frontier alongside their men. Just as the American West was pioneered by both men and women, Kuroda reasoned, Japanese women, as wives, mothers, and even hard laborers, should play their part in the birth of Japan as a great nation.

The Yamakawas, a venerable old samurai family, were in the service of the lord of Aizu. In the Japanese civil war, Aizu backed the declining Tokugawa shogunate and, along with several other northern domains that did the same, was branded an enemy of the imperial court. In August 1868, in one of the final and fiercest battles of the war, Stematz, eight years old, fought together with the men and women of Aizu, who were under siege by enemy forces. She was in charge of preventing explosions in the domain's castle by covering unexploded cannon shells with futon mattresses. Those shells were fired by a Satsuma battalion led by her future husband, Army Minister Oyama.

The northern rebel domains proved utterly powerless in the face of the British-backed technologies of the southern forces. With the fall of Aizu, the fortunes of the Yamakawa family declined as well. Something drastic had to be done to regain social respectability. Education was the best, and often the only, way to recover one's status. At the time, the government was calling for applicants to study abroad, urging young people to acquire knowledge in the West. Many young men from the formerly well-to-do families of those fallen domains took on the challenge. Although very few families were willing to send their daughters so far away for so long, the Yamakawas, in dire straits, decided to send theirs.

Stematz thrived in the home of Leonard Bacon, an abolitionist clergyman in New Haven, Connecticut. Growing up with his fourteen children, she attended local schools before enrolling at Vassar. Her best friend was Bacon's youngest daughter, Alice Mabel, who would help establish a women's college in Japan many years later. Unlike some other Japanese students, who assimilated to the extent of almost losing their mother tongue altogether, Stematz, determined to keep her Japanese language skills, wrote letters home every day.

In the early summer of 1882, Stematz's loyalties were many: to the new

Japanese government, which enabled her to study in the United States; to her family, who tried to clear its rebel name; to the Bacons, who raised her as one of their own; and to Vassar, which enabled her to become an independent-thinking woman. She was eager to be of use in the real world.

Stematz's homecoming at the end of 1882, after eleven years abroad, would be something of a disappointment. She was overeducated and over-qualified for the jobs available to women in Meiji Japan. Then she married one of the most powerful men in the Meiji government. Oyama Iwao was a widower eighteen years her senior. He was also the general responsible for bringing down her family's feudal domain. This would have been a union unimaginable in less enlightened circles. After the marriage, Stematz was able to initiate various philanthropic and educational enterprises.

The story of Prince Oyama and his Vassar bride was an example of how individual innovation, industry, grand ambition, and imagination could overcome the historical wounds that divided Japan. It was a union in which Japan's future enemy, the United States, was a prime inspiration. Both Japan and the United States were emerging powers coming into their own just as the world itself was going through profound change. In the words of one historian, it was "a world of empires gained and maintained by military power," and yet it was also "an internationalizing world; a world yearly more conscious of its one-ness" owing to economic interdependence, peace movements, and mass media (though the term "globalization" had not yet been coined). In a world of competing agendas and great uncertainties, Japan looked to the United States as a sympathetic mentor. "To catch up to and surpass the West" was the mantra of Japan's national quest. And more often than not, the West meant the United States, not old Europe.

In the following decades, Oyama took the Imperial Rescript to Soldiers and Sailors to heart and shied away from being invested with too much political power, preferring to live as an army man. Self-made successes in both their public and private lives, however, the Oyamas were entrenched in the heart of the Meiji establishment. Through their son, who married a younger sister of Prince Konoe Fumimaro, they even became closely tied to an ancient aristocratic family. The innovative Meiji spirit gradually disappeared into this new version of the old order.

The Meiji era ended in 1912 with the death of Emperor Mutsuhito. His rule had lasted forty-five years (superseding the reign of Queen Elizabeth I of England by one year). Japan, starting as an isolated feudal country on the periphery of Asia, had become a powerful industrial state. It now boasted institutions of higher education, efficient railway service, and a superior postal system. Meiji's greatest pride, though, was its modern army and navy, which won two wars in succession, against Qing China and czarist Russia. By the end of the Meiji era, the new Japan was looking more and more like an old power, or at least a superior imitation of one. And the pioneering ethos and individual initiatives of the United States that so impressed the builders of the Meiji state began to feel more and more like a threat to the glorious imperialist future of Japan, obstructing its bid to lead the Asia-Pacific region.

Japan under Emperor Mutsuhito's son, Yoshihito, is often characterized by its positive and creative energy. The period witnessed the rise of a flawed but vibrant parliamentary system. Abroad, Japan was securing its status as an emerging great power. A hope-filled time known as the Taisho Democracy had commenced. (Taisho, meaning "great righteousness," is the name given to Yoshihito's reign, which lasted from 1912 to 1926.)

It was not just the stirrings of democratic institutions that characterized this period. Japanese life became freer in many respects. Especially in cities, more people enjoyed for less money the pleasures of dance halls, cafés, department stores, theaters, and cinemas. As one poet observed, the mark of civilization was that anyone could get a cup of coffee in the morning and afford a newspaper every day.

Alas, Yoshihito was hopelessly unfit for the job. Lacking in personal charisma and physical strength, he was, in his formidable father's eyes, an unsatisfactory heir to the throne. He was emperor by default, since all his elder brothers had died in infancy. He had suffered from meningitis as a young boy, and his increasingly frail physical and mental health led the statesmen around him to conclude, around 1921, that his imperial role should be a passive one. Above all else, his first son, Hirohito, should take over the throne sooner rather than later.

In anticipation of his greater role, from March to September 1921, Hirohito made a grand tour of Europe, during which he visited Britain, France, Belgium, and Italy. He learned proper Western table manners aboard the *Katori,* on whose deck he also enjoyed practicing his golf. No Japanese crown prince had ever been to Europe before. Hirohito, who turned twenty during the trip, returned home a great Anglophile. He had received an enthusiastic welcome in Britain, partly owing to the Anglo-Japanese Alliance of 1902—an alliance of equals. A Japanese documentary film proudly reported that the British monarch, King George V, attended to the young crown prince with "fatherly kindness." The bespectacled crown prince appeared reserved yet unquestionably cheerful. He exuded a pleasant air of boyish curiosity.

One of the highlights of Hirohito's trip was his stay, at the invitation of the Duke of Atholl, at Blair Castle in Perthshire. The crown prince was genuinely moved by the Scottish nobleman's life of simplicity and frugality. Toward the end of a ball thrown in Hirohito's honor, common folk from the estate flooded onto the dance floor. "Let me show you how we Scots really dance," the duke reportedly said as he and his wife joined hands with the tenant farmers. Hirohito's astonishment turned to appreciation, and he concluded that as long as aristocrats and wealthy people lived a simple life, there would be no concern about class struggle. In addition to acquiring the lifelong habit of having a traditional English breakfast every morning, Hirohito appeared to be strongly drawn to the British monarchy's "reign but not rule" dictum. That preference would loom large for the rest of his life.

Soon after his return to Japan, because of his father's rapidly declining health, Hirohito was made the regent, a virtual sovereign, exercising comparable authority to the emperor. Hirohito was now commander in chief of Japan's armed forces. Forty years after the Imperial Rescript to Soldiers and Sailors, the Imperial Army and Navy had grown into formidable institutions.

Hirohito had strong views on military matters. He had come back from Europe convinced of the horrors of war. After salmon fishing in the Scottish Highlands, he was taken to the infamous battlefield of Ypres, in Flanders. Three years after the end of the Great War, those bleak fields were still filled with the remnants of bloody battles that had cost the lives of hundreds of thousands of young men. Numerous broken shells and bullets were scattered about, as if they were a permanent fixture of the landscape. The English poet Laurence Binyon, who would teach at Tokyo Imperial University in the late 1920s, famously memorialized the war dead in his 1914 poem "For the Fallen": "They shall grow not old, as we that are left grow old / Age shall not weary them, nor the years condemn." It was not simply the business of dying young that so impressed the impressionable crown prince, but also the continued mourning. The Belgian army officer who acted as his tour guide broke down in the middle of explaining something to Hirohito. When he learned that the man's son had perished on that field, the crown prince's eyes welled up.

Hirohito's monarchical philosophy and his aversion to war would soon be tested. In late 1923, a young anarchist revolutionary tried to assassinate him. (This would be followed by another assassination attempt by a Korean nationalist in 1932.) Hirohito's confidence in garnering popular support by mingling with ordinary people was dented. Because of the paradoxical ambiguities of a divine commander in chief who chose to reign but not rule, Hirohito's imperial role and his personal responsibility would become ever more complicated. He reigned over both the government and the armed services, and on several occasions he chose to exercise his power over them, but it was not customary for him to do so. Still, during that short time of tranquillity in Japan that followed World War I, Hirohito seemed to be as much at ease as anyone who was essentially lonely and anxious could be. He had carefully prepared himself to ascend to the imperial throne and to maintain and preserve what had been achieved since the time of the grandfather he worshiped. In December 1926, Yoshihito died at the age of forty-seven, and Hirohito officially became Japan's emperor.

CHAPTER 4

The Soldier's Dilemmas

I n October 1921, shortly after Hirohito had returned from his European tour, a quiet revolution in the Japanese army was set in motion. It started in the most unlikely of places, the scenic Black Forest spa town of Baden-Baden, where Nagata Tetsuzan, Obata Toshiro, and Okamura Yasuji, three members of the class of 1904 of the Imperial Japanese Army Academy, had gathered in secrecy. None of the officers—in their late thirties, on elite career tracks in the army, and in Europe on assignment—looked like fighting men. Their skinny physiques and owlish glasses suggested they preferred books to rigorous outdoor exercise, let alone combat. The men, known for their brilliant academic records and political skills in a huge military institution that was beginning to function like an impersonal bureaucratic organ, were dubbed "the three pillars of the army." A day later, they were joined by another like-minded officer stationed in Germany: Tojo Hideki, from the class of 1905.

Away from suspicious eyes, they all took a secret oath concerning the internal reform of the Imperial Army. The four of them agreed to eliminate regional factionalism within the service, to carry out a radical reorganization of personnel and the military system, and to establish a method for general mobilization. A large-scale reform was attempted step by step over the following decade as the four officers progressed, fully according to their expectations, on their executive paths. In their different ways, they all advocated a stronger and more united army—and, consequently, a stronger Japan for it to lead.

The scars of the civil war and rapid modernization of the Meiji period lingered in many places, including the army. In 1921, the power structure of the Meiji Restoration seemed secure. One of the two founding fathers of the modern Japanese army, Prince Yamagata Aritomo, now in his eighties, remained active politically. So long as he was alive, it was believed, anyone outside the southern Choshu clique that he headed could not dream of advancing to the army's exclusive executive corps. The dominance of Yamagata's faction was, in fact, less and less true, as more outsiders came to be represented in the top echelons. But its sway still annoyed those officers meeting in Baden-Baden, all non-Choshu men.

Tojo's father was a victim of that factionalism, coming as he did from one of the rebel northern domains that fought against the Choshu-Satsuma alliance in the 1860s. Even though the senior Tojo graduated first in his class at the Army War College, his career never flourished. Tojo was sensitive to his father's professional disappointments and was determined to settle old scores with the establishment that had so mistreated the man he loved.

Prince Yamagata's death in early 1922, only a few months after the Black Forest rendezvous, solved the problem of Choshu predominance. The army culture, though, became more rigid and unimaginative as a result. In the name of meritocracy, an increasing emphasis was placed on school records, which was to the benefit of the four officers who met at Baden-Baden, all of whom excelled in academics, especially Nagata Tetsuzan. Over time, it became clear that Nagata was destined to head the army in the not-too-distant future. Obata did not wholeheartedly welcome his fellow conspirator's ascension. Though agreeing with Nagata on the necessity of army reform, he disagreed with him dramatically on what form that reform should take. Obata was one of the main backers of the Imperial Way faction, founded by the bombastic ultranationalist general Araki Sadao and his ally Masaki Jinzaburo. The group's younger followers tended to be disgruntled ultranationalistic officers known for their advocacy of radicalized and terroristic methods. They saw an idealized Japan united under the divine power of the emperor, who would be assisted by the army in his practical duty of guiding the nation. They argued that the new Japan had to rise above all the political corruption and corporate influence. They blamed Japan's plight since the 1920s on the existing regime.

Nagata represented a rival reformist group, usually called the Control faction, though there was no official founding of this group, and it broadly included most of those who were against the Imperial Way agenda. Nagata, who did not like participating in any factional politics, conceived of Japan in the future as a highly efficient defensive nation-state centralized under the army, a nation reorganized as an efficient war machine equipped for total war. The Control faction was ruthlessly pragmatic, unsentimental, and Machiavellian. Nagata had sympathetic colleagues in other ministries who also wanted to "rebrand" Japan on the basis of efficiency. Many of those so-called New Bureaucrats, incidentally, would support Konoe's New Order Movement when he returned as prime minister in 1940.

The Imperial Way faction, on the other hand, was prone to sentimentality, invoked pseudotraditionalist values, and portrayed the army as the guardian of Japan's martial spirit. It saw Japanese society as too corrupt to be salvaged and believed that it needed to be built up from scratch. Both factions, though, agreed on militarizing Japan's political life. Whichever faction won out, Japan was assured of having an army eager to meddle in politics, in defiance of the imperial precepts of 1882.

By the mid-1930s, Nagata, supported by two other Baden-Baden pledge makers, Okamura and Tojo, had come out on top, having survived numerous setbacks with sheer cunning and alliance-making skills. Appointed chief of the Army Ministry's Military Affairs Bureau in early 1934, Nagata was perfectly placed to make some significant changes, including in personnel. His dreams suddenly died on the morning of August 12, 1935, when an intruder burst into his beautiful mahogany-paneled office in the Army Ministry and slashed him with a samurai sword. Nagata, unarmed, was cut once on the forehead, twice on the back, and again in the throat. He died on the floor of his office.

The killer, Aizawa Saburo, was a lieutenant colonel in his forties who was enraged by some of Nagata's personnel decisions affecting top figures in the Imperial Way faction, including its leader, Araki. Nagata was fifty-one years old and in the prime of his career. Ironically, he was in a meeting to discuss how best to control the disorderly behavior of radicalized officers when his killer forced his way in. In the course of his trial, Aizawa received much popular support and sympathy. Though he was found guilty and executed, some were as shocked by the level of support he received as they were by the murder.

The violence continued, climaxing with the aforementioned coup attempt of February 26, 1936, instigated by young Imperial Way–inspired officers (they claimed to be a separate group) who held especially ultranationalist values. After mobilizing almost fifteen hundred soldiers in snow-blanketed Tokyo, they killed several key government figures, including the finance minister and the lord keeper of the privy seal. Many of the soldiers who took part in this failed putsch were not overly politicized; they simply had to obey orders. It was the rebel officers, not the soldiers, who believed that revolutionary violence provided a way to change the status quo. But the officers could easily tap into the grievances of lower-ranking soldiers, many of whom were hapless victims of the endemic poverty that began to affect the Japanese countryside long before the worldwide economic depression. Stories of young women and children being sold off to seedy middlemen who shipped them off to city brothels were heard too often.

The rebel officers who plotted the coup claimed not to be out for political control themselves, justifying their acts as a legitimate means to save the emperor from the corrupt influences of democracy and capitalism. In fact, the main plotters wanted Imperial Prince Chichibu, the eldest of Hirohito's younger brothers, to be their new leader. The prince was an army man who enjoyed immense popularity within the service.

Hirohito exhibited more resolve than usual, immediately denouncing the coup. He was both horrified and enraged by the cowardly nocturnal attacks; unarmed men in their seventies and eighties had been murdered in their pajamas. Oddly, the emperor's uncommon public display of condemnation was soon matched by another outpouring of popular sympathy for the killers. Like Nagata's murderer, the coup plotters were praised for their supposedly pure and selfless motives in wishing to save the emperor and the empire from taking a wrong course. The execution of the key plotters made martyrs out of them. The Imperial Way philosophy remained popular, though no major terrorist takeovers would be attempted by the army after this incident.

This meant that, despite all the blood spilled, there was no clear-cut winner in the factional battle and that the army leadership would have to live with a built-in bomb—the latent fear of an upheaval from below—that might detonate at any moment. As Nagata's successor as the leader of the Control faction, Tojo faced the recurrent problem of having to tame the violent impetuosity of younger officers. His position was further complicated by the fact that he was a forever faithful servant of the emperor and would not have categorically rejected the cult of emperor worship exercised by the Imperial Way faction simply because it was the creed of his rivals. He had been raised in a military family and educated to be a soldier since boyhood, a product of the Imperial Rescript to Soldiers and Sailors taken to the extreme. He liked to say, "A soldier serves the emperor twenty-four hours a day. Even eating is part of his duty, so that one can better serve him." In Tojo's words, "His Majesty is not human. He is God."

Tojo was a man proud of having high principles. He was a hard worker who knew how to persevere. As a boy, he did not care much for schoolwork, but after being beaten up by a group of older boys, he set out to defeat them in test scores and did exactly that. He was an egalitarian of sorts who despised nepotism and preferred to eat the same meals that lower-ranking officers were given. His fastidiousness was almost neurotic. A compulsive notetaker who would jot things down on three different kinds of note cards, he meticulously itemized and organized those notes in chronological order every day of his life, without any secretarial assistance.

Though neither evil nor corrupt, Tojo was petty and thin-skinned. He was hypersensitive to criticism and was known to penalize those who dared to cross him. Every slight was remembered, and retribution often followed. At home, he was a disciplinarian to his sons. With his daughters, he was a typically doting and indulgent father. He did not smoke. There were no stories of womanizing. He drank only rarely. He certainly wasn't known for his personal charm, but he was a very able bureaucrat. Discipline and devotion to the emperor defined his life, and he demanded the same of others.

In July 1940, Tojo became army minister in Prince Konoe's second cabinet, the post the brilliant Nagata would have filled better. From that exalted place, the ever-loyal servant of the emperor issued an educational document to his soldiers. On January 8, 1941, almost sixty years after the Meiji emperor issued the Rescript to Soldiers and Sailors, Tojo introduced "Instructions for the Battlefield," elaborating on ideal soldierly conduct. The code was meant to instill and inspire the kind of self-control he himself constantly strived for. It included the notorious passage "Do not suffer the shame of being captured alive." This order glorifying death would be taken as a command to commit suicide in the face of impending capture and would come to have a devastating impact. It was printed in a booklet form, and was distributed to every soldier despite the country's serious paper shortage. And ordinary citizens could purchase the phonograph recording of Tojo's recitation of it.

Only two days before Tojo's announcement, President Roosevelt gave a memorable State of the Union address that came to be known as his "Four

Freedoms" speech and was pictorially immortalized in Norman Rockwell's work of the same name in *The Saturday Evening Post*. It advanced freedom of speech and expression, freedom of worship, freedom from want, and freedom from fear for people all over the world. Presaging the Universal Declaration of Human Rights, Roosevelt's speech clarified the core value of his administration: that a state exists to ensure the safety of its citizens, not to endanger and sacrifice it. Moreover, the president suggested individual freedoms had to be safeguarded from threats, even beyond the borders of the United States.

But in Japan, that sort of individualistic—and thus "selfish"—thinking was wholly discouraged as unpatriotic by 1941. This was true even in an all-boys preparatory school in Morioka, Tojo's ancestral domain, that was known in the past for its highly creative and liberal culture and had produced some formidable literary talents. According to one successful applicant, then twelve, the school's oral entrance exam that took place over three days in March 1941 consisted of questions such as "When was the Imperial Rescript on Education issued?" "The Rescript says, 'Our subjects ever united in loyalty and filial piety.' What does that mean?" "Can you think of some other slogans just like it?" These types of questions showed the limit of creative thinking allowed under the circumstances.

As the examiners' questions became more and more specific, the fear of economic encirclement and a possible war with the West was very much in the background: "How many years since the start of the China Incident?" "What is the name of the shrine where we honor our heroic war dead?" "Which countries are obstructing Japan's effort to build a 'New East Asian Order'?" "Name two European countries that are Japan's good friends." "What resource does Japan want to buy from the Dutch East Indies?"

Another section of the exam was meant to shed light on the moral character of the candidate: "Why must we be frugal now?" "What efforts are you making in everyday life to be frugal?" "How does it save energy if we use a lampshade?" "Do you know the exact figure of Japan's national savings target?"

This boy passed the exam, but he would soon be disappointed to find out that the school's uniform, a mark of achievement and distinction for the boys who wore it, was to be abolished in favor of a nationwide dress code of bland khakis, reminiscent of army uniforms, making all students look like little soldiers. By his second year, the prep school's once-rigorous curriculum had changed drastically, as more and more teachers were drafted to serve as soldiers. Instead of classroom learning, the students were expected to cultivate fields and participate in military drills, in anticipation of the day when they, too, would have to serve the emperor as soldiers.

THE IMPERIAL JAPANESE ARMY had always been a self-confident institution because of its role as the main engine behind the Meiji Restoration. The Imperial Navy, without which Japan's war with the United States and its allies in 1941 could not have even been contemplated, developed more slowly. When the Naval Academy was founded in 1876, Japan had no battleships. In 1888, six years after the army founded an elite war college, the navy founded its own for the education of its future executive officers. The navy college's student body was smaller, but that imbalance moved toward parity after Japan formed an alliance in 1902 with Britain, from whom the navy acquired battleships and shipbuilding and strategic knowledge.

On May 28, 1905, the Battle of Tsushima, one of the most decisive battles of the Russo-Japanese War, was won by Japan at sea. It sealed Japan's ultimate victory over czarist Russia, which was fighting Japan over its sphere of influence in Northeast China and Korea. Tsushima was the Imperial Navy's long-awaited moment in the sun. Unusual movement of Russia's Baltic Fleet had been deftly spotted by a twenty-five-year-old diplomat stationed in the Japanese consulate in Shanghai. Matsuoka Yosuke's timely warning cost the Russians numerous vessels, including eight battleships, as well as the lives of more than five thousand men, leading them to sue for peace.

Through the mediation of President Theodore Roosevelt, a treaty was signed on September 5, 1905, at Kittery, Maine, near Portsmouth. Roosevelt would win the Nobel Peace Prize for his good deed. Japan needed the treaty because it had been incurring huge war debts and could not have afforded the war for much longer. At home, there was considerable rage directed at the terms of the treaty, especially Japan's relinquishing of its right to demand indemnities from Russia. Ignorant of how financially and militarily overstretched their government was, many took to the streets to demonstrate against their leaders' diplomacy. The later popular embrace of Foreign Minister Matsuoka as a refreshingly dependable, hardnosed negotiator makes sense in the context of such a historical disappointment. Japan's unrealistic expectations that the United States would act as a sympathetic mediator of the China War, the resolution of which would become the sticking point in the U.S.-Japan negotiations of 1941, also likely had origins in this U.S. presidential mediation.

Popular discontent over the terms of the Portsmouth peace treaty notwithstanding, the news of Japan's victory had a confidence-boosting impact on many. Fuchida Mitsuo, a bomber pilot who would lead the Imperial Navy's aerial forces to Pearl Harbor—his plane sent out the famous coded signal of *"Tora! Tora! Tora!"* at the time of the surprise attack—was barely three years old in 1905. He was but one of a whole generation of youngsters who were enthralled by the sweet victory and aspired to a career in a navy uniform as a result. The victory over Russia had a profound legacy that went well beyond the creation of future Japanese soldiers. It was touted as the first major modern war won by a colored people over a white one. Japan's victory discredited the prevalent myth of the inborn racial supremacy of Westerners and in so doing helped encourage anticolonial aspirations in colonized parts of the world. Jawaharlal Nehru, India's first prime minister, was much affected as a boy. "Japanese victories stirred up my enthusiasm and I waited eagerly for the papers for fresh news daily," he recalled. "I invested in a large number of books on Japan and tried to read some of them. . . . Nationalistic ideas filled my mind. I mused of Indian freedom and Asiatic freedom from the thralldom of Europe."

Japan's victory spoke of the strength of material and cultural advancements. The Imperial Navy fed its men plenty of nutritious barley, which prevented the spread of beriberi, a disease caused by vitamin B deficiency that afflicted many Russian sailors. (Barley was often credited as one of the reasons the navy outperformed the army, which fed its soldiers overly processed white rice.) By the time of the Russo-Japanese War, Japan had achieved a staggering literacy rate of 75 percent, higher than anywhere in the West, which greatly aided in the training of its soldiers. The Japanese armed forces could employ manuals to teach the handling of complicated weapons. More than half of the Russian soldiers, on the other hand, were believed to be illiterate. Around seventy thousand Russian POWs in Japan were treated with dignity and were housed in relative comfort. The Japanese stuck to the spirit of the Hague Convention of 1899, ensuring the humane treatment of their prisoners. This impressed the international community.

Now the modernization and enlargement of the Imperial Navy began in full force. So did the rivalry between the two armed services, which vied for more money and more glory. The army, fearing a Russian retribution after 1905, saw its most dangerous threat lying to the north of Japan. The navy was increasingly alarmed by the United States, which seemed keen on expanding its sphere of influence in the Pacific Ocean, especially after it had gained control of Guam and the Philippines as a result of the 1898 Spanish-American War. Whatever their differences, the Russo-Japanese War made the emperor's army and navy equal competitors.

JAPAN'S NAVAL VICTORY CAME at a tremendous price for a twenty-one-year-old cadet ensign aboard the *Nisshin*. Assigned to frontline duty at the bow of the Japanese cruiser in the Battle of Tsushima, he was hit by a shell fragment that set his lower body on fire. It also scooped a hole as big as a newborn's head from his right thigh and cost him the index and middle fingers of his left hand. He recuperated at a naval hospital in Nagasaki for the next 160 days. When infection set in, the doctor suggested amputating his left arm. "I entered the navy with the great ambition of becoming a naval soldier and going to war," the sailor said. "Either I die from this festering wound—because I refuse to have my arm amputated—or I recover from it and continue being a soldier. I have a one-in-two chance, and I shall bet my life on it!" He won the bet. He recovered without losing his arm. This was not the last great gamble in the life of Yamamoto Isoroku, who would one day mastermind Japan's attack on Pearl Harbor.

Throughout his life, Yamamoto regarded his war wounds as a badge of honor. He was also very conscious of the handicap they imposed on him. He tried hard not to lag behind, not to let others feel he required special assistance. When he first started playing catch with his young son, he kept dropping the ball from his three-fingered hand. But with his quiet tenacity, he was soon able to catch the ball from any angle with that hand. He remained fit and could climb onto a battleship with lithe, rhythmic steps. Up to a point, Yamamoto, whom many regard as one of the greatest strategists in the history of the Imperial Navy, followed a typical elite career path, one similar to Tojo Hideki's. Both were born in 1884. They received their higher education in the colleges open only to a handful of military academy graduates with stellar school records. Both came from former samurai families from the northern "rebel" provinces, which resisted the Meiji Restoration. By the accident of birth, they inherited the grievances of lost honor and the need to prove themselves worthy members of the new Japanese state.

As a reward for their hard work, both were given prestigious postings abroad—Yamamoto in the United States and Tojo in Germany. Their direct encounters with the West led them to endorse radical modernization of the military services. From the 1920s on, Yamamoto became especially aware of the importance of aerial power for the navy. Though he himself was never trained as a pilot, he played a vital role in the development of the naval aerial division; the experience helped him shape the backbone of his later Pacific strategies.

Their personalities could not have been more different, though. Unlike Tojo, Yamamoto had an open, fun-loving temperament. Even into his fifties, he looked like a curious and inquisitive boy for whom the world was still full of new discoveries. Yamamoto did not wear glasses or have any facial hair. His youthful looks were further emphasized by his brilliant eyes and full lips. The only conspicuous marks of his increasing age were the deepening lines in his forehead and his closely cropped graying hair. He exuded a charisma and confidence that many found attractive. He was only five feet three, but his well-proportioned physique and self-assured manner belied his short stature. Again unlike the straight-and-narrow Tojo, Yamamoto loved to gamble. He was known to spend his leisure time playing poker and bridge, even aboard a battleship on duty. (Foreign Minister Matsuoka also had a reputation for his poker-playing skills.) He joked that in his retirement he would like to live in Monaco and play roulette; he was said to have won so much on the one occasion he visited Monte Carlo that he was barred from the casino. Yamamoto was a gifted bluffer, used to deftly concealing his greatest weaknesses. As with any good gambler, he had enough daring to take risks when the moment arrived. He thought that gambling was almost a mark of manhood: "Man is not a man if he does not gamble," he reportedly remarked.

Yamamoto ultimately saw life as a series of simple choices that eventually came down to the choice between life and death. He was always ready to die so that he could live more fully. He wanted his junior soldiers to be similarly prepared for death. Profoundly affected by the great injuries he had incurred as a young man, he felt that soldiers, especially those who fought on the front line, should have as few personal attachments to this world as possible, which was why he liked to advise young officers to marry late in life. (He himself married at thirty-four and had his first son at forty.) Not that Yamamoto treated death casually. In the black leather-bound pocket agenda he always carried with him, he listed the names and family records of all those who died under his command. Whenever he happened by the neighborhood of a fallen sailor, he would drop in on the family, praying in front of its ancestral altar, sometimes even breaking down uncontrollably.

Yamamoto appreciated the United States. He was at Harvard from 1919 to 1921 and was posted to the Japanese embassy in Washington as a naval attaché from 1926 to 1928. He recognized in the American people an abundant energy similar to his own. In his correspondence home, he reported on everyday American life, and the photographs he took as he traveled the country captured its people and landscapes with a moving intimacy. Whenever young Japanese asked him how to improve their English, he said they should read Carl Sandburg's biography of Abraham Lincoln. He very much identified with Lincoln as a fellow self-made man and underdog (Yamamoto's family was very poor, having fallen from grace after the Meiji Restoration) and admired his industry, high aspirations, and imagination. He would presumably have admired FDR as well, another strong-willed man who had overcome his physical disability.

Yamamoto's stimulating American years coincided with the heyday of interwar liberal internationalism. The question of how to cohabit peacefully with other powers loomed large in the minds of many thinking men and women. Numerous international and intergovernmental movements arose, such as President Wilson's cherished League of Nations. How does one square the soldierly duty of making war, or at least preparing one's country for war, with the ideal of a world without war? This serious dilemma had to be confronted by men in uniform, and Yamamoto was often a navy representative at international conferences to reduce arms. For a while, Japan seemed to be well on its way to becoming one of the leaders in the search for a more peace-loving world.

AT THE LONDON NAVAL CONFERENCE, held from January 21 to April 22, 1930, which Yamamoto attended as a naval adviser, the Japanese commitment to internationalism was severely tested and prevailed. At that point, Japan was led by Prime Minister Hamaguchi Osachi of the Constitutional Democratic Party, a hugely popular liberal whose dignified demeanor and mane-like hair had earned him the nickname of the Lion Premier. He vowed to maintain Japan's reputation as a respectable and cooperative member of the international community when many countries, mired in the Great Depression, had turned inward. Hamaguchi was determined to ratify the London Naval Treaty, which outlined the rules concerning naval engagement and limited the number of vessels to be maintained by major naval powers. Elaborating on the agreements reached at the Washington Conference, those gathered in London proposed that the ratio of battleship tonnage among the United States, Britain, and Japan be adjusted from 5:5:3 to approximately 10:10:7.

Given its increased quota, the Japanese Navy Ministry favored ratifying the new treaty. But aware of Premier Hamaguchi's strong leadership and fearing that he might undermine the authority of the armed services, the Naval General Staff—the military men rather than appointed government officials—launched an all-out campaign against it. With the backing of the right wing, of the opposition party Friends of Constitutional Government, and, in the final stages, of conservatives within the Privy Council—an advisory group to the emperor—the Naval General Staff quibbled that the proposed number was 0.4 percent short of their original target. (Yamamoto supported the general staff's argument at this point, as he was yet to be converted to the creed of arms reduction.) Knowing that the supreme commander of the armed forces—Emperor Hirohito—backed his policy, Hamaguchi stood his ground: "It doesn't matter if the Privy Council opposes us. I intend to request an imperial sanction [against the council] and will take no steps toward reaching a compromise." On September 19, the Privy Council gave in. On October 27, the formal ratification was announced on the radio by the premiers of Britain and Japan and the president of the United States simultaneously. It was an unprecedented and hugely successful publicity coup that displayed the spirit of international cooperation and goodwill, which remained even in hard times.

The triumph of Japan's parliamentary politics under Hamaguchi came at great cost, however. The Friends of Constitutional Government, in league with the hard-liners, picked up the Naval General Staff's argument and accused Hamaguchi of violating the independence of the supreme command (which was, of course, originally meant to keep soldiers out of politics). The most damaging of such attacks came from Friends parliamentarian Hatoyama Ichiro, who helped found Japan's conservative Liberal Democratic Party after the war and would serve as prime minister from 1954 to 1956. Hatoyama in the spring of 1930 claimed that arms control did not fall under the jurisdiction of the Navy Ministry. He insisted that a distinct political power be given to the general staffs of the armed services in such matters. Rather than restraining the military and strengthening the basis of party politics, Hatoyama, to win political advantage, was helping to undermine parliamentary politics.

The degeneration of party politics accelerated after this episode. Later in 1930, as the controversy lingered, Prime Minister Hamaguchi was gravely wounded by an ultranationalist gunman who was dissatisfied with the treaty's ratification. Taking advantage of the situation, Hatoyama demanded that the wounded premier attend the upcoming parliamentary sessions to defend his views. The session turned out to be one of the most hostile in Japanese history and marked the lowest point in the country's parliamentary politics to date. Friends members, in a continuing effort to topple the party's rival, disrupted the sessions and physically assaulted the acting prime minister when Hamaguchi did not attend. Determined to pass the cabinet's social reform bills, Hamaguchi did attend the sessions in March 1931, against medical advice. The bills affected labor unions and farm tenancy, lowered taxes and created more equitable redistribution (made possible by the savings resulting from a decreased military budget), lowered the male voting age from twenty-five to twenty, and enfranchised women in local elections.

In a pair of felt slippers made to look like regular shoes—the pain of wearing leather shoes was far too great—the once sturdy but now tragically emaciated Hamaguchi stumbled toward the podium to answer questions in a barely audible voice. The opposition shouted "Speak louder" and "Get lost and die." After attending ten such sessions, the prime minister resigned in April, four months before his death. Japan's far-reaching reform efforts died, too.

During the 1930s, social restiveness and uncertainties grew in Japan, as if filling the void left by a failed democratic experiment. More assassination plots ended the lives of liberal and moderate opponents of blind militarism. The targets even included military men, such as the army's own Nagata Tetsuzan, as we have seen, in the summer of 1935. The fear of such violent outbursts was widespread. When the Kwantung Army occupied northeastern China in September 1931, its commanders, too, claimed that their unauthorized actions had selfless and sacrosanct motives. Like the parliamentarian Hatoyama, they cited the inviolable independence of the supreme command to fend off any criticism of their behavior.

As noted previously, Hamaguchi's successor as prime minister, Wakatsuki Reijiro, proved inadequate in this emergency. "Had the government resigned within a few days of the crisis . . . had the government issued a statement of protest and treated the matter with the same spirit," said the Japanese consul general in Mukden at the time of the Manchurian Incident, "all—including the dignity of the government, Japan's international position, its economy, and its party politics—could have been salvaged." Instead, the government dithered for almost three months "even though they knew very well that the situation [in Manchuria] was deteriorating minute by minute."

By 1936, Nagano Osami was navy minister (the highest political post in the Navy Ministry); Yamamoto was his vice minister. Nagano was a balding man with an intimidating glare; he could have passed for a gangster boss. He had preceded Yamamoto in the much-envied elite course of studies and appointments, including a stint at Harvard and participation in various international conferences. He graduated second in his class from the Naval Academy, which almost assured him of a bright career. But he was not an engaging leader, lacking Yamamoto's charisma and magnetism. Known as the Dozing Admiral, he napped in his office a great deal. Journalists said behind his back that he needed his daytime rest because he couldn't possibly keep up with his fourth wife (the three others had died), who was thirty years younger than him.

Admiral Yonai Mitsumasa, navy minister from April 1937 to August 1939, was a more appealing superior for Yamamoto. When Yonai became prime minister in early 1940, *Time* magazine described his physical appearance:

His nickname—The White Elephant—[is] one of awe. . . . It refer[s] to his size; his exceptionally fair and aristocratic complexion, accented in its whiteness by his hair, black and shiny as a phonograph record; and his appearance of strength and wisdom.

This view was far more complimentary than that of the Japanese army, which called him the Goldfish Minister—pleasant to look at but essentially ill suited for a big government role.

The army underestimated Yonai's political abilities. He served in three different cabinets as navy minister. He made his share of political misjudgments, especially when he initially supported Prince Konoe in his hard-line policy against Chiang Kai-shek. But he became a consistent and staunch opponent of Japan's fascist alliance when the general mood in the government was becoming overwhelmingly pro-Germany. In a key ministerial conference held in August 1939, the finance minister asked Yonai what would happen if Japan, as a consequence of allying with the fascist powers, had to fight a war against the united front of Britain, France, the Soviet Union, and the United States. Such a war was bound to be a heavily naval one, and therefore Yonai's answer was of pivotal importance. He said there was absolutely no likelihood of victory because the Japanese navy was not built to fight a war against the combined Anglo-American powers. Yonai kept Japan from the unseemly alliance, at least for the time being, prompting Hirohito to tell him, "Thanks to the navy, our nation was saved." Yonai was fully aware that his defiance would put his life in danger. His courage and straight talk would be conspicuously absent in the Japanese leadership in 1941.

Despite the fight some naval leaders put up against the Tripartite Pact, it would be wrong to assume that the navy, as an institution, was more cautious and rational than the army about Japan's drawing close to the fascist powers. Yonai and his strongest allies, Yamamoto and Inoue Shigeyoshi, the chief of military affairs, were increasingly in the minority. Yonai's right-hand man and a self-proclaimed radical liberal, Inoue grasped the shallowness and danger of the Nazi ideology very quickly. Having read *Mein Kampf* in German, Inoue was aware of its disparaging references to his country, which were omitted in the Japanese translation. But Yonai and his allies had to counter not only the army but also the navy's own Nazi admirers, who were multiplying as a result of Hitler's blitzkrieg successes and pushing for the Axis alliance.

Rear Admiral Oka Takazumi, who would head the Navy Ministry's Naval Affairs Bureau and appoint its fiercest prowar advocate, Ishikawa Shingo, its sectional chief in the fall of 1940, thought that the Axis alliance was a good idea, arguing that Japan could end the China War by intimidating Britain. By allying with Germany and Italy, he claimed, Japan would be able to corner Britain into brokering peace between Japan and China. Yonai, Yamamoto, and Inoue dismissed such a wishful suggestion. They felt that an Axis alliance would surely lead to a war not only with Britain but also with the United States. "The historically isolationist United States would not try to counter the powerful German-Italian-Japanese alliance by siding with Britain, whose moon is already waning," insisted Oka.

The resultant debate with the pro-Axis camp was so intense that Yonai grew fearful for his younger associate's life. In August 1939, on Yonai's strong recommendation, Yamamoto, who insisted on staying in the Navy Ministry, was appointed commander in chief of the Combined Fleet. Ironically, Yonai's protectiveness in giving Yamamoto a military appointment eliminated the opportunity for Yamamoto to oppose the government's dubious policy choices. Moreover, he would later feel compelled to devise his plan for the sneak attack on Pearl Harbor. Inoue was also transferred to duties away from Tokyo's politics. Beginning in January 1940, Yonai would continue his fight against the Axis alliance as prime minister, an appointment on which Hirohito was said to be especially keen. But Yonai was quickly dragged down. Inspired by the Nazi successes in Europe, Konoe and other advocates of pro-Axis policy, many of them army men, would in June 1940 launch a campaign to undermine Yonai. Army Minister Hata Shunroku resigned from the cabinet, and the army refused to nominate his replacement. The lack of army cooperation meant that the cabinet had to be dissolved. That was how, in July, Konoe came back to rule as premier for the second time, along with his bombastic foreign minister, Matsuoka.

For a while, Navy Minister Yoshida continued in Yonai's footsteps, opposing the Axis alliance. But he was soon taken ill. He was replaced by Oikawa Koshiro in September 1940. Oikawa was an agreeable-looking man, with closely cropped salt-and-pepper hair and a copious mustache, though his big, beady eyes made him appear rather lost and unconfident. While he sympathized with the pro-Anglo-American view of the Yonai-Yamamoto school, Oikawa was known for his silence, which would often prove detrimental during political discussions of a most critical nature. He was from northern Japan, where reticence was a prized trait—a result, outsiders often joked, of its extremely cold weather freezing one's mouth shut. Oikawa exhibited the local tendency to such an extent that people wondered if he had any opinions of his own. Compounding this inclination to silence was his belief that politics was not the business of a navy man, an institutional view shared by many in the service. Personally, he hated confrontation and avoided arguments at all costs. Yonai's defiant rejection of the Axis alliance since 1939 was an act unimaginable to Oikawa. It was no surprise, then, that Oikawa did not resist the Tripartite Pact in the fall of 1940. He was not about to alienate Konoe and Matsuoka, let alone those in the navy newly converted to the pact and the army at large.

In April 1941, the navy had to recommend a successor to Imperial

Prince Fushimi Hiroyasu, who was retiring as chief of the Navy General Staff, to be appointed by Hirohito. For those in the navy who did not want Japan to clash with the West, this was a chance to reclaim their voice. Fushimi was a German-trained veteran of the Russo-Japanese War who for some time had exercised tremendous authority in naval affairs. An old-fashioned sailor, he believed that the strength and prestige of a nation was directly proportionate to the number of fighting ships it possessed (hence the Naval General Staff's opposition in 1930 to Hamaguchi's signing of the London Naval Treaty). This meant that Fushimi and his cohorts—often called the Squadron Group because of their traditionalist views—were in outright disagreement with Yonai, Yamamoto, and Inoue, who argued for conciliation with other powers (while at the same time working to develop newer technologies, such as airpower).

To the dismay of those who, wishing for a rapprochement with the United States, lobbied for Yonai's appointment, Oikawa, perfectly placed to recommend a name to the emperor, chose the Dozing Admiral to succeed Fushimi. This was done in accordance with the wishes of the exiting prince, whose experience in combat coupled with his imperial pedigree had made him too venerable a figure to be defied, at least in Oikawa's mind. When Yamamoto heard the news of his former boss Nagano's appointment, he lamented, "The man who believes himself to be a strate gic genius—when he is far from it—is now the chief of staff. . . . It is as if the war has already begun!"

Yamamoto's damning assessment of Nagano could also be read as a declaration of his partial resignation to a war that he publicly opposed, and would continue to oppose, but also wished to plan. To be sure, the cool, critical side of Yamamoto believed that it was impossible for Japan to win such a war. But if it had to be fought, he could not see anyone but himself in charge of it. He could try to prepare for it as best he could, and his best efforts would, in turn, maximize the strategic feasibility of a bold operation nobody else could have conceived—a gambler's plan with the slimmest chance for victory. Yamamoto understood that if Japan were to stand any chance of success, it had to gain the upper hand at the very beginning so that the United States just *might* be enticed to the negotiating table.

When Grew wrote to Hull on January 27, 1941, amid "the rumors of war" in Tokyo, he noted that his embassy colleague had heard "from many quarters, including a Japanese one" that "a surprise mass attack on Pearl Harbor was planned by the Japanese military forces." According to Grew, "the plan seemed fantastic," and it actually was. But Yamamoto was determined to make the fantasy come true. From late 1940 on, in the wake of the signing of the Tripartite Pact, he became immersed in the planning of Japan's Pacific strategies. No ordinary strategy would suffice, and for his extraordinary plan he would need extraordinary support.

IN EARLY FEBRUARY 1941, Lieutenant Commander Genda Minoru, a staff officer of the First Aerial Division, was aboard a Japanese aircraft carrier anchored near Shibushi Bay, in the prefecture of Kagoshima, at the southeastern tip of the southern island of Kyushu. Genda, an agile thirty-six-year-old, was the navy's star pilot. In the past, he had led a team of acrobatic pilots across the country for pageants, promoting the popularity of naval aviation. On this particular winter day, he disembarked from the *Kaga* at Kanoya, a major naval installation in southern Japan, after being summoned by Rear Admiral Onishi Takijiro, the chief of staff of the Eleventh Aerial Division. As the two men sat on a sofa in Onishi's office, the senior officer casually produced a letter from his breast pocket. "Why don't you take a look at this," Onishi urged him. Genda glanced at the back of the envelope and noted with surprise the signature of Yamamoto Isoroku, in the skillful calligraphy for which the commander was well known. Yamamoto's letter, as Genda recalled, said:

> Depending on the changes in the international situation, we might be driven to fight a war with the United States. If Japan and the United States were to go to war, we would have to resort to a radical tactic. . . . We would have to try, with all the might of our First and Second Aerial Divisions, to deal a blow to the U.S. Fleet in Hawaii, so that for a while, the United States would be kept from advancing to the western Pacific [where Japan would be facing other enemies, namely the Dutch and the British]. Our target would be a group of U.S. battleships. . . . This will not be easy to carry out. But I am determined to give everything to the completion of this plan, supervising the aerial divisions myself. I would like you to research the feasibility of such a plan in detail.

Since the founding of a U.S. naval base in Pearl Harbor, Hawaii, in 1908, the Japanese navy had felt threatened by a possible U.S. attack. The designation of Pearl Harbor in May 1940 as the main base for the U.S.

Pacific Fleet reinforced that feeling. The existing consensus was that a U.S.-Japan war would be a lopsided battle in favor of the United States and that the Japanese navy's strategic planning had to be a purely defensive one. The best the Japanese could hope to do was to ward off a U.S. naval advance with air strikes and submarines launched from the Japanese coast. Yamamoto, clearly, felt differently.

Upon finishing Yamamoto's letter, Genda, at a loss for words, merely said, "What an idea!" As he looked up in astonishment, Onishi asked, "Well now . . . I want you to find out if it could be done or not." Genda was flabbergasted, but he was also very intrigued.

The most apparent obstacle to the plan was the feasibility of torpedo attacks on enemy ships. Japan's state-of-the-art aerial torpedo required around ninety-eight feet (thirty meters) to sink and sail before it could adjust to the negotiated depth. Given Pearl Harbor's shallow water, averaging twelve meters (thirty-nine feet) deep, it was obvious the torpedoes would pierce the seabed, rendering them harmless. Then there was the difficulty of getting aircraft carriers to the target area without them being spotted. This operation was not going to be easy. In early April, two months after Genda was presented with Yamamoto's letter, Onishi submitted a plan of attack. It fell far short of Yamamoto's expectations. The plan eliminated the use of aerial torpedo attacks, replacing them with dive-bombing and level bombings—the kind carried out from a plane flying horizontally, which required complex calculations to negotiate the target range and so were often inaccurate. Yamamoto responded that if the existing torpedoes did not work, they had to be made to work by improving them and the pilots. He insisted that it was feasible.

CHAPTER 5

Good Riddance, Good Friends

The new alliance of Japan, Germany, Italy, and the Soviet Union, thanks to what Foreign Minister Matsuoka liked to call blitzkrieg diplomacy, was supposed to bring a quick and peaceful solution to all of Japan's problems abroad, including the war with China and the increasing diplomatic tensions with the United States. No such luck. And nothing had happened in the weeks since Matsuoka responded to Washington on May 12, 1941. Regardless of this inaction on the situation in the Pacific, the war in Europe was raging.

Following the fall of Yugoslavia, Athens caved in to invading German forces on April 27, prompting the Greek government and King George II— aided by British Commonwealth forces—to leave for Crete, where they sustained another huge defeat in the face of the Luftwaffe's onslaught (though Germany also suffered heavy losses). By the end of May, the Greek rulers had evacuated to Egypt. But Egypt wouldn't be safe for long, either. Starting in February, the newly formed German expeditionary force Afrika Korps had begun arriving in Libya—under the command of the Desert Fox, Erwin Rommel—to aid Italy, which was poised to capture North Africa.

In the meantime, the British Isles continued to be bombed; Belfast, Hull, and then Liverpool, which was devastated by seven consecutive nights of air raids in early May. But this would be the tail end of intense German bombings of Britain, as Hitler's attention turned eastward.

ON JUNE 22, 1941, a hot Sunday in Tokyo, Foreign Minister Matsuoka was treating Wang Jingwei to a matinee at the Kabukiza, a theater for traditional arts in the Ginza district. The building was a Japanese nativist answer to the Rokumeikan of the previous century. Despite its exaggerated traditional looks, including slated roofs in the style of a medieval Japanese castle, this relatively new edifice, finished in 1925, was made of concrete and boasted a seating capacity of twenty-seven hundred, as if to impress on its visitors Japan's modern achievements.

The country had less and less to boast about of late. In April, the steel industry was "unified" under the Steel Control Association—a virtual centralization under the National Mobilization Law. This was followed by the merger of other major industries, giving the state more control over resource allocation and pricing. As a result, the use of metals by citizens was especially restricted, and even metal buttons from school uniforms were confiscated and replaced by ones made of glass. For the traditional boys' festival celebration in May, the most coveted toys were planes, tanks, and helmets, but they were all made of wood, bamboo, and celluloid.

That Sunday matinee at the Kabukiza attracted Tokyo's most privileged citizens, dressed colorfully and appropriately for the special occasion commemorating the establishment of a Japanese-backed Chinese government in Nanjing under Wang's leadership. Throughout the performance, Kase Toshikazu, a young diplomat and Matsuoka's secretary, was fidgety, desperate to confirm a report that had reached his ears earlier that day. He slipped in and out of his seat in order to talk to the Foreign Ministry, calling from the basement cloakroom. Finally, as applause was breaking out at the end of the first act, he passed a note to Matsuoka. It confirmed that Germany had unleashed attacks on the Soviet Union that morning.

Matsuoka had expected that Germany would at some point attack the Soviet Union and had even said so on occasion. There had been reports of an impending German offensive from the Japanese ambassador in Berlin, Oshima Hiroshi. But Matsuoka had reacted to them with skepticism, believing he would hear directly from the Germans. Matsuoka was now taken aback.

Operation Barbarossa, the code name for the Nazi invasion of the Soviet Union, made Hitler something of a prophet: "The world will hold its breath and make no comment," he'd said. Indeed, on that fateful day, much of the world was left speechless. Stalin had repeatedly ignored warnings about German mobilization, convinced that the Molotov-Ribbentrop Pact of August 1939 would keep his country safe for the time being, that

Hitler, preoccupied as he was with Britain, would not instigate a war on two fronts. One of the numerous conflicting accounts (due to the shifting and unreliable nature of Kremlin historiography) asserts that Stalin was fishing in the Black Sea near dacha in Sochi. It was a warm Sunday. When news of the German offensive reached his sailboat, he lifted his rod quietly from the water and said: "Who would have thought now?" This was perhaps apocryphal, and he might have actually been in or near Moscow as is more generally believed, but what is certain is that Stalin was not heard from for days, consolidating the perception that he was completely caught off guard.

Army Minister Tojo and other Japanese leaders who believed their country to be a loyal ally of Germany faced a difficult question. Suzuki Teiichi was sent by Prime Minister Konoe to find out what Tojo thought of the news. Suzuki, a retired army lieutenant general, held the post of minister of state and also served as the general director of the Cabinet Planning Board, which was created in 1937 to unify and oversee cabinet policy for resource mobilization. The board's importance had increased in proportion to the escalation of the China War, and Suzuki, an ambitious political operator, would play a critical role in assessing the feasibility of Japan's war with the West. He addressed Tojo, a few years his senior, in a carefully deferential manner, telling him that Konoe believed Germany's attack on the Soviet Union provided a welcome opportunity for Japan to abandon the Tripartite Pact. Acquiring a less partisan diplomatic position was essential for Japan to achieve peace with the rest of the world, he felt. Upon hearing this, Tojo grew angry and barked at Suzuki, "Do you really think we can act in such an immoral way, against humanity and justice?" The Germans had of course violated the kind of loyalty Japanese soldiers were trained to prize as most important. The 1882 Imperial Rescript to Soldiers and Sailors said that "the soldier and sailor should consider loyalty their essential duty." Nonetheless, Tojo would not be dissuaded from his view.

Otto D. Tolischus, a Prussian-born Pulitzer Prize–winning journalist for *The New York Times* who was expelled from Nazi Germany in March 1940 and was now reporting from Tokyo, wrote on June 22: "The outbreak of war between Germany and Russia . . . froze official Japan into icy silence. The only official comment was that there would be no comment."

WELL BEFORE OPERATION Barbarossa forced him to accept the irreversible collapse of his quadruple diplomacy, Matsuoka had started losing his political clout within the Konoe government. But the bigger the rift between

Konoe and Matsuoka over the Draft Understanding, the greater Matsuoka's ambition for Japan's premiership and the more openly he criticized the cabinet of which he was still a part. Matsuoka deluded himself into believing he had the emperor's support, which he most assuredly did not. "Matsuoka has been likely bribed by Hitler" was Hirohito's reaction to the foreign minister's blatantly pro-German pronouncements since his return.

At the May 3 liaison conference, the first important meeting after his European tour, Matsuoka had vigorously pushed for his new pet project—a Japanese attack on Singapore—while brushing aside the more vital topic of how to respond to the United States regarding the Draft Understanding. Both Hermann Göring—who entertained the foreign minister with a lavish meal at his private villa, Carinhall—and Hitler himself were pressing for a Japanese commitment to attack the British in Singapore to help their war. "I would if I were the leader of Japan," Matsuoka had told them. Back in Japan, Matsuoka now insisted that Singapore had to be struck immediately. Upon hearing this proposal in the meeting, Army Chief of Staff Sugiyama was aghast. He had already told Matsuoka, before the foreign minister's European tour, that an attack on Singapore was out of the question. Besides, Sugiyama did not share Matsuoka's confidence that Germany would dominate Europe at any moment. "Germany and Italy have been preparing for the invasion of the British Isles, building so many bases in northern France," Sugiyama pointed out, noting that even there "they have not been able to succeed." "Germany says it could take care of Russia in two months," argued Matsuoka, even though he was in the dark on Germany's plan. "Singapore should not be such a big deal," he added.

Unfazed by the categorical rejection of his proposal, Matsuoka revisited the Singapore question in the next liaison conference, on May 8. Time and speediness were of the essence, he insisted. "Roosevelt is keen to go to war [in Europe]. You see, he is a huge gambler," he said. Victory over Britain in Singapore, Matsuoka maintained, would lead the United States to reconsider a direct confrontation with Japan: "If Britain surrenders [to Japan] an hour *before* the United States enters the war in Europe, the United States would change its mind and refrain from going to war. [But] if Britain surrenders [to Japan] an hour *after* the United States enters the war [in Europe], the United States would continue fighting [and also start a war against Japan]. . . . If the United States were ever to enter this war, the war will be prolonged, and the world civilization will be destroyed." He asked the roomful of key ministers and top military leaders, "If the war were to continue for ten years . . . then what would Japan do?"

Nobody responded. Matsuoka was encouraged that he could again force one of his policies through, as he had often done since his appointment the previous summer. He went to the palace that same day to make his argument to the emperor. Matsuoka had built his credibility on the assurance that Japan could become more powerful not by use of force but through deft and assertive diplomacy. Now he was advocating outright military engagement. Hirohito was alarmed enough to summon Konoe, who reassured the emperor that Matsuoka's view did not represent the rest of the government's.

Matsuoka's misunderstanding of America's national character seriously clouded his vision, wedded as he was to the notion that only defiance would garner U.S. respect. He relied too much on brinksmanship and bluff without knowing when or where to stop. That no one in the government had restrained him had only aggravated the diplomatic stalemate over the Pacific. As noted, the "Matsuoka Plan" was relayed to Hull on May 12, but nothing happened for more than a month afterward. There were some good reasons for this lack of diplomatic movement. On May 3, Matsuoka had sent Washington a bold oral statement (a type of diplomatic statement made orally, though usually submitted on paper) announcing, in his typical histrionic way, that U.S. entry into the European war would bring tragedy. He stated that Japan had no intention of leaving the Tripartite Pact. Ambassador Nomura was invested with the task of having to communicate this information, though Hull already knew of it from decoded intelligence information, thanks to the allied cryptanalysis Magic.

Matsuoka had also ordered Nomura to propose a neutrality pact between Japan and the United States. Hull summarily dismissed it ("I did not hesitate but promptly brushed it aside") as impractical and irrelevant to the issues at hand. Many of Matsuoka's actions were seen that way. On April 16, the day Washington decided to approach Tokyo with the Draft Understanding, Hull told Nomura that he "had not become unduly concerned" about the Soviet-Japanese Neutrality Pact, signed a few days earlier, because

for some time, I have acted on the view that the Soviet policy was not to have war with any country unless in actual self-defense, and that, on the other hand, I did not see wherein Japan could have a policy based on the disposition to attack the Soviet Union. It was one of those circumstances in which I felt that the written document merely reduced to writing the relationships and policies already existing between the two Governments.

Washington was not about to rush into a neutrality pact with Tokyo. The Roosevelt administration had predicated its policy on "the information which early in 1941 had come to the knowledge of the Government from reliable and confidential sources that Germany had decided to attack Russia." It even "communicated this information confidentially to the Soviet Ambassador." That would change everything, including American-Japanese relations.

The Roosevelt administration took its time in responding to the "Matsuoka Plan" precisely because of this expectation that Japan would be more amenable to making concessions with the United States after the opening of a German-Soviet war. On June 21, almost coinciding with Operation Barbarossa, the United States replied. Matching Matsuoka's defiant tone, the United States became noticeably tougher. The recognition of Manchukuo, mentioned in the Draft Understanding of April to the delight of the Japanese leaders, was nowhere to be seen. Washington now stressed that maintaining peace in the Pacific was its utmost concern and that neither Japan nor the United States was to entertain territorial designs in the region, thus categorically rejecting the Japanese right to resort to force in Southeast Asia, as was insisted upon by Matsuoka in his plan.

On the whole, the U.S. counterproposal depicted the Asia-Pacific region as one governed by the principles of free trade and equal opportunity. This ideal reflected Hull's basic worldview. The self-made lawyer from Tennessee who had served as Roosevelt's secretary of state since 1933 was a tireless critic of protectionism and the bloc economies that had emerged to the detriment of international trade since the Great Depression. But his uncompromising reply, coming as it did on the heels of the generally accommodating Draft Understanding—which had not been drafted by the U.S. government, of course—put off the Japanese.

Hull's reply was accompanied by an oral statement aimed explicitly at an unnamed Matsuoka. While commending the earnest efforts being made by the Japanese ambassador and his associates, Hull complained that

some Japanese leaders in influential official positions are definitely committed to a course which calls for support of Nazi Germany and its policies of conquest and that the only kind of understanding with the United States which they would endorse is one that would envisage Japan's fighting on the side of Hitler should the United States become involved in the European hostilities through carrying out its present policy of self-defense. . . . So long as such leaders maintain this attitude in their official positions and apparently seek to influence public opinion in Japan in the direction indicated, is it not illusory to expect that adoption of a proposal such as the one under consideration offers a basis for achieving substantial results along the desired lines?

This constituted a strong condemnation of Matsuoka's defiant remark of May 3 that Japan would stick to its Tripartite Pact obligations no matter what. Hull's statement continued: "This government must await some clearer indication than has yet been given that the Japanese Government as a whole desires to pursue courses of peace." It was a call to replace Matsuoka. On his way back from Geneva in 1933, Matsuoka met both Roosevelt and Hull. Roosevelt was said to have taken an instant dislike to him. Self-absorption probably made Matsuoka as oblivious to that as he was to the actions and feelings of most people. He could think quickly and use words and gestures to great effect, but his inability to read others and his often unpredictable behavior made him essentially ill suited to a political post that required patience, deliberation, and dexterity. His lack of self-awareness and restraint was remarkable. "Of all the world's statesmen, there is nobody before or after me who understands and loves Christianity as much as I do," he told Pius XII in the Vatican in April 1941. In Moscow, he confounded Stalin by lecturing him on communism.

The complete control Matsuoka once possessed over Japan's foreign policy was suddenly slipping away. But when the news of the German attack on the Soviet Union reached him, he quickly tried to regain his political influence at home. Rightly sensing that he would have no backers in the government, Matsuoka bypassed it, appealing directly to the emperor to attack Stalin immediately. Hirohito was astonished. Just recently, Matsuoka had advocated attacking Singapore. Now he was saying that Japan should be attacking the Soviets in the north. ("Heroes change their minds decisively. I have earlier advanced the southward move, but I am now switching to the north" was the brazen excuse Matsuoka gave for the retraction of his words.) There was no obligation for Japan under the Tripartite Pact to join forces with Germany in such a military action, and yet Matsuoka spoke as if it were an unquestioned necessity. Then, in a meeting with the Soviet ambassador to Japan, Constantin Smetanin, who was pale and panic-stricken, Matsuoka announced that the Tripartite Pact "had priority" over the Soviet-Japanese Neutrality Pact.

When Konoe found out about Matsuoka's direct appeal for war on the Soviet Union, the prince was again greatly embarrassed. He went to the palace the next day to explain his foreign minister's action. Konoe assured the emperor that a military expedition against the Soviet Union was Matsuoka's imaginary scenario. Operation Barbarossa only accentuated Matsuoka's isolation.

THE DIARIST KAFU COULD NOT have known the exact nature of Japan's domestic and diplomatic challenges around the time of the German attack on the Soviet Union. But he knew that the country was headed in the wrong direction. He could feel it most acutely as his creative freedom became increasingly compromised by the day. He lamented the fall of Paris and noted its first anniversary in his journal in red ink. The next day, June 15, 1941, nursing a cold, he was reading in bed when he came across the words of Kicho, an eighteenth-century author known for his essays and social critiques. When asked in his old age by a younger writer why he was fearless in his work, Kicho grew very serious: "It's fine to be extremely well mannered and reserved in your everyday conduct. But once you pick up your pen, you mustn't be in any way inhibited." He admitted that over the years family and friends had warned him against doing so, worried that he would end up in prison for writing things that might easily be construed as being aimed at the authorities. In the end, he was glad he had stuck to his creed of always recording the truth of what he saw around him.

This passage, which Kafu copied in his diary, made him "very ashamed" of his own conduct. Earlier that year, through one of his published works, some people had figured out that Kafu had been keeping a diary for many years. Fearing persecution, he "stayed up late one night to cut out angry and complaining words [against the authorities] from my diary. And when I went out, I hid it in the shoe storage cabinet just to be sure." Apparently moved by Kicho's words, Kafu now wanted to make up for his cowardly act of self-censorship. Declaring that future historians should refer to his summary of his political views on Japan as something true, coming from his heart, written without fear—at least in the confines of his diary—he wrote:

When the Japanese army first started invading Chinese land, Japan claimed that it was there to "punish unruly China." But when the war became unexpectedly prolonged, [the government] was completely at a loss as to what to do next and decided to call it a "holy war"—an utterly empty phrase. Now the Japanese government is looking to expand to the South Seas . . . trying to exploit the plight of the British army in Europe. Ignorant soldiers and fiendish schemers are responsible, and people at heart do not take joy in this development.

Kafu thought people were not protesting for fear of persecution. But he knew that such fear alone could not account for everything that had unfolded in Japan during the past decade. Shamefully, he noted, there were "those who try to advertise their loyalty and allegiance to the state in order to profit from its approval," which led him to conclude that the "Japanese, fundamentally, are a nation of 'happy-go-lucky' people whose primary pursuit is to pass one day at a time without encountering too much trouble, possessing no high ideals." For these indifferent citizens, the enormous political changes that "the present [militarization], or the Meiji Restoration has brought" did not have much meaning.

Five days after this cathartic entry, on June 20—two days before Operation Barbarossa—Kafu complained further about the deplorable effect bad politics were having on the way people read and wrote, the two things he cared most about. An unsolicited sales letter from a new magazine called *Friends of Italy* infuriated him. And so did a letter from Tokyo Imperial University's college newspaper, students talking out of turn, high-handedly telling him to contribute. "People these days . . . I find it so lamentable that such an arrogant nation as ours goes terrorizing our neighbors." He then concluded, "Oh, Americans, why don't you stand up now and make this brutal nation repent?"

REGARDLESS OF Japan's uncertain direction, a swift regrouping of alliances started to take place in the rest of the world after Operation Barbarossa. The Allies, especially Britain, felt that the fate of the Soviet Union was now closely intertwined with their own. On the evening of June 22, Prime Minister Winston Churchill took to the radio, giving what would come to be known as his "Fourth Climacteric" speech. It was also broadcast in the United States. "I have taken occasion to speak to you to-night because we have reached one of the climacterics of the war," he began. After listing the three previous "intense turning-points"—the fall of France, the attempted Nazi invasion of the British Isles, and the U.S. commencement of the Lend-Lease Act earlier that year to help the Allies—he named the fourth: Hitler's war in the Soviet Union. "German bombs rained down from the air upon the Russian cities," said Churchill, dramatically recounting the German stealth attack. The invasion of Britain had only been suspended temporarily, and the attack on the Soviet Union was Hitler's tactic to reestablish his power so that he could "once again repeat, upon a greater scale than ever before," his onslaught on the Western world. Churchill's Britain was determined to aid the Soviet Union—though compared with the United States, there was substantially little it could do.

Churchill knew that Roosevelt would have a hard time convincing his domestic opponents—the isolationists and anti-Communists—of the necessity of U.S. support for the Soviet Union. While conceding that it was "not for me to speak of the action of the United States," Churchill stressed that "the Russian danger is therefore our danger, and the danger of the United States, just as the cause of any Russian fighting for his hearth and home is the cause of free men and free peoples in every quarter of the globe."

Roosevelt felt the same and wished to encourage and support Soviet resistance, but he was keenly aware he had to approach the new situation cautiously. He had by this time come to the conclusion that the United States would have to go to war in Europe at some point, but he also knew this was not the time. He believed that asking for a declaration of war from Congress would mean a certain political defeat for his administration. The military men around him, including Secretary of War Henry Stimson and Secretary of the Navy Frank Knox, urged him to take immediate strategic action against Germany by escorting ships in the Atlantic, as they projected that Germany would defeat the Soviet Union within a few months. Nonetheless, Roosevelt's preference was to step up his anti-Axis policy just short of war.

The first of such steps, too small a step from Stalin's perspective, was to free up around $40 million of Soviet funds in the United States that had been frozen after the Soviet attack on Finland in late 1939. Roosevelt did that on June 24. A special team was also established to deal with the Soviet orders for armaments, which would cost about $50 million. But because of institutional reluctance and the inability across various government agencies to deal with the sheer size of the orders—Roosevelt wanted the Soviets to purchase the armaments without any extended credit—the actual U.S. assistance to the Soviet Union in the summer of 1941 was marginal at best, and Stalin would have to hold out on his own for many more months.

The tenuous European situation made it all the more desirable for the Roosevelt administration to try to avoid going to war in the Pacific. The quadruple alliance shattered, Washington expected Tokyo to reconsider its negotiating position. When Nomura called on Hull the day of the German offensive, Hull asked "whether Germany's declaration of war against the Soviet Union might not affect the situation in such a way as to render it more easy for the Japanese Government to find some way [to rid itself of Hitler and Mussolini]."

There were certainly no legal obstacles for Japan. In international law, agreements are deemed nonbinding when there is an unforeseeable and drastic change in circumstances. Operation Barbarossa qualified. Had Japan parted company with the Axis powers then, it would have reassured the United States (and the Soviet Union, too) that Japan was serious about negotiating with the West and that Germany was not orchestrating Japan's expansionist policy. As evidenced by Konoe's immediate dispatch of his messenger Suzuki to Tojo, the prime minister desired to correct his missteps and come closer to the United States. (He later claimed that he also convoked a conference among selected ministers to talk about this very issue; no record of such a meeting exists, and there was certainly no liaison conference discussion on this topic.)

Matsuoka and Tojo stood in his way, as did Kido, the supposedly pro-Anglo-American lord keeper of the privy seal. Not considering at all the damage done to U.S.-Japanese relations by the Tripartite Pact, Kido told Hirohito nonsensically that it was important for Japan to remain Hitler's friend because the United States valued international treaties. Actually, Kido did not wish the emperor to voice any decisive political preferences one way or the other, hoping to prevent Hirohito and the imperial house from being implicated in a significant policy shift. In the end, Konoe chose to do nothing because he did not want to confront such internal obstacles. As the utmost proponent of the Tripartite Pact the previous fall, he likely thought that he would lose all political credibility if he abandoned it so quickly.

CHAPTER 6

Japan's North-South Problem

On June 23, 1941, the day after Germany attacked the Soviet Union, an intelligence order drafted in Moscow was sent to Richard Sorge, a German journalist based in Tokyo: "Report on the Japanese government's position toward the German war against the Soviet Union." Sorge, a tall, ruggedly attractive man in his midforties, was a Soviet agent operating in Japan. Born in Baku in 1895 to a Russian mother, he had been brought up mostly in Berlin and was an early enlistee for Germany in World War I, but his disillusionment with that war—which left him with a limp— had pushed him into the arms of communism. A few days after receiving this intelligence order, Sorge was instructed by the Soviet government to "report on [Japanese] army mobilization towards our borders." It must have struck Sorge as ironic that Moscow was now so anxious for his reports. A series of specific warnings he sent earlier about the impending German attack on the Soviet Union had been dismissed by Stalin as untrustworthy.

Sorge arrived in Japan in the fall of 1933. His mission, as he once summed it up, was to

> observe Japan's Soviet policy closely . . . and to find out if Japan was planning to attack the Soviet Union. This was the most important assignment given to me and to my group. . . . It would not be an overstatement to say that it was the entire purpose of my stay in Japan.

Sorge seemed to be enjoying his life in Japan. He lived in an unpretentious two-story house filled with history books and souvenirs from his travels, and he was often seen riding a motorcycle in a leather jacket. An easy man to get on with, he soon became a popular figure in Tokyo's community of German expatriates. He was able to win the confidence of important Germans, including Eugen Ott, the embassy attaché who would become Germany's ambassador to Japan in 1938. That probably explains Sorge's accurate foreknowledge, down to the day of the attack, of Operation Barbarossa.

Ott was so taken with Sorge that he allowed the journalist to install himself in an office in the German embassy, where Sorge edited a daily bulletin (and had an affair with Mrs. Ott). Sorge efficiently recruited members for what would be known as the Sorge spy ring, which consisted of at least thirteen men and three women, though very few of them had direct, consistent contact with Sorge. Among those in the ring were Max Clausen, a Prussian radio communications engineer educated in Moscow; Branko de Vukelic, a Serbian Jew raised in Croatia writing for French and Yugoslav journals; Miyagi Yotoku, a Japanese painter from Okinawa trained from a young age in California; and Ozaki Hotsumi, an adviser of Prince Konoe's and a journalist of some renown with notable Chinese expertise.

Ozaki was a pudgy-faced man with kindly eyes who disarmed all who met him. He was by far the most important figure in the Sorge spy ring. Born in 1901 and raised mostly in colonial Taiwan, where his father was assigned as a newspaper correspondent, he returned to Tokyo to obtain his higher education. He eventually became a reporter for the *Asahi*. From 1928 to 1932, he was based in Shanghai.

Ozaki's time in Taiwan and China was central to his ideological formation. He recalled that his close contact with the Chinese residents of Taiwan, and his having witnessed the "ruler-ruled" power dynamic of colonial imperialism in "everyday life and in very specific forms," were the only "extraordinary" experiences in his otherwise ordinary childhood. He was upset to see that even his usually mild-tempered father could act like any other arrogant colonial master, fighting off a rickshaw driver who demanded more money. He said that Shanghai had strengthened his already strong feeling for nationalist movements in general and the national liberation of China in particular. To him, communism provided Asian nations a road to liberation from Western and Japanese imperialism, as well as a way for Japan and China to cohabit and work toward the same goal.

Through the introduction of Agnes Smedley, an American writer and reporter known for her activism in the Indian independence movement (and another of Sorge's lovers), the young journalist Ozaki met Sorge in Shanghai in early 1930. Sorge was on a mission for Moscow to investigate China's state of affairs and its communism and asked Ozaki to educate him on the nature of Japanese activities there. Sorge described their relationship as "impeccable both personally and professionally" and Ozaki's departure for Tokyo in 1932 as "a terrible loss" to the execution of his mission. "Those people [Smedley and Sorge] were both loyal to their ideologies and profound in their principles, as well as being devoted to and talented in their work," said Ozaki. "If they were in any small way motivated by self-interest, or acted as if they were trying to use us, I at least would have refused and parted company."

In light of such mutual admiration, it is no surprise that Ozaki agreed to cooperate—on the condition that he would not receive any monetary compensation—when he was approached by Sorge in Japan in 1934. The two men had much in common. Their analytical skills, scholarly inclinations (Sorge had a doctorate in political science), and passionate and gregarious natures enabled them to become both successful journalists and skillful espionage agents.

In Japan, Sorge used his membership in the Nazi Party to conceal his allegiance to communism. Occasionally, he would stumble. On September 4, 1939, the day after Britain and France declared war on Germany, his cover was almost blown. Sorge was emerging from the office of the German news agency DNB when he bumped into Robert Guillain, head of the Tokyo bureau of the French news agency Havas. When Guillain caught sight of the "Nazi" reporter, the Frenchman started to curse at him: "My grandfather fought the Germans when France lost in the Franco-Prussian War in 1870. My father, too, fought the Germans in 1914. That was because Germany attacked us. You don't seem to be satisfied with those two wars with France. All right, we will fight you for the third time. And this time around, we will crush you. We will crush Hitler and we will bomb you all to death. You just watch. Germany will be in ruins." Sorge responded to the tirade of his much-younger colleague with a courteous invitation to lunch. As they ate, Sorge told him, "I despise this war as much as you do. . . . I, too, have gone and fought in the Great War. I believed that peace would come to this world. When Hitler emerged, I thought that he would bring order to Germany and peace to Europe." He even acknowledged, "I know that I have been mistaken," adding, after a moment's hesitation, "I am a pacifist, you see?"

Sorge could not have functioned without Ozaki. He lacked the necessary language skills to operate effectively in Japanese society; his spoken Japanese remained rudimentary at best. (He did not speak adequate Russian, either, and mostly used English and German for his communications with Moscow.) Ozaki was in high demand as a political analyst and as a commentator on current affairs, especially Sino-Japanese relations. It was on this subject that he now reported for the *Asahi* and carried out research at the South Manchurian Railway's think tank. With the escalation of Japan's China War, he became a celebrated public intellectual, and people from various professions, including those in the military and the police, were eager to hear his opinions. He was also an active member of the Showa Research Association, a brain trust that helped Prince Konoe form his policies. This alone would have provided Ozaki with significant sources of information. But far more important was his participation in the so-called Breakfast Club.

This exclusive club met twice a month at eight o'clock in the morning to exchange information and debate current political issues. Its membership inspired awe. Though Konoe was not a regular fixture at meetings, members prided themselves on forming the prince's innermost circle. Most were from Japan's privileged class, in their thirties and early forties, inclined toward liberalism and internationalism (far more than Konoe was), and recipients of an elite Anglo-American education. Members included Konoe's secretary, Ushiba Tomohiko; Saionji Kinkazu, a grandson of Prince Saionji (and Matsuoka's Red Arrow companion); the chief cabinet secretary, Kazami Akira; the international journalist Matsumoto Shigeharu; Inukai Takeru, a novelist and the third son of former prime minister Inukai Tsuyoshi; and Matsukata Saburo, son of Matsukata Masayoshi, a Meiji oligarch.

Probably because of their impeccable pedigrees, the club members did not feel the need to hold back their opinions in front of Konoe, and that was presumably why he valued them. Ozaki was included in this group because of his Chinese expertise and his close friendship with Saionji. The two had met aboard a ship bound for a conference in the United States in 1936. Saionji had no idea of Ozaki's true radicalism. In fact, Ozaki did not even confide it to his wife, to whom he was otherwise completely devoted.

After their return from the United States, the two men spent time together virtually every day. It seemed natural that they would discuss politics when they met. Both were all too aware that Japan's politics were going off course and that the China War should be ended immediately. Ozaki later said that he had associated with those whom he ended up using as information sources "with utmost sincerity, out of mutual concern for the nation's present crisis."

AFTER OPERATION BARBAROSSA, the Communist spies needed to learn if Japan intended to attack the Soviet Union. As we have seen, Matsuoka believed that Japan should, and he encouraged the Germans to think that his country's participation in their war was imminent, which added to Soviet anxiety. Now that he was relying on Ambassador Oshima's highly biased reports from Berlin, there was no question in Matsuoka's mind that Germany was going to prevail. By attacking the Soviet Union, Japan could gain territory while convincing the Nazis of its good faith. To him, Japan was in a situation similar to that of Italy in June 1940, when Mussolini decided to attack France after German victory had already become apparent. But there was a fundamental problem with Matsuoka's new policy preference: Not only was there no practical strategic outline to accompany his proposal of "striking north," but nobody else in the Japanese leadership wanted a war with the Soviet Union.

Though the Japanese army had always looked northward, seeing Russia—and then the Soviet Union—as Japan's primary enemy, it had some compelling reasons for not being at all keen to back Matsuoka. Soviet superiority over the Japanese army, which did not possess any of the heavy tanks necessary for fighting in Mongolia and Siberia, had already been demonstrated during the border battles in Nomonhan in 1939. Japan also did not have enough soldiers to fight in both China and Russia. In June 1941, the army joined the navy to push instead for an expansion into the southern half of French Indochina.

Military planners insisted that the transfer of control from French colonial authorities to Japan would be peaceful, with proper "diplomatic" pressure applied. After all, in the past ten months alone, Japan had managed to take over the northern half of French Indochina and to mediate a territorial dispute between Thailand and French Indochina (in the former's favor) through the use of diplomacy backed by threats and force. By occupying the whole of the Indochinese Peninsula, not only would Japan establish a strategic foothold much closer to British Malaya and the Dutch East Indies, but it would also gain access to more rice, tin, and rubber, enabling it to fight China in the short term, to build a self-sufficient economic bloc in the long term, and perhaps to fight a bigger war in the future. Also, the Dutch in the East Indies might be deterred by the Japanese presence in their backyard and finally agree to provide Japan with more oil. No further military adventures would be necessary south of the Indochinese border, it was said.

Matsuoka vehemently objected. He was wrongly convinced of a swift German victory over the Soviet Union (as were many others, including some in Britain and the United States), but he was now rightly worried about the risk of a severe Anglo-American retaliation should Japan decide to occupy even more of France's colonial territory. That would unduly advertise Japan's greater ambition in the region, sending up a flare in Washington. The question of whether to strike north (the Soviet Union) or go south became the focus of Tokyo's policy deliberations in late June 1941. The institutional forces and mechanisms that enabled such a debate would have a lasting impact on Tokyo's policy formulation in the following months.

Broadly, Japan's strategic outline was set by the Imperial General Headquarters, the highest organ of the high command of the Army and Navy General Staffs. The general staffs initiated strategic proposals, but so did the Army and Navy Ministries, which were part of the cabinet. In both these ministries, ministers resided at the top of the institutional hierarchy, followed by vice ministers, chiefs of various bureaus (including military affairs, personnel, legal affairs, and supply and accounts), and then chiefs of sections (subgroups within the bureaus). The general staffs had a similar chain of command, with the chiefs of staff at the top, followed by vice chiefs of staff, chiefs of divisions (including operations, information, and mobilization), and, finally, various section chiefs. Strategic proposals were rarely formulated at the top levels; they were usually initiated at the bureau and section levels of the ministries and at the division and section levels of the general staffs. With many specialist groups trying to advance their interests, arriving at a new policy was a very complicated business.

If, for example, one division or section of the Army General Staff proposed a new initiative, it would first have to be approved, modified, and endorsed by the other division and section chiefs. Only then would the proposal be discussed in a joint meeting of the Army General Staff (independent of the government) and the Army Ministry (part of the government), usually attended by the chief and vice chief of staff and minister and vice minister. Meanwhile, the bureau and section chiefs of the Army

Ministry would be introduced to the Army General Staff's proposal; if in agreement, they would all work toward convincing the navy (the general staff, as well as the ministry) and the Foreign Ministry, both of which had their own intricate groups and subgroups. After agreement from the Foreign Ministry and the navy was secured, the prime minister's cabinet would finally be approached by the chiefs of staff, as the representatives of the high command, to put the proposal on the agenda of a liaison conference.

This sort of painstaking institutional groundwork was carried out by middle-ranking military planners, most of whom did not even attend the liaison meetings of the top leaders. They were aptly called *bakuryo*, which literally means "officers behind the curtains." In the olden days, the word *baku* (curtains) had a double meaning in explaining concentration of power. One was political, synonymous with the government, as in *bakufu* (shogunate), meaning "a regime behind the curtains." The other was strategic, alluding to the makeshift curtains used in encampments during field combat to identify the headquarters, where strategies were secretly debated among the select few. In prewar Japan, *bakuryo* had come to assume both the political task of negotiating and liaising with different sources of power and the more practical task of planning strategies. Because of the pivotal role *bakuryo* would come to assume in directing Japan's policy after July, the term evoked the image of war planners furtively creating bellicose policies in the name of assisting and advising their superiors.

In the early summer of 1941, Japan's three most influential *bakuryo*, all about fifty years old, were the chief of the Army General Staff's Operations Division, Tanaka Shin'ichi; the chief of the Army Ministry's Military Affairs Bureau, Muto Akira; and the aforementioned chief of the Navy Ministry's Naval Affairs Bureau, Oka Takazumi. Muto and Oka had the crucial role of working together to create an interservice agreement. Tanaka, on the other hand, often worked alone, driven by a hostile worldview that made him the doomsday oracle of the Army General Staff. His division was the most aggressive.

Tanaka consistently promoted a hard-line stance in China. For him, total victory was the only option, and the willingness Japanese leaders had been showing of late to negotiate with the United States was a disgrace. Refraining from war equated to cowardly surrender and was worse than losing everything after having fought a proper war. Because of the strength of his convictions and his forceful personality, and even though he was only third in the chain of command, he would come to have a greater influence on policy than anyone else on the Army General Staff.

Tanaka was often frustrated by what he perceived as Muto's accommodationist tendencies (Muto was hardly a moderate). To Tanaka, Sato Kenryo, a section chief in the Military Affairs Bureau who worked immediately below Muto and was a close associate of Army Minister Tojo, held more promise. Sato, in his midforties, had a few years earlier gained national notoriety when he made a strong case for the National Mobilization Law in a parliamentary session. He grew upset when legislators jeered at him, shouting "Shut up!" before he stormed out of the room. The democratic process was clearly not to Sato's taste.

The navy, too, had its middle-ranking hawks. The primary example was Ishikawa Shingo, a section chief in the Navy Ministry's Military Affairs Bureau, also in his midforties. In 1931, around the time of the Manchurian Incident, he wrote a controversial book, *Japan's Crisis,* under a pseudonym (and without permission from the navy, grounds enough for dismissal from the service). In it, he warned that the United Sates had entertained ambitions to control the East since the middle of the previous century, and he urged Japan to embark on a "great national march to ensure its right to survival" in the face of impending American threats. He thought the conferences on naval reduction that had been held in Washington and London were part of a Western conspiracy to obstruct Japan's rise to prominence. Like the army's Ishiwara Kanji, who had conceived of the Manchurian takeover, Ishikawa greatly influenced younger officers with his polemical book, turning many in what had traditionally been the pro-British navy into Nazi sympathizers. His fanatical personality had long alarmed the top brass. Nicknamed Wild Shot, he had been consistently passed over for influential positions for much of his career. Now, in the fall of 1940, Oka, chief of the Naval Affairs Bureau and a strong advocate of Japan's Axis alliance, appointed Ishikawa leader of its Arms Division, overriding objections from the Personnel Bureau.

Ishikawa, along with other like-minded associates, formed the First Naval Defense Policy Committee (the so-called First Committee), which would shape the navy's prowar position on the eve of Pearl Harbor. He believed, like Tanaka, that war with the United States was something not to be avoided but to be faced heroically. In his thinking, Japan's military occupation of French Indochina was about preparing for an inevitable war rather than a possible one. Ishikawa, in fact, favored a forceful military advance beyond Indochinese borders and advocated the conquest of British Malaya within 1941. Ishikawa would later boast, "I am the one who brought Japan to the war course."

One could say that these *bakuryo* officers were simply doing their soldierly job of preparing for war while keeping an eye on the opportunity for strategic and territorial aggrandizement. The problem for Japan in mid-1941, however, was that war preparation became the sole focus in the absence of an overarching national policy guiding it. Those at the top were often too willing to be led by the junior officers they should have been restraining, adopting their urgent rhetoric uncritically. The navy's chief of staff, Nagano Osami, summarized that attitude unabashedly: "Because the section chiefs are the ones most in the know, I accept their views."

Five decades later, Ishii Akiho, a *bakuryo* officer in the Army Ministry who was responsible for drafting many of its successful proposals, reflected on the power he and his colleagues had once possessed in those crucial months leading up to Pearl Harbor: "Fools that we were, we could make an important policy decision as long as we took the initiative. Of course, our policy might have been modified along the way, but [our voice] was that important. . . . And so my sin is great." In his mind, the most fundamental problem of the time was that no one in the chain of command ever doubted that the Japanese empire was destined to achieve regional—if not global—leadership and thus needed to expand no matter what. This meant that even if one expansionist program was rejected, the planners would come up with another just as expansionist. Well, they would ask, "if we can't go there, where can we go instead?"

It is important to emphasize, though, that in June 1941 the fanatical designs of Tanaka, Ishikawa, and Japan's other most bellicose strategists were not seen as such by top military leaders or by many of their *bakuryo* colleagues in the planning bodies. Those leaders supported the occupation of southern Indochina because they believed it was a timely low-risk, high-return venture; the power vacuum in colonial Southeast Asia had to be taken advantage of while the rest of the world occupied itself with the developments in Europe. Just as Matsuoka called for immediate Japanese action in the north, before Germany finished its business with the Soviet Union, the *bakuryo* officers believed their opportunity in the south was fleeting. This was the backdrop to the critical north-south debate, the outcome of which would have great ramifications for Japan's international standing.

On June 24, the navy and the army agreed that Japan should occupy the southern half of French Indochina and leave the option open for the army to strike the Soviet Union if a convenient opportunity—such as the large-scale transfer of Soviet troops from the Far East to the European front—arose. Prime Minister Konoe gave his blessing to this quickly emerging consensus partly because he saw the shift in policy objectives as a much-needed expedient to oust Matsuoka. Not so long ago, Konoe had relied on Matsuoka's forcefulness to lead the government. Now the disenchanted Konoe was relying on the military, the very group he had tried to contain and check via Matsuoka, to bring about the foreign minister's downfall. The new plan, loaded with unarticulated political motives, had to be approved in a liaison conference for it to become policy.

Far from a ceremonial formality, liaison conferences provided a chance for leaders to put forward specific questions openly and ruthlessly. There was always a possibility that proposals could be rejected, and everyone believed that Matsuoka would oppose. That was why the Navy and Army General Staffs brought the vice chiefs of staff as reinforcements. They were the experts, it was claimed, with command of the details. (In the case of the army's vice chief of staff, Tsukada Osamu, this claim to expertise was certainly not true, as he reportedly told his junior officers, "I don't understand data, so I will leave them up to you.") Matsuoka would have to be confronted. Konoe called a liaison meeting for June 25.

Contrary to expectations, Matsuoka was surprisingly pliable. Without much quibbling, he endorsed the military occupation of southern French Indochina. "This matter requires speedy action," he said. "So long as we have decided, we'd better get on with it." It was announced that later in the afternoon a cabinet meeting would be called (to endorse the liaison conference resolution as a government decision, a matter of formality) and would be followed by the chiefs of staff's interview with the emperor, informing him of the approved plan of action. When the discussion shifted to Japan's Soviet policy, Matsuoka pushed for an attack on the Soviet Union.

Taken aback, Army Chief of Staff Sugiyama responded:

> The foreign minister is preaching aggressive policy, but the army isn't at all prepared. We can attack only when the conditions in China, the north, and the south become favorable in all three directions. . . . One must be aware that if we hasten our attack on the Soviet Union, the United States could join forces with the Soviet Union.

Sugiyama mistakenly spoke as if the proposed Indochinese invasion carried no risk of a U.S. intervention. Matsuoka answered Sugiyama by pushing for a "deterrence move" against the Soviet Union. He was going to be the biggest stumbling block after all. Another liaison meeting, the leaders grudgingly concluded, had to be called in order to resolve this disagreement.

The next day, June 26, Matsuoka appealed to the military men's sense of loyalty to their alliance partner Germany and pressed again for an immediate strike in the north. Vice Army Chief Tsukada became adamant in his opposition: "I don't know about politics, but as far as military affairs are concerned, Germany is doing whatever it wants to do. That's all the more reason for us not to consult [Germany]!" Army Minister Tojo agreed with Tsukada, but the decision to endorse an Indochinese takeover was not one he made easily. On June 23, he had met with an officer from the army's Fuel Division who suggested that the only way Japan could procure petroleum was by advancing into southern Indochina. Tojo blew up. "You are telling me that we ought to steal it?" he asked. He was furious that the army's engineers had not invented synthetic oil despite their generous budget. "I cannot possibly report to His Imperial Majesty and say, 'I am afraid we must succumb to being thieves,'" he complained.

In his narrow focus, Tojo had failed to consider the ominous political implications for Japan's diplomatic relations with the West. He eventually supported the Indochinese advance, abandoning too easily his professed moral objections. Though the liaison meeting of June 26 ended inconclusively, the infighting was beginning to take its toll on Matsuoka. He became uncharacteristically inarticulate by the end of that meeting, saying he agreed with the military plan "broadly," though he disagreed with it "fundamentally." He promised to explain himself the next day.

Another day, another conference. In the meeting of June 27, Matsuoka again tried to retract his impetuous endorsement of the Indochinese invasion. He said he understood the *broad* strategic logic behind it but felt it was a *fundamental* political mistake because it would provoke the Allies to retaliate. An invasion of southern Indochina would be feasible only after Nazi preponderance in Europe was firmly established (which he felt would happen soon). Matsuoka dismissed Sugiyama's earlier concern that the United States might join forces with the Soviet Union against Japan; the United States had always hated the Soviet Union, he said.

True, the Soviet Union had never been a preferred member of the international community. The very war Hitler was now waging in Europe was precipitated as much by Stalin's territorial ambitions in Poland, the Baltic, and the Balkan states as by Hitler's master plan. Western opinion favored Finland when it refused to cede territories to the Soviet Union and was then attacked in late 1939. This resulted in the Soviet Union's becoming the only member ever to be expelled from the League of Nations. All this was true. But no one in the liaison meeting even mentioned the possibility that the United States, like Britain, hated Nazi Germany more than it hated the Soviet Union.

Matsuoka kept hammering away in meetings on June 28, 30, and July 1. "My foretelling for the near future has never been wrong," he said at one point. "I predict that going south would bring a great disaster." Muto disagreed. Recognizing that the discussion was going nowhere, Matsuoka also resorted to placating his opponents. "Why not postpone [the southern Indochinese takeover] for another six months? If the high command and the prime minister are resolved to go through with it no matter what, however, I cannot object to their decision, having once endorsed the plan myself."

Matsuoka's rare nonconfrontational tone seemed to shake the resolve of some leaders. Navy Minister Oikawa proposed to Army Chief of Staff Sugiyama that the plan be postponed for six months. Kondo, the navy's vice chief of staff, whispered to his army counterpart, Tsukada, to consider delaying. But Tsukada was not about to be mollified so easily. He openly admonished his superior, urging Sugiyama to stick to the original proposal. He did, and Konoe concurred. The finance minister and minister of industry and commerce, who could have helped the leaders see the situation in a more practical light, were only invited to attend liaison meetings after June 30. It was too late.

THE FORMAL APPROVAL FOR Japan to occupy southern French Indochina (or to become thieves, in Tojo's words) was given at an imperial conference held on July 2. Imperial conferences were rare, marking, more often than not, the beginnings and endings of wars. They were attended by key ministers of state, the chief cabinet secretary to assist the cabinet ministers, the director of the Cabinet Planning Board, the president of the Privy Council, chiefs and vice chiefs of the Army and Navy General Staffs, and chiefs of the Military Affairs Bureaus of the Army and Navy Ministries (though the army's bureau chief was absent on July 2 because of illness)—all formally attired in either military uniforms or tails.

"Imperial conferences," Hirohito once said, "were a curious thing. . . . The emperor had no deciding power, unable to dictate the atmosphere of the conference [despite its name]." The emperor would listen to the background of the proposal to be approved, and the president of the Privy Council would question the leaders on his behalf. The imperial approval was a mere formality with no constitutionally binding power. Yet it bore the stamp of uncontested authority, and there was no historical precedent of its having been overturned. By acquiring imperial sanction, policy decisions would become divine, suddenly apolitical, and political leaders would be collectively relieved of any personal responsibility for the newly approved policy.

The July 2 conference was the first of four imperial conferences to be held before Japan's attack on the United States. It took place in the First Eastern Hall of the Meiji Palace, a proud edifice located on the vast Imperial Palace compound in central Tokyo, built in 1888. The hall represented a marriage of Eastern and Western aesthetic sensibilities—ceilings hung with glass chandeliers, walls adorned with purple silk embroidered in traditional Japanese floral patterns. The long conference tables were blanketed in silk with multicolored checkered stripes in various shades. The infusion of color produced the muted opulence seen in the best kimono designs.

The conference lasted from 10:00 a.m. to noon. The decision to move on southern Indochina was challenged and questioned by Hara Yoshimichi, the president of the Privy Council. The leaders were expected to demonstrate in front of the emperor that they had weighed their decision carefully; the session was not intended to be an occasion to scrutinize or reconsider their decision. On July 2, the greatest concern for Hara was a chilling passage in the policy outline for the southern Indochinese occupation: "The Empire shall not flinch from war with Britain and the United States." It first appeared in a military draft in early June, and at different stages of formulating the outline, the *bakuryo* planners had deleted and reinserted the sentence. It was directed specifically at Matsuoka and his opposition to the Indochinese occupation. "Going to [occupy] Thailand or Indochina requires the resolve to fight Britain and the United States," he'd said. "In the absence of that resolve, I am disinclined to discuss this matter further." In order to force the occupation plan through, its proponents wanted to convince Matsuoka of their determination.

The "shall not flinch" resolve was hardly built upon a thorough deliberation within the armed services. Hard-line strategists like the army's Tanaka and the navy's Ishikawa gladly adopted Matsuoka's uncompromising tone and formalized it in their draft. Others in the services—the majority—were put off by the passage. Most navy men shuddered at the possibility of having to fight Britain and the United States single-handedly at sea. Sawamoto Yorio, the vice navy minister at the time, recalled afterward:

> I was surprised [at the "shall not flinch" passage] and asked Navy Minister Oikawa about it. He said he was against war, but considering the army's general preoccupation with the north . . . we had to say that much to stop the policy from slipping out of [the traditionally south-inclined] navy's control. I've also asked Admiral Toyoda, minister of commerce and industry, about the passage, and he reassured me, "Don't worry, Minister Oikawa doesn't want [war]."

For the navy leadership, the inclusion of the passage was a means of putting up a bold front for not only the foreign minister but the army as well. Ostensibly preparing for the possibility of war also suggested an increase in the navy's share of the military budget.

At the imperial conference of July 2, rightly sensing the flippancy of the leaders' bellicose rhetoric, the septuagenarian Privy Council president asked the attendees a series of questions related to their determination to "not flinch" from war with the West. A bespectacled, mustached man with a background in law, Hara was known for his conservative and anti-Communist beliefs, which made him sympathetic to Matsuoka's advocacy of striking the Soviet Union instead of occupying French Indochina. But common sense now guided him in his questioning. He said to the leaders:

> We need to be careful with the use of force. . . . It's one thing to make French Indochina listen to our demands by hinting at our power. It's quite another to exercise it. . . . We don't want our action to be seen as an "invasion." . . . You say that you won't refrain from fighting Britain and the United States . . . but how do you square that resolve with the reality [of not having prepared for such a war]? I am inclined to think that Britain and the United States would react if we went ahead with [the occupation of southern] French Indochina. . . . What is the likeli-

hood of [the new policy] prompting them to join forces [against Japan]?
I would like a clear answer.

Sugiyama conceded that it was indeed a serious matter to consider.
Tojo supported this view. But they reassured Hara that the planned occupation would not employ force and would be a peaceful one. This is not
what Matsuoka really believed; at one point that day he pronounced that
the possibility of war "cannot be said is nil." But even he did not want to
derail the plan once it had reached this awe-inspiring formal stage. Hirohito, at the head of the long blanketed tables, listened silently.

The purportedly peaceful and noncoercive nature of the planned takeover was an important point for the leadership to harp on. In the previous year's occupation of the northern half of the Indochinese Peninsula,
despite Tokyo's agreed policy of peaceable, diplomatic transition, impetuous officers of the Japanese field army started firing at the local French
forces, who were refusing to leave. There were several hundred casualties
before the Japanese could settle the matter with the French authorities.
This event reinforced Japan's reputation as a rogue in the West and was
very much on Hara's mind when he asked his questions.

Each time Hara brought up the issue of war with Britain and the
United States, he received a vague reply. The leaders didn't feel compelled
to discuss matters in depth at an imperial conference. After a while, Sugiyama summarized the majority thinking. The army chief of staff said that
it was very necessary

to carry out the proposed plan to resist an Anglo-American plot [of cor-
nering Japan economically]. If Germany's plan [to dominate Europe]
suffers a setback, yes, it becomes conceivable that the United States
will go to war [with Japan]. But Germany is winning the war now. [With
such a powerful ally behind Japan], I think Americans are not going to
go to war with us over French Indochina. It goes without saying that we
must complete the occupation in a peaceful way. We are tempted to go
as far as Thailand, but that would be too close to [British] Malaya, causing a big problem, so we are stopping at the borders of French Indochina
this time. . . . We intend to carry out this plan very carefully.

Hara was reassured. He said they were in "basic agreement" as long as
it was clear to everyone present that Japan should avoid war with Britain

and the United States, despite the bold words in the proposal. Everyone was convincing himself that as long as the military occupation of southern Indochina did not involve any physical violence and did not go farther than the peninsula, the world was not going to quibble, let alone start a war, with Japan.

Hirohito had qualms about the occupation, as Hara's insistent questioning revealed. When the proposal was introduced on June 25, the day Matsuoka impulsively endorsed it, Hirohito said, "In terms of international law principles, this makes me wonder." But in the face of the leaders' confidence (and in defiance of Matsuoka, whom the emperor did not trust), those qualms were not great enough for him to consider putting a stop to the plan. Prime Minister Konoe kept silent. When political leadership was called for, he was nowhere to be heard.

THE JULY 2 IMPERIAL CONFERENCE RESOLUTION was a turning point for Richard Sorge. Though Matsuoka's frequent reassurances had led the German embassy in Tokyo to count on Japanese participation in the Soviet war, Sorge remained skeptical. He later recalled:

> Ozaki's observations of the state of affairs before the imperial conference were that Prime Minister Konoe and his nonmilitary cabinet members did not want war with the Soviet Union and also that the navy did not want the war, either. Within the army, there was a strong desire to join in the war [with Germany]; nonetheless, such a stance had been tilted toward one of observing the situation for the time being. . . . Foreign Minister Matsuoka alone was of the opinion that Japan should reject the Soviet-Japan neutrality pact, which he himself had concluded.

Matsuoka personally informed Ambassador Ott of the decision of the imperial conference, which was how Sorge heard about it. Sorge noted:

> Foreign Minister Matsuoka's message consisted of two important points from the imperial conference resolutions. They were: (1) In the north, Japan would expand militarily and prepare in every way to oust Bolshevism. (2) In the south, Japan would launch an active advancement program. . . . Ambassador Ott interpreted these points with most emphasis placed on the first point; hence he was of the view that Japan would

build up its forces in the north and Manchuria . . . understanding that this mobilization implied the beginning of Japan's war with the Soviet Union.

Ozaki, according to Sorge, "placed more emphasis on the aforementioned second point," meaning that he believed Japan would begin an active military venture only in French Indochina. Sorge knew which one to trust and notified Moscow that

> at the imperial conference it was decided that there was no change in the military action plan for Saigon [southern Indochina]. There it was also decided that *in case of the Red Army's destruction, Japan would consider military action against the Soviet Union.*

The Red Army's general staff took Sorge's report seriously, prompting it to underline Sorge's conclusion. But there was no guarantee that Japan would not change its mind, especially since Japan seemed adamant about remaining a German ally. This suspicion would draw the Soviet Union closer to the United States.

A few days after the imperial conference, top fleet commanders were summoned to Tokyo by the navy minister and the naval chief of staff. When the commanders were informed of what had been decided, including the passage declaring Japan's resolve not to flinch from war, they were, on the whole, astonished. "Are we really ready for an aerial war?" Yamamoto Isoroku asked. He knew the answer better than anyone. Koga Mineichi, the commander of the Second Fleet, was furious. "How could you have endorsed such a critical policy without consulting us? What if a war really broke out? You can't just tell us then, 'OK, you go ahead and fight.' We won't win!" he said.

Navy Chief of Staff Nagano, the leading proponent of the southern Indochinese plan, responded as if he had had no part in advancing the proposal: "What can I say? The government decided on it."

CHAPTER 7

A Quiet Crisis in July

The speed and optimism with which the occupation of southern Indochina was approved on July 2 revealed that most of Japan's leaders felt there was no immediate crisis. The nation was informed by Konoe's chief cabinet secretary in a press conference that "an important policy decision has been made recently, owing to the present situation." But the occupation plan, drafted for internal use only and communicated to the Japanese embassy in Washington, was decoded by the United States within a week. Roosevelt welcomed the Japanese reluctance to attack the Soviet Union, his fledgling ally, but was alarmed by Japan's stated willingness to risk war with Britain and the United States by going south. He remarked to Secretary of the Interior Harold Ickes on July 1 that it was "terribly important for the control of the Atlantic for us to help to keep peace in the Pacific," adding, "I simply have not got enough Navy to go round—and every little episode in the Pacific means fewer ships in the Atlantic."

While embracing warlike rhetoric, the Japanese leaders acted as if diplomacy with the United States were of secondary importance. On July 10, almost three weeks after receiving the U.S. counterproposal to combat Matsuoka's hardnosed approach, Konoe chaired a liaison conference to discuss Japan's U.S. policy. There was a pervasive sense that the content and the tone of the U.S. reply were unfairly harsh to Japan. The new demands were seen as condescending, touching the raw nerve of the nation's deep-seated, historically nurtured sense of inadequacy as an upstart, nonwhite power. Matsuoka argued that Washington's response was a provocation, only a step short of racist foreign policy.

Matsuoka, understandably, was upset by Hull's calling for his dismissal:

> Hull's statement is extremely aggressive. Nomura, despite being a close friend of mine, had the outrageous temerity to relay this "statement" to me. To meddle with another country's internal affairs, such as the reorganization of its cabinet, is simply astounding. That is especially true when dealing with a great world power like Japan.

Matsuoka restated his dissatisfaction with Hull and Nomura and the whole manner in which the "talks" with the United States had come about. He was furious with everyone involved—most of all Konoe, who was sitting silently a few yards away.

Matsuoka continued to fulminate at a liaison meeting held two days later. "Hull's oral statement should in fact have been returned to him immediately upon its being read," he said. "It is truly appalling what it says . . . [and] only confirms that the United States looks down on Japan as if it were its protectorate or territory. . . . So long as I am the foreign minister, I cannot accept such a statement." He proposed to discontinue the talks with the United States. This alarmed even the most conservative and anti-American in attendance.

After a period of silence, Sugiyama spoke up. "Even though I share the same opinion as the foreign minister," the army chief of staff started politely, "the military is facing a most critical situation" in both the south and the north. One could not afford making an enemy out of the United States, he said, irrespective of one's personal views: "[It is] inappropriate to talk of severing ties completely with the United States. It is proper that we leave some room for negotiations."

Home Minister Hiranuma Kiichiro took the floor after Sugiyama. Seventy-three years old, a slender, bespectacled man with a cold and detached air, scholarly and sure of himself, Hiranuma bore some physical resemblance to Woodrow Wilson. He was a Japanese chauvinist and Asia-firster who thought Japan had a preordained mission to lead Asia into a better, more just world. He had been prime minister briefly in 1939 and shared some of Konoe's rightist views. But he did not take to fascism the way Konoe did, believing that National Socialism and other forms of fascism were just variations of communism. He resisted Konoe's fascistic political programs, including the creation of the Imperial Rule Assistance Association in 1940.

Hiranuma's unexpected loquaciousness on this day signaled his concern over the possibility of confronting the West. "On this occasion," he began,

> the Empire has to avoid going to war with the United States at all costs. That is the most important thing. . . . [If a war broke out], it might continue for fifty or a hundred years. The foreign minister himself has repeatedly referred to the great Japanese spirit represented in our common aim of "harmonizing the eight corners of the world under one roof." According to that spirit, we had better avoid war. Japan is not a totalitarian country. Neither is it a liberal state. As far as our ideals go, our Imperial Way is to eliminate all wars from this world. The United States might not understand this, but to stop and refrain from war is the route that Japan should take. So it is our task to steer the United States to help us in that endeavor. . . . If the foreign minister is right in saying that Americans will inevitably go to war, I suppose my reasoning with you serves no real purpose. The foreign minister insists that Roosevelt is leading his people in that direction and that they are following him. But there are those among them who are opposed to such a war. . . . It is all right, as the foreign minister says, to criticize [Hull's oral statement]. But even if our hope is small, could we not make an effort [to seek a peaceful settlement]?

After Hiranuma's heartfelt plea, Matsuoka had no choice but to say he would be amenable to negotiations so long as the United States would retract Hull's criticism of him. "Even if there is no hope," Tojo said, "we should pursue [peace] until the very end. I understand how difficult this might be . . . but as long as we truthfully communicate [to Washington] what we Japanese think is right, our feelings will surely get through to them." Said Oikawa: "There is an assessment within the navy that Secretary of State Hull wishes to avoid war in the Pacific. Japan does not wish to have a war in the Pacific. So isn't there naturally room [for peace to be achieved]?"

Here were military leaders seeming to contradict the latest imperial conference decision not to refrain from war with Britain and the United States. Clearly, the leaders were not resolved to fight such a war. Matsuoka, strange as it may seem, was no exception. In suggesting the end of U.S.-Japan talks, he wanted to appear tough and resolute, hoping to restore his credibility. But he miscalculated. "Why are you military men such wimps?" he said to Tojo and the others. According to one account, he even called them "boneheads" for their conciliatory attitude toward the United States. He said that men in uniform simply did not understand diplomacy and so should stop meddling and think only about wars, like proper soldiers. With these words, Matsuoka had definitively offended and alienated his military colleagues.

The unpleasantness was accompanied by ironies. No one acknowledged that Japan had already taken a step closer to the cessation of ties with the United States with its decision to occupy southern Indochina. Matsuoka, of course, understood that risk. And here he was, a man who in many ways knew the United States more intimately than did anyone else in the room, threatening to abandon negotiations entirely. This led the more conservative elements of the leadership, including Hiranuma and Tojo, to plead with him not to speak so impetuously.

Yes, Matsuoka had earlier insisted that Japan claim its sovereign right to exercise force in the south and had said so to Washington. He had also argued for an immediate strike on Singapore after his return from Europe, so as to help the German war cause. Hard though it might have been for other leaders to comprehend, there was a clear distinction in Matsuoka's mind between the kind of action he had previously advocated and the recent southward expansion program he opposed. He had envisioned a Japanese attack on Singapore as a quick, targeted deterrence gesture, whereas the Indochinese occupation plan risked a bigger war in order, paradoxically, to be able to fight one.

IN THE ENSUING DISCUSSION, Japan's leaders continued to reveal their superficial understanding of the outside world, focusing primarily on the timing, rather than the substance, of Japan's belated reply to Washington. Sugiyama recommended that Japan should delay until the military takeover of southern Indochina was complete. Japan was due to commence its negotiations with the authorities in Vichy France in two days, on July 14. Sugiyama said that giving the United States a chance to embrace and influence French Indochina would be a mistake. If the occupation went smoothly, Washington might not like Japan's initiative, but it would not take any drastic action over a "peaceful" transition so far from the American mainland. Needless to say, Sugiyama did not suspect that the United States already knew about the Japanese plan.

The leaders' shortsighted and wishful thinking went hand in hand with ready references to Japan's high moral ideals, the superiority of the Japanese spirit, Japan's grand mission to liberate the whole of Asia from Western colonialism, and their wish for a peaceful resolution of the diplomatic and economic stalemate. None of these were conflicting aims in their minds—as long as they remained abstract. They created the illusion of ideological consistency and uniformity in Japan's leadership.

As the conference drew to a close, Nagano addressed the foreign minister: "Matsuoka, if you say that the Americans will not do anything to change their attitude no matter what we tell them, why not do as you say, eh?" Was he saying that Matsuoka should reject the proposal and Hull's oral statement altogether, thus severing ties with Washington? Or—more likely—that Japan should respond to the United States without waiting for the Indochina takeover to be completed? Nagano did not clarify. Whatever his true intention, his question prompted the Navy Ministry's Oka to reprimand Nagano, based on his interpretation of what the navy chief had just said: "I can understand that however limited the hope, we should strive to make further efforts. But, Your Excellency, you are now saying that we should stop making such efforts entirely." Nagano agreed that his suggestion should be ignored, acknowledging his improper understanding of the issue at stake.

On that strangely unsettling note, the tense liaison meeting of July 12 ended. All that was agreed upon was that no reply should be made to the United States until Japan occupied southern Indochina. Konoe continued to sit silently by.

ON JULY 14, Matsuoka, though ill, managed to draft Japan's second response to the United States. Based on the joint proposal by the military and the government, it was little changed in content from the May 12 plan. It announced to the United States that Japan did not admit to weakness in the wake of the collapse of the alliance between Japan, Germany, Italy, and the Soviet Union. It also said that Japan was not about to abandon the Tripartite Pact. It tasked the United States with urging Chiang Kai-shek to make peace with Japan and with not interfering in the negotiation.

Matsuoka wanted to reject Hull's oral statement first (with a lengthy reproach of Hull's behavior), then send the full response to the U.S. counterproposal a couple of days later. Konoe and others felt that rejecting the oral statement alone would be too provocative and might end the "informal conversations" between the two countries. They favored simultaneous delivery. Matsuoka communicated the rejection of Hull's oral statement to Nomura anyway, though exercising some self-restraint, without his long tirade against Hull. On July 15, Matsuoka sent the draft of Japan's full response to Germany for its approval. Konoe was beside himself and for once acted quickly. He wanted an end to Matsuoka's one-man show.

On July 16—almost a year since Konoe's comeback as prime minister of Japan and Matsuoka's debut as his foreign minister—the second Konoe cabinet resigned en masse. Matsuoka would not have resigned voluntarily, as Konoe had hoped and as a minister who suffered a political defeat like the one Matsuoka experienced on July 2 would normally have done. Under the Meiji Constitution, Konoe could not fire a minister—hence this roundabout way of ousting Matsuoka. Illness kept Matsuoka from the emergency cabinet meeting where the decision was made. Konoe immediately formed a new cabinet, its key members unchanged save for the new foreign minister, replacing the old cabinet formally on July 18.

A crowd gathered to watch the celebrated national hero, ill as he was, make a symbolic final trip to his office. Asked by reporters to comment on his state of mind, Matsuoka composed a self-deprecating haiku that made reference to his trademark shaved head. In between puffing his pipe and coughing, he recited: "Baldie collapses by the roadside amid a rainy season journey."

The Japanese people, in the dark as to exactly why Matsuoka had been dismissed, felt a sense of loss. The self-confident and efficient manner in which he'd carried out diplomacy for their country had impressed and captivated them. He was also a public relations genius, knowing instinctively what to say and how to move in the public eye. And the Japanese loved him for it. Some citizens guessed, wrongly but understandably, that Matsuoka's removal signaled an imminent war with the Soviet Union. The novelist Nogami Yaeko speculated in her diary that Konoe probably wanted to attack the Soviet Union right away but Matsuoka could not accept it, considering "how chummy Mr. Matsuoka is with Stalin." As usual, Kafu was more perspicacious, observing that the latest development was the result of a power squabble within the government rather than a herald of a profound shift in foreign policy. "This shake-up smacks of a put-up job," he wrote in his diary on July 18.

That day was an unseasonably cold and windy day for mid-July. Kafu saw leaves being raked and burned in the fields, making him imagine it was late autumn already. His thoughts then drifted to World War I as he read Léon Bloy's wartime diary *La Porte des Humbles* (*The Gate of the Humble*). He noted how lucky he was not to have any family or friends for whose safety he would have to fear. "The rice tastes awful and sugar is scarce, but one can live with that. After all, it's not as if one's in prison without having committed a crime"—an everyday occurrence in the existing political climate. His diary represented what was left of his fast-diminishing freedom, which he was determined to keep.

Shortly after his fall, Matsuoka was visited by Saionji Kinkazu. The once-boastful foreign minister was a thoroughly deflated figure now— literally so. He had lost nearly thirty pounds since his return from Europe, likely owing to the relapse of the tuberculosis he had suffered from in his youth. His house, the former villa of a marquis, had always been filled with flatterers and power brokers; it was suddenly deserted. For about two hours, Saionji comforted him over whiskey. In just twelve months in office, Matsuoka had managed to entrench Japan in the very crisis with the United States that he claimed to know how to avoid. With his brinksmanship, he'd done more damage to Japan's international position than anyone with much less knowledge of the world ever could have.

OUT WENT a singular and explosive personality and in came Admiral Toyoda Teijiro. But the Oxford-educated naval officer was not the right man for the job. Though self-confident to the point of smugness, he had no diplomatic experience. He did, however, have the necessary connections in the military, including Ambassador Nomura, a navy veteran. Familiar with Japan's disadvantageous material situation from having served as minister of commerce and industry in Konoe's second cabinet, he could also make a convincing case to his colleagues that going to war in the Pacific would be inadvisable. Yet Toyoda's record suggested that he tended to be more interested in preserving his own as well as the navy's position than in Japan's political future. In the fall of 1940, as vice navy minister to Oikawa Koshiro, he pushed aggressively for the conclusion of the Tripartite Pact primarily because it would mean a budget increase for the navy.

In Washington, Nomura was hopeful. Overestimating Konoe's political will, he concluded that Matsuoka's departure was arranged so that there could be a clear shift in foreign policy, including Japan's exit from the Axis alliance and its suspension of the southern Indochinese incursion. The United States was hopeful, too. On the day of the German attack on the Soviet Union, *The New York Times* reported that "high circles in Washington hope that the German-Soviet phase of the war may lead to a new policy in Japan. The hope, in fact, is that Japan not only will break her Axis ties in the near future but actually face about and oppose Germany in the war." Such hopes were fleeting. By July 18, Washington had correctly surmised that there would be no change in Japan's policy. The Japanese leaders seemed to think that the personnel reshuffling alone would suffice to restore their country's credibility with the United States. The new foreign minister was already coercing the Vichy government to hand over its southern Indochinese possessions. When the French declined, Toyoda intimated that Japan would be willing to use force to achieve its goal. The French finally gave in to a "peaceful" Japanese takeover on July 22. This would bring Japan access to eight air bases and two naval ports in the area.

The Roosevelt administration became quickly aware of the Japanese agreement with the French (again thanks to intelligence information) and Acting Secretary of State Sumner Welles (filling in for Hull, who was ill) informed Nomura of the termination of U.S.-Japan talks on July 23. Two days later, Roosevelt froze Japanese assets in the United States. The Dutch East Indies, Britain, Canada, New Zealand, and the Philippines followed suit. Looking to guard the Philippines, Roosevelt then established the U.S. Army Forces in the Far East under the command of Douglas MacArthur. There was talk of a petroleum embargo. The British were extremely concerned about Singapore's precarious position. Visiting Toyoda before Japan's formal announcement, British ambassador Robert Craigie objected to the occupation in an uncharacteristically excited manner: "You say that we are encircling Japan in Burma, Malaya, China, and so on. That is simply not true! If you go ahead with this occupation, we must think of other ways to deal with you."

Japan was caught completely off guard, but its self-delusion persisted. In a liaison meeting on July 24—in the Imperial Palace, rather than at the prime minister's official residence, presumably for more confidentiality— Toyoda said that it would be a "great problem" if the United States resorted to a total petroleum embargo. The Army General Staff's log recorded that

Toyoda's worries were an overreaction to Nomura's "hysterical" reports warning of U.S. retaliation. The next day's log definitively repeated the old mantra: "We are convinced there will be no [petroleum] embargo as long as we don't go further than the military occupation of French Indochina."

The Navy Ministry's chief of the First Division of Military Affairs, Takada Toshitane—who, along with his belligerent colleague Ishikawa Shingo, had a big role in drafting the southward expansion plan—reflected on the situation many years later.

> We had no inkling that the United States would be so angry over our going into southern French Indochina. We, myself included, thought that advancing as far as southern French Indochina would—and should—be all right. It was a groundless conviction. . . . No, I did not solicit anybody else's opinions, like the Foreign Ministry's. Somehow, we seemed to believe it. . . . That is inexcusable. That was inexcusable.

Nomura, who had been warning the government of such a U.S. reaction all along, now had to try to minimize the damage. On the day Roosevelt froze Japanese assets, July 24, Nomura visited the president at 5:00 p.m. in the Oval Office. Admiral Harold Stark and Undersecretary of State Welles were present. Welles kept a record of the meeting. Roosevelt told the anxious ambassador, not for the first time, that his government suspected that Hitler was behind Japan's policy in the south. Nomura fiercely denied this. Roosevelt hinted at further U.S. sanctions against Japan, and even the possibility of war, should Japan try to seize oil by force in the Dutch East Indies.

Nomura responded that he was personally against his country's recent actions in Indochina. Roosevelt mentioned that he was happy to know that Toyoda was an old navy friend of Nomura's. This presumably was the basis of Roosevelt's hope that Japan's planned southward advance could yet be reversed. According to Welles, he then made the following bold proposal:

> If the Japanese Government would refrain from occupying Indochina with its military and naval forces, or, had such steps actually been commenced, if the Japanese Government would withdraw such forces, the President could assure the Japanese Government that he would do everything within his power to obtain from the Governments of China, Great Britain, the Netherlands, and of course the United States itself

a binding and solemn declaration, provided Japan would undertake the same commitment, to regard Indochina as a neutralized country in the same way in which Switzerland had up to now been regarded by the powers as a neutralized country.

This was the most remarkably conciliatory proposal ever made by Washington. It reflected the strategic importance of French Indochina, which provided the United States tin, rubber, and other critical raw materials. More than that, Roosevelt was eager to dissociate Japan from Hitler's regime in any way he could. With Roosevelt's overarching priority of providing optimal aid to Britain—and to the Soviet Union now, too—peace in the Pacific had to be secured, and that would require some creativity. The president, it is important to point out, was also conspicuously avoiding linking the Japanese actions in French Indochina to the bigger issue of Japan's war with China. This indicated Roosevelt's eagerness to make his plan appealing to the Japanese.

Nomura was moved by the offer, but he did not strike Welles as being optimistic about its chance for acceptance. Nomura suggested that only a great statesman would be able to reverse the Indochinese policy. It was apparent to the Americans that Japan was under pressure from the Nazi regime, Roosevelt responded, and it disturbed him greatly that the Japanese government did not see that Hitler was bent on world domination. Nomura's denials that Germany had influenced Japan continued to fall on deaf ears. The ambassador then told the assembled party that he would convey the president's proposal to his government at once.

JOSEPH GREW, Nomura's U.S. counterpart in Tokyo, cut a dashing figure at age sixty. Before arriving in Tokyo in 1932, he had served as ambassador to Denmark, Switzerland, and Turkey. His posting to Japan was particularly important to him because he was married to a grandniece of Matthew Perry, the commodore who forced an end to Japan's self-imposed isolation under the Tokugawa shogunate. After eight years in Japan, the Grews had formed a close attachment to the country and were fixtures in Tokyo's high society.

Grew was a Boston Brahmin with all the right social connections. Like Roosevelt and Welles (who were related to one another by marriage), he attended Groton. Also like Roosevelt and Welles, he went on to study at Harvard. They all spoke the same language, as it were. Grew immediately comprehended the meaning of the president's proposal for neutralizing French Indochina. He was excited and felt this could lead to a breakthrough.

Grew received the report of Roosevelt's meeting with Nomura two days after the fact. He immediately went to see Toyoda, on the morning of July 27, "with a view," in his words, "to neglecting nothing which might bring about an acceptance of the President's proposal." The ambassador acted entirely on his own initiative, acutely conscious that haste was vital and convinced that neither country wanted a war. Considering the nature of the proposal, he was sure its content had been received with a sigh of relief by the Japanese leaders. He could not have been more mistaken.

To Grew's astonishment, the foreign minister had no idea what the ambassador was talking about. Toyoda left the room to double-check whether a communication of that nature had been received from Nomura. It had not. It is possible that there had been a willful obstruction of information by pro-Axis elements in the Foreign Ministry, or it might simply have been a case of incompetence. Nomura had twice reported to Tokyo on his meeting with Roosevelt: immediately on July 24 and again on July 27.

Grew, naturally, was taken aback. Now it unexpectedly became his task to explain to Toyoda the gist of what the president had proposed. Toyoda's initial reaction was lukewarm at best. He said he regretted that the president's suggestion came too late, after public opinion had already been turned against the United States as a result of Washington's freezing of Japanese assets. He did not see his government reversing its course.

What Toyoda told Grew was only partially correct. True, the Japanese press had begun to employ the term "ABCD encirclement"—with the letters standing for American, British, Chinese, and Dutch—to sensationally describe Japan's economic plight and had ramped up its frenzied tone of late. That kind of sycophantic alarmist coverage in an undemocratic society was not unusual. It is somewhat surprising, though, that in the face of Roosevelt's offer, Toyoda seemed disinclined to respond more positively. Nonetheless, he said that the proposal would be discussed with other leaders and a definitive answer would be given.

Grew knew that the kind of concessions made by Roosevelt did not come easily from the United States. He tried to convince Toyoda then and there that the reversal of Japanese policy would mean a better future for Japan. Speaking in an unofficial capacity and strictly off the record, he even hinted at the unfreezing of Japanese assets should Japan respond favorably to the president's offer. He "fully recognized," he told Toyoda, "that the element of 'face-saving' must of necessity enter into the question." He added that Toyoda was now

> presented with an opportunity to rise above such considerations and to act in conformity with the highest statesmanship and to take a decision which would not only permit him to be relieved of the truly appalling situation . . . but which might well result in his being regarded by history as one of the greatest statesmen of Japan.

Grew misjudged the foreign minister. Such flattery would have appealed to Matsuoka, but Toyoda preferred to play it safe in the world he knew. Grew also hugely underestimated the problems deriving from the complicated workings of Japanese leadership. As far as the existing records show, the Roosevelt proposal was never even put forward for discussion at a liaison meeting. It seems that Konoe decided to keep this extremely sensitive proposal within the highest circles of government.

Konoe later claimed that he did not act on Roosevelt's proposal because of its timing. He improperly criticized Nomura for not having reported sooner. If Nomura was guilty of anything, it was his failure to emphasize sufficiently the proposal's importance. He had also failed to stress, in his earlier communications, the importance, from the U.S. perspective, of Hull's Four Principles. He should have made clear at the outset of the U.S.-Japan talks that if his government was even remotely serious about reaching a diplomatic settlement with the United States, those points could not be trifled with. Historians have characterized Nomura as a good negotiator but a bad communicator. Perhaps so. But one must take into consideration how the rudimentary nature of communication—primarily by telegram—made it hard to communicate quickly and sufficiently.

According to Konoe, he had done his utmost to find ways of accepting Roosevelt's proposal once he received it. He said he tried "in a hundred different directions." No illuminating record of such efforts exists. Konoe certainly did meet with Toyoda, Navy Minister Oikawa, and Army Minister Tojo. It is not difficult to imagine that Tojo, who was initially against "thieving" in the south, resisted a policy reversal on principle: As an already imperially approved matter, the occupation of southern Indochina was sacrosanct.

The president's proposal had come a bit late, but Konoe was hardly aggressive in taking advantage of the opportunity. No minister in Konoe's government, for that matter, was man enough to "rise above such considerations" of face-saving and internal conflict, as Grew had hoped, to dislodge a policy that was already in place.

Japan's leaders let the diplomatic crisis brew. Meanwhile, its people remained ignorant of such developments. In a sweeping national campaign to raise money, citizens were urged to buy national life insurance. In mid-July, it was announced with great fanfare that fifty million policies had been sold (Japan's population was about seventy-three million), raising 10 billion yen (almost 40 percent of the country's gross national product for 1941). Most of that money went to purchase government bonds to fund Japan's war in China. Little did people know that their lives would become very cheap, even worthless, thanks to the government they so earnestly supported with their hard-earned, hard-saved money.

On July 28, the Japanese occupation of southern Indochina formally commenced, putting Singapore within Japan's reach. The effortless take-over compelled some military men to start talking tough, despite their earlier claim that they were not looking any farther than the Indochinese Peninsula. On the last day of the month, Nagano went to see Hirohito at the palace, carrying a new war plan. The navy chief of staff told Hirohito that a war with the United States should be avoided and that he was vehemently against the Tripartite Pact, which he felt was obstructing Japan's diplomacy with the United States. But rather than suggesting a Japanese withdrawal from the pact (presumably because that would be a political decision that didn't concern him or the high command), Nagano warned, "If our petroleum supplies were cut off, we would lose our stock in two years. If a war broke out, we would use it all up in eighteen months." To maximize Japan's chance for survival beyond that limited time frame, he concluded, there was "no choice but to strike."

"Could we expect a big victory, such as our victory [over Russia] in the Sea of Japan?" Hirohito asked.

"I am uncertain as to any victory," Nagano replied, "let alone the kind of huge victory won in the Sea of Japan."

"What a reckless war that would be!" Hirohito exclaimed.

CHAPTER 8

"Meet Me in Juneau"

Ishii Hanako, a woman with luminous, feline eyes and a round face, had never seen her man, Richard Sorge, so devastated in the five years she had known him. Entering his study—a simply furnished and cozy room cut off from the outside world by dark red drapes over the window—on that late-June evening, she saw him lying perfectly still on the daybed, his hand on his forehead. She sat beside him and was surprised to see tears in his eyes. Sorge buried his head in her lap and started to cry uncontrollably. "Why, why are you crying?" she asked, embracing him and patting his back, not knowing what else she could do to comfort him.

Hanako, whom Sorge sometimes addressed by her adoptive German name Agnes, was a petite woman who looked quite a bit younger than her twenty-nine years. Though not a great beauty, she was pretty in the way a child is pretty. Despite wearing heavy eye makeup and luscious lip color, she could not help seeming innocent. Sorge, tall and blue-eyed, was more than fifteen years her senior. Their age difference appeared even greater because of the deep wrinkles that lined his world-weary face. Sorge had been crying over the recent news of Germany's invasion of the Soviet Union.

Sorge had met Hanako while she was working at the Rheingold, a beer hall in the Ginza. They had been together since the summer of 1936, though they kept separate homes. Hanako knew he was exhausted, and she sensed that his exhaustion was not of the usual kind. Her memory of Sorge losing control that day stayed with her for a long time.

Sorge was tired of his double life. As a German, his position in Soviet intelligence was becoming increasingly tenuous. The Communist doctrine that he wholeheartedly subscribed to was supposed to transcend the petty differences between countries, but the longer he spied for the Soviets, the more he found himself entrapped by the very differences he judged to be undesirable. Sorge's brand of Communist ideology, more in line with the Comintern or utopian Marxism, was becoming a liability in Stalin's Sovietized—and Russified—Moscow. Almost all of Sorge's closest friends who were highly idealistic adherents of the Leninist doctrine had been purged by Stalin over the previous few years. He told a fellow spy in Tokyo, Branko de Vukelic, that he was convinced he would be killed if he were summoned back to Moscow.

Sorge took to drinking heavily. Hanako often stayed up late reading in his study, patiently waiting for her lover to come home, invariably drunk. On the day Germany opened fire on the Soviet Union, a member of the German embassy staff saw him inebriated at the Imperial Hotel. Sorge was trying to engage French, British, Americans, and others at the bar, but no one paid attention to the rambling drunk. He shouted in English that Hitler was a bastard to break the pact of nonaggression with Stalin. The man from the German embassy was sympathetic, and he booked a room for Sorge upstairs, lending him enough money for the stay. Sorge was lucky not to have been denounced.

In the wake of the Nazi invasion of the Soviet Union, as Sorge and Ozaki had correctly surmised, Japan put any northward plans on indefinite hold, seeing the south as its priority. But doubt persisted among some observers because of a qualification attached to the imperial resolution: "Should a favorable development arise for the empire due to the changing conditions of the German-Soviet war, we shall resolve the northern problem by military force . . . [after] preparing secretly for war with the Soviet Union." This, though, was primarily a face-saving clause for the army, which was unhappy that the navy was bragging of plans to fight a war with Britain and the United States in the Pacific.

To keep pace with the navy, and also for the sake of all-around preparedness, the army pushed for a major mobilization, effective July 7, aiming to transport 850,000 soldiers along with a large amount of military equipment to northern China by mid-August. As noted earlier, the Japanese army's dream scenario was for the Soviets to move their troops from the Far East to the European front, thus thinning their defense against the Japanese. The new army plan was called a "special demonstration," but in its sheer scale it seemed more like a mobilization for war. Ozaki later recalled that the development led him to think twice that a Japanese war with the Soviet Union was imminent after all. Germany hoped that was true. Stalin, of course, continued to be terrified by the prospect of a two-front war. With German troops close to Moscow, the Kremlin was desperate to know more about Japanese designs. Sorge and Ozaki would be busy.

Because of this new army policy, Soldier U, home from the Chinese front since March 1938 and now thirty-five years old, was called back up in mid-July. As it was explained to him, the conscription was only provisional (in bureaucratic terms, this meant that even those who had just been sent home after years of active service could be enlisted again). When Soldier U first left for China in the summer of 1937, he was given a great send-off. There was no such celebration this time. The thought of once more leaving his family made him despair, but he knew he simply had to close his shop, say good-bye, and report. He wished that he would be turned away after the physical exam, but he passed with flying colors and was soon getting ready for his new, unexplained duties in Manchuria.

WITH TOKYO NOT REACTING to the Indochinese neutralization proposal, Washington began enforcing a petroleum embargo on August 1. Technically, it was not meant to be the "total" embargo that had been proposed in congressional debates. Instead, oil trade with Japan was to be placed under a much stricter licensing procedure, with Japan still able to purchase low-grade oil unsuited for aircraft. Hawks like Dean Acheson, the assistant secretary of state for economic affairs, and Treasury Secretary Henry Morgenthau Jr. took full advantage of the bureaucratic complexities of the licensing system. Working together, the State, Treasury, and Justice Departments ensured that appropriate funds would not be released to complete any petroleum transactions with Japan. Hull, ill when the freezing of assets went into effect in late July, only grasped the full extent of the oil embargo in early September.

As the crisis with the United States precipitously heightened, Konoe's flaws became even more pronounced. He found more excuses not to act, especially when he felt cornered—as he was now by Arita Hachiro. The veteran diplomat, who had served in four different cabinets as foreign minister, including Konoe's first, wrote him on August 1 saying that Konoe should not have allowed the occupation of southern Indochina while Japan was engaged in negotiations with the United States. Arita had not always been accommodating toward the Anglo-American powers, so this was a significant condemnation.

Konoe responded to Arita on August 3, after the petroleum embargo began:

> It was a mistake to think that [the occupation of] French Indochina would not inflict serious damage. . . . [But] when the new cabinet [after Matsuoka's removal] was formed, [the Japanese navy ships bound for Indochina] had already reached the island of Hainan. It was as if an arrow had already been shot and nothing could have been done to stop it.

All he could do, he said, was "pray for a miracle and divine intervention."

Was it really too late to reverse the course of Japan's southern program at that stage? Broadly speaking, one of the biggest obstacles to withdrawing from a war, especially a war you are losing, is justifying the blood spilled and the money spent. For example, when the U.S. Senate was sharply divided over the withdrawal of troops from Iraq in June 2006, the Democrats argued that the war had cost the United States too much already. The Republican administration, maintaining that any kind of withdrawal would be as good as conceding defeat, made emotive claims about the importance of having "the courage of our convictions" to fight on so that "the deaths of more than 2,500 troops would not be in vain." An identical argument was repeatedly heard in late-1930s Japan against any suggestion of Japanese withdrawal from China.

In early August, however, a withdrawal from Indochina was still possible. No Japanese blood had been spilled in the most recent takeover, and unlike in the north the previous year, there had been no local resistance. Since the troops ostensibly went into Indochina to restore peace and order in the region, the government could have claimed it was retreating after having fully achieved its objective of making sure that no power, including France, would lay claim to neutral Indochina. Konoe's government could have presented this "decolonization" of its fellow Asian nation as a political victory. Konoe was not up to the task.

The U.S. oil embargo of August 1 became a turning point in U.S.-Japan relations because Japanese leaders had failed to take a chance on the proposal that had preceded it. Now, surprised and overwhelmed by what they saw as an undeservedly harsh punishment for the "peaceful" occupation, some began to see war with the United States in much less abstract terms. "The 'war' that's mentioned in the July 2 policy and others was primarily put in there to boost morale," Ishii Akiho, a senior staff officer in the Army Ministry's Military Affairs Bureau, recalled. But only a month later, he said, "that [war] phrase became a realistic problem, and we felt cornered into making things black and white."

The news of the U.S. embargo made it known to ordinary citizens that things were quickly deteriorating between the two countries. The media's continuing use of the term "ABCD encirclement" hammered at the idea that the United States, the primary bully, was bent on isolating Japan. To legitimize the Japanese claim of constructing the Greater East Asia Coprosperity Sphere, the major newspaper *Yomiuri* ran in mid-August a series of articles introducing the cultures of various Southeast Asian nations to its readers, contextualizing them in terms of their colonial history.

"The encirclement of Japan by the so-called ABCD camp is becoming increasingly blatant of late," one analysis read.

The peace of the Pacific is again being threatened by [Western] economic pressures, blackmail, and malicious propaganda [employed against Japan]. Those unnecessary deterrence measures are not only stopping our valiant march toward the Greater East Asia Coprosperity Sphere but are also revealing the depth of [Western] greed. All the [Western] military bases [in the Pacific]—forming a horseshoe shape starting from Burma to Singapore, the Dutch East Indies, the Philippine Islands, Australia, Samoa, Hawaii, and Guam—fall within the sphere of East Asian nations. But they have all been trampled upon by white people. . . . We must now pay attention to the five centuries of white invasion and face up to the realities.

This tone and the analyst's prejudices continued throughout. Malays and Indonesians were described as diligent, clean, compassionate, and sensitive: "They are remarkably like us Japanese, but they lack in financial savvy and political awareness, allowing overseas Chinese to dominate their economy, while politically they are unable to break free of the British and Dutch fetters." Filipinos were portrayed in a damning way because they had absorbed Western—especially American—culture:

Eighty-eight percent of the islands' population are of mixed origins, resulting from the union of the natives and Spaniards, or Americans, and they believe in Christianity. They are a vain, Americanized bunch, devoted to dance and jazz music. That they have some white blood makes them so proud, and they believe that they are superior to Japanese. But the truth is, they have no culture of their own, and they take everything from Americans.

The question of how to square the purported U.S. injustices with Japan's own arrogant and often appalling behavior toward its neighbors in its modern imperialist history was of course not addressed in these newspaper stories. But there was enough awareness—and some guilty consciences, too—about what was going on in China. A collector of rumors, Kafu one day recorded the story of a young man's combat experience in the China War.

In Hankou, this young soldier and his comrades broke into a house of a physician who had two beautiful daughters. The doctor and his wife begged the Japanese soldiers not to touch the girls, offering them all the gold and silver they had. But they refused and raped the girls right in front of their parents, eventually tying up the whole family and throwing them alive into a garden well.

The young man returned to his mother and wife in Japan. Though the two women seemed to act a bit strange, distracted, and unhappy, they wouldn't tell him why.

A few months passed, and while the wife was out, the mother confessed everything: One night, during his absence in China, their house was burglarized, and both the mother and the wife were tied up and raped by the burglar.

The young man went mad and started publicly recounting his stories, including his crimes in Hankou. He was incarcerated by the military police but was soon removed to the army's psychiatric institution outside Tokyo, locked up with the other thirty thousand to forty thousand "madmen" the war had produced.

ROOSEVELT WAS BEGINNING to wonder if Tokyo really was interested in reaching a peaceful solution in the Pacific. On July 26, he wrote to one of his most trusted advisers, Harry Hopkins, who had been instrumental in realizing the Lend-Lease Act to boost U.S. aid to the Allies and was in London en route to a meeting with Stalin in Moscow. Roosevelt said he'd "had no answer yet" from Japan concerning his Indochinese proposal. Though he suspected that Tokyo's reply would "probably be unfavorable," he knew that his government "at least made one more effort to avoid Japanese expansion to [the] South Pacific." In line with Roosevelt's preference for giving Japan a chance to respond, Washington reacted calmly to what could have been a grave diplomatic incident in China. On July 30, Japan came ever so close to mistakenly sinking a U.S. gunboat. The *Tutuila* was anchored at Chongqing, unable to travel down the Yangtze River, where it had been used to escort U.S. shipping. Japanese forces were raiding Chiang Kai-shek's capital in the hope of inducing his surrender when some of their bombs landed on the ship, damaging its outboard motor. There were no U.S. casualties, and Tokyo's immediate apologies, communicated by Nomura, were enough to pacify Washington, still awaiting Japan's answer to Roosevelt's proposal for the neutralization of French Indochina.

The reply was long in coming. Not until August 6 did Japan announce that it intended to withdraw its troops from Indochina only after the China War had been resolved. As with all its other replies to U.S. proposals since the spring, Japan also asked the United States to help negotiate a peace between China and Japan, but with the assurance that Japan's "special regional position" would not be compromised. Not only was Japan rejecting Roosevelt's proposal, but it was again linking the chronic problem of the China War to the immediate issue of Indochinese occupation, something that Roosevelt had been careful to avoid. Japan pledged not to occupy areas beyond Indochina, but after the failure of appeasement at Munich, that certainly sounded hollow to Roosevelt's ears.

Two days later, Konoe requested a meeting with the U.S. president. The idea for a summit meeting came from Konoe's closest aides and friends—among them the Breakfast Club regulars Saionji Kinkazu, Matsumoto Shigeharu, and Ushiba Tomohiko—who were hopeful of reaching a peace with Washington. Their idea was that an international conference far from Tokyo would physically prevent the hard-line elements in the military from quibbling with whatever agreement might arise between the top statesmen. It was also meant to allow the militarists to save face, as they would not be held responsible for whatever was decided there. The summit was to be a chance for Konoe to compensate for all his past failures.

This approach had been tested before. In 1930, the prestige of an international agreement coupled with its imperial backing helped Premier Hamaguchi when he endorsed the ratification of the London Naval Treaty. Konoe, though far less consistent, courageous, and principled in his actions and beliefs than Hamaguchi, seemed to realize that a tactic as drastic as a direct meeting with Roosevelt was necessary to reverse the downward spiral he'd helped to create. Something could still be done, he believed, despite the resignation he had expressed earlier to Arita.

The timing of and the manner in which Konoe went about proposing the summit meeting, however, were bafflingly inept. On August 4, two days before his government turned down Roosevelt's plan, Konoe informed both the army and navy ministers of his intention to propose the summit meeting. Despite surface bravado, there was now a growing sense within the military that the southward advance had been an error in judgment. Although no leaders would assume blame for the mistake, they would have conceded to a reversal, especially if diplomatically arranged. The navy, unprepared to risk a major war in the Pacific, agreed to Konoe's proposed summit meeting right away.

Army Minister Tojo's support was more qualified. According to Konoe (who kept records selectively, mostly to his advantage), Tojo declared in a signed document that he would not necessarily object to Konoe's seeing Roosevelt "if the prime minister goes to the meeting in full cognizance that war with the United States might be the eventual outcome." Tojo added that if the conference did not bear fruit, Konoe should continue leading the government in its war preparations. Tojo was checking the notoriously evasive prince, to ensure that Konoe would be made to accept his share of responsibility in Japan's possible war with the West. Tojo's bullying tone intimidated Konoe, which was presumably why the prince noted it, as proof of what he was up against in his own government. But the navy and army had consented to Konoe's initiative, so Japan's negative reply could certainly have been delayed. Instead, Japan rejected Roosevelt's neutralization proposal and *then* asked for a summit. From the U.S. perspective, there was nothing to discuss. Japan had rebuffed what in U.S. eyes was an unusually generous concession, without expressing any interest.

On August 8, in reply to Konoe's request for a meeting, Hull told Nomura that Japan's recent response precluded a summit. The Roosevelt administration regarded Japan's occupation of southern Indochina as an unequivocal expression of its expansionist intent, especially since the occupation was carried out *while* the United States was still waiting to hear back from Tokyo. Foreign Minister Toyoda, without referring to the specifics of the concessions Konoe was considering, instructed Nomura to tell Washington that the previous Japanese answer regarding the southern Indochinese occupation was actually not "rigid" and that Konoe wished to "have a heart-to-heart with the president, from the broader vantage point of maintaining world peace." Nomura could not convey this message immediately. President Roosevelt was at the time meeting the British premier, Winston Churchill, off the coast of Newfoundland.

THAT SUMMER, *49th Parallel,* a film set in Canada, was in the process of being completed. With a formidable cast including Laurence Olivier and Leslie Howard, this tour de force of dramatic propaganda tells the story of a U-boat crew stranded ashore in Canada. The forty-ninth parallel, which delineates much of the U.S.-Canadian border, constitutes for the German crew the fine line between a nation at war and a nation considering going to war. The Germans dash down Canada toward the border in order to flee to the still-neutral United States, where they cannot be captured. In their desperation, they steal and kill, terrorizing Canadians. By introducing the possibility of Germans landing on the North American shore, the makers of the film—Michael Powell, an Englishman, and Emeric Pressburger, a Hungarian Jewish refugee in Britain—were arguing that Hitler's war should not be seen as a strictly European affair. Like it or not, the war could very easily spill onto American soil from the North Atlantic. They called for timely U.S. participation in the war. Churchill was seeking the same in meeting with Roosevelt.

From August 9 to 12, the U.S. cruiser *Augusta* and the British battleship *Prince of Wales,* anchored side by side in Placentia Bay, became the venues of a historic Anglo-American summit meeting. Though Roosevelt was not ready to give Churchill a concrete promise, recent events in Europe were forcing him to think of U.S. entry into the European war in ever more realistic terms. At home, debates were raging in Congress over the amendment of the Selective Training and Service Act, passed in August 1940, which enabled the U.S. Army to draft up to nine hundred thousand men for a one-year period. The new resolutions, if passed, would lift that limit and would allow the army to retain draftees for the duration of the national emergency and to send them beyond the Western Hemisphere. The Senate passed the bill on August 7, but a great deal of resistance was expected in the House of Representatives. The outcome could dramatically affect America's war readiness.

Over the course of the conference, Roosevelt and Churchill developed a personal rapport, despite the president's fundamental dislike of old European imperialism. The joint declaration they drafted, widely known as the Atlantic Charter, detailed the Allied war aims and plans for the postwar world. Both leaders pledged to support Stalin to prevent a Soviet collapse. They were greatly influenced by the positive view of Stalin formed by Harry Hopkins, Roosevelt's emissary who had met the Soviet leader in Moscow before sailing back with Churchill to attend the conference. This proved to be a critical juncture for the Allied campaign against Hitler. Despite the initial projection by Washington strategists of a swift German victory in Russia, as the weeks passed, the Soviet Union was beginning to reveal its dogged resilience in the face of major military setbacks. More and more favorable images of the Soviet Union began circulating in mainstream U.S. media, and lend-lease, the privilege that Roosevelt was initially reluctant to grant the Soviet Union, would come into effect by November 1941.

While in Newfoundland, Roosevelt took another decisive step by approving U.S. armed escorts for all shipping as far as Iceland, effective September 16. The president's hawkish military advisers had been pushing for convoy escorting in the Atlantic ever since the German-Soviet war broke out. Chief of Naval Operations Harold Stark argued for it, acknowledging it "would almost certainly involve us in war." Churchill failed to gain a clear U.S. commitment to go to war, but it was the closest the cautious Roosevelt had ever come to accepting that his country's entry into the European war was just a matter of time. Roosevelt told Churchill that the United States would consider war in the Pacific if Japan's policies took on a more expansionistic character. However, both leaders were still willing to explore diplomatic solutions and even to give Japan a chance to save face over Indochina.

On the last day of the conference, Roosevelt was notified of the passage of the amended Selective Training and Service Act in the House by one vote. That would prove indispensable in mobilizing for war.

Finally, on August 17, Nomura was able to meet with Roosevelt. The president, just back from Placentia Bay, had agreed to receive the ever-anxious ambassador on a Sunday. Hull reported that Nomura took from his pocket an instruction he said was from his government. With painful earnestness, Nomura stressed that Tokyo "desired to see peaceful relations preserved between our two countries" and that

Prince Konoye feels so seriously and so earnestly about preserving such relations that he would be disposed to meet the President midway, geographically speaking, between our two countries and sit down together and talk the matter out in a peaceful spirit.

The president responded in even broader terms:

If the Japanese Government takes any further steps in pursuance of a policy or program of military domination by force or threat of force of neighboring countries, the Government of the United States will be compelled to take immediately any and all steps which it may deem necessary toward safeguarding the legitimate rights and interests of the United States and American nationals and toward insuring the safety and security of the United States.

Despite such strong words, Roosevelt did not reject the idea of a summit meeting. He said that Hawaii, the proposed location, would be too far for him to travel and suggested Juneau, Alaska, instead. He was never averse to the kind of statecraft in which great things got decided by great leaders, efficiently and gentlemanly, as he had proved in his meeting with Churchill. Konoe therefore had legitimate reason to think he still could avert a disastrous war.

RICHARD SORGE HAD NEWS for Moscow regarding the mobilization of the Japanese army in the north. It had slowed down conspicuously and was not yet completed by the mid-August deadline. In fact, the Army General Staff, on August 9, had decided that the army would not attack the Soviet Union, at least not in 1941. There still was no prospect of a decisive German win over the Soviet Union, and no strategist in his right mind would suggest starting a war when the Siberian winter was fast approaching. By the second half of August, even the German embassy in Tokyo had come to see Japanese participation in the war as highly unlikely.

All summer long, Soldier U waited at his base in central Japan to be mobilized. On August 24, a small transport ship carrying him and others finally left Osaka for China via Korea. It was barely possible for each soldier to secure enough space to lie down. They arrived in northern Manchuria in early September. Most of them were novice soldiers. Now regarded as an old hand, Soldier U was assigned to oversee their intensive training in anticipation of fighting yet-to-be-identified enemies. He and his comrades suffered from acute hunger, which was made worse by the demanding physical exercises. Desperate, they resorted to stealing a few vegetables every now and then from local farmers' fields.

Things weren't plentiful in Japan, either, but the power elites were getting by just fine. Ozaki met his friend Saionji on or around August 25, dining at Asia, a restaurant on the top floor of the Southern Manchurian Railway building where Ozaki worked. The sleek state-of-the-art structure of reinforced concrete was completed in 1936, as if to assert the success of Japan's Manchurian project. (It would be purchased by the United States in 1952 and turned into a U.S. embassy annex.) Over the meal, Ozaki asked, "Looks like they've decided?" "Yes, they have decided not to do it," replied Saionji, who had become a special aide to Konoe.

When Ozaki reported to Sorge that the Japanese army's northern operation was officially scrapped, an expression of joy and relief swept over Sorge's face. Little did Saionji know that he had casually revealed a piece of information vital to the Soviet Union. Though it is impossible to prove, Stalin, paranoid over the increased presence of Japanese soldiers (including Soldier U) in the north, might not have decided to transfer his troops to the western front had it not been for the trust he came to have in Sorge's communications from Tokyo. The Soviet comeback, especially in the absence of immediate U.S. assistance, might not have been achieved without his absolute confidence that Japan would not strike north. Only later would Saionji discover the unwitting role he had played in this espionage drama.

At that time, Saionji was preoccupied with helping Konoe arrange a meeting with Roosevelt. Saionji and many of his blue-blooded friends knew that a war with the West would be unwinnable. Matsumoto Shigeharu, the Yale-educated journalist who was a direct descendant of another illustrious Meiji oligarch, shared Saionji's concern. "I have made a big mistake on Japan's relations with China," Konoe had confided to him. In a show of vulnerability displayed only to his social equals, the prime minister went on to lament:

> I am so ashamed and cannot face up to my ancestors. I do not want to repeat such a mistake. And I want to avoid war with the United States at all costs. If at all possible, I want to improve Sino-Japanese relations as well. I will give it my best shot, so won't you help me?

At a liaison meeting on August 26, 1941, a message from Konoe to be delivered to the president was approved. The original English text of it read:

> The preliminary informal conversations, disrupted July last, were quite appropriate in both spirit and content. But the idea of continuing those conversations and to have their conclusion confirmed by the responsible heads of the two Governments does not meet the need of the present situation which is developing swiftly and may produce unforeseen contingencies. I consider it, therefore, of urgent necessity that the two heads of the Governments should meet first to discuss from a broad standpoint all important problems between Japan and America covering the entire Pacific area, and to explore the possibility of saving the situation. Adjustment of minor items may, if necessary, be left to negotiations between competent officials of the two countries, following the meeting. Such is my aim in making the present proposal. I sincerely hope my views in this regard are fully understood and reciprocated by Your Excellency. Because of the nature of the meeting as stated above, I would prefer that it will take place as soon as possible.

Nomura conveyed this message to the president on August 28. Roosevelt complimented the "tone and spirit of it" and again mentioned Juneau as a meeting place. To Nomura, the location mattered little. The ambassador was encouraged because, as Hull noted, Roosevelt explicitly told him that he considered the prime minister's message a "step forward," that he was "very hopeful," and that he would be "keenly interested in having three or four days with Prince Konoye."

Nomura called on Hull at his hotel apartment that evening to express his gratitude for having arranged the presidential interview. He said that Juneau should be as agreeable a location as any other and that all that mattered from the Japanese point of view was that the meeting take place very soon. He described the likely composition of the Japanese delegation: "about twenty persons, of whom five each would be from the Foreign Office, the Army, the Navy and the Japanese Embassy at Washington." The period between September 21 and 25 would be suitable for the meeting, the ambassador added, and the prime minister would leave Japan about five days before the president left Washington so that the two leaders would arrive simultaneously.

Nomura's enthusiasm was quickly dampened. Hull wasn't really keen on the idea of a summit. He alluded to the recent "difficulties [that] had been encountered in regard to certain fundamental points which had caused delays that finally culminated in Japan's taking action contrary to the conversations." He was, of course, talking about Indochina. Before a summit meeting could be held, he said, he would have to have clearer answers from the Japanese to the most pressing issues endangering U.S.-Japan ties—namely, Japan's Axis alliance, Japan's troops in northern China and Inner Mongolia, and Japan's commitment to the application of the principle of nondiscrimination in international commercial relations.

Nomura, while trying to regain his composure, said the China issue would, in his view, be the most difficult to reach a prior agreement on. He suggested that the matter be left for the conference itself. Hull correctly responded that the United States was involved in the matter because Japan had requested that it exercise its good offices. "We could work together, Japan and the United States," Hull said, "in order to make the most of the potentialities of the 500,000,000 people of China as a trading nation"—a sentiment fully shared by Roosevelt. He repeated that "there should be an agreement in principle on the outstanding questions of importance prior to the holding of the meeting" and that "the meeting would serve the purpose of ratifying agreement in principle already reached." Wouldn't that be better for everyone's peace of mind? Nomura felt that a Juneau conference was now much less likely than it had been just a few minutes earlier.

Konoe was still confident that a summit meeting would take place. On August 29, he and his supporters gathered at a resort at the foot of Mount Fuji to draft a proposal for a preconference agreement, just as Hull had requested. The banker Ikawa Tadao, who had recently returned from Washington, and Father Drought, one of the two Catholic priests who had begun the haphazard U.S.-Japan talks, dropped in to lend their moral support. For the last three days of August, those assembled at Fujiya, a luxury hotel known for its silver tea service and French cuisine, worked day and night to hone the proposal. The intensity of their work was relieved by a round or two of golf.

In their drafting sessions, two points emerged as most critical. One was that Japan should, "as a general principle," agree to withdraw from China. It would be the first time Japan committed itself to a categorical withdrawal. The second point was that should a war break out between the United States and Germany, Japan would exercise its own judgment over the terms of obligations in the Tripartite Pact. This was meant to reassure the United States that Japan would not automatically go to war against it. The drafters had to walk a fine line between enticing Washington and not being seen as weak by Japanese military leaders. Konoe took an active part in polishing the document, and by the end of their stay, the drafters felt they had achieved the proper balance.

The draft would have to go through a liaison conference on September 3 before Konoe could present it to the United States as Japan's official preconference proposal. Saionji laid the necessary groundwork, running the proposal by officials at both the Navy and Army Ministries, who ultimately approved it. It was now up to Konoe to do what he was least skilled at: confronting opposition and holding his own. He had to know that, in the end, all that mattered was the invitation from Roosevelt asking him to "meet me in Juneau."

CHAPTER 9

An Unwinnable, Inevitable War

On the morning of August 27, 1941, a group of graduate students at the Total War Research Institute gathered at the official residence of the prime minister of Japan. The atmosphere was subdued, even gloomy, a mood made even more so by the on-and-off late-summer rain. In a grand chandelier-lit hall, the researchers, whose average age was a mere thirty-three, came face-to-face with the cabinet. From nine o'clock in the morning until six in the evening, and then again the following day, they presented a lengthy report. After careful consideration of an array of ministerial data, and having simulated various diplomatic and strategic situations over the previous six weeks, the group concluded that should Japan go to war with the United States and its allies, Japan would *necessarily* lose. If such a war occurred, Japan might very well prevail in a few initial battles, but it would then be forced into a prolonged war that would see its resources dwindle and eventually run out.

The researchers making the predictions had had approximately ten years of professional experience before joining the Total War Research Institute. The institute was opened in April 1941 and was loosely modeled on Britain's Imperial Defence College, where officers and leaders were trained in an intensive one-year program. It was meant to be an elite educational institution that would prepare Japan's future leaders, both military and civilian, for greatness.

The high aspirations of its founders were never realized. Each ministry sent its top candidate, so the students were the crème de la crème of

Japan's midcareer civil servants. But despite the institute's prime location in central Tokyo, the building itself was enough to make the hearts of the newly arriving students sink. It was a two-story shanty that looked especially incongruous surrounded by the imposing redbrick buildings of the government district. Many recruits felt they had been dragged down to a lowly student existence.

The researchers liked the institute's first dean, Lieutenant General Iimura Jo. An amiable man and a formidable linguist fluent in French and Russian, he had lectured at an army academy in Turkey and had translated many strategic documents into Japanese. His magnetic personality attracted some interesting people to give special talks at the institute, including one by Ozaki Hotsumi, Sorge's fellow spy. Still, most students were dissatisfied with the life that had been suddenly forced upon them. They had expected to do high-level research but were instead reduced to attending basic physical education and other unoriginal and often ill-prepared classes.

So a trip to Japan's central region, starting on June 20, 1941, came as a much-needed breather. The group visited the navy's flagship, the *Nagato,* at Ise Bay, where Yamamoto Isoroku was headquartered. Aboard the *Nagato* and another warship, the *Hyuga,* both equipped with the navy's latest technologies, the researchers had special permission to observe maneuvers. Everything seemed to go beautifully. But the visitors were most impressed by the capacity of the ships to simulate torpedo attacks in total darkness with astonishing precision, guided by a lighting system embedded in the torpedo itself.

After the maneuvers, Yamamoto was eager to hear what the visitors thought of his fleet. He called on Higasa Hiroo, who'd come to the institute from the governor-general's office in Korea. He responded with due deference: "I was impressed with your defense system against submarines, sir. The same goes for your bombing strategies. But I sensed a certain vulnerability to aerial attacks."

Higasa was quite right. A lesser military man might have been irritated by the young civilian's impertinence, but Yamamoto instead rewarded Higasa with a bottle of whiskey, by then a prized commodity in Japan. Yamamoto was pleased that Higasa had looked beyond the obvious and spoken frankly, something he felt Japan's elites were generally incapable of. Yes, those impressive naval ships were not as unassailable as they appeared, and Yamamoto would have been the first to admit it.

The researchers remained with the fleet until it reached Shibushi Bay in southern Japan. (Adjacent to this bay was Kinko Bay, which is shaped remarkably like Pearl Harbor.) It was then that the radio informed them of Germany's surprise attack on the Soviet Union. That, and the resultant decision to occupy southern Indochina, suddenly made the researchers' work far more urgent.

Shortly after their return to Tokyo, the researchers were assigned a war game exercise. Each member was given a cabinet role to play in a hypothetical government of a hypothetical country (modeled on Japan). From their respective cabinet positions, they were to participate in a hypothetical war with a hypothetical enemy (the United States) and its allies. The exercise started on July 12; not so far away, Foreign Minister Matsuoka was attending his final liaison conference.

For this total war, the cabinet needed to develop policies covering all areas of military strategy, diplomacy, ideology, and economics. The guidelines presented to the researchers by their instructors noted that "the various plans need to correspond to the changes in both domestic and external situations anticipated in the coming two years. . . . Your policies need to be devised on a specific monthly basis or on a few-monthly basis." The researchers were meant to simulate real-world developments as accurately as possible, consulting actual data brought in by various ministers from their home ministries. In the end, this war seemed to be more real than imaginary.

At the start of the war game, Japan was on the cusp of declaring war on the United States. The U.S. and British governments having placed embargos against it, Japan was now completely isolated economically. Therefore, it would have to go farther into Southeast Asia to procure resources by force.

The researchers were uneasy with the premise provided by their instructors. They felt that going into Southeast Asia—most likely the Dutch East Indies—made war with the West inevitable, without giving diplomacy a chance to prevent it. Most cabinet members projected that the country would probably be able to secure the Indonesian oil fields but that the enemy fleet stationed in the Philippines would soon launch an all-out attack on Japanese ships, making the transport of resources impossible and defeating the whole purpose of accessing Indonesian oil. As a result, Japan would be provoked into a larger-scale war with the United States, which the country could ill afford. Most ministers had determined even before the simulation started that such a war would be unwinnable and should not be waged.

AS THE RESEARCHERS PRESENTED their report on the simulation exercise to Konoe's cabinet, Tojo, like the earnest student he once must have been, never stopped taking notes. When the report came to its unequivocal conclusion that the war was unwinnable, Tojo grew noticeably pale, as though his worst fears had been confirmed. And yet the report's conclusion should not have surprised him. His own ministry's War Economy Research Office, in conjunction with reports sent by the Army General Staff's intelligence agent stationed in New York, had recently declared that Japan's industrial power was a twentieth of the United States'. One only had to look at the buildings of central Tokyo to appreciate how dire Japan's material condition was. Since April, all the cast-iron ornamental fences and gates of the Meiji era had been dismantled. Among the last to come down, on June 23, were the gates of the Tokyo prefectural office. The former symbols of public authority had become nineteen hundred pounds of scrap metal to be used for armaments.

The redbrick buildings were still there, of course, but their newly installed wooden enclosures were unnerving. The Total War Research Institute's shanty didn't seem so shabby in this new version of Tokyo. It was hard to recall that only a few years earlier, the same city had successfully lobbied to host the 1940 Olympics.

At the end of the two-day presentation, Tojo would not succumb to the gloom. He commended the team's excellent efforts but noted that the research had one fatal flaw. "This is, after all, a desktop exercise," he said. "Actual wars do not go as you fellows imagine. We did not go to war with Russia thinking that we would win, but we did win." At pains to gloss over the harsh realities that had just been presented to him, he added, "Your work doesn't include elements of unpredictability, although I wouldn't go so far as to say it's an empty theory." He concluded his remarks by saying firmly that the researchers were to keep their opinions to themselves.

Was Tojo hoping for the sudden discovery of oil fields in Japan so that his country could forget that the United States had until recently been providing more than 90 percent of its petroleum? Was he counting on groundbreaking progress in the development of synthetic oil? Was he anticipating a series of natural disasters to work in the empire's favor, like the typhoons that had prevented the Mongols from invading Japan in the thirteenth century? Or was he banking on high levels of morale and resilience among the troops, which must be considered in any war, as well as faith in one's ability to fight on? The instructor Horiba Kazuo, an army man, had told his researchers, "The Yamato spirit is what the United States is lacking, and that is the greatest resource of our country." He was referring to a supposedly inborn trait that made the Japanese a unique, resilient, disciplined, and hardworking people. Such a metaphysical claim of uniqueness is almost obligatory in nationalistic mythologies.

Throughout the simulation exercise, the most vocal and consistent opposition to the war came from Lieutenant Commander Shimura of the Navy Ministry. He had graduated at the top of his class at the Naval War College, writing his dissertation on total war. He once said to his instructor: "Very well, sir, let the Japanese have their Yamato spirit. But Americans have their Yankee spirit, too. It's wrong to see it only on one side and ignore the other."

The Yamato spirit certainly had its limitations. By mid-August, Tokyo's sewage system had become a serious problem; the fuel shortage was the direct cause of this catastrophe. It was estimated that on average 1,900,000 gallons of human waste were created daily by the city's more than one million households. Flush toilets were still rare, and most of the waste had to be carried out to rural communities for composting. In ordinary times, this was done with motor vehicles. Now that fuel was an issue, the more than three hundred night-soil men had to improvise with bicycle-drawn carts and boats, though it was becoming abundantly clear that demand for this service far outpaced supply. The city's public welfare division was inundated with complaints, but frustrated with bureaucratic inertia, disgruntled citizens started appealing to the mayor's wife directly. On August 16, an article entitled "What to Do with Excrement?" appeared in the newspaper *Kokumin Shimbun,* explaining that the city government had convened an emergency meeting to deal with the malodorous situation. No definitive solution was found.

Besides, the wife of the mayor was not the best person for hapless citizens to approach, as Mayor Okubo Tomejiro was a powerful thug with concerns other than solving Tokyo's sewage problem. He was a former Home Ministry bureaucrat who once served as the divisional chief of the notorious Special Higher Police, leading the ministry's aggressive, large-scale persecution of communists—or simply suspected communists—in the

1920s. Kafu noted that Okubo was rumored to have blackmailed the major literary journal *Chuo Koron,* claiming he could deflect a possible defamatory lawsuit against it and extorting 5,000 yen from the publisher (for comparison, a public primary school superintendent in suburban Tokyo made 145 yen a month).

ON SEPTEMBER 3, Ambassador Nomura received an official U.S. communication regarding Konoe's request for a summit. The president, now echoing Hull, said he could not agree to a meeting without having negotiated and secured a prior understanding on the matters to be settled, though he was still favorable to a conference. That this was a deliberate tactic to delay any constructive efforts to reach peace (as some have inferred from Roosevelt's comment to Churchill in Placentia Bay that he could "baby" Japan for another three months) is uncertain. But Konoe took heart when Roosevelt said, "I am very desirous of collaborating with you in efforts to make these principles effective in practice."

Though the countries they led were fundamentally different, Konoe and Roosevelt themselves shared a fair number of personality traits. Both were averse to personal confrontation and surrounded themselves with advisers who held diverging and often outright contradictory opinions. In Konoe's case, they ranged from Marxists to ultranationalists; in Roosevelt's case, they ranged from interventionists to Europhobes. The two highborn leaders were equally guarded about their innermost thoughts, even in cabinet meetings, and were difficult to pin down for that reason. But at the same time, their most basic worldviews (Konoe's one of revisionist Japanese chauvinism, and Roosevelt's a Wilsonian liberal internationalism) remained surprisingly consistent.

What made Roosevelt a far superior statesman, however, was that even in the face of conflicting advice, and even while incorporating seemingly contradictory ideas in his policies (from which he had to backtrack from time to time), he held on to his excellent instinct and judgment about what was politically practicable and cautiously but determinedly pursued it. Konoe had a very delicate situation to deal with domestically, but so did Roosevelt, who had to persuade Congress, consider public opinion, and navigate bureaucratic constraints. Konoe woefully lacked Roosevelt's staying power and sense of priority, and since his lofty social status ensured that he could, he was too willing to blame his failure on others. The *New*

York Times correspondent Otto Tolischus accurately grasped the root cause of Konoe's lack of persistence, as well as his strange magnetism, in his August 3, 1941, profile of the Japanese premier. "As head of the second noblest family in the land," he wrote, "[Konoe] is above personal ambitions and the Premiership is rather a step down than an elevation for him." And despite his chronic habit of disappointing his supporters, he would continue to be supported because he gave off an aura of someone who had to be protected, advised, and sympathized with—Japan's second emperor.

Konoe felt that he had to concede to hard-line elements at home; it was an implicit barter he'd made with the military. The military would continue to plan for a war, backing it up with all its tough talk, while allowing the prime minister to meet with Roosevelt abroad. Konoe believed he could halt the march toward war once and for all at this summit. The militant *bakuryo* officers actually concurred with him, expecting that once in direct conference with Roosevelt, Konoe would reach some kind of a sweeping understanding with Washington to avert hostilities. An August 29 journal entry by an officer in the War Guidance Office of the Army General Staff expressed this conflicted feeling very well:

> Our military attaché in the United States tells us that the U.S. president received Prime Minister Konoe's message in high spirits. It looks as if the summit meeting in Hawaii [*sic*] is really going to happen. Once it does, we believe that the talks will not break down. . . . That means our first step to [psychologically] surrendering to the United States. . . . It will be many steps backward for our empire, but still, we don't want a long, drawn-out war, either.

Even those who made a living preparing for war knew that bluff alone would not carry Japan to victory. "What idiots they are in Washington!" said Sato Kenryo, a section chief in the Army Ministry's Military Affairs Bureau. "If they agreed to meet with Konoe without any conditions, everything would go their way."

A senior staff officer in Sato's section, Ishii Akiho, was confidentially appointed as a delegate to accompany Konoe to Juneau, even before a presidential invitation was secured. Ishii believed the likely sequence of events would be as follows: Konoe meets Roosevelt; Konoe conveys the Japanese conditions, preapproved by the military; Roosevelt refuses to accept such conditions; Konoe telegraphs the U.S. reply; the army gets furious; the emperor steps in to reprimand the army for its intransigence; and a peace—which was sure to include Japan's troop withdrawal from China and Indochina—is reached between the two countries.

In late August and early September, war preparations continued alongside summit meeting preparations. The inherent contradiction of this situation seems to have struck no one in Tokyo. Instead, the parallel paths were seen as all-around preparedness.

In a liaison conference on September 3—the day Roosevelt told Nomura a summit could not yet be arranged—the Japanese leaders agreed on a joint military plan, in the making since late August, that further elaborated on the plan, called "Outline of National Policies in View of the Changing Situation," of the July 2 imperial conference. This revised plan, "Essentials for Carrying Out the Empire's Policies," stated that while recommending the policy of continuing negotiations with the United States, Japan would go to war should the talks not bear fruit before an early-October deadline.

The prowar advocates, represented in the conference primarily by the general staffs, argued that war needed to be started within the year, before the enemy could build up its strength, before the monsoon season in the south, and while the severe winter weather kept the country safe from Soviet attacks in the north. "The empire is getting skinnier in every category of material resources," the navy's chief of staff, Nagano, said. It was better to go to war while the empire could still put up a decent fight—hence the need for a tight deadline for diplomacy.

The approved resolution was, on paper, a strong push for war. But a more sophisticated reading would be that it was a cloak of bravado for the militarists. They fully expected to make concessions involving troop withdrawal. By proposing and passing a step-by-step war plan against the United States, the high command leaders were saving face, remaining aggressive in the eventuality of huge diplomatic concessions.

Not all military leaders were comfortable with this new proposal, especially its specific deadline. The discussion involving the wording of the plan revealed that uneasiness. Navy Minister Oikawa did not want a strict definition of diplomatic failure; he wanted that to be debated later. Army Chief of Staff Sugiyama gave his word that no military movements, including the deployment of troops to Thailand, would take place while Konoe and Roosevelt were meeting. He also said he could not keep the army from shipping materials to French Indochina. This alarmed Tojo. "But that would reveal our intent [to prepare for war]," he protested. "Well, that cannot be helped," answered Sugiyama. Whatever was being said, most believed that a diplomatic solution was just around the corner. At the same liaison conference, that came up for discussion as well.

Konoe was supposed to introduce his own proposal, drafted and polished by his friends at the Fujiya Hotel, at the end of August. It emphasized the overall Japanese willingness to agree to a troop withdrawal from China in the hope of conciliating the United States. But Konoe never unveiled it. The Foreign Ministry had prepared its own proposal, and Konoe yielded to it. Saionji, one of the main engines behind Konoe's proposal, demanded an explanation afterward. "Tomita [the chief cabinet secretary] should have coordinated with them [the Foreign Ministry] beforehand," Konoe mumbled, and disappeared into his office without further explanation. Konoe felt that the Foreign Ministry's plan contained enough concessions for Roosevelt to be enticed to the negotiating table, so why make a fuss?

Konoe had, yet again, let down his strongest supporters, revealing that peace in the Pacific hinged on a man who could not even stand up for his own proposal in a liaison meeting he himself convoked! Meanwhile, war preparations continued.

The Foreign Ministry's proposal was sent by telegram to Nomura in Washington the next day. It proposed the peaceful settlement of tensions in the South Pacific, the promotion of nondiscriminatory commercial agreements, Japanese cooperation with the United States in its attempt to gain access to regional resources, and the unfreezing of Japanese assets. It also stated that Japan was prepared to withdraw promptly from China *once* Sino-Japanese agreements were reached—the greatest difference in nuance from Konoe's proposal, which committed Japan to a withdrawal from China as a matter of general principle. The Foreign Ministry's proposal would reach the Roosevelt administration on September 6.

While diplomacy stumbled, Tokyo's mobilization kept to its timetable with mechanical precision. On September 5, late in the afternoon, Konoe visited Hirohito at the palace to explain the "Essentials for Carrying Out the Empire's Policies," which had been agreed to on September 3 and stipulated that diplomatic efforts would cease in early October. An imperial conference had already been scheduled for the following day to obtain the emperor's blessing. Hirohito was flabbergasted by what he was told. The "Essentials" looked like a war mobilization plan, which is exactly what it was. Hirohito quickly understood that it could be reduced to the following three points, in order of importance:

1. The empire would not refrain from war with the United States, Britain, and the Netherlands and would prepare for war.
2. While those preparations moved forward, the empire would try its utmost in diplomatic efforts with the United States and Britain, guided by an attached document (see below).
3. If diplomatic efforts did not succeed by early October, the empire would launch a war at the end of October with the United States, Britain, and the Netherlands.

The separate attachment mentioned in the second point contained Japan's diplomatic demands, as well as the limits of its concessions, independent of the presummit agreement. They included noninterference by the United States in Japan's war settlement with China and a request to reclose the Burma Road, vital to relaying Western material aid to Chiang Kai-shek; in turn, Japan promised it would not use French Indochina as a base for further military advancement in the south. As long as the Soviet Union kept its neutrality, Japan would not use force against it. To reverse the argument, Japan would not withdraw from French Indochina or abandon the Tripartite Pact. The less diplomatic clout Japan possessed, the greater its stubbornness appeared to be. Still, it was assumed Konoe would be free to yield a great deal more to Roosevelt to avoid war.

Hirohito was disturbed all the same. He rightly sensed and complained that these guidelines put more emphasis on war. He asked Konoe to reverse the items so that diplomacy would become Japan's overwhelming priority. "That would be impossible," Konoe responded, presumably believing that he had to concede that much to enable his meeting with Roosevelt. Konoe was defying the doubtful emperor, just as he had when he endorsed signing the Tripartite Pact. Hirohito, always cautious of excessive political intervention, did not challenge Konoe enough then. This time, he responded more firmly. He said he had no idea until that moment that Japan's military preparations had advanced so far. Why, he asked, had he been kept in the dark? Konoe did not reply directly but suggested that Hirohito should summon the two chiefs of staff, strategic professionals, to better explain the exact situation. He acted as if politics had no place in this monumental resolution approved by his own government.

Nagano and Sugiyama were called immediately. At the end of July, Nagano had visited the palace with a war plan, though he said at the time, as we've seen, that he was uncertain Japan could win. Hirohito had been upset by that and consulted Navy Minister Oikawa about replacing Nagano. Nothing came of it. Now, only five weeks later, Nagano was back again with an advanced plan.

Displaying the incisiveness he was capable of when utterly compelled—which did not happen often—Hirohito asked devastating questions of the military leaders as Konoe listened. He told them that war and diplomacy could not be pursued in parallel and that diplomacy had to come first. He asked how long they estimated their planned war in the south would last.

> SUGIYAMA: Sir, we intend to complete [our mission] in the South Seas in three months.
> HIROHITO: When the China Incident broke out, you were our army minister. I remember you telling me then that the conflict would be over in about a month. But after four long years, it hasn't ended!
> SUGIYAMA: China has a huge hinterland. That was why we couldn't carry out our plans as we had originally envisioned.
> HIROHITO: If you say that China has a huge hinterland, the Pacific Ocean is even bigger. On what basis are you now telling me three months?

Sugiyama, deeply embarrassed, was at a loss for words and concealed his blushing by bowing his head.

Unable to stand the pathetic sight of his colleague, Nagano intervened to help. Despite the service rivalries, the two chiefs of staff got on well because Nagano was clearly in charge. "I speak broadly on behalf of the high command," Nagano began.

> If we were to compare today's U.S.-Japanese relations to a sick patient, the patient is in dire need of an operation. If we don't operate, and instead leave him be, the patient will gradually be weaker and weaker. Not that there isn't any hope of recovery. But we must decide while there still is a chance [for the success of the operation]. The high command desires diplomatic negotiations to reach a successful conclusion. But in case of its failure, I am afraid that we must pluck up enough courage and operate.

Trying to adjust to the idea of such a war, Hirohito had a hard time squaring Nagano's projected chance of success with his earlier admission that he had no confidence in victory. He asked Nagano the same question he had put to him not so long ago: "Will we win? Can you say we will definitely win?" To this, Nagano replied, "I cannot say 'definitely' because it depends not on just manpower but on divine power, too." He insisted that war was not the high command's preference, but that it felt compelled to prepare Japan for war in the face of the present crisis. "If there is even a remote chance of [war] working out, we must do it," he said.

This led to Hirohito's final question: "Then I'll ask you again: Is it correct for me to understand that the high command intends to put more emphasis on diplomacy as of today?" The two chiefs responded affirmatively.

The forty-year-old emperor intuited the feebleness of the prowar argument, the utter irresponsibility of the two much-older men in uniform who were justifying it, and the potentially devastating impact of his imperial approval. Hirohito discerned the plan's recklessness because he was basically an outsider to Tokyo's strange decision-making process. His natural instinct to avoid war as the peace-loving patriarch of Japan's family-state conflicted with his responsibility as the supreme commander of the armed forces, whose role was to ensure Japan's survival through military preparedness; on this occasion, the latter ultimately prevailed, leading him to acquiesce to the war plan.

Konoe, who had remained silent throughout the emperor's interview, was now belatedly waking up to the enormity of the decisions being made. He felt a growing sense of panic when he returned to the palace the next morning for the imperial conference. Konoe now wished that Hirohito would try to tilt the opinion of the conference toward peace, and he asked Kido, the emperor's closest adviser, for his help.

The imperial conference began promptly at 10:00 a.m. As before, the prime minister, the foreign minister, the home minister, the finance minister, and the army and navy ministers were joined by the chiefs of staff, the vice chiefs of staff, the chiefs of the Military Affairs Bureau and the Naval Affairs Bureau, the chief cabinet secretary, and the director of the Cabinet Planning Board. Asking questions on behalf of the emperor, again, was Hara Yoshimichi, president of the Privy Council.

As if to reenact Hirohito's exchange, Hara asked the two chiefs of staff whether strategy or diplomacy had priority in Japan's foreign policy. Neither replied, setting off an awkward silence. Hirohito, sitting in front of a ceremonious gold screen at the head of the table, was expected to remain silent, but now, to everyone's astonishment, he spoke up. "President Hara's question just now was truly appropriate. It is regrettable that both chiefs of the general staff are unable to answer it." He then took a piece of paper from the breast pocket of his khaki army uniform. On it was a poem written by his late grandfather, the great Meiji. Because of his less-than-satisfactory interview with the two chiefs of staff, and also because of Konoe's request that morning for some kind of imperial intervention, he had brought it with him. The emperor recited:

> *In all four seas all are brothers and sisters.*
> *Then why, oh why, these rough winds and waves?*

This pacifist lament, distilled into thirty-one Japanese syllables, was penned at the onset of the Russo-Japanese War. By reading it aloud, Hirohito was expressing his fundamental uneasiness with the new proposal and his desire for Japan to avoid war—or at least that was what he intended his indirect communication to convey to his audience. But the recital of the poem merely created a bizarre and self-pitying atmosphere of passive resistance. The emperor became a metaphor for Japan, a nation that was pressured into taking an undesirable action because of some uncontrollable external forces, despite its peaceful preferences. The peace poem did not free Hirohito from his customary imperial obligation; he approved the proposal all the same.

One cannot help wondering what would have happened had Hirohito been more explicit in his opposition to war or simply refused to approve the plan. Rather than read a poem open to many interpretations, why could he not have instead said that war was not an option? It is likely that the ever-cautious Kido, who communicated Konoe's wish for imperial intervention that morning, advised Hirohito to refrain from expressing any definitive political judgment, worried that the emperor would be held responsible for whatever happened to Japan next. That neither Kido nor Hirohito believed in excessive imperial political mediation was certainly one reason for Hirohito's muted objection. Another was the emperor's personality—he was too meek to oppose the general momentum for war preparations, especially since there was no historical precedent for an imperial veto. (Though it was not clearly sanctioned by the Meiji Constitution, it was deemed theoretically possible—most critically by Hirohito himself.) Carefully navigating between his divine role and his earthly one, the emperor chose to merely recite a poem.

That evening, after the early-October diplomatic deadline had received imperial sanction, Konoe invited Ambassador Grew to a surreptitious dinner at the home of a friend. Konoe was accompanied by Breakfast Club member Ushiba Tomohiko, who was fluent in English. Also present was the Osaka-born Eugene Dooman from the U.S. embassy. Konoe's geisha mistress attended to them.

The secrecy was necessary because on August 15 the seasoned politician Hiranuma Kiichiro, a minister in Konoe's second and current cabinets, was attacked in his home by an ultranationalist would-be assassin. Despite being shot six times, including once in the head, Hiranuma miraculously survived and would fully recover. He had been targeted because he was drawing too close to Grew in the hope of avoiding war with the United States. That gave Konoe pause.

Over the course of three hours, Konoe tried to impress on Grew how much he longed to see Roosevelt. Afterward, Grew wrote a lengthy report to the president, summarizing the meeting and relaying Konoe's wish that "his statements be transmitted personally to the President in the belief that they might amplify and clarify the approach through diplomatic channels which he had made in Washington through Admiral Nomura." It was theoretically still possible for Konoe to reach sweeping diplomatic settlements with Washington, but time was running out, and the prowar faction had just surmounted a big obstacle by winning the emperor's assent.

Or, more accurately, the military, though divided and unsure about the feasibility of a hastily envisioned war, was becoming a prisoner of its own bellicose rhetoric. Now that a specific deadline had been set, the rush to war had acquired an internally driven dynamic.

The recommendation of the hypothetical cabinet at the Total War Research Institute, in contrast, was based on a detached analysis of relative capabilities. True, the researchers did not know exactly how much petroleum Japan still possessed, but in all other respects they could materially assess that Japan did not have the means to win a war with the United States. Konoe and his ministers could not plead ignorance of their findings. In the late summer of 1941, the war that was declared unwinnable by a hypothetical government was, in only ten days, made almost inevitable by the real one.

CHAPTER 10

One Last Opportunity

Army Minister Tojo was growing vociferous about the necessity of preparing for war. In order to slow the momentum, Konoe arranged a meeting between Tojo and Higashikuni Naruhiko. Higashikuni was a liberal—some would say libertarian—prince who had spent much of his youth in Europe, mostly in France. He was one of the few vocal opponents of Japan's going to war with the West. Because he was an army general, it was presumed his cautionary words to Tojo would be seriously considered. Higashikuni was also an uncle by marriage of Emperor Hirohito and a member of the imperial household, which strengthened his position. Tojo's dedication to the imperial institution was known to be almost servile, as if to atone for his ancestors' sins in fighting against the court-backed samurai.

Konoe's timing was again baffling. The meeting came the day after the momentous imperial resolution for an early-October diplomatic deadline for a late-October war, so nothing short of its retraction by the emperor would have stopped Tojo from sticking to that decision. Tojo was said to have shed tears as he recounted to his junior staff Hirohito's recitation of the peace poem. But he did not think the emperor was objecting to war. To him, the poem represented imperial encouragement for the military in the face of long odds.

Tojo was determined to travel the path that was mapped out for him—and to drag the nation with him if he must. "The United States in the end demands that Japan withdraw from the Tripartite alliance and join the Anglo-American camp," he would say to Higashikuni. But even if Japan abandoned the fascists and joined the Allies, he continued, "the Anglo-Americans would surely attack Japan once they finished their business with Germany."

Tojo's perception of Western menace was highly speculative, but his fear was genuine and not uncommon. He believed that the liberal West was interested in brokering peace between Japan and China only because it had designs on Japan and wanted to become a hegemonic power throughout Asia. Secretary of State Hull's pet project of spreading free trade and equal commercial opportunities had to be distrusted given America's greater ambitions. Tojo also insisted that it was inconceivable for Japan to withdraw troops from China in light of "all the heroic souls who have fallen in Japanese wars," repeating the phrase popularized by Matsuoka when he first emerged as a populist politician in the early 1930s. Tojo was echoing a pervasive military sentiment. But he was no ordinary soldier; he was the army minister, answerable to the cabinet. Blinded by his service allegiance, he refused to see that war was hardly inevitable or advisable. What defined Tojo was his tremendous single-mindedness about pursuing goals he deemed to be right and righteous. Could Higashikuni ameliorate his obstinacy, as Konoe hoped?

Higashikuni was a slim, effete man with the weak chin characteristic of highborn Japanese. He had pleasing, if plain, features, and unlike many of his army colleagues, he was clean-shaven. The cosmopolitan fifty-three-year-old did have the penetrating voice of a natural orator, which alone sufficed to make people pay attention the minute he opened his mouth. He said to Tojo that Japan's situation reminded him of something that the French statesmen Marshal Pétain and Georges Clemenceau once told him. Both men had said the United States would eventually try to provoke Japan into a war. To the Frenchmen, this was an easily foreseeable geopolitical consequence of a power scramble for control of Asia. But it was equally inevitable that Japan would lose that war because of its relative material weaknesses. The best thing Japan could do was to be patient and to minimize its losses. Higashikuni then made his most important point: Since the emperor and the prime minister were both keen on reaching an agreement with Roosevelt, Tojo, as their army minister, should comply with that higher wish. If he could not follow a policy of nonconfrontation, he should quit his job.

Tojo was utterly unfazed by Higashikuni's suggestion—one no doubt endorsed by Konoe, who didn't want to confront Tojo directly—that he was being a troublemaker. He responded that if the ABCD encirclement of Japan continued, Japan was doomed to disappear. If Japan took a risk now, the chance of Japan winning a war was one in two. (He was right only to the extent that one could either win or lose.) Surely it was better to take that risk than to perish without resistance. Tojo's emotions had clearly overcome his reason. He told the prince he had no inclination to put a stop to the war planning.

On September 8 and 9, Army Chief of Staff Sugiyama visited the palace to explain to Hirohito the tactical details of the army's plan. The emperor wondered on both occasions what would happen if a military clash transpired on the Soviet-Manchukuo border after Japan went to war with the West. Sugiyama reassured him that the chances of anything happening in the winter months were slim, and if anything did happen, the army could always redirect its troops from China to the north. But the winter months would not last forever, and Japan could hardly afford to transfer men from China to fight the Soviet Union. (Within ten days of Sugiyama's irresponsible words, the Japanese army launched Operation Changsha in its bid to control the south-central region of China, only to be met with fierce Chinese opposition.) Hirohito should have protested that waging another war was unimaginable. But instead, he told Sugiyama that he "understood the logistics behind" the decision, as if Hirohito saw it as a purely conceptual strategic exercise divorced from political realities. Perhaps he was still counting on the Konoe-Roosevelt summit.

Five times in September and on October 3, the army announced provisional unit formation and mobilization plans for the south. Its paratrooper unit, the key to conquering the Indonesian island of Sumatra, stepped up its intensive training. The unit was founded only the previous fall. Its organizers had had to rely on photographs of U.S. Army parachutes in order to make their own. Having trained at a free-fall tower in an amusement park, passing as university students enjoying what was still left of Japan's leisurely activities, the paratroopers completed their first successful landing in late February.

The navy also intensified its preparations. War games for a southern invasion were carried out from September 11 to 20 at the Naval War College. A desktop simulation for an attack on Hawaii had taken place on September 16, but the Naval General Staff deemed the plan too risky and impracticable and rejected it.

AS JAPAN'S ARMED FORCES WERE desperately trying to parallel the war-ready rhetoric of its strategists and leaders, the United States almost went to war—in Iceland. When Germany invaded Denmark in April 1940, Iceland, near critical Atlantic shipping lanes, was tied to Denmark by the Act of Union. Britain dispatched forces to Iceland in May, and Canada sent reinforcements. Churchill hoped that the United States would take over Icelandic defense. By the spring of 1941, the Roosevelt administration had agreed to assume such responsibility in the event of U.S. war entry. Even after the German invasion of the Soviet Union, when Roosevelt's hawkish strategists started calling for immediate deployment of U.S. troops to the region, Roosevelt remained cautious. He agreed to dispatch forty-four hundred marines on July 7, 1941, at the request of the Icelandic government. He was carefully circumventing the Selective Training and Service Act, whose future was still uncertain at that point. By sending professional soldiers rather than draftees—who were not allowed to serve outside the Western Hemisphere—he avoided antagonizing the public, sticking to his earlier pledge that their "boys" would not be made to fight in foreign wars. This would, however, be followed by Roosevelt's critical decision during the Atlantic Conference, as we have seen, to allow U.S. armed escorts to protect all shipping as far as Iceland. This series of events was highly relevant to Japan. The U.S. preoccupation with the western Atlantic accounted for Washington's initial willingness in the spring of 1941 to reach some kind of peace with Tokyo that would ensure that Japan stayed out of the imminent American war with the Nazis. Japan, of course, squandered that opportunity.

On September 4, 1941, the waters off the coast of Iceland became a theater in an undeclared war between Germany and the United States. The *Greer,* a U.S. destroyer with a few military passengers and mail on board, was approaching Iceland at 8:40 a.m. when the ship was alerted by a British bomber that a German submarine was lurking in the vicinity. The British plane dropped four depth charges, which missed the target, and retreated after nearly running out of fuel. The *Greer,* without any authority to attack, opted to pursue the submarine rather than report back to base. Three hours after it was first detected, the German submarine came within 330 feet of the U.S. ship and released a torpedo, likely anxious to come to the surface as its batteries ran out. It, too, missed the target. The *Greer* then dropped eight depth charges, none of which did much damage to the submarine. A second torpedo from the German submarine went awry. A dozen more depth charges were dropped by the *Greer* and another reinforcement British bomber. The two sides came out of the very close encounter, which lasted about ten hours, unscathed.

The *Greer* incident was the first significant U.S. skirmish with a German submarine. In a powerful attempt at selling a war that Roosevelt was resolved to enter, the president used this episode in his September 11 radio address to mobilize public opinion against Hitler. He did not mention that the first depth charges were dropped by the British plane, enabling the German torpedo attack to be interpreted as an act of self-defense, nor did he mention the *Greer's* insistent and unauthorized retaliation. (These details became clear after a Senate committee investigation the following month.) But his speech made abundantly clear his hatred of the Nazi regime. "This was piracy—piracy legally and morally," he declared to the nation with a thespian's intonation. "It was not the first nor the last act of piracy which the Nazi Government has committed against the American flag in this war. For attack has followed attack."

Citing four other instances of suspected German attacks on U.S. ships and one on a Panamanian ship in the preceding months, Roosevelt warned that these were not isolated incidents but "part of a general plan." These were acts of "international lawlessness," he said, and constituted a "Nazi design to abolish the freedom of the seas, and to acquire absolute control and domination of these seas for themselves." He continued:

> This Nazi attempt to seize control of the oceans is but a counterpart of the Nazi plots now being carried on throughout the Western Hemisphere—all designed toward the same end. For Hitler's advance guards—not only his avowed agents but also his dupes among us—have sought to make ready for him footholds, [and] bridgeheads in the New World, to be used as soon as he has gained control of the oceans. His intrigues, his plots, his machinations, his sabotage in this New World are all known to the Government of the United States. Conspiracy has followed conspiracy. . . . This attack on the *Greer* was no localized military operation in the North Atlantic. This was no mere episode in a struggle between two nations. This was one determined step towards creating a permanent world system based on force, on terror and on murder.

Roosevelt told the American people that note writing and other "normal practices of diplomacy" were no longer of use in dealing with Germany. To protect the line of supply of war materials to defeat Hitler, as well as to ensure the freedom of U.S. shipping on the high seas, the United States had to strike, without hesitation, at Nazi submarines and raiders. They were the "rattlesnakes of the Atlantic," and "when you see a rattlesnake poised to strike, you do not wait until he has struck before you crush him." The time for "active defense" had come. This meant that U.S. ships could attack German submarines in waters vital to U.S. self-defense. Moreover, these vital waters would be defined by the U.S. government. Roosevelt also used this occasion to introduce the nation to his new program of allowing U.S. escorts of Allied shipping in the Atlantic, which he had approved at Placentia Bay and was going into effect in five days.

Roosevelt had confirmed his oratorical genius; a poll after this fireside chat indicated that 62 percent of Americans supported his shoot-on-sight policy regarding German vessels in the Atlantic. And yet, as the British ambassador to the United States, Lord Halifax, incisively reported to Churchill, the majority of Americans wished to stay out of the European war despite their approval of the president's new Atlantic policy and their desire to defeat Hitler.

For some strategists in Washington, the possibility of war had become a pressing concern. At the behest of the army's chief of staff, General George Marshall, a team of middle-ranking officers led by Major Albert Wedemeyer set out in July 1941 to prepare an extensive war plan, which would come to be known as the Victory Program. Completed by September 25, it projected the necessary scale of military and industrial mobilization and recommended strategic guidelines to defeat the Axis powers. The plan would prove indispensable within a few months, though until the very last minute, Germany was the country's primary enemy in the eyes of these planners, and they urged leaders to hold Japan in check.

The Japanese government should have wondered if the day might soon come when Washington deemed "note writing" between Japan and the United States no longer a viable option and what might be done to prevent that deterioration. Instead, it planned for "active defense" on its own terms.

AFTER HEARING FROM Sorge that there was no risk of Japan attacking the Soviet Union, Stalin moved twenty divisions from the Far Eastern front to Moscow within the month of September. Stalin could now concentrate on his battle with Germany. He would ultimately reduce his troops in the Far East by half, and the situation on the Soviet western front would steadily improve.

That was all the more reason for Japan to reassess its approach to the United States. The pact that entrenched Japan in fascist company was entirely predicated on Germany prevailing. Japan's strategic plans continued to rest on that assumption, even though many in the Army General Staff were taking note of the surprising resilience of the Soviet Union. Despite that, and the fact that they did not subscribe to a true fascist ideology, Japan's leaders refused to do anything to extricate itself from the Axis alliance. This was presumably because nobody dared to own up to their mistakes in having uncritically endorsed German invincibility. Instead, Japan would remain a fascist power by association and would have a diminished chance of reaching any diplomatic settlement with the United States.

On September 10, Nomura met with Hull in his new apartment, in the famous Wardman Park Hotel, a fortress of a building with a thousand rooms built in commemoration of the end of World War I. He asked what Hull thought of the latest Japanese proposal (the one devised by the Foreign Ministry) for the preliminary agreement. Hull replied that this proposal "narrowed down the spirit and the scope of the proposed understanding," whereas their earlier conversations "had related to a broad and liberal understanding covering the entire Pacific area." It was, in short, a step backward.

The apparent narrowing down could only have reinforced Hull's suspicions of Konoe's feeble leadership and his inability to deliver any meaningful concessions. For Nomura, this meeting confirmed his view that Tokyo had to commit to concrete concessions before any summit could take place. Specifically, he warned his government that the issue of troop withdrawal from China was critical to the United States. The leaders in Tokyo had a difficult time openly accepting this view.

From the initial stages of the U.S.-Japan negotiations, the presence of Japanese troops in China was surely an issue, but its importance seemed to have grown enormously in American eyes of late. In May, Hull was certainly more accommodating on Japan's military occupation of China, at least off the record, and Nomura had conveyed that impression to Tokyo. The banker and amateur diplomat Ikawa Tadao had noted that Hull even suggested rephrasing Japan's ostensible purpose for its military occupation of China from "anticommunist occupation" to "peacekeeping occupation." That change would enable Japan to continue to occupy the Chinese island of Hainan, which faced no immediate Communist threat.

The developments during the summer of 1941—the German attack on the Soviet Union, Japan's advance into southern Indochina in the face of Roosevelt's proposal, its insistence on remaining in the fascist camp, and the subsequent intensification of U.S. public opinion against Japan—appeared to have eliminated such conciliatory U.S. inclinations regarding China. Unlike with Czechoslovakia, China could not be sold down the river. Negotiating a U.S.-Japanese understanding without settling the China question had now become, in Sumner Welles's words, like "asking whether the play of *Hamlet* could be given on the stage without the character of Hamlet." If Konoe had proposed, as outlined by his friends, that "Japan *in principle* agrees to withdraw its troops from China," things might have been quite different. Konoe had only himself to blame for that.

Following Hull's rejection, a liaison meeting on September 20 passed another presummit proposal to be submitted to Washington. The reworked proposal was identical in its basic outline to the September 6 version, specifying that the United States would broker a peace between Japan and Chiang Kai-shek's regime without interfering in Japan's initiatives to resolve the China War in the meantime; Japanese assets would be unfrozen and normal trade restored; and Japan would not venture beyond French Indochina.

The new proposal included more detailed demands regarding the terms of any peace with China and was far firmer in tone, reflecting the prowar strategists increased involvement. Sensing an even further narrowing of his government's scope, Nomura felt there was nothing in the new proposal to help him in his negotiations. It clearly revealed the limits of his influence over Tokyo and the limits of Konoe's courage.

Nomura was particularly troubled by one Japanese condition for its desired peace with China. Tokyo continued to insist on the merger of the governments of Chiang Kai-shek and Wang Jingwei, the Japanese puppet loathed by Chiang. There was no way the United States would agree to that. Nomura also sensed that any pleading for Japan's regional interests in Asia would be counterproductive, only adding to U.S. alarm. He sent a telegram to Tokyo: "I do not believe that this proposal will do." Again, Nomura's appeal was dismissed.

AT LEAST ONE military insider was appalled by the excessive interference of his *bakuryo* colleagues in the drafting of such diplomatic proposals. "The general staff is an organ that should be dedicated to the nation's defense and mobilization," Ishii Akiho of the Army Ministry's Military Affairs Bureau later lamented. "Why [it] quibbled so relentlessly with a diplomatic document, I do not understand."

Even Admiral Toyoda, a foreign minister who was essentially a military partisan, had to admit that the "new" plan of September 20 did not represent a compelling proposal for Washington. He nonetheless passed it on to Ambassador Grew as a reference material, which was then relayed to the State Department by September 27.

WITH NO DISCERNIBLE PROGRESS being made for a Konoe-Roosevelt summit, Saionji Kinkazu was not sure what he should be doing to help. The prime minister had appointed him an adviser presumably because he trusted him unconditionally. Saionji reciprocated his trust, worked hard on Konoe's projects, and, most recently, helped draft Konoe's aborted proposal. The exhilaration he felt about the proposal only a few weeks earlier had faded. Saionji had experienced Konoe's mercurial temper and dithering too often and was frustrated, though he still believed Konoe's desire for a summit meeting was heartfelt.

In late September, Saionji received a telephone call from his best friend, Ozaki Hotsumi. Ozaki had just come back from a two-week lecture trip in Manchukuo. It had been a busy summer for the journalist and spy. That evening, Saionji and Ozaki dined together in a Japanese inn, exchanging their views on Japan's negotiations with the United States. Ozaki was thoroughly pessimistic. He felt the Americans did not trust the current Japanese leadership. The United States was unlikely to take any Japanese proposal seriously, he said, including the proposal for a summit meeting. Saionji told him that, at Konoe's request, he had participated in drawing up a new proposal, one Saionji hoped might still move things along.

On September 24, Ozaki invited Saionji for a drink at the same Japanese inn. The summer was lingering, and the two felt like a beer. (Unlike many others, they could still afford it. According to the official rationing schedule in Tokyo, as of April 1941, each household could purchase only two to four bottles of beer every six months.) They met in a private dining room, though there was nothing furtive in the air. Saionji brought with him the draft of the proposal that he and his friends had produced at the foot of Mount Fuji, the one Konoe failed to present. Ozaki had not asked to see it, but it seemed only natural for Saionji to share it with his best friend. Ozaki read through the draft without comment. He then begged off from a dinner Saionji had arranged with other friends and left, presumably to keep Sorge informed. This meeting added one more count to the charge of espionage Saionji would later face.

The next day, September 25, started out sunny and mild, with the temperature hanging in the seventies, but by early afternoon it was rainy and cold. The liaison conference that day only increased the gloom for Konoe. Chiefs of Staff Sugiyama and Nagano now jointly made a case to do away with the vague early-October deadline and set a specific date for the termination of diplomacy.

> The timing of the opening of war is hugely dependent on our tactical requirements. Therefore, we cannot afford to waste another day before passing a final judgment on the success or failure of the U.S.-Japan diplomatic negotiations. We need to choose between diplomacy and war by October 15 at the very latest.

With the chiefs' new and more exacting demand, Konoe began to panic, albeit quietly. He declined to stay on for a customary luncheon organized by the high command and took his key cabinet ministers back to the prime minister's residence. "Is the October 15 deadline a very rigid demand?" he asked of the foreign, navy, and army ministers. The query was really directed at Tojo, who sided with the chiefs of staff regarding the need for immediate war preparations. Tojo scoffed at Konoe and said that the matter had been formally decided in an imperial conference—early October was to be the end of Nomura's mission in Washington.

Adept at masking his innermost feelings, Konoe was not the easiest man to read. But the change in him after the liaison conference did not go unnoticed. A *bakuryo* officer in the War Guidance Office, taking his turn keeping the group's journal, noted the following day: "Superficially, it appears that yesterday's request by the high command [to set a mid-October deadline for diplomacy] had not created a huge sensation. But facts beg to differ. Prime Minister Konoe seems to have undergone a tremendous change in his state of mind." Konoe's ostensible desire to have everyone save face was really a failure to confront opponents, and it had taken its toll. It was finally becoming clear to him that the United States was not keen on the summit. Konoe, terrified, instantly began to act on his strongest instinct: self-preservation.

In a private conference with Kido in the late afternoon of September 26, Konoe spoke of quitting the government. Schoolmates at the Peers Academy, the two men had literally rubbed shoulders with one another growing up, standing side by side in assemblies. "If the military insists on the October 15 deadline to begin war," Konoe complained to Kido, "I do not have any confidence. I have no other choice but to think of resigning." Kido responded:

> You are the one who called the September 6 imperial conference [that set the early-October deadline for diplomacy]. You cannot leave that decision hanging and just disappear. That's irresponsible. Why not propose a reconsideration of the resolution? You cannot start talking like that before crossing swords with the military. To leave the mess this way is irresponsible.

Kido's strong admonishment kept Konoe from resigning. Instead, he fled to a villa in the ancient samurai capital of Kamakura, only thirty miles away but safely enclosed by a range of mountains and the sea. He did not emerge from it until October 2.

With the prince absent from Tokyo, Foreign Minister Toyoda had to lobby for a Konoe-Roosevelt meeting on his own. Rather than heeding Nomura's advice to try to fundamentally reorient Japan's policy and come up with a more enticing plan, Toyoda had passed on to U.S. ambassador Grew an insufficiently reworked proposal for a presummit agreement, as we have seen. Assuming that the ambassador had tremendous influence over the president because they were old friends, Toyoda hoped to gain from Grew some behind-the-scenes intervention. But by adding another diplomatic channel and treating it as if it were a more powerful line of communication to the White House, Toyoda, in effect, discredited Nomura.

Toyoda pleaded with Grew on September 27 to explain to Washington the complicated workings of Tokyo's leadership, making excuses for Konoe's and his own lack of mettle to confront and negotiate with domestic opposition. He insinuated that the "official" presummit proposals from Tokyo should not be taken as the limits of concessions Konoe could make in Juneau.

In a lengthy eleven-point communication on September 29, Grew wrote to Roosevelt that he had been "emphatically told on numerous occasions" that prior to the proposed meeting and formal negotiations, it would be "impossible for the Japanese Government to define its future assurances and commitments more specifically than hitherto stated." One reason for this, he explained, was that

> former Foreign Minister Matsuoka, after his retirement in July, recounted in complete detail to the German Ambassador in Japan the course of the Washington conversations up to that time. Because many supporters of Matsuoka remain in the Tokyo Foreign Office, the fear has been expressed that these men will not scruple to reveal to both the Germans and the Japanese extremists any information which would render the present Cabinet's position untenable. Although certain basic principles have been accepted provisionally by the Japanese Government, the definitions and formulae of Japan's future objectives and policy . . . are so abstract or equivocal and are open to such wide interpretation that they rather create confusion than clarify commitments which the Japanese Government is ready to undertake.

Grew therefore advised that the United States should trust Konoe's good intentions and arrange a summit. He suggested as much in a carefully cushioned double-negative supposition:

> [I do not] consider unlikely the possibility of Prince Konoye's being in a position to give President Roosevelt directly a more explicit and satisfactory engagement than has already been vouchsafed in the course of the preliminary conversations.

Grew further stressed that a gradualist approach should be pursued. He agreed with Toyoda that "the only alternative . . . is an attempt to produce a regeneration of Japanese thought and outlook through constructive conciliation, along the lines of American efforts at present."

Foreign-policy makers are famous for referring to recent crises to inform their next move. To some members of the U.S. administration, Grew's communication urging "constructive conciliation" must have smacked of appeasement. No matter how different the Japanese situation was from Hitler's Third Reich in the autumn of 1938, the Munich Conference was too fresh and too disheartening a memory to be easily dismissed. Though Toyoda did a remarkable job painting a false picture of the Konoe cabinet being surrounded predominantly by pro-Matsuoka, pro-German enemies, he could blame only so much on his predecessor. With or without Matsuoka, Japan could not escape identification with the Nazi regime. It was, after all, an Axis ally. Grew, aware of this, insisted that the method he was advocating to Washington was "not so-called appeasement."

Konoe, alas, hardly had the kind of track record to convince Washington that he could be trusted. Both Konoe and Toyoda continued to suggest that Konoe would bring satisfactory, even surprising, concessions with him to Juneau. The U.S. administration remained unconvinced.

Konoe had first come to attention in the West as the author of a jingoistic article speaking against the "Anglo-American" dictatorship of the Paris Peace Conference in early 1919. He was prime minister when the China War broke out in 1937 and was responsible for its escalation, including Japan's brutal conquest of China's major cities and industrial areas, most notably Nanjing. He was the prime minister who formally approved the establishment of Wang Jingwei's puppet regime. He pushed for Japan's alliance with Germany and Italy. "If the United States continues to deliberately misread the true intentions of Japan, Germany, and Italy," he said in a press conference after the Tripartite Pact was signed, "we won't be left with any other choices but war." Konoe felt none of these words or deeds affected his credibility. He was a prince after all. He was also deluded.

THE SEPTEMBER 25 LIAISON meeting that set off Konoe's sense of gloom had also stirred up Navy Minister Oikawa's greatest fear—that of a titanic naval war with the United States. True, in trying to oust Matsuoka, the usually overcautious and reticent Oikawa boasted, in a conference in late June, that "the navy is confident about war with Britain and the United States." Oikawa was then merely trying to force the southern Indochinese plan through. "If you are confident enough to fight Britain and the United States," responded Matsuoka, "how much more extra trouble would it be for you to fight the Soviet Union, too?" With his wit not up to Matsuoka's sarcasm, he could only reply in earnest: "Don't you see if the Soviet Union joined, that means one more extra country for us to fight?" Exactly three months after his exchange with Matsuoka, Oikawa faced the likelihood of Japan having to confront all those enemies.

To his credit, Oikawa, unlike Konoe, openly resisted the navy and army chiefs of staff when they tried to set a mid-October diplomatic deadline at the liaison meeting of September 25. He hoped to slow, if not put a stop to, the momentum for war. Army Vice Chief of Staff Tsukada, the most hawkish voice in liaison conferences since the north-south debate, was clearly unhappy with Oikawa's obstruction. A fanatical believer in Japan's inherent greatness, he was convinced that Japan's war, a necessary one, was based not on rational, strategic thinking but on the "morally just spirit of our divine land." Though many Japanese, both military men and civilians, were socialized to a certain extent into accepting this pseudoreligious view of Japan's national destiny, the level Tsukada had taken it to was alarming for a senior strategist. After the meeting, he complained to his subordinates that Tojo should urge Oikawa to come to his senses so that they could *all* get on with war preparations—as if Oikawa were the one without any common sense. Still, even Tsukada had to concede that Japan could not fight the United States if the navy was not willing.

Not everyone in the army shared Tsukada's single-minded desire for war. There had been a renewed sense of hesitation brewing in the army, notably among those in the Army Ministry's Military Affairs Bureau. Because the bureau was responsible for the allocation of resources within the army and for setting the overall tenor of army policy making in consultation with the general staff, its chief was the third most influential man in the Army Ministry (after the minister and vice minister). On September 29, bureau members gathered in the office of the chief, Muto Akira, to discuss possible future scenarios in some detail. The terrain was familiar. The army couldn't publicly concede to Washington's demands—especially the withdrawal of troops from China—but in Muto's mind, war would be even more deplorable. "The likely prospect might be war after all," he said. "But you see, one misstep and war can end up destroying the state. I just cannot make up my mind for war. I don't want war, all the more so since the emperor also said so [by reciting the poem]." Muto had heartily supported the war against China when it broke out in 1937, but he had come to realize it had been a "misstep" for Japan. He knew another one could wreck it.

The same day, Yamamoto Isoroku, the commander in chief of the Combined Fleet, sent a warning to Chief of Staff Nagano. Though he had been studiously planning a devastating attack on the United States for the past ten months, Yamamoto remained convinced that winning a battle or two would not ensure a victory in a long and protracted war. Hence his assessment to Nagano:

> Our war games suggest that the southern operation should settle more or less in four months, but at the cost of losing 650 planes. Certainly, there would be many more losses that are not related to actual combat.

This means that we would have to replenish a sufficient number [of air-craft] in order to continue fighting. . . . If we were to fight at our present level of strength, [the only chance for our ultimate victory is] to achieve considerable success in initial battles.

Yamamoto surely wanted to prove to the world that he was capable of pulling off "considerable success." That was the boastful gambler in him. But a rational Yamamoto advised Nagano:

If I might add . . . it is evident that a U.S.-Japanese war is bound to be protracted. The United States will not give up fighting as long as Japan has the upper hand. The war will last for several years. In the mean-time, Japan's resources will be depleted, battleships and weaponry will be damaged, replenishing materials will be impossible. . . . Japan will be impoverished.

He then famously concluded: "A war with so little chance of success should not be fought." The hesitations of the top commander of the navy, a strategic mastermind, proved that the momentum for war set by the general staffs was fairly detached from Japan's strategic reality. The mili-tary's push for war was far from universal. Konoe's only hope, other than an invitation from Roosevelt, was to exploit such differences of opinion. In the early evening of October 1, Oikawa was summoned by Konoe to the Kamakura villa to which he had retreated. Konoe asked the navy minister what he thought of the new development calling for a firm deadline for diplomacy. Oikawa responded:

Your Excellency, you say that you are definitely against war. [But not going to war] would require being prepared to swallow all the U.S. demands in order for us to normalize our relations. . . . If you have made up your mind to go down that route, the navy will back you up fully, and the army should follow.

Konoe, visibly happy, told Oikawa that he felt reassured.

In Tokyo, Oikawa then met with Navy Chief of Staff Nagano, who, according to Vice Navy Minister Sawamoto, agreed to lend his support to the policy of war avoidance, which suggests that Nagano's hard-line state-ments in liaison conferences should not be taken at face value. Oikawa, for his part, had always been diffident about the potential war with the West and must have welcomed this emerging agreement with Konoe and Nagano with a sigh of relief. Foreign Minister Toyoda, a navy admiral, also agreed that diplomatic settlement with the United States should be pursued. He was regretting the hastiness with which the imperial conference had set a diplomatic deadline—after only one liaison conference. Konoe now felt brave enough to emerge from his self-imposed exile and return to Tokyo.

ON OCTOBER 2, Ambassador Nomura was summoned to Hull's apartment at 9:00 p.m. He was handed a statement urging Japan to accept the secretary of state's Four Principles, which, again, were (1) respect for the territorial integrity and the sovereignty of each and all nations, (2) support for the principle of noninterference in the internal affairs of other countries, (3) support for the principle of equality, including equality of commercial opportunity, and (4) nondisturbance of the status quo in the Pacific except as the status quo may be altered by peaceful means. Hull then asked Japan to present the United States with "a clear-cut manifestation of Japan's intention in regard to the withdrawal of Japanese troops from China and French Indochina." As for Japan's affiliation with the Axis powers, he said, "It would be helpful if the Japanese Government could give further study to the question of possible additional clarification of its position." Most emphatically, there would be no summit until there was "a meeting of minds on essential points." Nomura was repeatedly reminded that the administration believed that "no patchwork arrangement would meet the situation of establishing peace in the Pacific area." Nomura was also told that Washington believed that to minimize adverse public opinion it needed to "insure the success of any meeting that we might hold."

Nomura, asked by Hull to comment on the document, initially expressed fear that his government would be disappointed. Hull's Four Principles were demanding of Japan a fundamental change in the nation's outlook impossible to achieve on such short notice. The United States itself had taken, and was still taking, its time to become a righteous power, after all. Its unequal treaties with Japan (which had expired only in 1911), its alliances with Britain and other old imperialist powers, and its policies toward people of color all made U.S. professions of high moral standards seem hypocritical to many Japanese.

The logistics of withdrawing all Japanese troops from China were chal-

lenging. Because of the Soviet proximity to Inner Mongolia and northern China, some in the Japanese army believed that signs of Japanese
retreat would prompt an imminent Bolshevist advance—fears that would
be proved correct in four years' time.

The most practical solution in Nomura's mind was to hold a summit
meeting at which all these issues could be discussed. He told Hull again
that his government was earnest and sincere in its desire for such a meeting. He also said that because of the domestic situation in Japan, it was
difficult for the government to commit to anything in advance of the talks.
Nomura stressed that the Konoe cabinet was in a "comparatively strong
position" and that he did not think there was a very high likelihood of
reactionary groups coming into power. Nomura was trying hard to explain
Konoe's characteristic unwillingness to confront his opponents head-on—
which, paradoxically, gave his premiership power and longevity—without
fundamentally discrediting Konoe's leadership. This was hard to do.

THE OCTOBER 4 LIAISON conference, the first since Nomura's unsatisfactory conversation with Hull, lacked vigor. Nomura's telegram reporting
Hull's communication had not been completely translated by the time of
the meeting, so it could not be discussed in detail. The leaders instead
expressed their general opinions. Army Chief of Staff Sugiyama warned
that the ultimate decision to dispense with diplomacy should not be
delayed:

> [We] cannot afford to waste time. If the decision doesn't get made soon
> and we waste more time, we'll end up not being able to launch a war at
> all, either in the south or in the north. We won't have to decide today,
> but we must decide [soon].

Immediately after Sugiyama finished, Navy Chief of Staff Nagano
said: "It is no longer time for discussion. We should [set a timetable for
war] right away!"

Nagano, of course, had told Oikawa two days previously that he preferred to avert a military confrontation with the West. Though Nagano was
the master of speaking out of both sides of his mouth, all of Japan's leaders
did it to a certain extent, switching effortlessly between public and private personas without feeling dishonest. Moreover, such a habit of double-

talking—encapsulated by the phrase *honne to tatemae,* or "true voice and façade"—had a tendency to be regarded as a virtue used to stave off embarrassing social situations. Nagano's bullying, almost thug-like public personality predominated whenever he spoke on behalf of the high command, representing Japan's strategic interests. Oikawa's efforts to oppose war on behalf of the navy—and Japan—became all the more difficult in the absence of any collegial support in liaison meetings. And because Oikawa intrinsically understood the importance to Nagano of keeping up his façade as a confident navy chief of staff, and also because Oikawa was a weak man, he would not call Nagano out. The liaison conferences were becoming a tragic farce of keeping up appearances for appearances' sake. In the face of such misplaced priorities, the fate of the Japanese nation was secondary.

No words from Oikawa were recorded that day, presumably because he kept silent. In January 1946, in a roundtable discussion attended by former senior naval officers, he said that he believed the prime minister, not navy representatives, should have taken the lead in shifting the government's policy away from war. The suspicion that Konoe was trying to assign all the responsibility for a policy switch to the navy put Oikawa on guard, and made him even more reticent than usual around this time. A dedicated and narrow-minded military man with no grasp of the world beyond the naval institution, Oikawa refused to risk being blamed for avoiding war, not accepting that his lack of assertiveness was, in large part, a sign of cowardice. Oikawa was not alone in deluding himself—everyone in the leadership took part in this utterly futile game of passing the buck.

At the same postwar roundtable, Vice Navy Minister Sawamoto sympathetically spoke of the delicacy of the situation that had confronted Oikawa. As hard as it was to imagine in 1946, he said, in the fall of 1941 one simply couldn't have said: "The navy cannot fight." This would have been demoralizing to officers at sea. Again, with military leaders taking a position against Japan's best interests, the idiocy of protecting one's own and institutional positions had gone much too far.

Another roundtable attendee, Inoue Shigeyoshi, a self-described radical liberal and a close associate of Admirals Yonai and Yamamoto who was sidelined from Tokyo's decision making in 1941, did not accept such postwar explanations and asked Oikawa directly: "The navy should have fought it all out with the army [over the war decision]. Instead, [by going to war] we ended up losing everything, *including* the army and the navy.

Why didn't you [do or say anything]?" He pressed: "Are you saying that you didn't oppose the war because Konoe should have instead?" Oikawa feebly defended himself: "How could the navy have contained [the hard-liners] when the prime minister could not?"

Inoue felt it would have been well within Oikawa's power to stop the march toward war. He could have quit his post, and the navy could have refused to appoint a new minister—who had to be chosen from admirals on active duty. The navy could then have delayed the deadline for war. That neither Oikawa nor other top navy leaders employed this tactic shows that regardless of what was said after the war, no one used his power—or courage—to resist a war he knew would be calamitous for Japan.

The liaison conference of October 4 accomplished nothing. The more time that passed, the greater the courage required for anyone to say no to war. On October 5, the navy held a top-level meeting between the ministry and the general staff and managed to agree that "with unflinching resolve, the prime minister should meet the army minister," in order to "discuss with him the extension of the time limit for [U.S.-Japan diplomatic] negotiations and relaxation of our conditions [to the United States]." Vice Minister Sawamoto had originally suggested that the prime minister, army minister, navy minister, and foreign minister should attend the conference, but Oikawa was reluctant to take part, presumably because he did not want to be seen as the sole opponent of going to war.

Oikawa's fear was not unwarranted. The Army General Staff now mistakenly believed that Konoe had come to support the war option, simply because he hadn't expressed strong opposition. The army's middle-ranking *bakuryo* strategists, now gearing themselves up for war, attacked Oikawa for the navy's seeming indecision. The October 5 entry of the War Guidance Office journal conveyed their feelings:

> The prime minister appears to have decided for war. He is holding separate meetings with his key ministers this evening. There are those among us in the general staff who are all excited and feel relieved. Our only enemy is the navy minister.

Konoe met with Tojo early that evening to try to talk him out of war. The venue was Konoe's favorite private villa, Tekigaiso, on the western outskirts of metropolitan Tokyo with a scenic view of Mount Fuji. He liked to conduct his most intimate political business there. This, however, was to be

Tojo's show from beginning to end. "The United States demands us to leave the Tripartite Pact, to embrace its Four Principles unconditionally, and to stop our military occupation. Japan cannot stomach all these," Tojo said.

"The central issue is troop withdrawal [from China]. Why not agree to withdrawal in principle but leave some troops for the purpose of protecting resources?" said Konoe.

"That sort of thing is called scheming," Tojo said.

Konoe, exasperated, changed his tactics. "Let us consider the atmosphere of the imperial conference," he said, referring to Hirohito's hesitation when he read the poem. He asked if Tojo thought a war with Britain could be fought without inviting U.S. involvement. The idea had surfaced of late in certain parts of the navy, betraying their fundamental unwillingness to confront the United States. Tojo rebuffed Konoe. He said that "after a great deal of research," the high command had already reached the unequivocal conclusion that "from the perspective of naval strategies, a separate war could not be fought."

Both armed services held independent meetings the next day, October 6, without discussing Japan's readiness for war. At the top level, Sugiyama saw Tojo in the evening and confirmed his opposition to conceding to any of the U.S. demands, while insisting on committing the government to an October 15 diplomatic deadline. They agreed that the Army General Staff should "categorically" stop the navy's possible attempt to "back out of war."

The navy's top-level meeting was attended by the navy minister and vice minister, the chief and vice chief of the Navy General Staff, and the chief of the Navy Ministry's Military Affairs Bureau. Nagano was brought up to speed on the last meeting, which he'd missed. Their evasive public attitude notwithstanding, the navy leaders had managed to form a broad consensus the previous day that it was "folly to start a war with the United States." Furthermore, they agreed "in principle" to a withdrawal of Japanese forces "from the parts [of China] where peace and stability were assured, one by one." This would surely enrage the army. According to Vice Minister Sawamoto, Oikawa was

half coaxing himself to make up his own mind and half talking to the chief of staff [Nagano] for encouragement when he said: "Is it all right, then, that I venture to have a quarrel with the army?" To this, Nagano answered: "I doubt the wisdom of it." This put a brake on the navy minister's decision, which had taken him considerable courage to reach, and spoiled the atmosphere of heightened [antiwar] morale in an instant.

Oikawa's weakness of character was clear for all to see. He'd gotten to his present position by not making enemies and by the default of seniority when his predecessor, Yoshida Zengo, became ill. It took only Nagano's vague opposition to dampen Oikawa's courage because he was diffident about confronting the army in the first place. And nobody else tried to help Oikawa regain his ground.

The army's War Guidance Office log of October 6 reporting on a joint army/navy meeting of midlevel officers, summarized where things stood:

The army and navy are still in disagreement. The army is saying that there is no hope [for diplomacy]. The navy still thinks there is hope, saying that if [the army] would only reconsider the question of military occupation [and withdraw troops from China and Indochina], there would be hope. We are left to wonder what the Navy General Staff is thinking [by suggesting such nonsense]. It was only the day before yesterday, at the liaison conference, that [Nagano] declared there was no longer any time for "discussion." But what now? . . . The navy is an enigma. . . . One cannot but feel anger [at the navy's suggestion]. . . . [One navy division chief says] he anticipates the loss of 1.4 million tons of vessels. . . . [Another] wonders if there is a way to avoid attacking the Philippines [so as to avoid risking U.S. intervention]. What are they talking about at this stage? The navy is selfishly trying to nullify the sacrosanct decision made at the imperial conference. Unspeakable! How irresponsible the navy is! How untrustworthy! The navy is actually destroying our nation!

Though it is hard to judge how representative this staff officer's views were of the entire army, what is clear is that there were serious interservice tensions.

The navy's unusually frank admission in this forum was made by the chief of its Operations Division, Fukudome Shigeru:

As far as losses of ships are concerned, [it is believed that] 1.4 million tons will be sunk in the first year of the war. The results of the new war games conducted by the Combined Fleet [show] that there will be no ships left for civilian requirements in the third year of the war. I have no confidence [in this war].

The following day, October 7, the ministers of the two armed services finally came face-to-face. In a cabinet meeting, Tojo announced: "I know it is painful to your ears, but I must say this. Today's economy is not a normal economy. Nor is the current state of diplomacy. . . . It should be our top priority now to fight our way through." He then conferred with Oikawa one on one. He insisted, as Sugiyama had, that the army would not allow Japan to accept Hull's Four Principles. Nor would it be possible, in his view, for Japan to withdraw troops from China entirely or immediately.

Oikawa suggested that it was the army that should reconsider its uncompromising posture. He pointed out that the U.S. proposal of October 2 was not as rigid as it appeared on paper and that there was still hope for a diplomatic settlement. Tojo asked specifically if the navy had not changed its mind about the September 6 imperial conference resolution. Oikawa replied: "No, our mind hasn't changed. As far as our resolve for war is concerned, we've still got it." Perhaps for Oikawa, "resolve for war" did not automatically lead to war. It was an evasive and dangerous attitude nonetheless, especially when Tojo was seeking straightforward clarification.

Tojo did not let Oikawa off the hook. Should a war actually come to pass, he pressed, did the navy minister have confidence in victory? Oikawa now replied with some measure of honesty, revealing his *honne* (true voice): "That, I am afraid, I do not have. . . . If the war continues for a few years, we do not know what the outcome would be. . . . What I have said should not go beyond this room."

Tojo, the foremost proponent of war within the year, now became surprisingly conciliatory. "If the navy is not confident," Tojo told Oikawa, "we must reconsider it. What must be reversed must be reversed, though it of course has to be done with the humble admission of our greatest responsibilities." This meant that the responsible ministers in the cabinet should all resign.

However awkwardly and uneasily, the navy and army ministers were getting closer to the elusive heart of the matter: Japan—most vitally the navy—was not ready to fight the war mapped out by the hastily passed resolution of early September. But just as this tenuous meeting of the minds was emerging between the two ministers, Navy Chief of Staff Nagano continued to talk tough; next to him, as we've seen, Oikawa was regarded as timid and overcautious. When Nagano met his army counterpart, Sugiyama, that day, Nagano pushed harder for war. But even he could not help occasionally revealing his doubts:

NAGANO: I don't think matters can be settled diplomatically. But if the Foreign Ministry thinks that there is still hope, I am in favor of continuing negotiations. . . . That doesn't change our belief that October 15 should be the day of decision for war or peace. [At the same time] we must be careful not to miss any strategic opportunities. . . . [We must prepare for war as we negotiate because] we wouldn't be able to fight if [the government leaders] came to us [later] and said: "We have tried our best with diplomacy, and we didn't succeed. Now it's your turn. . . ."

SUGIYAMA: But am I to understand that the navy is not confident about war?

NAGANO: What? Not confident about war? That is not true. Of course, we have never said that victory is assured. I've told the emperor this too, but we are saying that there is a chance of winning for now. As far as the future is concerned, the question of victory or defeat will depend on the total combination of material and psychological strengths. . . . If you follow the navy minister's belief that it would be difficult to fight, well, that kind of attitude would put to question the need for any military preparations. . . . As far as the deadline for deciding between war or no war is concerned, the navy wouldn't mind extending it a bit. . . . But that's not the army's position, is it? You seem to be charging right ahead.

SUGIYAMA: That's not true. We are going about it very cautiously. . . .

NAGANO: It's not for nothing that the emperor reached the September 6 decision. . . . We musn't now hesitate to pour more soldiers into southern French Indochina.

SUGIYAMA: I agree with you completely.

That evening, Tojo again saw Konoe at Tekigaiso. This was the meeting that Oikawa had insisted Konoe conduct alone. As he had two nights previously, Konoe suggested that if Japan would agree to a troop withdrawal from China in principle—the timing would depend on the actual field conditions—diplomacy might succeed. "We absolutely cannot do that," responded Tojo. Konoe pointed out again that in his mind the question of troop withdrawal stood as the major obstacle to peace:

> As far as the Four Principles are concerned, we should accept the principle of equal opportunities. There are, of course, special interests in China due to our geographical proximity, but that could be acknowledged, I believe, by the United States. As for the Tripartite Pact, to pledge [Japan's withdrawal from the pact] on paper would be difficult, but I am optimistic that something could be worked out in a direct meeting with the president. There remains only the question of military occupation. Could one not go easier on military occupation and not call it that? What would you do if this question alone became the stumbling block of the negotiations? Can we not find a way to stick to the substance of military occupation and still agree to troop withdrawal?

Tojo responded that the overall problem was much more difficult than Konoe tried to make it sound. Tojo thought it was wishful to think that the United States would agree to Japan's special regional interests in regard to China. Besides, he refused to voluntarily commit the army to such a huge concession when all other issues, including the realization of a summit meeting itself, were in doubt. To this, Konoe could say only: "Military men take wars too lightly."

Tojo insisted that the September 6 resolution was sacrosanct and that the October 15 deadline had to be honored. "You say that military men take wars too lightly. Occasionally," Tojo said in one of his most memorable (and previously cited) utterances, "one must conjure up enough courage, close one's eyes, and jump off the platform of the Kiyomizu." Jumping into the abyss was all well and good if one were talking only about oneself, Konoe responded, "but if I think of the national polity that has lasted twenty-six hundred years and of the hundred million Japanese belonging to this nation, I, as a person in the position of great responsibility, cannot do such a thing."

Beneath his bravado, Tojo's doubts lingered. The following day, Oikawa visited him to find out how his meeting with Konoe had gone. "We've lost tens of thousands of lives over the China Incident. To withdraw [from China] seems an unbearable option," said Tojo, looking pained. "And yet if we do go to war with the United States, we will lose tens of thousands more. I am thinking about withdrawing troops, but I just cannot decide."

The most ironic aspect of Tojo's fixation with those who had perished in China was that senior Japanese commanding officers in China were strongly urging Japan to avoid war with the United States. In early October, the commander in chief of Japanese forces in China, General Hata Shunroku, dispatched an officer bearing his message to Tokyo. Hata argued that the Japanese nation had already been drained of its fighting resources and should therefore accept the U.S. demands and settle its war with China once and for all. Tojo was fully aware of the toll the China War was taking on Japan. But as his subsequent actions would repeatedly show, dead souls always seemed to count more for him than living ones.

Hull's damning postwar assessment of Tojo as "rather stupid" with a "small-bore, straight-laced, one-track mind" was not inaccurate, yet the reasons for Tojo's internal conflict in the fall of 1941 were slightly more complex. As a professional soldier, he considered troop withdrawal a humiliating defeat. His inflexible way of being and set of principles kept him from allowing Japan to accept Hull's Four Principles. Most damagingly, Tojo—and most other military colleagues alike—did not seem to understand how provisional international understandings worked, that practical details were often fudged. Or he was simply incapable of diverging from his precise military way of life.

OCTOBER 12, Konoe's fiftieth birthday, was no festive occasion. Still tempted to resign at any moment, the prime minister decided to make one last attempt to buy time for diplomacy by holding a conference with the foreign minister, the army minister, the navy minister, and the general director of the Cabinet Planning Board, Suzuki Teiichi, a retired lieutenant general close to both Konoe and Tojo. In this small group, Konoe felt he had the best chance of making an impact.

At two o'clock in the afternoon, Konoe convened the meeting in the beautiful reception room of Tekigaiso. Though the house was built in a traditional Japanese style, the room's décor was eclectic. The furniture was Chinese, and the large windows, the door, and the ceiling were latticed in an art deco fashion. "We must continue to seek a diplomatic settlement," he told the attendees. "I have no confidence in a war such as this. If we were to start a war, it has to be done by someone who believes in it."

Oikawa kept his views vague and insisted that the decision to start—or stop—a war was entirely Konoe's. "We are at the crossroads of pursuing a diplomatic approach or war," he said. "The deadline is approaching. The prime minister has to decide. If he decides not to go to war, that would be fine by [the navy]."

As so many times in the recent past, Oikawa should have told his colleagues what he sincerely believed. Besides, he was wrong in relegating the decision to Konoe alone. Under the constitution, the prime minister did not have the executive prerogative to decide between war and peace—the whole cabinet had to agree. Especially because the success of Japanese operations against the Western allies depended on the navy, Oikawa's fact-based opposition would have carried tremendous weight. And, as the "radical liberal" Inoue would point out five years later, Oikawa had the power and responsibility to question the cabinet's war decision and, if necessary, to simply resign his post. It is no surprise that Oikawa, still again, could not in certain circles risk disgracing himself or the entire naval service.

Oikawa felt he could be evasive because he was convinced that Konoe would carry the ball. At half past midnight the night before the conference, two men had called on him at the navy minister's official residence so unexpectedly that he greeted them in his pajamas. They were Tomita Kenji, the chief cabinet secretary sent as Konoe's emissary, and Oka, the chief of the Navy Ministry's Military Affairs Bureau. Tomita said he hoped the navy would make a clear case against war so that the prime minister would not be put on the spot.

Oikawa, supported by Oka, dodged the issue. He told Tomita that the matter was essentially a "political" problem.

> It's not up to the military to say that we can or cannot go to war. That decision is a political one, to be made by the government. If the government decides on war, the military will have to follow, no matter how disadvantageous that war may be. Tomorrow, at the conference, I will repeat that, as the navy minister, I will go along with any decision the prime minister makes. . . . Prince Konoe would then have to take charge, stating that he would like [diplomatic] negotiations to continue and [to stop the war preparations].

When Oikawa hit the ball back into Konoe's court at the conference, he believed the navy had given Konoe carte blanche to declare that the war option had to be abandoned once and for all. He had told Konoe, at their secretive meeting in Kamakura, that the prince had to be "prepared to swallow" U.S. demands if he really wanted to give diplomacy a chance and that the navy would support his decision. Konoe may have had the desire to forestall the war, but he didn't have the nerve to say it. He also believed that ultimately it was the navy's responsibility, not his. That was why, at the very last minute, Konoe had asked Tomita to extract from Oikawa a clear commitment that the navy would directly intervene. Their dealings had turned into a bigger farce, courage utterly and devastatingly missing.

When Konoe could not pass the responsibility on to Oikawa, he had little else to say. The last thing on his mind at this small conference was to question his own wisdom in having endorsed the imperial conference decision. Foreign Minister Toyoda was the only one who came close to scrutinizing the subject. He faced up to their joint "mistake" and urged the continuation of diplomatic talks. "If I am allowed to be brutally frank, the imperial conference resolution [of September 6] was impetuous," he said. "We did it even though the relevant documents reached us only two days before [and decided it after only one liaison meeting]."

Now Tojo became vexed with Konoe. In response to Konoe's statement that he had "no confidence in a war such as this," Tojo barked at him: "You surprise me. What do you mean you have no confidence? Isn't that something you should have brought up when we decided on the 'Essentials for Carrying Out the Empire's Policies'?" Tojo insisted that the government had to stick to the September 6 resolution simply because it had been decided. He was, as ever, forceful in his indictment of others, not betraying for a moment the internal conflict he had recently revealed to Oikawa. He was showing his public face, his *tatemae*. "This is unbelievable!" he exclaimed. It was too late now to alter such an important and, most significant to him, "imperially sanctioned" resolution, regardless of the vaguely expressed imperial opinion.

This meeting would be remembered as the Tekigaiso Conference, known not for what it had achieved but for what it had not. October 15 was only three days away.

CHAPTER 11

A Soldier Takes Over

On January 11, 1941, the government issued, as a supplement to the National Mobilization Law, a set of regulations concerning newspapers and other media. Sensitive matters of military, diplomatic, and fiscal policies could no longer be officially written or spoken about, and there were detailed instructions regarding the coverage of resource shortages, weather forecasts (because of their potential strategic sensitivity), family problems (such as adultery committed by wives of soldiers fighting in China), and many other social topics that might obstruct successful mobilization on the home front. Though these rules certainly restricted newspaper reporting, freedom of the press in Japan was, and had been, nonexistent for some time.

As noted earlier, from the Manchurian Incident onward, major newspapers had been especially blatant in their support of state policies, appealing to patriotic fervor to compete in a fierce circulation war. When the Japanese invaded Manchuria, military men and journalists actively cultivated one another, drawing closer as more and more journalists were dispatched to the battlefront. Objective reporting was abandoned. The policy of selective reporting, concentrating on Japanese victories, continued after the outbreak of the China War, and by 1941, it had become impossible for the Japanese media to disentangle themselves from their dangerous liaison with the military.

The national radio monopoly NHK had always surpassed the newspapers in its self-conscious role as the mouthpiece of official policy. One day in May 1938, it aired what it touted as the first-ever live broadcast of a battle, from an unnamed site in Xuzhou in the eastern coastal province of Jiangsu in China. The announcer's excited voice echoed all over Japan, describing what was developing in front of him as "the hell of victory." In reality, the enemy forces had quickly retreated, and there had been little combat. But that was not what the listeners were told. "The fall of Xuzhou! The fall of Xuzhou! Dear listeners on the home front, it is, however, premature to hear your joyous cheers. The joy of victory still awaits us. Our greatest search-and-destroy mission goes on as I speak. So please, everyone back home, stay up all night tonight and pray for Japan's greatest victory!" Under the spell of this adrenaline-filled call, many gathered at the Yasukuni Shrine, forming a long line to say midnight prayers. This was a dress rehearsal for the greater radio announcement of the morning of December 8, 1941.

Not all media had been as overtly uncritical as NHK or the major newspapers. The so-called general magazines, appealing to middlebrow and highbrow audiences and usually published monthly, featured political commentaries as well as literary pieces. They now were especially vulnerable. Their publishers were given the names of banned liberal contributors and were made to submit a list of subscribers, in addition to the detailed outlines of upcoming issues, to be approved by the Information Division of the government. Magazines for children were no exception. Japan's young audience was dispirited in the fall of 1941 when a hugely successful ten-year-old cartoon serialized in a boys' magazine came to an abrupt end; the tales of the adventures and exploits of the stray-dog soldier Norakuro were deemed disrespectful to the military not so much because they were critical of Japanese militarism but because the soldiers were all animals.

The practical problem of obtaining paper also made publishing too difficult a business, forcing many magazines to close down. (Saionji Kinkazu, who edited a glossy photographic journal, ceased its publication earlier that year.) But some people seemed to manage. Kafu was surprised to see several new magazines advertised one day. "How utterly bizarre. Haven't they been telling us to save paper? Why new magazines now?" They all had fascist-sounding titles.

The all-female theater troupe Takarazuka, whose extremely popular repertoire included American-style revues, was now finding itself under tremendous pressure to produce more shows with patriotic themes. Its main attraction that fall was *Mothers of the Big Sky* (*Taiku no Haha*), a musical about women protecting their homes in the absence of their pilot husbands and sons.

But even in this climate of censorship, the Japanese love of certain things American continued unabated—and unchecked. In early October, an annual American football tournament was held in Tokyo. American films were still being shown in theaters, though less often. That wouldn't last for long.

RICHARD SORGE WAS a frequent customer at a fancy delicatessen in the Ginza with a basement dining room. On October 4, Sorge chose to celebrate his forty-sixth birthday there. The owner, August Lohmeyer, was a former German prisoner of war captured by the Japanese in the Battle of Qingdao, when Japan fought Germany alongside Britain in World War I. A sausage maker by training, Lohmeyer built a successful business selling an array of processed meats then still rare in Japan. Had it not been for the Great War, Lohmeyer, a peasant boy from Westphalia, would not have wound up in Japan. Had it not been for his disillusioning wartime experiences, Sorge, a bourgeois Berliner with a doctorate, would not have turned to communism and become a spy for the Soviet Union. Now war was very much on Sorge's mind again.

Sorge and Hanako were drinking cocktails at the bar when he spotted plainclothes detectives. It was not unusual for the Japanese police to have foreign journalists followed. But this night, Sorge was clearly alarmed by their presence. He took Hanako to a table in the back, where he whispered to her that Japan would soon attack the United States in a blitzkrieg.

"But Ambassador Nomura is an able man," Hanako protested, as if to say diplomacy would win out. Possessed of a literary penchant and romantic disposition that might have made her particularly oblivious to the tense political situation, she had no idea how bad things were between Japan and the United States. But her opinion of Nomura was reflective of the wishful thinking of the majority of Japanese.

"The United States has many things in abundance," Sorge had once told her. "Japan can never win. If Japan goes to war, defeat is a sure thing." Sorge was happy that Japan's acrimonious relationship with the United States at least made it certain that Japan would not attack the Soviet Union. He had accomplished his mission in the best way possible. "If the United States does not make any compromise by mid-October, Japan will attack the United States, and then Malaya, Singapore, and Sumatra as well," he said in an authoritative message he had dispatched to Moscow earlier that day. The Soviet Union was no longer an enemy in Japanese strategic thinking. After eight years, Sorge felt his mission was officially over. He decided he would ask Moscow if he could return to the Soviet Union or even to Germany.

After dinner, Sorge went to the German embassy to meet his "friends," including Ambassador Ott, to continue celebrating his birthday. Hanako watched him walk into the darkness. She would never see her lover again.

THINGS COULD NOT have looked worse for Konoe. He had led Japan to the brink of another war. His leadership challenged by Tojo, he focused on finding a way out for himself. The Roosevelt administration could hardly be blamed for its reluctance to trust Konoe. He had repeatedly failed to establish himself as a credible leader. There was a slim chance that a summit would prevent war, but it was understandable why the United States wanted to avoid the meeting.

Two days after the Tekigaiso Conference and only a day before the deadline for diplomacy, Tojo saw Konoe prior to a cabinet meeting. One last time, Konoe tried to convince Tojo to accept a troop withdrawal. Now, for a change, Konoe spoke frankly and openly, showing he felt he had nothing to lose. He said:

> I am greatly responsible for the China Incident. After four years, the incident has not ended. I simply cannot agree to starting yet another great war whose outlook is very vague. I suggest that we now concede to the U.S. withdrawal formula and avoid opening fire between Japan and the United States. We really need to end the China Incident. . . . Japan's future growth is doubtless desirable, but in order to make a great leap, we must sometimes concede [to greater forces] so that we can preserve and nurture our national strength.

"I believe the prime minister's argument is too pessimistic," Tojo responded unabashedly. "That's because we know our country's weak points all too well. But don't you see that the United States has its own weaknesses, too?" Tojo had already made up his mind that withdrawal, at least under the current government, was out of the question.

"It comes down to a difference in our opinions," Konoe replied. "I would insist that you reconsider."

"I would say it's a difference in our personalities," said Tojo with deep emotion.

In the cabinet meeting that followed, Tojo made a speech in an excessively affected fashion. It was archaic in tone and often employed the phrase "thus there exists." The formality of the speech was strangely effective in communicating the inflexibility of the army minister's position and the depth of his determination to end Konoe's leadership. The speech went as follows:

> With all due respect to the efforts of the foreign ministers to normalize relations during the six months since last April, I must say that we have reached a limit. If we were to continue with diplomacy, we must be sure of its success. . . . The army's actions have been based on the decision of the September 4 [sic] imperial conference. The decision followed sufficient deliberation by each cabinet minister. That decision dictated: "If diplomatic negotiations do not bear fruit by early October and there is still no likelihood of our demands getting through, we would make up our minds to go to war with the United States, Britain, and the Netherlands." Today is October 14. We mentioned early October. But it is already the fourteenth! . . . The army, with late October in mind, is mobilizing several hundred thousand troops, and we are in the process of moving soldiers from both China and Manchuria. . . . As we speak, they are moving! If there were to be a breakthrough in diplomacy . . . we would have to stop the movement [of troops]. I would like you to please consider how to proceed from here.

After the meeting, Tojo went to see Lord Keeper of the Privy Seal Kido in his office in the palace. He wanted to legitimize the case he was now openly making against Konoe and to push for his resignation. Tojo complained about the navy leaders' insistence that they had not changed their minds concerning September 6, despite Oikawa's perceptible diffidence. Tojo and Kido agreed that to avoid war they had to ensure that the next prime minister would move away from the problematic imperial resolution. Kido insisted that the army and the navy needed to stop quarrelling and act as one. Tojo, going right against the theatrical, hard-hitting prowar tone of the speech he had just delivered, said as much: "What has been decided has been decided, and we should simply stop wasting time trying to figure out who is to blame [for having endorsed the September 6 decision]." He felt that, at this late stage, they had to consider its actual feasibility.

Later that afternoon, when Tojo met Sugiyama in his office at the Army General Staff headquarters to report on his interview with Kido, he was still complaining about the conflicting messages he was getting from Oikawa as to the navy's readiness for war. "The navy minister doesn't say clearly that he is not confident," Tojo said, "but he certainly talks as if he hasn't got any confidence. If the navy doesn't want to [go to war], we must think of some other way."

So it had come to this: The navy would not say it did not want war, suggesting there was no need to articulate its unwillingness when the army seemed to fully comprehend the navy's hesitations. The army, which would bear the bulk of public humiliation of troop withdrawal in the case of diplomatic settlement, was accusing the navy of not clearly stating its opposition to the new war so that the army, too, would have to admit to weakness by saying it could not fight.

Tojo thought the easiest way to start anew was to put an end to Konoe's premiership. That evening, he sent the director of the Cabinet Planning Board, Suzuki Teiichi, to Konoe with a message asking him to make up his mind about quitting. Suzuki explained that because of the navy's diffidence regarding the prospects of war, the September 6 resolution had to be reversed. The correct procedure to bring that about, in Tojo's mind, was for the cabinet, which had presided over the decision, to own up to its complicity and resign. Tojo recommended that the next prime minister be the antiwar Higashikuni, who, ironically, had recently admonished Tojo for his dogged reluctance to extend support for diplomatic efforts and suggested, on Konoe's behalf, that he resign his army minister's post. The choice of Higashikuni divulged Tojo's new and surprising acceptance that the war option had to be discarded. Tojo felt only an imperial personage with military experience, like Prince Higashikuni, could possibly manage the reversal of the imperial decision of early September.

Tojo's suggestion appalled Privy Seal Kido, a man ever so dedicated to the imperial institution. With the death of Prince Saionji in late 1940, Kido now wielded a great deal of influence over the selection of the next prime minister. To Kido, the imperial institution unfailingly came before the national interest, a belief predicated on the circular argument that the imperial institution *was* Japan's national interest. Kido had no inclination to involve the empress's uncle in politics, especially at this very sensitive time.

A small man with a mustache and glasses, Kido looked the part of the perfect courtier, always clad formally and impeccably in dark suits. He lurked in the shadow of the emperor like a master puppeteer. Kido prided himself on being the guardian of the palace, which had been transformed in the second half of the nineteenth century to cater to the new needs of modern Japan. His grandfather Kido Takayoshi, a Choshu samurai and later a Meiji oligarch of high renown, had been instrumental in Japan's centralization under the emperor. It is often said that it takes three generations to make a gentleman. Marquis Kido, as a rightful third-generation gentleman, claimed to know what was best for the political system that his grandfather had so deftly helped to create.

Although considered a liberal influence on the emperor, Kido had, as the late prince Saionji had once noted, a right-leaning streak (after all, he supported Konoe's New Order Movement to centralize Japan in 1940). Perhaps he was simply overcompensating for not being a "real" aristocrat, like Konoe or Saionji, who could claim imperial ancestries going back over a thousand years. Whatever his pedigree, he had become the gatekeeper of the palace. He would not allow Higashikuni to assume Japan's premiership.

Throughout the turmoil, the Breakfast Club of Konoe's advisers continued to meet. On October 15, its members gathered in a restaurant to enjoy a lunch of grilled eel—a luxury at any time, but especially now. Ozaki Hotsumi was conspicuously late. As the others started to eat without him, Konoe's secretary, Kishi Dozo, burst into the private dining room. "I've got some awful news!" he shouted. "Ozaki's been arrested. They say he's been charged with spying."

THE JAPANESE POLICE HAD no idea about the existence of Sorge's international spy ring before they arrested the painter Miyagi Yotoku. Originally from Okinawa, Miyagi spent his adolescent years in California and became attracted to Marxist-Leninist doctrine while attending art school. He joined the Communist Party of the United States of America, which then dispatched him to Japan. There he operated on the periphery of Sorge's group. He was arrested on October 10 because of his connection to another Japanese member of the party who had been implicated in underground activities unrelated to Sorge's work. Miyagi unsuccessfully tried to commit suicide by jumping from the window of his second-floor interrogation room. Then he confessed everything, including his work for Sorge's group, which led to Ozaki's arrest.

The accusation that one of the better known and more popular intellectuals in Konoe's intimate circle was a communist and a spy shocked the prime minister and those around him. It would have taken someone much stronger than Konoe to stand up to the inevitable criticism. (Given the press censorship, Ozaki's activities would not be made public until June 1942.) Konoe resigned the post of prime minister the next day, October 16.

Actually, Konoe's mind had already been made up. He was weary of being charged with the responsibility to reverse the September 6 decision and was unable to face the possibility of war with the United States under his leadership. No matter how he or his cohorts tried to justify his exit and win sympathy for his frustrations, he had clearly failed, and failed miserably. His blue blood and intellectual background had proved no guarantee of effective leadership. Konoe retained his premiership by keeping his thoughts to himself, often agreeing to proposals that he did not embrace, in the hope that things would get fixed in a less confrontational, more furtive manner, without his having to dirty his hands.

Konoe had switched his political creeds with alarming facility between right and left, ostensibly to create a stronger and more united Japan. He had been prime minister for nearly three of the preceding four years of Japan's looming international crisis, during which an unwinnable war with China escalated and an improbable war with the West became a "legitimate" policy alternative carrying the seal of imperial approval.

As cabinet changes were being planned in high secrecy, young subjects of the empire were made to feel the urgency of Japan's situation in a very practical sense. The Ministry of Health and Welfare announced a "patriotic marriages" campaign to help the China War effort. On October 9, fifty or so bureaucrats, academics, physicians, and educators gathered in the ministry's conference room and for the entire afternoon discussed the goals to be achieved. In the end, they agreed on the need to lower the average age of first marriages by three years for men and four years for women, and encourage couples to have more than five children; to eliminate feudal notions of marriage based on family pedigrees and fortunes; and to simplify marriage-related celebrations and lower their cost.

Of all the problems highlighted that day, the increasing tendency to marry late, especially in women, was deemed most grievous. On October 10, the *Asahi* published an article on this conference entitled "Let Us Marry to March!" in which the well-known female doctor and activist Takeuchi Shigeyo echoed the patriotic sentiment:

> Parents tend to be overprotective of their daughters. . . . They tend to keep their girls at home for a few years after they finish school, in order to train them in domestic skills like flower arranging, sewing, and just generally keeping the house. But that kind of training should be done while they are still in school so that they can get married right after graduation. School education, especially in domestic science, should not be focused so much on teaching them how to cook Western-style meals. First and foremost, educators must realize that it is imperative to teach them how to cook nutritious vegetable-rich meals economically.

It didn't take expert commentary like this to know that Japan's traditional social arrangements—especially in courtship and marriage—were rapidly breaking down in a time of crisis. One day in early October, Kafu chatted with an elderly man about some of those changes. The man said that during the Russo-Japanese War, people were not expected to send care packages to soldiers they didn't know. Nowadays, as a result of the formation of neighborhood associations, the practice had become compulsory, and people were required to enclose a letter of moral support in each package bound for China. (It was not for nothing that the care packages were selling so well in department stores. They had become the most immediate link between the home and war fronts and an obvious symbol of one's patriotism. A melodramatic story of a soldier dying in combat as he held the pebbles from the Imperial Palace's plaza that had come in his care package won first prize in a nationwide literary competition in September.)

Such letter writing was vigorously encouraged in schools, too, Kafu was told, and young female students sometimes ended up corresponding with soldiers unbeknownst to their parents. This led to all sorts of problems, including unrequited love, stalking, and incompatible unions of those who would otherwise never have met (that is, of course, if the soldier was lucky enough to come home alive). Soldiers were just as vulnerable as young girls, as some women took advantage of the new social opportunities. Bar hostesses and others in the service sector were known to send support letters in the hope of acquiring future clients. Kafu, who had cultivated a sort of obsessive admiration for women on the margin of society, was impressed by their survival instincts.

IN THE MIDAFTERNOON of October 17, Tojo received a telephone call from the palace, requesting his presence immediately. This was an intimidating summons. Tojo suspected that he was going to be admonished by Hirohito for his part in bringing down the Konoe cabinet. "Minister, you cornered Prince Konoe. . . . You said you would quit the post of army minister if a troop withdrawal from China was mentioned," said Sato Kenryo, Tojo's close aide and the hard-line section chief of the Army Ministry's Military Affairs Bureau. "That's why His Majesty is about to admonish you."

"I dare not argue with His Imperial Majesty," said Tojo. "Whatever he says is final."

Tojo was aware that as an army minister he, too, had been a critical part of the failed Konoe government. For the September 6 imperial resolution to be reversed honorably, the government that had proposed it had to be dismantled completely. Tojo had already started to move out of the army minister's official residence, sending his belongings back to his private home in a Tokyo suburb.

With a heavy heart but fully prepared, Tojo came face-to-face with Hirohito at 5:00 p.m. He was stunned when the emperor nominated him as the next prime minister of Japan. The nominee for the premiership was traditionally supposed to reply: "Let me please have a little time to accept the command." But even those few words escaped Tojo. Hirohito covered for his subject's embarrassing silence: "Let us give you a little while to think it over." This was, of course, a rubber-stamping formality.

It was all happening so fast. The day before, Konoe and his entire cabinet had resigned. This very day, a conference of senior statesmen was hastily convened to discuss prime ministerial candidates. The conference was instituted less than ten years before to fill the vacuum left by the deaths of the Meiji oligarchs, who'd effectively run Japan's modern state. It was attended mostly by former prime ministers, and they were meant to advise and assist the palace in its selection of the next premier. They were surprised when Kido announced: "Under the circumstances, we must try to unify the policies of the army and the navy and, moreover, to reexamine the September 6 imperial conference decision. From that perspective, I insist that Army Minister Tojo be appointed the next prime minister."

No one openly objected, according to Kido. He was acting on his belief that one should "pick a thief to catch a thief." Because Tojo was the person who had insisted on the sanctity of the September 6 imperial conference resolution, Kido thought it best to have him take charge of the difficult task of reversing it. But Tojo's professional loyalties and institutional obligations rested with the military. The logic behind making the most publicly bellicose voice of the preceding cabinet Japan's next prime minister in order to avoid war was certainly questionable. Besides, the problematic imperial decision was a collaborative one made by the cabinet *and* the high command. If the government had to own up to its share of the responsibility for September 6, so did the two chiefs of staff. Kido made no effort to have either Sugiyama or Nagano dismissed to create a clean break.

Contrary to Kido's record of the unanimous acceptance of Tojo, some of those senior statesmen present at the October 17 conference seconded Higashikuni or another army candidate, General Ugaki Kazushige, as Japan's next premier. None, however, delivered as forceful an argument as Kido did for Tojo. Kido had prevailed, and the emperor, who placed utmost trust in Kido, effected Tojo's nomination. "No pain, no gain, wouldn't you say?" the emperor said to Kido. The comment was a reference to the Chinese proverb "One must enter the tiger's den in order to catch his cubs." The tiger's den was presumably Japan's high command, filled with restless, bloodthirsty warmongers. The cubs were a metaphor for Japan's peaceful settlement of the crisis with the United States.

Kido made sure that the army and navy were in no doubt about the true reason for Tojo's surprise appointment, made to "wipe the slate clean." He summoned Oikawa to the palace and spoke to him and Tojo in the waiting room of the salon where Tojo had just accepted the imperial nomination.

> I gather that you [Tojo] have now received the imperial words concerning the need for the army and navy to cooperate. I must stress that it is the emperor's wish that in formulating the nation's policy, you would not be a slave to the September 6 imperial resolution. You must consider both domestic and external situations, deeply and broadly. The emperor wishes you to take a cautious approach.

Upon leaving the palace, Tojo directed his car first to the Meiji Shrine, then to the Togo Shrine (built in honor of the Russo-Japanese War hero Admiral Togo Heihachiro, who defeated the czar's Baltic Fleet), and finally to the Yasukuni Shrine (where the souls of soldiers who died in the empire's past wars were enshrined). After an hour or so of hopping between shrines in central Tokyo, Tojo returned to the army minister's official residence. The news of his appointment had already reached the members of his staff, who congratulated him. But Japan's new prime minister was in no mood to celebrate. He realized the enormity of the task he now faced. That evening, in his absurdly principled way, he ordered that no one from the army should enter his office, which he now declared to be purely civilian territory. He made telephone calls in an effort to fill ministerial positions. He appointed himself army minister and home minister. Then he tapped Togo Shigenori, the veteran diplomat who had served as the ambassador to the Soviet Union, to be his foreign minister.

Togo, a sixty-year-old dandy with copious graying hair, was married to a German woman and had once wished to become a German literature scholar. He was averse to Nazism; his brief tenure as an ambassador to Germany from 1937 to 1938 was terminated partly because of his frosty relationship with Foreign Minister Joachim von Ribbentrop. Neither pro-Anglo-American nor pro-Axis, Togo was a genuine Japanese patriot. He wore his patriotism on his sleeve perhaps because he felt that no matter how successful he was in his professional career, he was vulnerable to being labeled an outsider. Born as Park Shigenori in Kagoshima, a southwestern city on the southern island of Kyushu, he came from a long line of Korean potters who were forcibly brought to Japan at the end of the sixteenth century and had remarkably preserved their language and culture over many generations. His father, a successful businessman, bought the Japanese family name Togo when Shigenori was five. (Contrary to popular belief, Togo was no relation to Admiral Togo, the Nelson of the East.)

On the whole, Togo was a much more reasonable and sensible choice than Toyoda, the departing foreign minister, had been. He was an experienced diplomat whose skills could be put to good use. Togo had his reservations. Before midnight, he went to see Tojo and asked whether the would-be premier was ready to make difficult concessions to avoid war. The stiff army man responded to the suave diplomat that things were very different now. "I do not have any problem reexamining the issue once again," Tojo said. The reexamination implied extracting concessions from the army, including the withdrawal of already mobilized troops, in order to give the new foreign minister more room for diplomatic maneuver with the United States. Upon this pledge of honor, the unlikely Tojo-Togo team was born.

Tojo's top candidates for finance minister and navy minister also wanted to be assured that the new prime minister was committed to averting war with the United States. Kaya Okinori was satisfied and undertook to manage the economy. Shimada Shigetaro, known for his antiwar stance, required much persuasion but finally became navy minister.

THAT SAME DAY, October 17, Richard Sorge was fast asleep when he was suddenly awakened at 6:00 a.m. by a vaguely familiar voice calling his name from outside. While riding his motorcycle, Sorge had gotten into a traffic accident and through its settlement had become acquainted with a policeman named Saito. Now Saito was yelling: "Mr. Sorge! It's Saito from the police department here. I came because of the other day."

When Sorge opened the door, he was greeted by a different voice exclaiming in German: "I am a public prosecutor. With this warrant, I am arresting you!" The German was surrounded by a squad of ten or so Japanese police officers. Sorge's hands were securely cuffed. His spy ring associates Vukelic and Clausen were arrested that day as well. Sorge and some others had been preparing to leave Japan for good.

Even with the news of more arrests of foreign spies, Saionji Kinkazu remained adamantly in denial. He refused to believe any of the charges against Ozaki or that his friend was connected with Sorge. Ozaki's misfortune had to be somehow linked to the fall of the Konoe cabinet, Saionji told himself, and concluded that Ozaki was a victim of some kind of political conspiracy.

Saionji, who considered Tojo the man least fit to keep his country out of war, went to see him on the first morning of his premiership. "I have three things to say to you," Saionji said. "One, you must not make Japan into a police state. Two, you must hurry to make peace with China. Three, you must see to the success of the U.S.-Japan negotiations." Tojo was smugly calm. The emperor had bestowed upon him the leadership of his divine nation. This descendant of rebels who had fought against the court in the Boshin War had come a very long way indeed. "Mr. Saionji, thank you for your advice," Tojo said with frosty politeness. "I shall have my secretary contact you from now on."

Less than a year earlier, Saionji's grandfather was still alive, the most venerated man in the country after the emperor. Now his onetime protégé, Konoe, the man who'd inadequately filled his shoes, had fallen, and Saionji's grandson with him. Not so long before, Tojo had complained to

Konoe that people like Saionji Kinkazu, the journalist Matsumoto Shige-haru, and the now incarcerated Ozaki—the Breakfast Clubbers—should not be meddling in Japan's political decisions. Konoe had defended his friends, and Tojo had to let the matter drop. Now the tables had turned.

Tojo infelicitously began a routine of checking the contents of ordinary citizens' household rubbish on his morning strolls. This was meant as a publicity stunt to make sure that the ration system was working properly and equitably, that there was enough to eat and, moreover, that people were eating well. (Tojo looked for signs of "good" food waste, such as fish bones.) Some Japanese thought it admirable that a prime minister should take in such minor details. But most were put off, and they would give their new prime minister a thankless nickname: the Dumpster Minister.

CHAPTER 12

Winding Back the Clock

From October 23 to 30, Tojo convoked one liaison conference after another to reconsider the September 6 resolution. Essential concerns ignored in preceding conferences, including the feasibility of total war and its possible impact on Japan's economy, were on the agenda. Unlike before, the finance minister, Kaya, and the general director of the Cabinet Planning Board, Suzuki, attended those conferences; economic consequences of a possible war were finally to be addressed in an open forum. The most boisterous voices calling for war preparations—the chiefs and vice chiefs of staff—were still very much in evidence.

In these more ambitious liaison meetings of late October, there were assessments of the wars in Europe and China, the U.S.-Japan diplomatic negotiations, and the wisdom of Japan's remaining a German ally. At the first such meeting during Tojo's leadership, on October 23, Foreign Minister Togo challenged the assumption of eventual German victory. He did not mince his words:

> Britain has gained some time and room because of the German war with the Soviet Union. Next year, the prospect [of German victory over Britain] will be fifty-fifty. The year after that, I believe the odds favor a victory for Britain. Germany will want a peace settlement sooner rather than later. But Japan should not formulate its policy counting on such a peace.

In fact, Togo deemed it highly unlikely that Germany would be able to extract a peaceful settlement from Britain. The Navy General Staff believed the Germans would probably have a difficult time fighting Britain on land but said that Germany might defeat Britain in the air and at sea. An army representative (exactly who is not recorded) added: "[A German invasion of Britain] would be difficult but not impossible." Such a truism hardly contributed to a meaningful discussion. It was this kind of thinking that could allow such unhelpful statements as "Japan's winning a war against the United States would be difficult but not impossible."

Nagano, who had commented earlier that it was "no longer a time for discussion," reiterated his view:

> We've passed the [original early] October deadline already. Why don't you simply finish this kind of study meeting? Every hour, we are expending four hundred tons of petroleum. The situation is urgent. You must decide quickly whether or not we are going to war.

His counterpart, Army Chief of Staff Sugiyama, agreed. "We have already been dragged along for a month. We cannot bear to spend another four or five days studying this subject. Do it quickly!"

Tojo's position, as we've seen, was far more nuanced and complicated now. He was torn between his roles as army minister (which meant he was still on active military duty), prime minister, and home minister. "I do understand the strong argument made by the high command for a swift decision," Tojo said in an effort to conciliate the chiefs of staff. "But this government includes some new ministers, such as the navy, finance, and foreign ministers, [and for their sake] we must thoroughly explore [the issues at stake] so that we can fully own up to the responsibility [for our ultimate decision]."

Kaya stood his ground in the face of the combined general staffs' insistence that war preparations should simply go ahead because time and resources were running out. At fifty-two, Kaya was relatively young for a key minister, though his deportment made him seem older. In fact, he shared certain physical resemblances with Togo, who had a square face, a full head of swept-back hair, and a thick mustache. Togo, though, was slim and elegant; Kaya was round, and suffered from facial tics.

Kaya was not a man to be taken lightly. As a Finance Ministry bureaucrat, he had developed expertise in the National Budget Bureau and had attended a couple of international arms reduction conferences in the 1920s as the ministry's delegate. The son of a nationalistic father and a hawkish mother, he had nevertheless been a staunch believer in international treaties and liberal internationalism in his early days. In 1929, in London during the preliminary round of the London Naval Conference scheduled for the following year, he quarreled with Yamamoto Isoroku, who was representing the navy and had yet to be converted to the credo of arms reduction. During the 1930s, however, his and Yamamoto's political beliefs were reversed to a certain extent. An ambitious man, Kaya, as finance minister in Konoe's first cabinet, helped turn the Japanese economy into a wartime one after the China War broke out; he also supported Konoe's New Order Movement for increased centralization. Yamamoto, meanwhile, became more and more accepting of the general trend toward liberal internationalism and criticized Konoe's perilous flirtation with totalitarian philosophy.

Whatever his political views, Kaya was not about to approve of a war that did not make any sense to him numbers-wise. "Could you explain to me in a way that I can understand?" was the first of Kaya's insistent queries in those late-October conferences.

My questions are, What would happen to the material situation if we go to war? What would happen if we do not go to war and carry on just as we are carrying on right now? What should we do if diplomatic negotiations with the United States fail? Et cetera, et cetera. These are the issues we need to concentrate on now. I believe the question of the budget is not our biggest concern. Matters regarding the budget could be settled once the relationship between demand and supply of materials becomes clearer [depending on which course Japan takes and the amount of resources that are available].

Kaya's questions were straightforward enough. But they were most difficult to answer for those who built their prowar argument on a series of convenient assumptions that included Germany's continued predominance in Europe as well as Japan's ability to secure *and* transport sufficient materials from Southeast Asia once the war in the Pacific began. What if these assumptions did not stand?

Other than marking the first day of Tojo's efforts to revisit the question of going to war, October 23 was a symbolic day for Japan at the crossroads. The North Pacific Fur Seal Convention, an important endeavor in liberal internationalism of an earlier era, came to an end that day at Japan's initiative. The treaty, signed by the United States, Britain, Japan, and Russia in 1911, limited the harvest of furred sea mammals. Caring about the fate of seals was asking too much of a nation-state that could not even ensure the safety of its own citizens. Gone were the days when Japan aspired to be a model citizen of the world.

AT THE LIAISON MEETINGS of October 24 and 25, the Navy General Staff continued to maintain that the initial battles in a war with the United States could be won but that victory would ultimately depend on the international situation and the psychological strength of the Japanese nation. There appeared to be a general awareness that the enemy could not be conquered by military force alone; that would somehow have to happen through diplomacy. Ironies and contradictions abounded: A war was to be declared because diplomacy could not deliver a satisfactory outcome for Japan at present, and yet once the war began, diplomacy would have to be quickly reintroduced to end it because Japan did not have sufficient resources for a drawn-out conflict. And this diplomatic settlement would hopefully be initiated by a United States shaken and intimidated enough by early Japanese victories to sue for peace.

But what if the United States refused to succumb, as Yamamoto had already warned Nagano was more likely? What if Japan's military offensive made the United States more resolute, like Britain against Hitler? No reasonable attempt to debate or answer these uncomfortable questions is to be found in the record of these conferences.

The prowar argument, no matter how it was presented, required self-delusion and false accounting to make Japan seem prepared for a drawn-out war. Inconvenient numbers were brushed aside. The lack of critical debate over Japan's projected shipping losses is a telling example. Needless to say, any loss of ships affects a warring country's immediate fighting and convoying abilities, especially in a predominantly naval war. But the estimation of wartime losses allowed for creative distortion. In preparing new data to be presented at the late-October liaison meetings, the chief of the Army Ministry's Resource Office, Nakahara Shigetoshi, was astonished when he first saw the navy estimates predicting enormous losses. With numbers like that, he felt, Japan couldn't start, let alone fight, a war. The next day, the navy came back with new estimates. These numbers satisfied the two chiefs of staff and served as the basis of the high command's argument for war throughout Tojo's reexamination. The projected annual losses for the first three years of war averaged 700,000 tons. Three years in, Japan could fully compensate for the losses, it was said. (As it turned out, Japan's shipping losses would surpass its shipbuilding capacity by 4 million tons after the first three years of the war.)

The chiefs of staff did not question the reliability of the numbers that had emerged literally overnight. Instead, Nagano used them to the navy's advantage, ignoring the bigger question of what good a strong navy was if Japan lost the war. Nagano declared:

> For the navy to be able to keep fighting a long war, the replenishment of naval power is very important, and so is the acquisition of strategic resources. In order to sustain our positions in the critical area in the south, the navy would require, at all times, a thousand bomber planes, a thousand fighter planes, and another thousand planes for the defense of those areas.

Nagano didn't get into the question of Japan's practical ability to replenish its losses, including the loss of well-trained pilots, who were almost impossible to replace quickly. The navy had been compelled to concentrate on training a small number of elite pilots. The United States, on the other hand, had the resources and capacity to train many pilots to passable fighting standards and to produce hundreds of thousands of planes. The relative advantage for the United States would be only too clear the longer the war lasted. These realities did not seem to trouble Nagano, at least on the surface.

Kaya wasn't so cavalier. In the meeting of October 27, he tried to direct the leaders' attention to these fundamental issues. When Suzuki was invited to share his views, he immediately admitted to Japan's dire material situation:

> Japan has not established a defensive system, has no long-term plans for material sustenance of the state, and has dealt with the distribution of materials on a year-by-year basis. . . . That is the truth of our material situation. For 1942, we project the material supply to be 90 percent of what it was for this year. . . . That would mean depleting all the present stocks.

Suzuki said that Japan would have a hard time sustaining a conflict materially but stopped short of voicing definitive objection to the war. He could have made better use of the figures at hand to make a powerful case against it. In 1940, the Cabinet Planning Board had compared the industrial outputs of Japan and the United States. According to its research, the United States produced more than five hundred times as much petroleum, twelve times as much pig iron, nine times as much steel ingot and copper, and seven times as much aluminum as Japan. Including other areas of production, such as coal, mercury, zinc, and lead, the average industrial output of the United States was thought to be more than seventy-four times (whereas the army had estimated more optimistically twenty times) that of Japan. These overwhelming figures were at the time available even to a junior researcher working for a steel manufacturer. Presumably, Suzuki had more detailed, up-to-date figures than these, which alone would have forced most leaders to confront the hard realities. Yet Suzuki did not present them. Later, when he was ninety-three, Suzuki tried to explain why: "I was depressed. . . . It was as though they had already decided to go to war. My task was basically to provide numbers to fit that decision. But in my mind, I didn't want [Japan] to go to war."

Suzuki was initially seen as a key figure in Tojo's attempt to reexamine the September 6 decision, having been asked personally by Konoe to remain in his post after the prince's departure. But Suzuki quickly concluded that he was too powerless to effect a policy shift and chose to side with what he regarded as mainstream opinion. As an army partisan (he was a recently retired lieutenant general) and a deft political operator, he was also annoyed that he was expected, implicitly, to save the navy's neck by suggesting that the war could not be fought successfully. In the same postwar interview, Suzuki said as much: "The navy should have been the one to decide [against war] in the end, because it was the navy who had to fight it. But the navy refused to say clearly it could not!"

So Suzuki simply skated over Kaya's questions, explaining how Japan could go about securing goods for domestic demands.

> [For civilian consumption], if we were to set aside three million tons of shipping at all times, it would be possible to sustain the present level of national strength. However, in order to sustain the use of three million tons, we would have to build four hundred thousand tons of ships in 1942 and six hundred thousand tons in 1943. Navy Minister Shimada has commented [in the previous liaison meeting] that only half that number would be realistic. . . . In that case, it would be difficult to sustain the present level.

These numbers, too, reflected wishful thinking. No one could guarantee that the sea routes used for transporting both military and civilian goods would be safe from obstacles. The Navy General Staff had not put forward any specific plans to establish a secure convoying system to minimize expected shipping losses.

So despite the pertinence of Kaya's questions, and Tojo's original intentions, little progress was made. The Army General Staff record of October 27 summarized the state of affairs: "(1) It seems the prime minister has not changed his mind [for war]; (2) the navy minister continues to be vague, but mostly talks in a negative way [about war]; (3) the navy on the whole has the tendency to advertise its need for more resource allocation; (4) the foreign minister is straightforward and to the point [against war], and he seems very confident." (Togo's remarks on that particular day were not kept, but the log was accurate. Togo would provide the most formidable voice of opposition in the final set of meetings.)

Navy Minister Shimada had joined the Tojo cabinet on the condition that it would do its best to avoid war. He was expected to express far more opposition to war than his predecessor, Oikawa, had. But his private conference with Admiral of the Fleet Imperial Prince Fushimi on October 27 seems to have shaken his resolve. "Unless we decide quickly, we'll lose an opportunity," the sixty-six-year-old veteran of the Russo-Japanese War told Shimada. Fushimi, like other shortsighted war planners, believed that the navy should fight while it could still afford to and that a diplomatic resolution after a quick blitzkrieg attack on the United States would be feasible. Fushimi remained too popular, too influential, and too powerful a figure—an imperial figure—in the navy to be ignored even after he retired as its chief of staff in the spring of 1941. (Presumably, the biggest obstacle to replacing Nagano as chief of staff despite Hirohito's earlier recommendation was that he was safely protected under Fushimi's wing.)

The War Guidance Office of the Army General Staff noted in its journal entry that day:

Conference proceedings show no signs of progress. . . . As we speak, precious strategic opportunities are being lost, which, as members of the high command, we regret very much. It is first and foremost necessary, at this point, to make up our minds. Then and only then can we calibrate our national capabilities and direct the nation to prepare for war. Nonetheless, the present situation is one of protracted debate and dithering over the question of "Can we or can we not?" without making up our minds. This does not achieve anything.

The resolve to "not flinch from war" made in July at the first imperial conference of that year had come to be regarded, beyond logic, as an inviolable priority in Japan's foreign policy agenda. The second imperial resolution of September added to the importance of such resolve by giving it a time-sensitive dimension. The momentum had built and it was proving hard to counteract.

THE CONFERENCE ON OCTOBER 28 addressed the idea of delaying a conflict with the United States until March 1942. The Foreign Ministry as well as the general staffs felt it was advantageous for Japan to wait and see how the fortunes of war changed in Europe. It was suggested that the United States was preoccupied with the war in Europe and that Japan's strategic and diplomatic opportunities would improve as more time was allowed to pass. The implicit basis for this suggestion was that the United States would likely go to war with Hitler soon and that Japan would benefit from knowing who the winner of that war would be, rather than blindly assuming Germany's continued preponderance in Europe.

Despite their open admission of such advantages, however, the strategic sticking point for the warmongers on the general staffs remained the same: that the longer Japan waited, the worse Japan's material situation would become. Nothing could deter them. They declared at the meeting, having agreed among themselves beforehand, that "the start of war has to be November. By October 31, we must decide to go to war. We emphasize that the depletion of resources [while we wait] is fatal to the navy." Tojo could not hold the line and apologized to the two chiefs of staff for taking too much time with his reexamination. The delaying option was shelved after only one session.

The meetings of October 29 and 30 were reserved for further assessing the material feasibility of war and, at long last, the prospect of diplomacy with the United States. On the material front, Kaya had earlier requested that he needed to know, "in actual numbers, what the relationship between supply and demand of matériel would be in the event of war and of not going to war." Suzuki was again invited to make his case on behalf of the Cabinet Planning Board. He estimated that the country would have 2.55

million tons of petroleum at the end of the first year of war, 150,000 tons at the end of the second year, and, slightly recovering, 700,000 tons at the end of the third year. Japan would barely be keeping up its subsistence level. Suzuki's latest interpretation, however, was that fighting the war would be difficult yet possible.

Once again, Kaya's attempt to make rational sense out of the war plan was dodged and sabotaged by the parties concerned. Inertia, self-preservation, institutional material gain, and irrational conviction were all at work. Then it was Togo's turn to question the wisdom of war.

If Kaya could not make others see the tenuousness of the prowar argument from a material standpoint, perhaps Togo could do so from a diplomatic one. The two perspectives were, of course, closely related. First, Togo made clear his position that diplomacy should prevail and that even if Japan were to make greater concessions than it would like (including withdrawing its troops from Indochina and China), the peace gained would be well worth the sacrifice.

Almost everyone in the room reacted harshly to this suggestion. Such conciliatory behavior would make Japan a third-rate country and an easy target for Western bullies, critics claimed. Togo openly and daringly pushed for a troop withdrawal from China. "Our economy would survive even if we withdrew," he insisted. "The sooner it is done, the better." His attitude stirred up such strong resistance from the Army General Staff that Tojo proposed a tortured compromise: Japan might agree to retreat from large parts of China on the condition that it would take its time to do so in certain parts, "allowing something close to 'forever.'"

This sparked a surreal argument over the acceptable time frame for completing a withdrawal from China; suggestions ranged from twenty-five to ninety-nine years. After a haggling match between the parties, they eventually and broadly settled on twenty-five years for the withdrawal of troops from northern China, Inner Mongolia, and the island of Hainan, should the United States demand a specific time frame; other troops stationed in China would be withdrawn within two years of securing an agreement with China. The withdrawal from French Indochina would take place after "the establishment of peace" and "the resolution of Japan's war with China." For Togo, it was better than nothing.

On October 30, it was also decided that the Tripartite Pact would continue as it was. Concerning the terms proposed by the United States, most leaders opted not to accept Hull's Four Principles as official preconditions for further negotiations, though they recognized that whatever Tokyo had already told Washington in favor of them could not be undone. Deeds should count more than words, they appeared to believe. They stressed that a shift in attitude toward free trade could not possibly occur overnight, as though discarding one style of dress for another, more fashionable one. The predominance of this kind of argument proved that Japanese leaders in 1941 were, on the whole, ineffective international negotiators. They failed to see that in diplomatic negotiations words often counted more than deeds—or at least that words were expected to come before deeds.

Togo still insisted that the government needed to signal that the Four Principles could be accepted in principle, without attaching any preconditions, to impress on the United States the seriousness of Japan's desire to avoid armed conflict. Tojo again offered a compromise between the general staffs and Togo, suggesting that Japan propose that free trade principles be applied to the rest of the world before the United States could demand their exclusive application by Japan in China. At the same time, any claims of Japan's special regional interests were to be dropped.

The general diplomatic outline, or Plan A, was thus drawn. It included timed troop withdrawal, free trade in China if first applied to the rest of the world, and the maintenance of the Tripartite alliance while avoiding a categorical acceptance of Hull's Four Principles. Togo's tenaciousness made it clear that military concessions were possible, and that the previous cabinet had been conceding too easily to the high command. Still, Togo was nervous because he knew too well that good diplomacy could not be pursued in parallel with urgent war preparations. He was also surprised that the navy had not come to his aid during his fight against the hard-liners:

> I had expected that the army would take a hard line. But I was expecting the navy to have a more moderate attitude, and my various efforts were made on the assumption that the navy people would be on my side. However, at the liaison conference, I was astonished to see that they were quite adamant about the issue of troop withdrawal, among other things.

Togo was not getting help from the navy in large part because Navy Minister Shimada, following his meeting with Prince Fushimi, had made up his mind to support war preparations. Shimada confided in Vice Navy

Minister Sawamoto: "I would not be able to forgive myself if we lost an opportunity for war because of my single opposition as the navy minister." Togo did not know of Shimada's change of heart. He tried to win over the Navy Ministry through his network of powerful, more liberal-minded navy veterans, including a former prime minister and a navy minister, to no avail.

Ironically, only Nagano appeared somewhat sympathetic to Togo's attempt to resuscitate Japan's diplomacy. When the discussion had stalled at one point on the Army General Staff's intransigence over the principle of nondiscrimination in trade in China, Nagano abruptly asked: "Why not do it? Why not just agree to nondiscriminatory commercial policies? Why not show them how magnanimous we are?" He may well have wanted to make sure diplomacy was given a proper chance so that there would still be a way to avoid war without the navy—or him—being seen as shrinking from it. His words and actions two days later would support such a reading.

At the end of the October 30 meeting, the two key antiwar ministers of Tojo's cabinet, Kaya and Togo, were exhausted. The leaders had been meeting almost every day for a week. Tojo, in his meticulous bureaucratic manner, had covered all the topics he said he was going to at the first meeting. But it would be a gross exaggeration to say that all available alternatives had been carefully reconsidered and honestly debated.

The fate of the country was to be decided on November 1.

CHAPTER 13

On the Brink

When Tojo saw Army Chief of Staff Sugiyama at 7:30 a.m. on November 1, the prime minister's increasing doubts about war were evident. He tried to persuade Sugiyama to reconsider his prowar position and explained that three policy options needed to be discussed at the liaison meeting later that morning: to not go to war, to go to war and prepare quickly, or to continue with diplomatic negotiations without dismissing the possibility of war entirely. "I intend to take the third route," Tojo said. He offered reassurances that Japan would not make any unnecessary diplomatic concessions to the United States.

The previous evening, Tojo had conferred with key members of his cabinet, including Shimada, Togo, Kaya, and Suzuki. Tojo now told Sugiyama that "the navy minister, the finance minister, and the director of the Cabinet Planning Board have all agreed to endorse the third scenario." Tojo and Sugiyama both knew Togo preferred the first option but might accept the third. Tojo suggested that Sugiyama, too, should go along with the third option.

Shimada's conditions were noted in the War Guidance Office log: "As was expected, the navy [minister] kept saying, 'We need steel. We need aluminum. And we need nickel. And unless you give us them all, we cannot fight the war.'" The log was filled with jealous fury (the army and navy, rivals to the end), but there was no hint of awareness that advocating a reckless war might be the ultimate act of selfishness and a disservice to the nation.

It is hard to believe in hindsight, but Sugiyama's greatest fear at this turning point in history was still that the navy would fight for a larger share of military resources without committing itself to war. "We have started directing two hundred thousand troops from Japan and from China [southward in preparation for battles in Southeast Asia]," he told Tojo, "giving priority to this mobilization over other necessary campaigns that need to be fought elsewhere. If we dispatch soldiers to the South Seas, only to call them back without waging a war, that would dampen their morale." This was a strange justification indeed for war. He said that he would demand that (1) the idea of normalizing relations with the United States be abandoned, (2) the decision be made to go to war, (3) the start date for war be set for early December, (4) the strategy be finalized; and (5) a (duplicitous) diplomacy be conducted in a way that would help place the military in an advantageous position for war.

"I am not going to change the opinion of the high command," Tojo responded. "However, I believe it would be difficult to convince His Imperial Majesty." Ironically, the palace was hoping that Tojo would do exactly what he hoped the emperor would do: restrain the warmongers.

THE LIAISON CONFERENCE BEGAN at nine in the morning, soon after Tojo's private meeting with Sugiyama. It would last seventeen hours and become one of the most notorious in Japan's history.

The first topic to be introduced that day was the question of resource distribution among the navy, the army, and the Cabinet Planning Board should a war come to pass. It was proposed that for 1942, the navy would be given 1.1 million tons of ordinary steel; the army, 790,000 tons; and the Cabinet Planning Board, for domestic consumption, 2.6 million tons. Humiliated, Sugiyama asked Shimada: "If you get this much steel, will you for once make up your mind [for war]?" The navy minister merely nodded at Sugiyama. After several hours of discussion, the tacit agreement had been made, and the allocation plan was ratified.

Tojo now tried to bring things to a head: Would Japan go to war or not? In his formalistic way, he pursued the answer by examining the three alternative scenarios he'd outlined earlier to Sugiyama: no war, war, or diplomacy and war pursued in parallel. Kaya, in a scene of déjà vu, reopened his critical line of questioning. He asked the navy leaders impatiently: "If we went to war right now, would Japan still be able to continue fighting after

232 · JAPAN 1941

a few years? Would the United States still be likely to attack Japan after three years if Japan didn't go to war?"

"The chances of victory [for the immediate war option] are unclear," Admiral Nagano replied. He was "fifty-fifty."

On the possibility of a U.S. attack, Kaya said: "I don't know if we could manage to win a naval war."

Nagano responded that it would be much better for Japan to fight "now rather than waiting for three years . . . because the necessary foundation for continuing the war will have been under our control." By the "necessary foundation," he meant Southeast Asian resources.

"If the chances of victory in the third year of war were still to be high," said Kaya, "I say it would be all right to go to war. But according to Nagano, that point remains unclear. Moreover, I doubt the likelihood of the United States launching war on us. I just don't think it would be wise to go to war now."

Contrary to Tojo's remark to Sugiyama earlier that morning, Kaya categorically did not want to go to war. Togo agreed: "I don't think that the U.S. fleets would come to our shores. It is unnecessary to go to war now."

"There is a saying: 'Do not simply wait for enemy attacks,'" said Nagano. "The future is unclear. One cannot feel too safe. In three years' time, the defense in the south will be harder to overcome and enemy fleets will have expanded."

Nagano's invocation of a passage from *The Art of War* by Sunzi (Sun Tzu) was a self-serving misreading of the text. Sunzi's dictum preaches an all-around general preparedness, even for the unlikely case of being attacked. (It does not advocate provoking a very risky war that would not otherwise have come one's way either, and even warns against going to war out of a sense of humiliation and irritation, urging one to try to subjugate the enemy without fighting and to attain political goals by nonviolent means. Above all, it stipulates the need to fully understand the enemy's power before finally launching a war.) Kaya replied: "Well then, when would you say we start that war in order to win it?" Either ignoring or failing to perceive the irony of Kaya's question, Nagano said firmly: "Now! No more opportunities for war will arrive later."

Tojo thought he had secured Suzuki's support for continuing diplomacy, but he was wrong. Suzuki betrayed no diffidence about the war he later said he was privately against and depressed by. Suzuki now said that war was desirable after all: "Kaya is worried about securing enough war matériel and seems to think that we would be disadvantaged in the years 1941 and 1942. But there is no need to worry. By 1943, things will look better if we go to war." The high command had told him so. Coming from a man who had recently said that Japan had no "defensive system" and "no long-term plans for material sustenance of the state," Suzuki's advocacy was indeed surprising and irresponsible.

Kaya and Togo did not hide their disgust at the thought of diplomacy becoming a tool of deception for the sake of secret war preparations. The navy's vice chief of staff, Ito Seiichi, disagreed: "From the navy's perspective, I would say you may carry on diplomacy until November 20." His army counterpart, Tsukada, thought that was too generous a deadline for the government. "From the army's perspective, you may [engage in diplomacy] until November 13, but we cannot agree to a day beyond that date!"

"Diplomacy by nature requires many days and nights for its goals to be fulfilled," interjected Togo. "As foreign minister, I cannot conduct diplomacy without any likelihood of success. I need to be assured that I would be given the time and conditions required to make it a success. War, needless to say, must be avoided." Togo asked how much time he would have to engage in real diplomacy, which gave rise to the following exchange between him and the army's vice chief of staff.

> TSUKADA: We insist that diplomacy not interfere with strategies. We would not want the fickle conditions of diplomacy to dictate and affect our strategic plans, and therefore we demand that November 13 be the final deadline for diplomacy.
>
> TOGO: November 13. That is awful! The navy is saying November 20.
>
> TSUKADA: Preparing for strategic operations implies "strategic conduct." . . . November 13 is the final day before all the preparation would start being seen as "strategic conduct."

Tsukada argued that mobilizing the military in anticipation of war, even without actually declaring war, was bound to invite clashes with enemy forces. Therefore, he insisted, war preparations in and of themselves were tantamount to "strategic conduct," or going to war. This was an overstretched argument, even for a military man, and prompted Nagano to remark: "Small clashes only mean local conflicts. They are not the same as wars." Tojo and Togo made clear their view that diplomacy had to be conducted honorably, with full hope for its success. Tsukada bitterly accepted the point, though he made sure that the diplomatic deadline would be honored, too: "It is all right to seek diplomatic solutions until November 13, but anything beyond that date would be an infringement on the authority of the supreme command."

As the day darkened into night, the atmosphere became even more suffocating. Long silences were punctuated by the faint songs of the crickets outside and by the bickering that erupted every now and then. Unable to agree on a timetable for diplomacy, the leaders took a twenty-minute break, during which the Army General Staff called in the chief of its Operations Division, Tanaka Shin'ichi, to strategize for the rest of the conference. The Navy General Staff did the same, summoning Fukudome Shigeru, the naval operations chief. It was agreed, finally, that the high command would set November 30 as the final deadline for diplomacy.

DURING THIS BREAK, the chief of the Foreign Ministry's American Affairs Bureau, Yamamoto Kumaichi, there to assist Togo, bumped into Nagano in the hallway. Nagano patted his back. "Well, my dear Yamamoto," he asked, "would the Foreign Ministry take it upon itself to settle this mess through diplomacy? If so, the navy would be glad to entrust everything to the Foreign Ministry. What do you think?" Yamamoto, surprised, could only repeat Togo's view that the existing conditions were not good enough to produce a successful diplomatic outcome.

Nagano's abrupt proposition revealed that he was the greatest vacillator of them all, despite his hawkish façade. At the past few conferences, he had hinted at his preference for giving diplomacy a chance. He was finding it harder and harder to conceal his diffidence. Worse, Nagano was fundamentally unsure of the offensive plan that he had recently approved. During the previous months, Admiral Yamamoto Isoroku had been trying to perfect his offensive plan, helped mostly by two pilots, Rear Admiral Onishi Takijiro and Lieutenant Commander Genda Minoru. He also relied on Kuroshima Kameto, an eccentric officer in his late forties whose powerful push for the naval offensive plan overwhelmed even Nagano.

Born into an impoverished stonemason's family in Hiroshima in 1893, Kuroshima lost his father young and was raised by his uncle and aunt from the age of three. He was a loner who rarely revealed his emotions. After putting himself through night school, he was admitted first to the Naval Academy and then to the elite Naval War College. This must have been a dream come true for a socially disadvantaged orphan with minimal formal schooling whose formative years coincided with the rise of the navy after the Russo-Japanese War. He came to be recognized for his unusual proposals in strategic studies discussions.

It was presumably in response to a request from his old classmate Yamamoto that Shimada, then the commander of the Second Fleet, recommended Kuroshima for a critical planning post. In October 1939, though lacking seniority, he was appointed as Yamamoto's staff officer. Kuroshima was an odd choice by any ordinary standard. A tall, willowy man with a gaunt face and a bald head, he had an ascetic aura that prompted his colleagues to call him Gandhi. But his habits would have made Mahatma shudder in horror. He bathed only rarely and smoked cigarettes incessantly, dropping ashes everywhere he went. In order to concentrate, he would lock himself up in a dark, incense-filled room, naked, for days on end. When inspiration finally arrived, he would jot down his plans like a man possessed.

Such eccentricities should have seriously hampered his career. But they did not appear to disturb Yamamoto in the least. In fact, the man's strangeness seemed to encourage Yamamoto to think that this was no ordinary strategist. He observed that Kuroshima was the only officer who would dare disagree with him, the only one who would suggest to him things Yamamoto himself would never have come up with on his own. He conceded that there were many other excellent staff officers, but he was disappointed when they gave him identical answers to a question. In the planning of his special Pacific operation, he grew tired of hearing words of caution and arguments that what he proposed was technically and logistically impossible. Kuroshima, on the other hand, was determined to help Yamamoto make the impossible come true.

Kuroshima, aided by Onishi and Genda on the technical details, perfected what became Yamamoto's final plan for Hawaii. The operation was unconventional—a gamble—and as such entailed great risks. The most apparent obstacle, as mentioned earlier, was the feasibility of aerial torpedo attacks in Pearl Harbor's shallow waters, which averaged just shy of forty feet. But by the autumn of 1941, improvements had been made on the torpedoes themselves, so that the depth they would have to sink before they could sail was drastically reduced, making it less likely they would get stuck in the seabed. Pilots had been superbly trained to fly at an extremely low altitude, which would prevent the torpedoes from plunging too deeply. The training that had begun in September in southern Japan—in and around Kinko Bay in Kagoshima, chosen because it resembled Pearl Harbor—had become more intense in October. But none of the pilots, except for their two leaders, knew the real purpose of their hard work.

When the Hawaii plan was presented for approval in Tokyo, the Naval General Staff was dead set against it. The plan was predicated on deploying a huge proportion of Japan's naval resources, including six aircraft carriers (out of ten, though more were under construction). Japan's Southeast Asian operation would be compromised by diverting the much-needed help from the air, and the navy would risk losing its command of the sea and skies altogether. The war games carried out in September at the Naval War College only confirmed the general staff's belief that the plan was too risky.

Yamamoto would not budge. Kuroshima traveled to Tokyo to lobby passionately for the plan. He eventually resorted to threats, saying that Yamamoto and all his supporters were prepared to quit if the Hawaii plan was not adopted. Desperate not to lose Yamamoto, Nagano reluctantly approved the plan on October 20, just as the Tojo cabinet was being formed. Such was Nagano's total reliance on Yamamoto's ability to command this one-of-a-kind operation. He had no other strategists to turn to, even though he remained unconvinced of the feasibility of Yamamoto's daring plan. This helps explain Nagano's sudden plea for the Foreign Ministry's help, in spite of all his loud calls for war in the liaison meetings. In contrast, Navy Minister Shimada, who'd joined the Tojo cabinet wanting to stop the war, had now completely made up his mind for war.

"COULDN'T THE DEADLINE be extended to December 1? Couldn't we let diplomacy pursue its course a bit longer?" Tojo asked the military officers as the meeting reconvened after the break. Tsukada was mortified. "Absolutely not. Anything more than the last day of November is out of the question. Out of the question!" The navy minister pathetically asked Tsukada: "When you say November 30, what time exactly do you mean? Surely, you would give us until the twenty-fourth hour?" Tsukada answered Shimada coldly: "Yes, until twelve midnight would be all right." War was feeling more and more unstoppable.

The discussion now moved to the terms of diplomatic negotiations with the United States. Togo knew that Plan A would be insufficient from the U.S. perspective. So, on the morning of November 1, he had the Foreign Ministry submit Plan B in the hope of creating more room for diplomatic maneuver. He devised it with the help of a veteran diplomat, Shidehara Kijuro, and a former ambassador to Britain, Yoshida Shigeru, both desperate to avoid war. The alternative plan was brought to the discussion table at 10:00 p.m., thirteen hours after the opening of the day's conference. It stipulated that both Japan and the United States would refrain from advancing militarily into the South Pacific, would cooperate with one another to secure access to needed materials from the Dutch East Indies, and would revert their commercial relations to the conditions before the U.S. freezing of Japanese assets, and that the United States would promise a supply of petroleum to Japan.

The greatest concession requested of the military was buried in a separate note. It clarified that Japan was prepared to relocate its southern Indochinese troops immediately to the northern half of the peninsula. Japan would also pledge to withdraw entirely from Indochina when peace in either the Pacific in general or China in particular was established. And, if necessary, the present plan would include further explorations of the principle of global nondiscrimination in trade and of the Tripartite Pact. Plan B was Togo's attempt to eliminate the ever-sticky question of how to exclude the China War from the negotiation, at least for the time being, and to restore diplomatic relations to where they had been before July, when the Roosevelt administration felt that it could do business with Tokyo for the sake of concentrating U.S. strategic efforts on the Atlantic and keeping things in check in the Pacific.

Unsurprisingly, the hard-liners Tsukada and Sugiyama vehemently objected to an immediate, unconditional withdrawal of Japanese troops from southern French Indochina. This gave rise to another heated argument between Tsukada and Togo. "On the whole, I believe the way we have handled the negotiations so far has been misguided," Togo began. "We should narrow down our conditions and settle the 'South Problem' in order to handle the China situation on our own terms." He knew that Japan's troop withdrawal from Indochina might be a stopgap measure, but he saw it as one of the only concrete actions Japan could take within the little time given him.

Tsukada objected: "A troop withdrawal from southern Indochina won't happen . . . [because] if we withdrew, the United States would have its way. Then it could interfere with us anytime it wanted." He didn't think commercial relations between the two countries would be restored because "the United States would not stop supporting Chiang Kai-shek. Petroleum, especially, would not flow into Japan [even after the Indochinese withdrawal]." He asserted that "half a year later, a war opportunity will have already passed us by."

In the end, a kind of compromise was suggested: the insertion of a fourth condition into Plan B. It maintained that the U.S. government would not interfere in the peacemaking efforts between Japan and China. Togo hoped that if the United States rejected this Japanese demand, he would be able to drop it at a later date. But reintroducing the China issue and presenting it together with the "South Problem" kept Tojo from simplifying his diplomacy, defeating the main objective of having a more manageable alternative plan.

Even with this concession, Tsukada remained furious over the suggestion of an Indochinese withdrawal. He demanded that Plan B be scrapped completely, shouting at Togo to just "make do with Plan A." But Togo was equally adamant and was not about to be bullied. The escalating tension caused Tojo to halt the meeting again for ten minutes.

During this break, the army participants tried to come to terms with Plan B, with what most regarded as the shocking concession of transferring occupation forces from southern to northern Indochina. But it was speculated that the China factors would likely sabotage the success of Plan B anyway. What was more worrying, from the general staff's perspective, was having to spend an extra few days deliberating Plan B while compromising Japan's fleeting opportunity for a decisive attack. In the end, even Tsukada was persuaded to accept Plan B, if only because he believed it made it more likely that diplomacy would fail.

Ultimately, the longest liaison conference in history ended with only a tentative agreement. The proposed date for starting military action was to be the beginning of December, and strategies were to be prepared accordingly. If a diplomatic settlement could be reached with the United States by the zero hour of December 1, military action would cease, no matter what. Togo now had Plan A and Plan B at his disposal, but not much time left for diplomacy. Kaya and Togo remained fundamentally unconvinced by the prowar argument and were mystified as to why other attendees did not feel the same.

The conference ended at 1:30 in the morning on November 2.

TOGO DID NOT have to approve the tentative conference resolution. He or Finance Minister Kaya or any other minister could have vetoed the resolution, preventing its passage requiring unanimity. Under the Meiji Constitution, a minister was directly answerable to the emperor, which meant that a prime minister could not simply fire a minister. (In reality, when prodded by a prime minister, a minister would usually resign, but this was not the case, as we've seen, with Konoe and Matsuoka and, to an extent, with Konoe and Tojo.) A defiant action to veto the resolution and then to refuse to resign could have possibly led to the demise of the cabinet. Another means to sabotage the resolution was for a minister to simply resign on his own. This wouldn't cause a collapse of the resolution, but it could greatly discredit it. Pursuing either one of these two options in early November 1941 meant overtly attacking the government and the high command, because of the sheer damage it could inflict on time-sensitive war preparations already under way. After the final conference, Togo contemplated resigning. That appeared to be the simplest and most effective way for him to continue his valiant resistance, and this possibility was clearly worrying the hard-liners in the army. By resigning his post, Togo would have rejected Tojo's "reexamination" attempt while stalling the war planning.

Togo now sought advice from Hirota Koki, a former prime minister who had served as foreign minister in four different cabinets. A famously cautious man, Hirota advised against Togo's resignation, warning that the post might be filled by a prowar candidate. This was, of course, possible. It would be better if Togo kept working for peace with the United States, Hirota insisted. Togo decided to stay on after all. This also meant that the concessions he had won from the military would not go to waste.

At noon on November 2, Togo told Tojo he would act on the previous night's decisions. Kaya had accepted the tentative decisions, too. Tojo promised his full support for the momentous diplomatic undertaking at hand. He said he would help find ways to make more compromises when and if the United States showed any interest in either Plan A or Plan B. He reassured Togo that no matter how far the military preparations had proceeded, they would be stopped immediately in the event of a diplomatic breakthrough. Togo said that if Japan could not reach a diplomatic settlement to avoid war, he would resign. Both Togo and Kaya were beginning to accept the unthinkable.

At five o'clock that afternoon, Nagano and Sugiyama presented the emperor with a detailed war plan, which was not revealed at the liaison conferences for confidentiality reasons. This imperial interview was meant merely to prep Hirohito for yet another imperial conference, scheduled for November 5. The operational details included Yamamoto's plan for Hawaii, with the date of the attack definitively set for December 8 (December 7 local time). The weather that Sunday was predicted to be ideal, with the moon casting favorable light into the morning hours, aiding Japan's predawn attack.

Hirohito, visibly sad, reiterated his preference for a diplomatic resolution. He also questioned the chiefs of staff on some technical issues, conceding that "perhaps it is unavoidable that we continue preparations for military operations." He expressed concern over the weather predicted for the Southeast Asian campaigns, to be undertaken in conjunction with the Pearl Harbor attack ("You have told me that monsoons would impede the landing of our troops. . . . Would you be able to land?" "How's the weather in Malaya?"). Though Hirohito continued to entertain hopes for diplomacy, he, too, seemed to be adjusting to the idea of imminent war. One could rationalize that by going to war, Japan would be preserving its control over its future. Wasn't taking action, taking the initiative, better than sitting still?

On November 4, the Supreme War Council met. The emperor was present, as were his military advisers, including Prince Higashikuni. No one objected to the new liaison conference resolution stipulating that diplomacy and military preparations would be pursued in parallel. If a diplomatic settlement could not be reached with the United States by the zero hour of December 1, it would mean war. Tojo, addressing the attendees, spoke as though he had a split personality. Despite his recent pledge to Togo to support his diplomatic efforts, Tojo was now intimating that the war was a certainty, and a good thing at that. This was his *tatemae,* the face he put on for this formal occasion attended by military heavyweights and the emperor. He was acting the part of a heroic soldier rather than a conflicted political leader. "If we just stand by with our arms folded," he said, "and allow our country to revert to the 'little Japan' that we once were, we would be tainting its brilliant twenty-six-hundred-year history."

On November 5, the elegant First Eastern Hall of the Meiji Palace became the venue for yet more political theater when the third imperial conference of the year was convened. In the presence of the emperor, Togo was called to explain the prospect of Japan's diplomacy. His role was to fully and categorically support the latest resolution that was now being authorized by the emperor. Rather than pushing an antiwar agenda, Togo couched his speech in the anticolonialist claim that Japan was embarking on a grand mission to save Asia. He pledged his commitment to the survival of not only Japan but also the whole of Asia, thereby ideologically justifying his support for the war he had so vehemently opposed in the liaison conferences. Togo, the most courageous and rational of the top leaders, was now beginning to sound like all the others who claimed not to want war while helping to make it inevitable. The failure since April to produce an understanding with the United States was blamed on the other side. Japan was a persecuted country, Togo insisted.

> President Roosevelt is taking advantage of America's strong economic position. As if it had already entered the war, it is helping Britain and is resorting to a harshly oppressive economic policy against Japan. Since mid-April this year, we have been engaging in unofficial negotiations concerning the general normalization of U.S.-Japan relations. The imperial government has been honest and just in its attitude in those negotiations from the very beginning, desiring the stability of East Asia and world peace.

On he went about how Japan had patiently tried to reach an understanding, but its efforts, including the new proposal submitted in late September, had been in vain. "If things go as they are going now," he said, "I regret that the negotiations do not have any prospect of a quick resolution." Even if this speech might not have faithfully reflected Togo's innermost voice (*honne*), these official pronouncements showed that Togo was abandoning the courage of his convictions—though, to be sure, he had done more than anybody in the top decision-making circles to resist war.

All the leaders asserted their right to decide Japan's fate by initiating a war, while paradoxically insinuating that they had no ultimate control over the fate of the country they led. Above all, they were eager to absolve themselves of the responsibility for whatever consequences might follow from their tortured decision, sensing that they would truly be devastating. The imperial conference, a ceremonial pseudo-religious rite meant to depoliticize huge political decisions, ensured that no one party or individual would be forced to shoulder the enormous burden of Japan's grave future.

CHAPTER 14

"No Last Word Between Friends"

T here is no last word between friends," President Roosevelt, with the effortless charm of a patrician statesman, remarked to his two Japanese visitors. It was late on the morning of November 17, 1941. One of the visitors was Ambassador Nomura, a frequent guest at the White House over the past half year. The other was less familiar: Kurusu Saburo. Kurusu was much shorter than Nomura, who was as tall as many of his U.S. colleagues, but possessed an air of quiet authority. Everything about him was urbane and sophisticated. At fifty-five, he had a full head of slightly graying hair, neatly combed back. His well-cut suits, his fine mustache, his silver-rimmed glasses, his tipping of his hat to greet journalists, all spoke to his polished personality. But precisely because of his impeccable demeanor, Kurusu could seem somewhat distant, even cold, to those who did not know him. A seasoned diplomat, he had been dispatched by Tojo's government as a special envoy to the United States and had arrived in Washington only two days earlier.

Kurusu's new responsibilities had begun, in effect, on the night of November 3. Asleep after a pleasant if exhausting day of visiting museums and walking around old Tokyo with his son, an aeronautical engineer for the army, he was awakened at midnight by a policeman from a nearby police station. "Please report immediately to the foreign minister's official residence," said the policeman, who had been sent because the telephone line to Kurusu's house was not working properly. Though Kurusu wondered at first if this summons might have something to do with his private antiwar pronouncements, it would soon become clear that he was mistaken. He hurried himself to Togo's official residence. There he found, in a brightly lit room, the tense-looking foreign minister and several of his closest aides, all with equally serious faces.

Togo summarized the history of the informal talks between the United States and Japan, noting that the situation needed to be drastically improved at once. For that, Ambassador Nomura needed an able man with a proven track record in international negotiations. As Japan's first consul general in Manila, Kurusu had established excellent Japan-Philippines relations and in 1919 famously prevented the passage of a bill that would have resulted in the confiscation of Japanese-developed agricultural properties. Though semiretired, Kurusu was eminently qualified. He was asked if he would go to Washington.

When Tojo took over the government from Konoe, Nomura requested to be sent back home, and not for the first time. Once again, he was turned down. One can only imagine Nomura's frustration as he almost single-handedly continued to campaign for a peaceful settlement in Washington, where he was regarded as an outsider within his own embassy. His frustration might have gotten the best of him if he had known of the deadline for a diplomatic settlement. He had no idea that a specific date for war mobilization had been discussed in Tokyo, decided upon, reexamined, and then reapproved. With the new deadline set for the end of November, Tokyo could not afford to replace Nomura. Rather, the overworked ambassador would now be sent someone to assist him.

The official explanation for Kurusu's dispatch was Nomura's poor English; the truth was that Togo did not have a high opinion of Nomura as a diplomat. "In this dangerous emergency," Togo later wrote, "one could not afford to discharge him or to be too hesitant." That was why Togo "sent him almost excessively detailed instructions concerning the treaty formats, for instance, where the ambassador was weak." Togo came to feel that the telegrams loaded with such instructions would not suffice.

In that midnight conference with Togo, Kurusu was briefed on the contents of Plans A and B, which were to be proposed to the United States in the coming weeks. When Kurusu returned home around two in the morning, he stunned his family by announcing that he would be leaving for the United States almost immediately.

Kurusu spent the next twenty or so hours trying to acquaint himself with the "informal conversations" held between Japan and the United

States since the spring. Reading through documents and meeting with informed parties at the Foreign Ministry, he learned that the talks had, in fact, been thought to be going well at first. The definite turning point, it was clear to him, was the Japanese occupation of southern French Indochina in July. Kurusu was reassured by Yamamoto Kumaichi of the American Affairs Bureau that he would make every conceivable effort to persuade the military to halt its march to war should Kurusu recognize even a glimmer of hope for the success of the negotiations. Yamamoto had a good reason to think it could be done, remembering that Nagano had told him that "the navy would be glad to entrust everything to the Foreign Ministry."

Later that evening, his departure imminent, Kurusu went to see Tojo. They had never met before. To Kurusu, the prime minister appeared relatively relaxed. He had changed from his usual khaki army uniform into a kimono, though it was still a rather formal one. Tojo told him that he had reported to the emperor about Kurusu's special appointment. He went on to say that in his estimation "the chance of success in the negotiations with the United States is 30 percent." But he felt there was still time. He believed that the United States was not yet prepared for war and that U.S. public opinion was clearly against it. The United States lacked natural resources such as rubber and tin, Tojo said, making it unlikely that it would jeopardize its access to Southeast Asia by going to war with Japan.

"Be sure to give it your best effort," Tojo said, "and come to an agreement." To the diplomat's dismay, he added: "But Japan could not possibly concede on the point of troop withdrawal." If that concession were made, he would not be able to face the souls of the men who had died for the emperor in all of Japan's modern wars. This was Tojo's customary line, of course, which had prevented Konoe's third cabinet from pursuing a diplomatic settlement with the United States. And yet Tojo was not as intransigent on this issue as his words suggested. He had helped Togo win some significant concessions from the militarists in the recent liaison conferences. Plan A promised at least a timed withdrawal from China; Plan B committed Japan to a swift withdrawal from southern Indochina as a preliminary step toward withdrawing from all of French Indochina and China. Tojo had indeed come a long way on the issue of troop withdrawal, probably because he understood its importance, despite his continued references to the heroic souls of the war dead.

Kurusu felt Tojo was too optimistic. He explained that he had agreed to the difficult mission in the belief that trying to avoid war was the service he was expected to render to the people of Japan as well as to the emperor. His mission was meant for the living, not the dead. "Will you be prepared to back up the diplomatic effort if an agreement were to be reached between the two countries, despite the expected opposition?" Kurusu asked. Tojo answered: "Yes, I surely will." Japan's top diplomat now quickly grasped the tremendous delicacy of the situation: Even though Tojo, as a soldier, could not overtly promise humiliating military concessions, Kurusu understood him to be saying that, in effect, he would be prepared to stomach them as long as Kurusu could engage the other side. This gave Kurusu some hope.

As they were wrapping up their meeting, Tojo told Kurusu that the negotiations could proceed only until the end of November. He said it in a chillingly casual manner. Togo had not mentioned that to Kurusu. With less than two weeks left, Kurusu belatedly realized, the true obstacle was the time frame.

DESPITE HIS UNQUESTIONED INTELLECT and experience, Kurusu was an unfortunate choice in a public relations sense. To the outside world, Kurusu was known only as the man who signed the Tripartite Pact, having been photographed next to Hitler at the height of German-Japanese friendship. He was actually strongly opposed to the pact but was obliged to sign it as Japan's ambassador to Germany in the autumn of 1940. Kurusu never wanted the Berlin job and had turned it down several times. He was ready to retire after his tenure in Belgium, where he was posted from 1936 to 1939. His time in Brussels coincided with the outbreak and intensification of the China War under the first Konoe government. He tried in his capacity as ambassador to initiate a settlement of the China conflict through the mediation of the Belgian and French governments. He knew that Japan lacked any coherent plans for that war and, more damningly, an effective leader. The escalation, in his words, came about because "the government always allowed itself to be dragged along by the faits accomplis in the field without any prospects of long-term solution." Worse, there was "no coordination within and between the army and the navy" and everyone was "preoccupied with saving face and evading responsibilities."

Kurusu could not have envisioned that things would get so bad so fast when he and his family, along with a crowd of enthused spectators, welcomed the record-setting *Kamikaze* aviators at the Brussels airport in April 1937. Kurusu accepted the ambassadorship to Berlin in 1939 only in the hope that he might prevent Japan's diplomatic course from going further astray. Once in Berlin, he continued to seek ways to settle the China War through the third-party intervention of Germany. But just as things seemed to be moving in the right direction, Konoe, in his second premiership, recognized Wang Jingwei's China, thereby alienating Chiang Kai-shek forever.

Kurusu was soon left out of all key communications between German and Japanese officials. Hitler's government judged that Japan could not be wooed sufficiently through Kurusu, and the agreement on the Tripartite Pact was hastily reached between Matsuoka and a German envoy visiting Tokyo. Nonetheless, because Kurusu was photographed standing side by side with Hitler, his reputation became forever tainted.

Kurusu was so disgusted by that and other experiences in Germany that he requested to be relieved of his post and was allowed to leave Berlin in February 1941. Back in Japan, he led the life of a recluse, turning down government appointments, including a position in Tojo's cabinet. Kurusu, however, could not reject the emergency call to Washington. A peaceful settlement of U.S.-Japanese differences was something he truly desired. He was pro-Anglo-American at heart. Perhaps as the son of the successful industrialist who had developed the cosmopolitan port of Yokohama, he had the appreciation of mercantile liberalism in his blood. The port town served as the window to the world during Japan's rapid modernization and was known for its unsentimental, practical people like Kurusu.

Kurusu also had a personal stake in the future of the United States and Japan. He was married to an American from New York City born to British parents (her father was an Anglican clergyman). Kurusu wanted to do everything in his power to avoid a war between the two countries that meant the most to his family. It was to be a perilous mission. There were some on the Army General Staff who openly said they wished Kurusu's plane would crash. With such ill wishes behind him, he departed for Taiwan in the early morning of November 7.

NOMURA WOULD HAVE to continue on his own until midmonth, given the length of Kurusu's journey. Togo gave Nomura an overview of Plans A and B. "'The negotiations at hand represent our last-ditch attempt," wrote Togo. "Our counterproposal is literally the final one in both name and substance. . . . If we cannot bring about a swift compromise, regrettably, it will only mean the collapse of the negotiations and the relations between the two countries." While the actual deadline was zero hour of December 1, Nomura was told that an agreement had to be reached by November 25. Nomura was also kept in the dark about the significant military concession Togo had won for Plan B: the immediate troop withdrawal from southern Indochina. If all else failed, Togo reasoned, he could deal this card at the very last possible moment for maximum effect in the negotiations.

Nomura charged ahead. On November 7, he met with Secretary of State Hull and presented him with Plan A. Hull already knew its contents from intelligence sources but told the ambassador he needed some time to study and consider it. On November 10, Nomura met with Roosevelt. The president made no specific references to Plan A but used the term "modus vivendi" to describe what the two countries were trying to achieve. Roosevelt said that he, Nomura, and Hull "had only consumed some six months in discussing a solution of our relations and those of other countries in the Pacific." More patience was necessary. A modus vivendi, in his mind, "was not merely an expedient and temporary agreement, but also one which takes into account actual human existence." Nomura left the meeting sensing that the president was now considering a provisional accommodation of disagreements with Japan, rather than demanding their permanent resolution in the form of a complete and immediate policy shift.

From the U.S. perspective, given Roosevelt's preoccupation with the war in Europe, deterring any kind of conflict in another, faraway theater made sense. Washington was in no hurry. Nomura was. In order to achieve something concrete before Tokyo's self-imposed deadline, he needed a more definitive response from Roosevelt to the items listed in Plan A, which he requested from the president on November 10 and again from Hull on November 12. When Wakasugi Kaname, the minister-counselor, visited Undersecretary of State Joseph Ballantine on November 13, he said the "[Japanese] public was becoming impatient and almost desperate." This was a gross misrepresentation, portraying Japan as if it were an informed and open democracy whose "public" knew of what was now at stake in Washington.

Wakasugi had told Ballantine that Tokyo considered their talks to be of a formal nature, since Ambassador Nomura presented his instructions from Tokyo to the president in person. The U.S. government, on the other hand, according to Ballantine, regarded their talks as "still being in a stage of informal exploratory discussions." He elaborated that the U.S. government would expect to talk to China and other concerned parties, if need be, and "a stage of negotiations" between Japan and the United States could then and only then be reached.

On November 14, an exasperated Nomura dispatched a telegram to Togo. "If the situation allows," the ambassador pleaded with the foreign minister, "we should not feel rushed by a matter of one or two months. We must sit back and look at the whole world in its entirety, and wait and persevere until we have a better idea of a future course." This perfectly reasonable argument was almost beside the point, given the looming deadline, and irritated Togo because he knew, at heart, that Nomura was right.

On November 15, Nomura, accompanied by Wakasugi, met Hull in his apartment. Nomura was handed an oral statement and an unofficial draft of a proposed joint declaration by the United States and Japan on economic policy and equal commercial opportunities. Hull had not accepted the Japanese point that the equal opportunity principle should be applied to the rest of the world before it was enforced in China: "[Japan could not possibility expect] the United States to assume responsibility for discriminatory practices in areas outside of its sovereign jurisdiction, or to propose including in an arrangement with the United States a condition which could be fulfilled only with the consent and cooperation of all other Governments," he explained. But he was at last engaging with a specific item outlined in Plan A. Wakasugi asked if Japan could get speedy U.S. replies on the remaining questions as well. Nomura asked whether one could now legitimately say that the "informal conversations" had passed an exploratory state and the two countries were engaged in formal negotiations. That would have had some impact in Tokyo. Hull responded negatively and asked Wakasugi to take careful note of what he was going to say. "If we are to work out a peaceful settlement in the Pacific area," the U.S. administration could do so "only on the basis of carrying on exploratory conversations." Only after Hull deemed it appropriate to go to "Great Britain, to China, and to the Dutch" would he feel comfortable to call "what took place thereafter a negotiation." What would he say to his friends, he asked the Japanese, if those countries concerned read in the newspapers that he was formally "negotiating with Japan on matters affecting them without their being consulted"? At the end of the meeting, Hull sounded the encouraging note that as long as Japan's peaceful intentions concerning nondiscrimination in commercial affairs as well as the Tripartite Pact became clear, Hull thought they "could sit down like brothers and reach some solution of the question of stationing Japanese troops in China."

ON NOVEMBER 16, Togo responded to Nomura's telegram that urged abandoning a deadline. "Regrettably," wrote Togo, "because of various existing factors, we cannot wait and persevere until we know better what the world would look like in the future. . . . We cannot alter the fact that we will need to reach a compromise in this negotiation speedily."

The day before, Kurusu had finally arrived in Washington. In Tokyo, Togo had given him elaborate instructions concerning various formats in which Plan B—in the event of Plan A's failure—was to be presented to the White House, each offering slightly different terms. The first of the three versions of Plan B was the one decided on at the imperial conference of November 5, which pledged (1) no further military advance into East Asia and the South Pacific, (2) cooperation to secure the needed resources from the Dutch East Indies, (3) reversion of commercial relations to the conditions before the U.S. freezing of Japanese assets, and (4) no U.S. interference in a Sino-Japanese peace. In this version, Japan's preparedness to withdraw from Indochina, to make concessions on nondiscriminatory commercial policy, and to explore the Japanese interpretations of the Tripartite Pact were all listed only as "additional remarks."

In the second version, the first four headings remained the same, and these three "additional remarks" were upgraded to formal headings (numbers 5 to 7, respectively). These new headings also had various qualifications in the form of "additional remarks," the most notable of which were the conditions attached to troop withdrawal: Japan would be willing to transfer its troops from southern French Indochina to the north immediately "in case of an agreement being reached" between the United States and Japan.

The third version, which Togo believed would have the greatest favorable impact on Washington, clearly stated under heading 5 (rather than as an "additional remark") that Japan would be prepared to "transfer the existing Japanese troops stationed in southern French Indochina into northern French Indochina."

The most critical job entrusted to Kurusu, then, was to make sure that the different versions are used to maximum effect, according to Togo's orders. Nomura and Kurusu had next to no diplomatic freedom.

Right before he left Tokyo, Kurusu stopped by the U.S. embassy. He wanted to thank Joseph Grew for arranging a transpacific Clipper flight to carry him to Washington. "Are you bringing a new proposal?" Grew asked him with apparent eagerness. Still fresh in his memory was his attempt over the summer to convince his government to let Konoe have his chance at a summit meeting. Grew had insisted then that although no definitive deals could be made on paper in advance, the prince was sure to bring terms favorable to the United States in person. He had hoped that Kurusu was bringing some notable concession. "No," Kurusu responded. Grew was visibly discouraged. Together with a tearful Mrs. Grew, he wished Kurusu the best of luck.

Kurusu wondered if the U.S. administration would be kindly disposed toward him. Not only had he signed the Tripartite Pact, albeit unwillingly, but he also lacked the political importance of a cabinet member. Would he be able to impress upon the Americans that the Japanese leadership truly wished to avoid a military confrontation? Would Plan B, in whichever form, be sufficient if it came to that?

On November 17, Kurusu, led by Hull and accompanied by Nomura, walked over from Hull's office in the State Department to the White House to meet Roosevelt for the first time. Though not exactly relaxed, the atmosphere was not especially tense, either. Kurusu came out of the meeting encouraged by what he saw as U.S. willingness to continue the "conversations." He communicated to Roosevelt that his arrival represented not added pressure but an extra effort on the part of Japan to find common ground. In describing the Japanese point of view, Kurusu pleaded with the president to see the situation from the Japanese "frame of mind." That was when Roosevelt remarked, "There is no last word between friends."

The phrase had a particular resonance with the Japanese. Roosevelt had repeated the words spoken almost three decades earlier by Secretary of State William Jennings Bryan to Chinda Sutemi, the Japanese ambassador to the United States. Chinda's historic service to the two countries was to bring cherry trees and have them planted on the banks of the Potomac. But for the Japanese, Chinda's name was equally linked to California's Alien Land Law of 1913, which he spoke out against. The law, mainly aimed at the burgeoning Japanese community, prevented foreign nationals who were not eligible for citizenship from owning property. (The Naturalization Act of 1870 stipulated that all people of Asian descent not born in the United States were ineligible for citizenship.) Chinda's protest to President Wilson did not produce a satisfactory result; the state law proved to be only a precursor to the federal Immigration Act of 1924, which included the Asian Exclusion Act.

To many Japanese, these measures were a clear manifestation of the ingrained racism of white Americans toward nonwhite peoples. Such exclusionary measures in part propelled Japanese to emigrate elsewhere, and were used, self-servingly, as a pretext for Japan's imperialist expansion into the rest of Asia. Despite various setbacks in their diplomatic relations over the years, however, Japan, as a government, had always found solace in Bryan's diplomatic mantra when dealing with the United States. Kurusu was deeply moved by Roosevelt's citing it.

Roosevelt appeared more than responsive to Kurusu's efforts. He sounded most amenable on the topic of China, claiming to understand the sensitivities and logistical difficulties of immediate troop withdrawal from the Japanese point of view. Though he did not know whether such a diplomatic term existed, he expressed his willingness to act as an "introducer" between China and Japan. The United States would not "mediate," let alone "intervene," in the terms of a peace agreement but would merely bring the two negotiating parties together, just as Japan had requested.

So far, so good. Kurusu sensed that the most problematic topic from Roosevelt's perspective, superseding the China withdrawal issue, was Japan's status in the Tripartite Pact, and he moved on to that subject now. It would be difficult for Japan to disengage itself from the pact, at least in a formal sense, Kurusu admitted. But if Japan were to reach a "general understanding" with the United States, that understanding would surely "outshine" the Tripartite Pact, making it a dead letter. For the U.S. leaders, who were fundamentally against the Nazi regime and its ideology, this claim, made by the very man who signed Japan's pact with Hitler, was difficult to appreciate. Never one to hold back his thoughts on this topic, Hull intervened at this point to express his vehement disagreement with what Kurusu had just said.

At the meeting's end, Kurusu thought it had been an overall success. Nomura was reassured by his younger colleague's social and linguistic fluency. Their dispatch to Tokyo accordingly reported some signs of significant U.S. keenness. But this optimistic impression was not shared by the other side. Hull could not contain his displeasure when he wrote a memorandum summarizing the meeting. He would not accept anything less than Japan's formal abandonment of the Axis alliance. He was dismissive of Kurusu's "specious attempt to explain away the Tripartite Pact."

Joseph Grew was always willing, and went out of his way, to try to comprehend and communicate the Japanese perspective. Hull, though he was showing tremendous patience, was more inclined to listen to Stanley Hornbeck of the State Department, a staunch believer in using a stick rather than a carrot as far as Tokyo was concerned. Hull had said in a previous meeting with Nomura that it would be very difficult for him to "make the people of this country and the people of all peaceful nations believe that Japan was pursuing a peaceful course." Japan, after all, "was tied in an alliance with the most flagrant aggressor who has appeared on this planet in the last 2,000 years." If the government of the United States "went into an agreement with Japan, while Japan had an outstanding obligation to Germany," Hull believed he "might well be lynched."

Given Hull's aversion to the Nazis and, by extension, their "friends," Kurusu's appointment as a special ambassador was viewed skeptically by the secretary of state. Kurusu didn't help himself by declining Hull's invitation to continue to discuss the Tripartite Pact, among other things, immediately following the meeting with Roosevelt. This was a decision that Kurusu would come to regret deeply, though he never gave a clear explanation of why he had turned Hull down. Perhaps he felt he needed an extra day to prepare for the meeting or, more likely, to wait for further instructions from Togo. He also must have been physically exhausted from his long journey. Whatever the reason, Hull's opinion of Kurusu from that day forward would be forever fixed, as he recorded in his memorandum of their meeting:

> All in all, there was nothing new brought out by the Japanese Ambassador and Ambassador Kurusu. Ambassador Kurusu constantly made the plea that there was no reason why there should be serious differences between the two countries and that ways must be found to solve the present situation. He referred to Prime Minister Tojo as being very desirous of bringing about a peaceful adjustment notwithstanding he is an Army Man. . . . The President frequently parried the remarks of Ambassador Nomura and also of Ambassador Kurusu, especially in regard to the three main points of difference between our two countries [equal trade opportunities, the China withdrawal, and the Tripartite Pact]. There was no effort to solve these questions at the conference.

Looking back in 1948, Hull said he "felt from the start that [Kurusu] was deceitful."

INCREASING REPORTS in Washington of Japanese politicians making bellicose public speeches were not going to make Kurusu's mission any easier. Tojo's policy speech in the Diet on November 17, just as Kurusu was getting started, was particularly damaging because of the wide publicity it received. Tojo was addressing the first "parliamentary" session to be recorded and filmed. (Japan's parliamentary system, as noted, had been defunct since the formation of the Imperial Rule Assistance Association under Konoe's second premiership.) It was broadcast on NHK and then released as a news reel to the general audience the following day. A student of Nazi propaganda, Tojo made an active attempt to rouse and mobilize the Japanese nation through the use of audio and visual media.

Though Tojo said that Japan's political situation was now "critical," the speech, lacking as it was in specific details, was not particularly news to the Japanese. It broadly pointed out that things were not going so well because Japan continued to be bullied by those who didn't understand Japan's peaceful intentions. He thanked the soldiers fighting in China and reassured the nation that the fall of Chiang Kai-shek's regime was near and that, in light of the unstable condition of the Soviet Union since June, certain measures were being undertaken to safeguard Japan's northern frontiers. As for the south, Tojo insisted that Japan was forced into the occupation of northern French Indochina because "Britain, the United States, and the Netherlands had stepped up their exclusionary economic policies against Japan." Japan's occupation of the southern half of Indochina was meant as an additional "defensive step" to counter these policies. But that, too, was "received with suspicion and fear by those same countries, which led them to freeze Japanese assets and enforce a de facto total sanction." This, in his view, "was an aggressive and hostile action tantamount to an armed conflict."

Tojo told the nation that his government was still trying its best to bring about a peaceful resolution, but he also suggested that it was not going to be easy. Therefore, the nation had to come together as one, "no matter how the situation might develop," for the sake of a brighter future for Japan, for Asia, and for the world. He ended his speech by thanking the Japanese for their mobilization effort and expressed his respect and gratitude to the "heroic souls of the war dead" for protecting their nation.

Tojo's speech was given to preface a ceremonious bicameral approval of a new policy accompanied by a special increase in the military budget, which was, in the words of the reporter Otto Tolischus, characterized by "something of that super-deftness in language that often baffles translators." Tolischus's report for *The New York Times* on November 18, 1941, quoted Tojo's speech as follows:

> To settle the troubles in East Asia as speedily as possible and to secure co-prosperity among East Asiatic nations forever and thereby contribute to world peace are the immovable national policies of the Japanese Empire. The government is requested to effect a break in the current critical situation while properly meeting the situations at home and abroad and thereby not make a single mistake in the execution of the national policies.

The Japanese could not have been too alarmed by the forcefulness of this resolution or of Tojo's speech. Such strong language had lost its impact through habitual overuse. To the extent that it introduced the people of Japan to Tojo's voice, the speech was a success. Tojo's distinct, affectedly formal way of talking—characterized by his fondness for the words "therefore" and "thus"—became so familiar to the Japanese ear that schoolchildren soon started imitating him.

The impact of this well-publicized session was greater in the United States. These were no utterances of peace-loving politicians. While claiming to prefer peace, Japanese leaders from Tojo down seemed to be doing everything in their power to prepare for war and to blatantly publicize their warlike intentions. Tolischus observed that the policy speeches delivered by Tojo and Togo in the Diet "make it evident that a final showdown between Japan and the United States is at hand." Though Togo was quoted as saying that "amicable conclusion of the negotiations is by no means impossible," the reporter conveyed that "the general impression in both foreign and diplomatic quarters here" was that the speeches "contributed nothing toward that peaceful settlement in the Pacific which, Japan says, she desires."

The next day, November 19, Tolischus dispatched another report, citing a speech made by Shimada Toshio. The veteran politician and former minister of agriculture explained the current policy as vital to treating the "cancer of the Pacific [that] lies in the minds of arrogant American leaders who are seeking world hegemony for themselves and are meddling even in Europe by assisting Britain." It was Japan's mission to remove this cancer by wielding a big knife and to carry on with its "disinterested holy war." Most chillingly, he added that "there are other ways to make such a party understand."

In Washington, it seemed that Japan had decided to go to war. There were almost no Americans left in Tokyo now. For some time, despite the diplomatic tensions and the China War, the number of Americans residing in Tokyo had been on the rise, reaching its peak of more than a thousand in June 1940. But in November 1941, there were only two hundred U.S. nationals left, the lowest figure of the past three decades.

Kurusu had far more than his own tainted public image to overcome in Washington.

DESPITE U.S.-GERMAN HOSTILITIES, the United States was keeping out of Hitler's war. Following the *Greer* incident, the U.S. destroyer *Kearny* was torpedoed by a U-boat off the coast of Iceland on October 17, causing eleven deaths. Roosevelt spoke then as if a war were imminent, but he did not follow up with a request for a congressional declaration of war. On October 31, the United States suffered another blow when a U-boat attacked the destroyer *Reuben James*, acting as part of the convoy escort force, near Iceland. It sank, and 115 men perished. Again, there was no request for a declaration of war; in fact, Roosevelt's reaction to this disaster was surprisingly measured. He was ever mindful of domestic isolationist opposition, antiwar public opinion, the country's unpreparedness for war mobilization, and, increasingly, the uncertainty of the U.S.-Japanese relations in the Pacific.

In the wake of the *Reuben James* incident, a resolution to repeal sections of the Neutrality Acts was passed by the Senate on November 7, followed by the House on November 13. Both votes were close (50–37 in the Senate and 212–194 in the House), which justified Roosevelt's continued caution. The United States could now arm its merchant ships and travel to combat zones carrying any type of cargo. Just as Washington's legislators were finally acting to remove legal obstacles to entering the war they thought likely in the Atlantic, things were beginning to heat up in the Pacific, too. Japanese troops in French Indochina increased by the day. In response, Britain and the United States stepped up their defenses in

Malaya and the Philippines. There was an unsettling atmosphere in the South Seas.

Yet again, Soldier U was directly affected by Japan's new mobilization plan. He had been called up for a possible attack on the Soviet Union in the summer of 1941, which, as we know, never took place. Instead, he was assigned to oversee the training of his less experienced comrades in northern Manchuria into early fall, all the while fighting constant hunger and bedbugs. In late October, he and his unit were moved to the Russian-developed cosmopolitan city of Harbin. There he was given a spade and pickax and made to engage in rigorous construction work, day in and day out for forty days, to help build army bunkers. The effort left him with a chronic limp in his left leg. In mid-November, his unit was ordered to leave Harbin immediately; he could not even say good-bye to his sister-in-law, a Harbin resident. Nonetheless, Soldier U and his friends departed the railroad station with light hearts. They believed that their "provisional call" had finally come to an end and that they were being sent home. They remained cheerful throughout the three-day journey in packed train cars.

Their spirits sank when they arrived in Dalian, a major Manchurian seaport. They were ordered to exchange their winter clothes for summer ones and were given masks and gloves made of mosquito nets. They had no idea where they were being taken, but it was clear they were not going home. They boarded a big ship, along with a few other units. At sea, they lived on a little bit of rice, supplemented with seaweed, which hardly satiated their hunger. They felt it getting hotter as each day passed. The ship finally stopped. The rumor was that they were in the Taiwan Strait. As the men climbed on deck, they were astonished to see an impressive fleet of Japanese navy vessels. After all the ships were refueled, they set out together. The navy escort, which included warplanes and warships, made the soldiers feel safe. As the temperature rose even higher and their thirst and hunger grew, Soldier U still had no idea where he was going.

This southward mobilization represented only one aspect of Japan's offensive program. Earlier, on November 7, the Navy General Staff had issued the first order for war mobilization. On November 10, ten sailors were selected for a special submarine mission to aid the aerial attack on Pearl Harbor. The mission involved five midget submarines, each bearing two men and two torpedoes, which would act as "manned torpedoes." They had limited range, and once they were inside the harbor, the chance of survival for the crews was deemed extremely small. Yamamoto, averse to any strategies that presupposed the death of his sailors, had repeatedly rejected the plan over the previous months. But the young officers who developed it insisted on its execution. Finally, Yamamoto gave in—on the condition that the officers would continue researching the possibility of a safe return and would pledge themselves to maximizing that possibility.

What would effectively be a suicide mission was thus approved. This echoed the whole rationale for the war decision itself: As long as there was even the slightest chance of success, it was a gamble worth taking. On November 18, having completed their final exercise, a group of six aircraft carriers ultimately bound for Hawaii left for Hitokappu Bay, located at the northernmost end of the Japanese island chain. The carriers would set off from there so as to avoid being spotted by other ships. Fifty-four-year-old Vice Admiral Nagumo Chuichi commanded this First Air Fleet. An old-school fleet commander with no experience in aviation to speak of, he was appointed solely on the basis of seniority.

THAT SAME DAY in Washington, Nomura and Kurusu met Hull. Hull was as strident as he had been the previous day about the inadvisability of Japan's remaining in the fascist alliance. He said once again that he could not understand why Japan should be so adamant about honoring its treaty with Hitler. Germany did not exactly have a great track record as far as honoring friendships was concerned. Hull impressed on the Japanese envoys that so long as Japan remained a fascist ally, he did not know whether "anything could be done in the matter of reaching a satisfactory agreement with Japan." He said that the United States could "go so far but rather than go beyond a certain point it would be better for us to stand and take the consequences." He was not about to compromise what he regarded as his most basic moral principles. Kurusu could only repeat that an agreement between Japan and the United States would "outshine" the Tripartite Pact, and he begged Hull to understand that "big ships cannot turn around too quickly, that they have to be eased around slowly and gradually."

Then came by far the most remarkable moment for Nomura in his dealings with Washington. Nomura suggested to Hull that Japan would withdraw its troops from southern Indochina so that the two countries could "[go] back to the status which existed before the date in July . . . before [the U.S.] freezing measures were put into effect." Nomura was playing his trump card—the concession Togo had obtained from the military. Kurusu had likely informed him of it.

Hull appeared unmoved by Nomura's suggestion. He expressed his misgivings that Japan might simply divert the withdrawn troops to its advantage, "to some equally objectionable" places, and said that it would be difficult for his government to remove the embargo unless it "believed that the Japanese were definitely started on a peaceful course and had renounced purposes of conquest." Nomura persisted. He explained that the Japanese people were sick of fighting in China and that the U.S. government could be assured of Japan's sincere intention to take a first tangible step toward peace.

Nomura proposed to seek a détente—the easing of immediate tensions—rather than striving for a complete, idealistic plan that could hardly be agreed upon, let alone carried out, anytime soon. It was his way of demonstrating to Washington that Japan took the business of creating a modus vivendi—Roosevelt's idea—very seriously. By the end of the meeting, Hull had come around to promising that he would consult with the British and the Dutch about the new Japanese proposal. This was a sign that, in Hull's earlier words, the discussions were progressing beyond the "exploratory conversations" toward "formal negotiations." The two Japanese negotiators were greatly encouraged by the prospect.

KURUSU SENT a message to Tokyo immediately after this meeting with Hull. He wrote compellingly that both he and Nomura thought Washington was open to negotiations and that it would be foolish to resort to some reckless, irreversible action simply because the other party would not at once agree to all of Japan's proposed terms. Kurusu's communication also emphasized that Roosevelt and Hull were becoming firmer in their demand for Japan to sever ties with Germany. Though it might be impossible for Japan to leave the pact right away, he felt Japan had to show a clearer sign that it was moving toward parting ways with Hitler. Given the time constraints placed on the negotiations, Kurusu argued, it would be wise to continue pursuing an agreement along the lines of Nomura's latest proposal and to withdraw from southern French Indochina. The more conditions Japan attached to its proposal, the more difficult it would be for the two governments to engage in a meaningful exchange. He ended the message by saying that he and Nomura would like to reach some kind of an understanding with Roosevelt before November 22, when the president was due to leave Washington.

For the next two days, everything seemed to take an upward turn for the Japanese envoys. They kept receiving informal news that the Roosevelt administration was considering Nomura's proposal seriously. On the morning of November 19, Father Walsh, one of the two priests who had set the U.S.-Japan "informal conversations" in motion earlier that year, visited Kurusu at the Japanese embassy. Because of his close ties with Frank Walker, Roosevelt's postmaster general and a devout Catholic, he claimed to have access to insider information. Walsh congratulated Kurusu on the near completion of his mission, saying that the United States would probably accept Nomura's proposal.

Encouraged, Nomura and Kurusu visited Hull in his apartment later that night. Hull seemed optimistic indeed. He expressed his view that an agreement on this matter "might enable the leaders in Japan to hold their ground and organize public opinion in favor of a peaceful course"— though, he also sympathetically conceded, turning public opinion around "might take some time." The representatives of the two governments were finally speaking the same language and seemed about to take a concrete first step toward their shared objective.

THAT HOPEFUL ATMOSPHERE was dampened in an instant with the arrival of a telegram from Togo to Nomura, dispatched on November 20. Togo was furious that Nomura had veered from his meticulous instructions and taken such a diplomatic initiative. Since Togo still hadn't received a U.S. reply to Plan A, he had not yet authorized his Washington team to present Plan B. Nomura, said Togo, had no business separating the issue of Indochinese troop withdrawal from the other items in Plan B and turning it into a stand alone proposal.

Togo's outrage could partly be explained by what he regarded as the impudence of a nonprofessional diplomat. A proud man, he treated the talks as his own and the diplomats in Washington as mere conduits for his orders. In Togo's mind, Nomura's action was a typical case of an envoy forgetting that "his duty is to carry out orders" and promising the other side too much. Perhaps he was venting frustration, facing the reality that it was unlikely the military would unilaterally concede to a troop withdrawal. (The army, especially, wanted something in return, like a favorable settlement of the China War.) Perhaps he was simply exhausted and demoralized. Whatever the reasons, Togo was determined to sabotage Nomura's initiative instead of trying to further negotiate with the military, even though he had been promised Tojo's support.

"There is absolutely no room for such maneuver," Togo told the ambassadors in Washington. It was "regrettable, given the delicate situation at home," that Nomura should have gone beyond his brief. Togo instructed him to immediately submit Japan's so-called Final Proposal, a version of Plan B that entailed (1) no military advance beyond Indochina, (2) cooperation to secure resources from the Dutch East Indies, (3) reversion of commercial relations to the conditions prior to Japan's southern Indochinese occupation, (4) no U.S. intervention in a Sino-Japanese peace, and (5) withdrawal of Japanese troops from southern Indochina. The China issue was reintroduced after all. Nomura's attempt to get the diplomatic ball rolling had failed. "If we cannot gain U.S. approval for this plan [Plan B]," Togo had written, "we will simply have to accept the eventuality of talks falling apart."

CHAPTER 15

The Hull Note

There is no question that diplomacy, by the nature of its craft, requires patience. But Tokyo's self-imposed deadline for a U.S.-Japan understanding made the business of waiting exceptionally difficult, even for a seasoned diplomat. Kurusu, desperate for an answer from Hull to Plan B, submitted the previous day, visited the secretary of state at his apartment on November 21. It was now *his* turn to take a bold initiative, Togo be damned.

Kurusu handed Hull a draft letter pledging that Japan would act independently of its Tripartite Pact partners in the event that the United States went to war in Europe. It was presented as a strictly private proposal, but one that essentially mirrored the Japanese government's existing position. Indeed, Kurusu simply copied a passage from Togo's November 20 instructions on how to explain the government's stance on the Tripartite Pact. Togo had prohibited its immediate use; Kurusu and Nomura were "to refrain from presenting this explanation [to the United States] until an agreement is reached."

Togo did not want any references he made to Japan's exit from the fascist alliance to fall into U.S. hands. Should a U.S.-Japanese agreement fall through, he feared that it could be used for propaganda purposes by the U.S. administration to publicly drive a wedge into the enemy coalition. But Kurusu did not see any point in keeping this critical piece of information from the United States, as he strongly sensed that Tokyo's renunciation of the Tripartite Pact now could just possibly tip the balance of the negotiations. Kurusu suspected a written promise that Japan had "in substance" left the Tripartite Pact would mean a great deal more to the United States if it came from the very signer of that pact. Thus he presented Hull with his personal note:

> As Your Excellency is fully aware I am the one who signed the said treaty under the instructions of my Government; and I am very happy to make the following statement which I trust will serve to eradicate the aforesaid false impression [regarding Japan's Tripartite Pact obligations]
>
> It goes without saying that this treaty can not and does not infringe, in any way, upon the sovereign right of Japan as an independent state.
>
> Besides, as Article III of the Pact stands, Japan is in a position to interpret its obligation freely and independently and is not to be bound by the interpretation which the other high contracting parties may make of it. I should like to add that my Government is not obligated by the aforementioned treaty or any other international engagement to become a collaborator or cooperator in any aggression whatever by any third Power or Powers.
>
> My Government would never project the people of Japan into war at the behest of any foreign Power; it will accept warfare only as the ultimate, inescapable necessity for the maintenance of its security and the preservation of national life against active injustice.
>
> I hope that the above statement will assist you in removing entirely the popular suspicion which Your Excellency has repeatedly referred to. I have to add that, when a complete Understanding is reached between us, Your Excellency may feel perfectly free to publish the present communication.

Upon reading this statement, Hull said he wanted to show it to someone else and asked Kurusu if he could keep it. Kurusu, encouraged by this response, asked if that someone was the president. The answer was no. Did the secretary mean to present it at a cabinet meeting? Again, no. Hull volunteered no more information, but Kurusu took the risk and left the document in Hull's hands.

As far as Kurusu was concerned, his thirty-minute meeting with Hull provided some hope. Hull even engaged him in the kind of small talk for which Roosevelt was better known. "You came all this way, Ambassador, so it would be proper for me to invite you to a meal or to a round of golf," Hull told Kurusu. "But you know how busy we all are. And I find that golfing takes too much time anyway. I have come to believe that the game is not compatible with the affairs of state." Hull seemed unusually cheerful and compassionate. He complimented Kurusu on his clever use of the term "outshine" in describing the effective dead-lettering of the Tripartite Pact. He then went on to reminisce about his experiences working with Japanese delegates at the 1933 London Economic Conference with apparent nostalgia and fondness and even hinted at some sympathy for Japan's desire to create a regional order. (After all, Hull's Four Principles, too, were an attempt—though a more peaceful one—at creating a semblance of a regional order in Asia.) He said he could understand the concept very well, though he thought that East Asian Coprosperity Sphere was a rather clumsy name for it.

More important to Kurusu, Hull appeared to genuinely appreciate his and Nomura's efforts to reach a diplomatic solution, in spite of the tremendous pressures and restrictions placed upon them by the hard-line elements back home. Hull lamented that he was only too familiar with the frustrations of not being able to conduct diplomacy unfettered by various political obstructions. Hull was finally seeming to open up to Kurusu, and that was very good news. Shaking Hull's hand upon taking his leave, the Japanese envoy noticed that Hull had a fever. "Please, do take care of yourself," said Kurusu, and left, having played, with no certainty of its success, the only card he felt he still possessed.

Hull's memorandum of his tête-à-tête with Kurusu was extremely brief and not encouraging from the Japanese perspective:

> I looked at the paper and then asked Mr. Kurusu whether he had anything more on the whole subject of a peaceful settlement to offer. He replied that he did not. I said that I did not think this would be of any particular help and so dismissed it. This was virtually all that was said of importance.

When Kurusu and Nomura visited Hull the next day, November 22, the secretary of state had recovered from his cold and was his usual professional self. He gave no specific answers regarding Plan B. Instead, he expressed his distrust of Japan's peaceful intentions. He condemned Japan's entry into southern Indochina in the summer even as he was discussing the possibility of reversing it with Nomura. He said that oil purchased by Japan the previous spring "was not used for normal civilian consumption," as Hull had been led to believe it would be. He also made note of the increasing volume of anti-Anglo-American statements in the Japanese press.

Hull wondered why there was "not some Japanese statesman backing the two Ambassadors by preaching peace." Would it not be possible, the secretary inquired, "for a Japanese statesman now to come out and say that Japan wanted peace"? Wouldn't Japan "like to have a peace which she did not have to fight for to obtain and maintain" even though there was "much confusion in the world because of the war situation"? Why had Japan "pushed everything it wanted all at once into its proposal," he asked, "[when] a peaceful movement could be started in thirty or forty days by moving gradually"? He indicated that he much preferred Nomura's single-item approach to Togo's Plan B.

Hull also pointed to the blatantly obvious "danger arising from blocking progress by injecting the China matter in the proposal." This confirmed what Nomura and Kurusu had feared from the beginning: "The carrying out of such a point in the Japanese proposal would effectually prevent the United States from ever successfully extending its good offices in a peace settlement between Japan and China." By including the noninterference condition in the peace between Japan and China, the chances of Plan B ever moving forward were greatly diminished.

Nomura would not give up hope. Some response—any response—from the United States represented continued engagement. As long as there remained a remote chance of peace, he believed, a right-thinking government would not abandon diplomacy. Nomura felt that if he could get the United States to address even one aspect of Plan B directly, negotiations could carry on, despite Tokyo's deadline, which was only three days away. That was why Nomura asked Hull whether there were any points in the current Japanese proposal that the United States would either accept or like Japan to consider modifying. Alas, no clear reply was forthcoming. Hull said that he could not "carry the whole burden" and asked if the Japanese government could not wait until he had the time to confer with the representatives of other concerned parties (the Dutch, the Chinese, and the British). Not desiring to press Hull too much and alienate him even further, Nomura agreed to wait.

On the same day, Nomura received a telegram from Togo informing him that the negotiation deadline of November 25 had been mercifully extended to November 29. But there were to be "absolutely no more changes beyond that date." The situation would then press on "in an automatic fashion." The telegram explained that the extension was given because of "the waiting time necessary for the whole [diplomatic] procedure to complete." Within the given time, the Japanese diplomats were told to secure "not only the official signing but also the exchange of official documents with Britain and the Netherlands." Togo attached a draft of the official documents to be exchanged and signed by the concerned parties. This was unlikely to be put to use, and Togo knew it. But it was the formal procedure.

ON THE EVENING of November 25, Hull prepared a U.S. reply that proposed a truce, requesting Japan's immediate withdrawal from southern French Indochina (the concession already outlined in Plan B) and the reduction of Japan's northern French Indochinese troops to twenty-five thousand. In return, the United States would unfreeze Japanese assets and resume economic relations with Japan, albeit with some restrictions. The duration of the modus vivendi would be three months, but an extension could be initiated by either party.

However uncompromising Hull's moral ground, and whatever his personal views of Japan or its diplomats, he remained a pragmatic and extremely patient negotiator with the Japanese. And his new plan reflected his continuing effort to find a compromise—a modus vivendi, as suggested by Roosevelt to the Japanese—that would allow the United States more time to prop up its defenses in the Philippines and prepare itself for an anticipated war in Europe. By the morning of the next day, Hull had completely scrapped the plan. There were several explanations for this sudden shift. One was that the Chinese and the British opposed a U.S. compromise with Japan (the Dutch supported Hull's modus vivendi). Hull's own postwar explanation was that "the slight prospect of Japan's agreeing to the *modus vivendi* did not warrant assuming the risks involved in proceeding with it, especially the risk of collapse of Chinese morale and resistance, and even of disintegration in China." But given its timing, the most powerful reason for the reversal was almost certainly the report of Japanese troop mobilization in the South Seas, especially the movement south of Taiwan, which had led the Roosevelt administration to conclude that Japan was poised to strike any day.

It was, of course, no secret that both countries were already mobilizing in the South Seas. And Roosevelt knew of Togo's November 22 communication informing the Japanese embassy that things would proceed "in an automatic fashion" after November 29. Based on this intercepted communication, the president reportedly told his advisers on November 25 that Japan would likely attack the United States on December 1, "for the Japanese are notorious for making an attack without warning." Roosevelt's secretary of war, Henry Stimson, recorded in his diary that the central question at the meeting was how to "maneuver [the Japanese] into the position of firing the first shot without allowing too much danger to ourselves." Roosevelt fully anticipated a Japanese military offensive while at the same time underestimating Japan's ability to launch a truly crippling attack. The news of an increasing military buildup in the south probably led him to believe that a Japanese move against British, Dutch, or U.S. targets was imminent in Southeast Asia. When he reached this conclusion, his view of the Japanese negotiators in Washington must have hardened—either they were dunces or, worse, they were duplicitously trying to buy time.

In the dark early days of World War II, Roosevelt felt it vital for the United States to enter the war against Germany. Now he felt the time had come to take on Japan. This does not in any way endorse the so-called backdoor theory that Roosevelt and Churchill connived to have the United States enter the war in Europe by way of a war with Japan. Because Japan had refused to join forces with Germany against the Soviet Union, it was possible Germany could refuse to fight the United States on Japan's account. No one can say for sure what would have transpired. What is known is that when Nomura and Kurusu were summoned to the State Department in the late afternoon of November 26, they received not the modus vivendi but another document Hull had drafted alongside it. Officially titled "Outline of Proposed Basis for Agreement Between the United States and Japan," it would be better known in history as the Hull Note. The two Japanese envoys were urged by Hull to read it carefully.

The second section of the document, "Steps to Be Taken by the Government of the United States and by the Government of Japan," consisted of ten points and contained the most critical information. It proposed that an agreement of nonaggression be reached multilaterally by the United States, Japan, Britain, China, the Netherlands, the Soviet Union, and Thailand. There would be a similar multilateral agreement on the preservation of territorial integrity and equal commercial opportunities in French Indochina.

Negotiating a multilateral agreement, however, was not what the Japanese diplomats were supposed to be doing. Tokyo had made it very clear that Japan wanted a bilateral agreement with the United States, one to which the other governments could subsequently extend their approval, again, on a bilateral basis. The Japanese had neither the time nor the inclination to conceive of a grand international peace on the scale that the United States was now proposing.

The Japanese envoys were further discouraged by the U.S. demands on Japan regarding China. These were crystallized in the third, fourth, and fifth points: The government of Japan was to withdraw all military, naval, air, and police forces from China and from Indochina; the U.S. and Japanese governments would agree not to support militarily, politically, or economically any government or regime in China other than the national government of the Republic of China with its capital temporarily at Chongqing; and both governments would give up all extraterritorial rights in China, including rights and interests in, and with regard to, international settlements and concessions and rights under the Boxer Protocol of 1901.

The outline consisted of a list of proposals that both parties knew could not be negotiated and agreed to within a short period of time. It spelled out America's long-term vision of an Asia based on the principles of free trade and equal opportunity and was most likely drafted as a supplement to the scrapped modus vivendi plan that contained U.S. engagement with the specific terms of Plan B. As a stand-alone document, the outline read as if the United States were demanding an unconditional surrender without having fought and won a war with Japan. It "outshined" the Japanese in pushing "everything it wanted all at once into its proposal." Even though the outline was marked "tentative and without commitment," Hull knew fully, and later admitted, that "we had no serious thought that Japan would accept our proposal."

The Japanese delegates attempted to have Hull temper the U.S. demands before the document left the meeting room. Their efforts were in vain. When Kurusu pointed out that, practically speaking, the Japanese government could not possibly stand by and watch Wang Jingwei's government collapse, Hull suggested that Wang's government had no ability to unite China and that it was not worth wasting time discussing a failed regime. Kurusu protested that Japan could not at this point abruptly change its diplomatic methodology and agree to multilateral agreements. Hull did not want to have a dialogue on that matter, either.

Nomura asked if they could speak directly with the president, citing Roosevelt's recent remark about there being no last word between friends. With apparent reluctance, Hull agreed to set up a meeting. Kurusu expressed his grave fear that "[the] proposal could be interpreted as tantamount to meaning the end." Was there no chance that the United States might still be interested in agreeing to a modus vivendi? The answer was no. Hull said he had done his best.

On the day the Hull Note was issued, Japan's troop movement in the South Seas had caused a stern reaction in Washington. But far more significant that day was the furtive departure of Vice Admiral Nagumo's squadron, led by the flagship *Akagi,* from Hitokappu Bay. The crew had recently been notified, for the first time, of the goal of its mission. The plan was shrouded in such secrecy that even Tojo was not informed of its details. Should a diplomatic settlement be reached before the deadline, the ships were expected to turn around and go home. That now seemed highly unlikely.

CHAPTER 16

Jumping Off the High Platform

The Hull Note did not impose a specific deadline, but it was taken as an ultimatum when it reached the Japanese government around noon on November 27.

Togo was shocked by its content. "I was struck by despair," he later recalled. "I tried to imagine swallowing whole [the demands], but there was no way to force them down my throat." He felt that the note rejected willfully and categorically all the efforts that the two countries had been putting into their discussions, as though they had never taken place. For those restlessly itching for military action, the note was "nothing short of a miracle!" noted one *bakuryo* officer on the Army General Staff. It now seemed that no diplomatic settlement was possible.

Most Japanese leaders took the note as a provocation and a disgrace. Its cavalier tone, not to mention its difficult terms, confirmed in their minds that they were being bullied and humiliated. It also gave the leaders a chance to put a stop to the infighting and place responsibility squarely on the other side. More credence was given to the emotive story of Japan being persecuted by the ABCD powers. The United States was the primary bully, squeezing the life out of Japan while helping Chiang Kai-shek and the British in their respective wars behind the thinly veiled pretense of neutrality.

This Japanese reading, needless to say, was a case of selective memory. It was Japan that had occupied southern Indochina without responding to Roosevelt's proposal for neutralization. It was Japan that had not done enough to dispel the U.S. fear of its alliance with Germany, even after Operation Barbarossa provided Tokyo with a golden opportunity for divorce. It was Tojo whose tough public speeches gave the impression to the outside world that Japan was now a full-fledged military dictatorship—though, ironically, Japan's strange consensus building could hardly be called a dictatorship and the palace had appointed Tojo in the hope of reversing the war momentum. Above all, the fast-approaching deadline for the end of diplomatic negotiations was entirely of the Japanese leaders' making. Self-delusion now created in Japan an overwhelming sense of self-pity.

Togo's daughter, Ise, observed a physical change in her father. Until the arrival of the note, he had great energy; after November 27, he looked despondent. He saw the note not only as an insult to the Japanese government but also as a personal rejection. Contemplating resignation, he consulted with foreign policy officials, including the former foreign minister Sato Naotake. Sato tried to convince him that the note should not cause such despair and that his job now was to find a way around it.

Count Makino Nobuaki, a noted liberal internationalist of the Saionji school, reacted to the note with a sigh. "This is terribly written indeed!" the eighty-year-old said, lamenting the harshness of the U.S. tone and demands. Still, he believed Togo's mission was to avoid perceiving war as inevitable. He relayed his advice to Togo through his son-in-law Yoshida Shigeru, a former ambassador to Britain.

> The decision between war and peace requires utmost caution. I hope very much that the foreign minister would not make any mistakes in his treatment of the situation and his course of action. If we were to commence war with the United States, and instantly upset everything that we have accomplished since the Meiji Restoration, the foreign minister, as one of the leaders in charge, would not be able to justify himself.

Yoshida told Togo that whatever the true intentions of the Hull Note, in strictly diplomatic and legal terms, it did not constitute an ultimatum and did not place a time limit on Japanese actions. Yoshida encouraged the foreign minister to make a defiant political stand by resigning his post. "If you resign," he said to Togo, "the cabinet will be stalled and the imprudent military would have to think twice." Yoshida suggested that Togo should meet with Ambassador Grew, who was keen to explain that the note should not be seen as an ultimatum. Togo saw no use for such a talk. Thoroughly dispirited, a wronged hero (now wronged, in his mind, by Washington rather than by his domestic opponents), Togo felt there was nothing more to be done. Perhaps this was a conclusion he had gradually started reaching when he decided to back the latest imperial conference resolution. The Hull Note only helped him come to terms with it.

ROOSEVELT AND HULL RECEIVED Nomura and Kurusu in the Oval Office on November 27. Despite having warned his closest advisers that Japan might strike the United States on December 1, Roosevelt, the quintessential diplomat, welcomed the Japanese cheerfully, camouflaging his distrust. After the Japanese envoys sat down, the president offered them cigarettes, and Nomura gratefully accepted. The president struck a match to light Nomura's cigarette. Nomura, blind in his right eye as a result of an assault in China, struggled to find the match. Smiling, Roosevelt extended his arm farther and helped Nomura finally reach the light. The atmosphere was nothing but congenial.

After some initial chitchat about Roosevelt not being able to take any time off in the country, the president began to talk about Germany. He said that the United States and Japan, as partners during World War 1, together suffered from the German inability to understand the psychology of other nations. Kurusu understood that the remark was the president's indirect but unflinching way of criticizing the Japanese folly in remaining a German ally.

Nomura then came to the point of their visit, expressing his regret over the absence of an alternative to the most recent U.S. proposal. The president replied as if already lamenting the inevitable conclusion. He and his government were grateful for and appreciative of the effort of "the peace element in Japan," which had striven to support "the movement to establish a peaceful settlement in the Pacific area." Even though he had still not given up, the president thought the situation to be "serious" and said "that fact should be recognized."

Continuing as if he were ceremoniously recapping the past events to bring the meeting to an end, Roosevelt looked back on the conversations he had had with Nomura since April. He said that the Japanese occupation of southern Indochina had felt like "a cold bath" to his administration and that the more recent "movements and utterances of the Japanese slanting wholly in the direction of conquest by force and ignoring the whole question of a peaceful settlement and the principles underlying it" aroused fears that he might have to suffer through another one. In addition to the jingoistic pronouncements in Japan's media, the president had in mind the aforementioned Japanese troop movement detected in the south, as well as the rumor that Japan was about to reach a military pact with neutral Thailand. He stressed how disappointed he was with those Japanese leaders who "continued to express opposition to the fundamental principles of peace and order." Should Japan "unfortunately decide to follow Hitlerism and courses of aggression," he said, the United States was convinced that Japan would be "the ultimate loser."

In response, Nomura tried to appeal to the president's sense of nostalgia, reminding him of their thirty-year acquaintance, and asked for his help in finding some way out of the crisis. The congenial air that pervaded at the beginning of the meeting was no longer in evidence, however. No significant modifications to the Hull Note were to be made by the United States, and Hull flatly dismissed Nomura's suggestion. "Unless the opposition to the peace element in control of the Government should make up its mind definitely to act and talk and move in a peaceful direction," he said, "no conversations could or would get anywhere as has been so clearly demonstrated."

Following the Japanese envoys' departure, the State Department, usually cautious about divulging the details of U.S.-Japanese conversations, elaborated on the state of affairs in a press conference. Its intended message was that the United States had done everything it could. *The New York Times* on November 28 reported:

> All United States efforts to solve differences with Japan appeared exhausted yesterday, and the next move—either diplomatic or military—seemed up to Tokyo. President Roosevelt, with Secretary Hull at his side, held a forty-five-minute conference with the Japanese envoys . . . who now await official Tokyo reaction to Mr. Hull's note reaffirming this country's stand on its basic policy in the Far East. The conference followed the receipt of reports that Japanese reinforcements were moving into French Indo-China. . . . Secretary Hull's note, handed to the envoys Wednesday night, was received in informed Tokyo quarters with calmness that suggested the Japanese had been expecting such a reply to their demands.

The U.S. government was now on record saying that whether it was going to war or not was entirely up to Japan—exactly the opposite of what the leaders in Tokyo were telling themselves.

IT WAS CERTAINLY WRONG to say that the Hull Note was "received in informed Tokyo quarters with calmness." There had been errors in judgment on both sides. But the errors had been induced, amplified, and spun out of control largely by the erratic and inflexible fashion in which Tokyo had been carrying out its foreign policy over many months, especially since its occupation of northern Indochina and its signing of the Tripartite Pact with Germany and Italy. Roosevelt might very well have underrated Japan's military capabilities and tactical planning and overestimated its link with the Nazi regime. But in the end, it was still resoundingly up to Japan, not the United States, to avoid war, however humiliating, emasculating, and impossible that choice might have seemed to its leaders. The strategic timetable and bureaucratic rules that limited Tokyo's options were not created by the United States, no matter how easily the Japanese leaders came to convince themselves that they had been cornered into war. They could delude themselves into thinking that they were the wronged party, that despite everything, Japan had been accommodating with the United States. But even the Japanese concessions outlined in Plans A and B had surfaced only recently and belatedly, after much coaxing by Togo. As the Hull Note now helped the conflicted Japanese leaders catapult themselves into a dreaded war, the leaders had only self-pity, rage, and, most important, a gambler's daring on their side. The United States, on the other hand, could afford to fight a long war, even if it also had to fight Germany. "They would be ground to powder" was Churchill's unreserved prediction of Japan's fate.

Surely, not all Japanese feelings of injustice were imaginary. Moreover, those feelings were underpinned by the fear of the outside world rooted in Japan's modern history. But it is too facile to portray the war that Japan was about to launch as a war for Asia against the arrogant West. In the sweeping picture of a racial-civilizational clash, all Western (that is, white) powers were lumped together as Japan's potential enemy. In the same imperial conference of November 5 that sanctioned the final deadline for diplomatic negotiations, Hara, the president of the Privy Council, worked in close consultation with Privy Seal Kido to pose questions on behalf of

Hirohito: "If Japan is to join the war, we must consider what will happen to the relations between Germany and Britain and between Germany and the United States." Hara did not trust Germany—or any other "white" power, for that matter. He had been disturbed when Hitler said that the Japanese were a second-class race. Considering that Germany had not directly declared war on the United States, he feared that Japan might be placed in an awkward situation if it went to war.

> Would the U.S. popular attitude be the same against Japan as it is against Germany? Or would it be more outraged by Japan than it would be by Hitler? Once Japan launches a war against the United States, I fear that there would be an agreement between Germany, the United States, and Britain to leave Japan behind. Their hatred of the yellow race will immediately be transferred to Japan, superseding their hatred of Germany. We must be prepared for such an eventuality. . . . We must carefully consider the factors of race relations and must make sure that the Japanese empire would not be left alone, encircled by the Aryan races.

To Hara, the "Aryan races" embraced all white powers. A great deal of Japanese feeling was invested in its skin.

And yet racial humiliation and thin skin did not always deprive Japan's leaders of sensible judgment. At the conclusion of the Sino-Japanese War in 1895, as we've seen, Japan opted to brook the shame of the Triple Intervention. Then Russia, Germany, and France ganged up on Japan, intervening in the terms of the Treaty of Shimonoseki to suit their imperialist aims. Much against popular opinion in Japan at the time, the government, led by Prime Minister Ito Hirobumi and Foreign Minister Mutsu Munemitsu, decided not to launch a war of protest, aware of the slim chance of winning it. Instead, Japan opted to voluntarily withdraw from the Liaodong Peninsula for an additional indemnity. The leadership made a prudent policy choice consistent with Japan's greater goal of rapid modernization.

But there were no leaders of the caliber of those Meiji rulers in November 1941. This was plain for all to see when Japan's former prime ministers gathered for lunch with the emperor at his request on November 29 to discuss the Hull Note. None of them welcomed a war. But most shied away from making their opinions explicit, assuming they had no power to change the existing policy. Admiral Yonai, a consistent anti-Nazi advocate whose short-lived cabinet in 1940 was ended by Konoe's return as premier, did speak up. "Excuse me for speaking my mind in crude ways, but I think we mustn't become utterly poor in our quest to avoid becoming gradually poor," said Yonai. Such a cryptic, restrained comment could achieve nothing other than to impress on the rest of the leaders that he remained, at heart, antiwar.

Prince Konoe actually came closest to articulating any kind of objection. He asked whether it was really necessary for Japan to resort to war: "Can we not stick to the status quo? In other words, should we not wait out the hard times and see if we could break the deadlock?" But this was so little coming so pitifully late from the very man who should have asked the exact same question before he endorsed the imperial resolutions in July and again in September. There simply was no concerted effort among the former leaders of Japan to support and encourage the fearful emperor to rise up to the challenge, to use his authority to call a stop to war mobilization.

In the liaison conference that followed this imperial luncheon, it was announced that the war plan was going through its final stages of preparation, with the expectation of the immediate aid of Germany and Italy in Japan's upcoming clash. Togo had not even been told when the attack would commence. "Is there any time left for diplomacy?" he asked Nagano. "There is still some time left," answered the navy's chief of staff. Togo asked again: "On which day is the military planning to open fire? . . . Unless we know [the date], we cannot carry out diplomacy [to help the military cause]." "All right, then," said Nagano. "It is December 8. Why don't you engage in diplomacy in a way that would help us win battles?"

Across the ocean, insulated from the air of suicidal fatalism that was beginning to infect almost everyone in Tokyo, Nomura and Kurusu believed that if anyone could sway the course at this late stage, it was the emperor. They had repeatedly heard Roosevelt and Hull lament the lack of Japanese statesmen publicly professing their desire for peace. The Japanese envoys had come to learn that the U.S. distrust of Japan's peaceful intention ran deep.

On November 26, shortly before the Hull Note was delivered, Kurusu had taken it upon himself to tell Togo that, as a last resort, an imperial intervention should be requested in order to prevent the collapse of diplomatic negotiations. Kurusu's idea was to ask Roosevelt to send a message to the emperor indicating his desire for the maintenance of peace in the

Pacific and for U.S.-Japanese cooperation. The emperor could then simply reply in kind. (Kurusu knew the emperor could never initiate such a correspondence.) This, Kurusu hoped, would enable the negotiations to start anew.

Kurusu recommended to Togo that for a long-term solution in Southeast Asia, Japan should suggest the establishment of a neutralized zone encompassing French Indochina, the Dutch East Indies, and Thailand. This would benefit both parties by not only reducing the U.S. suspicions of Japanese designs on the south but also preempting any U.S. attempt to occupy the Dutch East Indies at the invitation of the Dutch colonizers. He concluded his message with a plea that he "sincerely desired that the message be communicated to Privy Seal Kido and be answered urgently."

Nomura supported Kurusu's plan wholeheartedly. Togo immediately rejected the idea—but consulted with Kido all the same. The lord keeper of the privy seal would have none of it, saying "it was not an appropriate time" for the emperor to get involved. There was, however, a palace insider who very much wanted Hirohito to intervene. On November 30, thirty-six-year-old Rear Admiral Takamatsu Nobuhito, who had recently been transferred to the Naval General Staff, visited his eldest brother, Hirohito, at the palace.

THE BROTHERS, four years apart, were close, despite Hirohito having been raised separately from his younger siblings in anticipation of his ascending the imperial throne. The sports-loving, energetic Prince Takamatsu was originally seen to be prowar. But what he had to say to Hirohito that day utterly betrayed his earlier reputation. "The navy cannot afford to fight," he told his brother, according to Kido's record. "There is a feeling that, if possible, the navy would want to avoid a Japanese-American war. If we pass up this opportunity, war will be impossible to avoid. The navy will start mobilizing for combat on December 1. After that, [war] cannot be contained."

Hirohito frankly confessed to his brother his fear of an eventual Japanese defeat. Takamatsu replied that this was all the more reason for the emperor to act now. Hirohito felt the burden acutely, but he said it was not his place to go against a decision that had been passed on to him by the government and the high command, especially when there was no clear constitutional procedure in place for an imperial veto. "If I did not approve of war, Tojo would resign, then a big coup d'état would erupt, and this would in turn give rise to absurd arguments for war," Hirohito would later explain. Of course, by failing to act, he had already allowed for the "absurd arguments for war" to reign. Kido summoned Tojo to the palace after Prince Takamatsu had left, so that the emperor could clarify any remaining questions he might have about the actual operation. Tojo would not comment on the details of the planned attack, recommending instead that Nagano and Navy Minister Shimada could do so more effectively. "Naval strategies are everything [in the upcoming war]," he said.

The two navy men arrived. Repeating the familiar official line about naval preparedness, they said they were awaiting the imperial command for war to descend upon them. Hirohito asked what would happen if Germany would not join Japan. (He was echoing Hara's fear that "Aryans" would gang up on Japan.) Shimada, in order to "reassure and calm his imperial mind," said that the Japanese empire was not counting on any German help.

Yet a Japanese war with the United States and its allies had always been predicated on German victory or, at the very least, German preponderance in Europe. The "Plan for the Facilitation of the Conclusion of War with the United States, Britain, and the Netherlands," approved at the November 15 liaison conference, said:

> We aim to demolish the Far Eastern bases belonging to the United States, Britain, and the Netherlands quickly so as to ensure our survival and defense, while actively seeking the surrender of the Chiang Kai-shek regime, cooperating with Germany and Italy to prompt British surrender first, and trying to deprive the United States of its will to continue the war.

A German defeat, or a German conciliation with the Allied powers, was never part of the official Japanese war plan.

The emperor wasn't getting any straight talk from his loyal subjects. Rather than being encouraged to halt the war, he was made to think that the wheels had already started moving "automatically" and that Japan must risk a drastic surgery to cure the "cancer of the Pacific."

Coincidentally, that same day, the newspaper *Hochi* reported, "Incredible Good News to Cancer Patients." A certain Professor Okada of Nagoya Imperial University had discovered a definitive cure for all kinds of cancer, the report said. The professor claimed to have achieved a complete remission in all of the dozen or so patients he had treated since April with a regime of homeopathic injections of cancerous cells. The professor modestly qualified his feat, saying there was still a possibility that their cancerous cells would come back, though he believed the chances were slim. He was confident that they could again be treated by the same method and achieve the same brilliant results.

Needless to say, there was no such dreamlike cure for Japan's cancer.

ON DECEMBER 1, 1941, Hirohito convened an imperial conference, the fourth in five months. There was a solemn atmosphere. The deadline for diplomatic negotiations had passed. This conference was to approve the decision to go to war with the United States, Britain, and the Netherlands. In "discussing" the matter, there was nothing new in the statements made by the government and the high command. Hirohito was silent throughout the proceedings. Hara asked questions pertaining to the neutrality of Thailand and, unexpectedly, the preparedness of Tokyo for aerial bombings, as if he foresaw the city's devastation. Hara also felt there were a few things that needed to be clarified in the Hull Note. To him, it was not so evident that its demand for a Japanese troop withdrawal from China also applied to Manchukuo, Japan's puppet state. If it didn't, Hara implied, could the note be considered less harsh than it first appeared to them? Togo wasn't sure. But it was too late for such details to be scrutinized. This imperial conference, like all the ones that had come before, was convened for a ceremonial purpose only.

Finally, Hirohito gave his approval:

> Our negotiations with the United States based on the resolution of [the revised] November 5 "Essentials for Carrying Out the Empire's Policies" did not come to a [successful] conclusion. The Empire will go to war with the United States, Britain, and the Netherlands.

On December 2, Yamamoto Isoroku sent out a radio message from aboard the *Nagato* anchored in the Inland Sea, not far from Hiroshima. It was addressed to Vice Admiral Nagumo's First Air Fleet, en route to Pearl Harbor and just about to cross the international date line along the 180th meridian. The communication read: "Climb Mount Niitaka 1208."

Japan was going to war on December 8.

The New Beginning

On the night of June 18, 1942, the *Gripsholm* of the Swedish American Line set sail from New York with a group of Japanese nationals aboard who had been detained in various makeshift camps, including one on Ellis Island. The Japanese government, in return, had dispatched the *Asama Maru* from the port of Yokohama, and later the Italian ship *Conte Verde* from Shanghai, carrying North and South American nationals home.

Some of the notable faces among the Japanese group were Nomura and Kurusu. On the day of Japan's attack on Pearl Harbor, December 7, 1941, the two men endured the most unnerving public humiliation imaginable for any diplomat. To ensure the success of the military operations in Hawaii and Malaya, the Japanese government kept the two ambassadors completely in the dark about its decision to go to war. They were notified of Tokyo's intention to terminate diplomatic relations only hours before the attack.

The Japanese embassy's inability to cope with the last-minute nature of Tokyo's instructions did not help Nomura and Kurusu in their final mission of communicating to the White House the end of diplomacy, either. Tokyo had ordered Nomura and Kurusu to see Hull at 1:00 p.m., shortly before the first bomb was to be dropped on Pearl Harbor. Because the diplomatic communication, consisting of fourteen parts, was late in being typed up for delivery, the two Japanese diplomats were shown into Hull's office at 2:20 p.m., utterly unaware that their country had already attacked the United States.

Hull was only a few pages into reading the official Japanese document when his hands began to shake. The two Japanese envoys could not understand Hull's apparent fury. After he had finished reading the entire document (not for the first time; the decoded telegrams had reached Roosevelt by 10:00 a.m.), he turned to Nomura and said:

I must say that in all my conversations with you . . . I have never uttered one word of untruth. This is borne out absolutely by the record. In all my fifty years of public service I have never seen a document that was more crowded with infamous falsehoods and distortions—infamous falsehoods and distortions on a scale so huge that I never imagined until today that any Government on this planet was capable of uttering them.

The two Japanese emissaries took their leave in speechless confusion, still ignorant of the enormous diplomatic duplicity in which they themselves had unknowingly been engaging.

Since it was a Sunday, there were very few staff members or journalists around when Nomura and Kurusu arrived at the State Department. But by the time they left the meeting, the two had to dodge reporters. They were driven back to their embassy. The heavy iron gates shut behind the diplomatic vehicle, and policemen had to restrain the angry mob congregating in front of the embassy building. It was only then that the two ambassadors were notified of Japan's attack on Pearl Harbor, and they realized that Hull had already been informed of the news when they met.

Before his departure for Washington, Nomura was forewarned by his old navy friend Admiral Yonai: "Be careful . . . the gang around today are the kind who won't hesitate to pull the ladder out from under you once they've got you to climb up it." Yonai was right.

IN THE MONTHS that followed the opening of the war in the Pacific, Nomura, Kurusu, and other Japanese nationals awaited deportation in cramped resort hotels that had been turned into temporary detention camps (luxurious lodgings compared with the internment camps that many Japanese immigrants and Americans of Japanese descent were forced to live in). In Hot Springs, Virginia, and then in White Sulphur Springs, West Virginia, Kurusu had ample time to reflect on what had gone wrong in his last-minute quest to secure peace between the two countries.

Although well aware of the urgency of their task, the two ambassadors had no idea—and Tokyo made sure they didn't—exactly how small their window of opportunity was. On November 30, Yamamoto Kumaichi of the Foreign Ministry's American Affairs Bureau telephoned them in Washington. They talked in a hastily constructed coded language. Tokyo wanted the diplomats to continue making every effort to avoid war, they were told. That's why Nomura and Kurusu feverishly worked past Tokyo's deadline of November 29, proposing on December 1 that the government ask the Roosevelt administration for an emergency meeting of representatives from the two countries, preferably in Honolulu. Nomura recommended that heavyweights be sent from Japan and hoped that Vice President Henry Wallace would attend from the U.S. side.

It was not until the summer of 1942 that Kurusu learned what had really been going on during those last ten days before Japan's attack. In Japanese-occupied Singapore, where the *Gripsholm* made a brief stop, Kurusu heard army officers recount how difficult it was for them to prepare for attacks in the run-up to the war since the military leaders in Tokyo had not decided to go to war until November 26.

This was a chilling and disheartening revelation for Kurusu. That the military leaders *had,* in fact, decided for war by November 26 confirmed that he and Nomura were told to continue diplomacy in a deliberate attempt to deceive and mislead the other side. To be sure, there were moments in the ambassadors' mission that tipped them off to Tokyo's impending decision to give up the diplomatic route, especially after the delivery of the Hull Note. In a communication from Tokyo on November 28, Togo expressed his "regret and surprise" at the content of the note and hinted to the Washington team that he would have to terminate the negotiations sometime soon. But Togo had then told the ambassadors to wait for official directives, to arrive within three days. That document, "Views of the Imperial Government," was to be delivered to the White House upon the termination of their talks. Until then, they were to carry on as normal.

That official document never arrived. On December 3, Togo directed the envoys to keep pressing the United States. Togo's exact words read: "[Plan B] constitutes, in my mind, the very best way forward to overcome this difficult situation, and so you must really explain that to the American side." Even the knotty problem of China, Togo claimed, could be settled by peaceful means: Tokyo was merely asking the United States to stop aiding Chiang Kai-shek only after the peace talks, "introduced" by President Roosevelt, had materialized. This had given Nomura and Kurusu a renewed hope for a diplomatic reconciliation. As late as December 5, Nomura and Kurusu were requesting that Hull reconsider Plan B, which the Roosevelt administration had not formally rejected, despite its issuing of the Hull Note. And on the same day, Roosevelt dispatched a peace telegram to Hirohito. All for naught.

THAT KURUSU AND NOMURA DELIVERED the message breaking off diplomatic relations after the Pearl Harbor attack has been a source of impassioned debate for decades in postwar Japan. There are some compelling, if contestable, reasons for the persistence of this debate. For one, the late delivery enabled Roosevelt to put forward a powerful indictment of Japan's duplicity, most famously memorialized in his "Day of Infamy" speech. The Japanese conduct legitimized the president's call for war, not only against Japan but also Japan's fascist allies in Europe. The proposition that Roosevelt and Churchill had known about the impending Japanese attack on Pearl Harbor but let it occur to serve their larger aim of getting the United States to enter the war in Europe continues to excite the imagination of some.

There are those who believe that certain *bakuryo* officers had arranged for the late delivery of the final message to ensure that the attack would commence with no forewarning. The fact that those embassy staff members who failed to prepare the documents in time were never punished—in some cases, their careers flourished after the war—fueled this view.

In fact, the delay in delivering the message was caused by a combination of the embassy's unpreparedness and Togo's compliance with the military demand to ensure the success of its offensive plans. Admiral Yamamoto had insisted that Tokyo notify the United States of Japan's belligerent intent in advance. So did Hirohito, who remained consistent in his desire for Japan to abide by the general principles of international law. On December 3, the Foreign Ministry drafted a final memorandum to be delivered to Hull that included a specific sentence indicating Japan's possible declaration of war in accordance with the Hague Convention. But Togo allowed that part of the document to be dropped. The dispatch of his sensitive communication to Washington was deliberately left until the very last minute for the sake of watertight confidentiality of military strategies.

Even if the document had been handed to Hull before the commencement of the Pearl Harbor attack, it would not have eliminated the element of surprise—as well as illegality—from Japan's offensive. The late delivery in Washington did strengthen Roosevelt's case, helping him rally the country around the flag, but he himself made clear that the stealth of the Pearl Harbor strategy and the accompanying use of diplomacy as its cloak were the most abominable part of Japan's conduct. And he got that message through to the nation forcefully and brilliantly when he addressed a joint session of Congress on December 8.

> One hour after Japanese air squadrons had commenced bombing in Oahu, the Japanese Ambassador to the United States and his colleague delivered to the Secretary of State a formal reply to a recent American message. While this reply stated that it seemed useless to continue the existing diplomatic negotiations, it contained no threat or hint of war or armed attack.

Three days after the Pearl Harbor attack, four of the largest and most beautiful Japanese cherry trees along the Tidal Basin in West Potomac Park were chopped down in an act of vandalism. The trees, once a symbol of friendship between the United States and Japan, between whom there should have been "no last word," now became the target of intense U.S. hatred. United under the national call to "remember Pearl Harbor," the United States went to war against Japan, the war that Tokyo's warmongers were keen to wage so as not to, in the words of the army chief of staff, "dampen [the soldiers'] morale."

ON JULY 20, 1942, the *Gripsholm,* having picked up and crammed aboard even more detained Japanese in Rio de Janeiro, entered the port of Lourenço Marques (Maputo) in Portuguese Mozambique. Two days later, the *Asama Maru* and the *Conte Verde,* flying Japan's Rising Sun flag, anchored at the same port in the Indian Ocean. It was there that the actual citizen exchange between the warring parties took place. The Japanese from North and South America quietly organized themselves and resettled on the two ships coming from Japan. There was no direct contact between the people from the Allied and Axis camps. But while waiting at the port, Nomura and Kurusu both spotted the tall figure of Ambassador Grew in the other group. He recognized them, too. Kurusu immediately recalled his interview with Grew the night before his departure for Washington in early November of the previous year. The uneasy physical distance between them was ample proof of the peace that had eluded them. The three men took their hats off in silent acknowledgment of one another.

The ships carrying the Japanese nationals reached Yokohama, Kurusu's hometown, on August 20, 1942. By then, Japan's preponderance at sea was declining precipitously. The balance of power had been tipped. From June 4 to 7, the Imperial Japanese Navy fought one of the most devastating naval battles in modern history, the Battle of Midway. The same men who planned the Pearl Harbor attack conceived of the Midway strategy, hoping to eliminate the United States from the Pacific once and for all. The operation ended in disaster for Japan. By this time, the Japanese military code had been broken by the United States (whereas at the time of the Pearl Harbor attack, only the diplomatic code had been broken). The Japanese navy was dragged down from its glorious pinnacle only six months after it had reached it.

All this was unknown to most Japanese. The euphoric afterglow of Pearl Harbor was still lingering when the ships bearing the returnees from the West arrived. Nomura and Kurusu were greeted with a series of celebratory homecoming events, including an imperial banquet and a prime ministerial luncheon. It was as though the government were eager to compensate for its gross maltreatment of Japan's top representatives at the height of its diplomatic crisis, which had turned them into public enemies in America. They were the targets of hatred in the detention camps: "Which one's Kurusu? I'll break his neck!" one graffitist wrote. Now back in Japan, they were suddenly elevated to the status of national heroes who had stood up to the bullies in Washington until the very end.

Kurusu likened the practice of diplomacy to drawing pictures in the sand on the beach. No matter how many treaties and alliances a diplomat might achieve, a single shift in government policy could wash them all away. "I want to leave something more tangible to posterity, something that lasts longer, even if that means leaving only one bridge," said his son, Ryo, who decided to study engineering rather than follow in his father's footsteps. Ryo never got to build a single bridge. The Chicago-born, half-American engineer pilot of the Imperial Japanese Army would lose his young life in February 1945 in the war his father was powerless to prevent.

Those two dashing airmen of the *Kamikaze,* whom Kurusu had the joy of welcoming to Brussels in April 1937, also lost their lives in the war. The younger, Iinuma, died in Phnom Penh shortly after Pearl Harbor. (He was killed by a propeller of a moving aircraft as he walked down a runway, leading some to speculate that his death was a suicide.) Less than two years later, his best friend and flying partner, Tsukagoshi, disappeared on a mission. In October 1944, the Japanese army's kamikaze pilot unit would launch its first attack on Leyte Gulf in the Philippines, under the command of Rear Admiral Onishi Takijiro, one of the chief architects of the Pearl Harbor attack. The notoriety of that deathly mission would quickly overshadow the accomplishments of the two original *Kamikaze* aviators.

The violinist Suwa Nejiko, a close friend of the Kurusus, with a blind dedication to her music and a political naïveté to which even the greatest artists are not immune, decided to continue her studies in occupied Paris with her Russian mentor, Boris Kamensky. The former child prodigy often traveled to Germany, where she played with Hans Knappertsbusch and the Berlin Philharmonic. Joseph Goebbels presented her with a Stradivarius in February 1943. She would be captured by the advancing U.S. troops and detained in the United States. She finally returned to Japan, after nearly a decade in Europe, in December 1945. It was by then a country in utter ruins.

When Kurusu and Nomura returned in the summer of 1942, however, Tokyo was poor but still standing. The two diplomats sat through the various homecoming events forced upon them. At one, Hirohito expressed no special feelings about Japan's situation and had no words other than to commend them for their professional efforts. Prince Takamatsu, more straightforward, told Kurusu he regretted that diplomacy did not prevail and that the war had had to begin.

At the prime minister's luncheon, Tojo spoke of the reservations the government—and he himself—had felt on the verge of finally deciding to go to war in late November 1941. Not surprisingly, he said his government was forced to choose that route because of incessant persecution by Washington. As far as Japan was concerned, he said, war was never the preferred option. He also said that had Roosevelt's message to the emperor arrived three days sooner, a war might have been avoided. (Roosevelt's peace message reached Ambassador Grew late on December 7 in Japan, after having been held up in Tokyo for ten hours by the Army General Staff's order, intended to sabotage any last-minute peace; Hirohito received it only half an hour before the Pearl Harbor attack. Kurusu had, in fact, proposed the exchange of peace messages between Roosevelt and Hirohito well in time, on November 26, but failed at that point to convince Togo and Kido it was worthwhile.)

Regardless of Tojo's self-serving reading of U.S. inflexibility, the root problem in the Japanese government remained consistent throughout 1941: None of the top leaders, their occasional protestations notwithstanding, had sufficient will, desire, or courage to stop the momentum for war.

Particularly for the chiefs and vice chiefs of the general staffs, it proved much easier to go along with the call for war preparedness initiated by the *bakuryo* planners than to try to restrain them. Talking tough gave these leaders an illusory sense of power and bravery when the rest of the leaders openly dithered and vacillated between war and peace, unable to articulate an emphatic no. The liaison conferences and imperial conferences helped every leader feel that he held no individual responsibility.

From April to December 1941, the Japanese leadership made a series of decisions that many at first failed to recognize as constituting a doomed path toward war. But with each step, room for maneuver was lost. The unwinnable war with the West was never an absolute inevitability, however. Despite the risk of losing all that had been achieved since Meiji, the leaders ultimately succumbed to a destructive—and self-destructive—course in the name of maximizing Japan's chance of survival and self-preservation in the short term and, more ambitiously, building an Asia for Asians under Japan's leadership in the long term. Neither the short-term nor the long-term goals were ever realizable because the planning for them was not realistic. Japan approached the war as a gambler would, taking comfort in the likelihood of initial advantages while deluding itself that it would be able to take the money and run, though running was never an option in this game.

True, Pearl Harbor was extolled by the generally uninformed nation as a dazzling victory, at least in the beginning. Many opted to see it as an honorable and heroic choice made by Japan for the brighter future of Asia. Even the emperor was said to have been delighted at the report of the Pearl Harbor victory. Most of those newly placed under Japanese control in Southeast Asia, however, despised Japan's gratuitous and self-serving leadership. If anything, they saw the occupation as more hypocritical than Western colonialism because of the gap between Japan's professed high ideals and the ill-orchestrated, haphazard nature of its rule, which frequently led to poverty and brutality. That is why it is often said that Pearl

Harbor was a brilliant tactical triumph but an awful strategic blunder. But was it even a tactical triumph? On the morning of December 7, 1941, Vice Admiral Nagumo curtailed his task force's attack, against the wishes of Fuchida Mitsuo, chief coordinator and the bomber pilot who led the first wave of attacks. Of the first group of 183 planes, only 9 were lost, having suffered minimal retaliatory attacks. But 20 planes out of 167 were lost in the second wave. Nagumo was discouraged by this increase and opted to turn back.

Consequently, as noted earlier, oil tanks, machine shops, and other U.S. facilities were mostly left untouched. Japan was also unable to inflict damage on any of the U.S. submarines and aircraft carriers, which were not present in the harbor at the time. This, along with the fact that the harbor's shallow waters made the repair of damaged crafts easier, enabled a speedy recovery of U.S. naval might in the Pacific.

As for Yamamoto's submariners who ventured to become human torpedoes immediately preceding the aerial attacks, their deaths served little purpose other than as Japanese propaganda. Major newspapers (not military headquarters) declared them "Nine Military Gods." (Ten were dispatched; one survived and was taken captive by the United States, unbeknownst to ordinary Japanese.) When the first anniversary of the opening of the war was celebrated, they became the centerpiece of the nation's hero worship.

Another highlight of the first anniversary was a film produced by the Navy Ministry, *The Naval Battle from Hawaii to Malaya (Hawai Mare Oki Kaisen)*, which was released to the general public on December 3, 1942. The main character is a cadet pilot, a country boy who, through absolute persistence and hard work, transforms himself into an elite pilot of the Imperial Navy. The film, with a swelling sound track of military marches and Wagnerian themes, climaxes in the Japanese attacks on Hawaii and the naval battle off Malaya, ending with the empire's declaration of war on the United States and its allies. But Tokyo's leaders could only ride the coattails of victories in Hawaii and Malaya for so long.

SOLDIER U KNEW too well that a life of combat was quite different from what was depicted in propaganda movies. The drifter's fate continued. On December 8, 1941, aboard the ship whose destination was still unannounced, his unit was informed of Japan's declaration of war. Sailing through Cam Ranh Bay in southeastern Indochina, entering the Mekong and refueling at Saigon, his ship finally deposited the soldiers in southern Thailand. They were to take part in the historic battle against the British over Malaya. He survived the battle.

After the fall of Singapore in February 1942, Soldier U was shifted to policing duties in Kota Medan, in northern Sumatra, where life was relatively calm and the Japanese occupiers, he believed, got along well with the locals. He was never hungry there, but he missed home, and so he was overjoyed when he was told in December 1942 that he was being discharged for being too old. His journey home proved to be another risky venture. His ship constantly had to dodge torpedo attacks, and when he and the other returning soldiers, full of anticipation, prepared to land in Hiroshima in small boats at night, pitch-darkness surrounded them because of the wartime blackout. Their boats collided with one another. Some men were thrown into the icy water and perished. Some were rescued. Soldier U was among them.

BY THE MIDDLE OF 1944, the anticipation of worse things to come on the home front led to a new policy. The government, still under Tojo's leadership, announced an evacuation program for primary schoolers from thirteen metropolitan cities. The children, ranging in age from eight to twelve, were moved to the countryside, where they lived in large groups; for many, it was the first time away from their parents. They were usually put up in extremely rudimentary and overcrowded rooms of Buddhist temples or traditional inns. In all, about eight hundred thousand city children experienced this collective evacuation, characterized by perpetual hunger, homesickness, and spartan living. It would form a major part of their generational memory.

Newspapers and magazines saw the evacuation program through rose-colored glasses; they reported that the children were enjoying fresh country air and featured photos of their smiling—though clearly undernourished—faces. One photo showed a group of small boys squatting on the bathroom floor in a big circle, each scrubbing the back of the boy in front of him. They look to be having fun, but their astonishingly skinny naked bodies make one wonder how they had any energy left for smiling, let alone back scrubbing.

Without access to food other than whatever little was given them, the evacuated children suffered from hunger first and foremost. The greatest pastime for them was to draw food. "Sponge cakes, dumplings, pastries, shortcakes, caramels, rice crackers . . . we drew them all—absolutely every snack in this world one could remember," one woman recalled. "Then we showed them to one another and enjoyed discussing how wonderful they would taste if we really were to eat them." Complaining, unhappy letters home were systematically discouraged, and their teachers checked all mail before it was sent out. State censorship and confiscation of correspondence, legalized in October 1941, were exercised even at this level voluntarily.

This haphazard evacuation program was a direct response to the threat of a U.S. landing on the Japanese mainland, which seemed especially likely after the United States captured Saipan, fifteen hundred miles south. The island fell on July 7, 1944, and more than 55,000 Japanese, including civilians, died there. (Made a Japanese mandate by the League of Nations in 1920, Saipan had a Japanese population, including colonial Taiwanese and Koreans classified as Japanese, of 29,348 in 1943.) Vice Admiral Nagumo and other navy commanders ordered their soldiers to "die a hero's death" and to become the "Pacific seawall" against the United States. Nagumo set a precedent by committing suicide on July 6, before the island's conquest. The same "ultimate sacrifice" was also expected of civilians in the absence of any protection offered by the military. Too many chose death over surrender, sometimes coaxed by the remaining Japanese soldiers, who made sure that nobody was to suffer the shame of being taken captive.

The haunting proof of patriotic allegiance was captured on film by the U.S. Marines. Civilians, many of them women and some with babies and children, stumbled toward the edge of volcanic cliffs to make their final leaps. One can feel their slight hesitation and momentary fear as they looked down into the abyss of black seawater. But by sheer force of determination, they overcame their fear and jumped. *"Banzai!"* ("Live forever!"—or, more accurately in this case, "Long live the emperor!") was often the last word of those loyal subjects of the empire. More civilians would commit suicide on the islands of Tinian, Guam, and Okinawa in the face of the U.S. advance.

Japanese losses in the Pacific were so great that they could not be kept a secret any longer. The Saipan calamity was reported to the Japanese nation on July 18, 1944, along with the resignation of the Tojo cabinet. Two days after Tojo's fall, on July 20, Operation Valkyrie, the most nearly successful of all the assassination attempts on Hitler, was carried out. With renewed fanaticism, the Führer would continue to lead Germany until his suicide.

Germany without Hitler would have been an immediately different country. But Japan without Tojo looked too much like Japan with him. The same institutional and cultural failings that led to its decision to go to war remained, and if anything, the material and human sacrifices of the war years made it even more difficult for any leader to end the conflict. Some hoped to deal another decisive blow to the United States so that Japan would not suffer a total defeat. Others, equally misguidedly, believed that either Germany or the Soviet Union could intervene and mediate a peace. Some fanatics in the leadership wanted to fight on whatever the consequences. Even with the general understanding at the top that Japan could only lose the war, it would take thirteen more months, two more prime ministers, the complete destruction of Japan's major cities, and two atomic bombs for the emperor to finally put his foot down—some say valiantly, some say all too belatedly—and end the war that had been waged without any concrete exit plan. The chronic preference of leaders for wishful thinking, self-preservation, and face-saving that in 1941 culminated in the country's most reckless decision had too familiar an echo in 1944 and 1945.

Meanwhile, life had to carry on, and children continued to be evacuated. On August 22, 1944, about seven hundred children, in transit from Okinawa to Kagoshima, perished at sea. The U.S. submarines were already that close. The ill-orchestrated evacuation program ended in early 1945 for younger students, and city families were urged to make individual arrangements to ensure the safety of their children. Family reunions were often brutally short-lived. Many children from Tokyo were sent back home just in time to experience the worst (but not the last) air raid unleashed on the city: the one in the early-morning hours of March 10, which cost Kafu his house.

With the destruction of almost every Japanese city and the constant announcements of soldiers' deaths, Japanese morale could not have been lower. Surviving death—from disease, hunger, or the incendiary bombs that grilled alive newborns and old people alike—had become the utmost national priority. A distraught mother who embraced her baby to the point of suffocation while seeking shelter during a bombing raid, a schoolgirl trying to float her way to safety down a river filled with dying people clinging to her, people navigating heaps of charred bodies as they looked for their missing family members—stories like these were becoming all too common. The Meiji Palace, where the imperial conferences had taken place, was burned down in May 1945, forcing the leaders to hold the final two imperial conferences before Japan's unconditional surrender in an air-raid shelter.

Life in the countryside was less pressed, though things were scarce. Toddlers innocently competed with one another to collect plant roots, a substitute staple for rice, and grasshoppers, an invaluable available source of protein and calcium for growing children. Students were sent into the forests for pine sap to make gasoline (which never quite worked), and all households were ordered to turn in their metal, including buckets and ladles, to make airplanes. "We must be losing the war," said one farm boy at the time, deducing that the government wouldn't otherwise sink so low as to take utensils from poor people's kitchens. But uncomplaining, and with a degree of fatalism, the nation endured the horrid times as if it were dealing with a series of relentless natural disasters rather than man-made ones.

In the midst of all this, a very select group of Japanese, mainly military officers but also some filmmakers, university students, and other civilians, had a rare chance to see films that the British had left behind in Southeast Asia. One of them was *Gone with the Wind*. The Japanese were amazed by the quality, technical superiority, and glamour of the nearly four-hour-long saga. They wondered how they could possibly defeat a country that had managed to produce such an astonishing film. (Another film left behind was Walt Disney's 1937 *Snow White and the Seven Dwarfs*, whose quality far surpassed that of Japanese animation technology.)

ON AUGUST 17, 1945, two days after the emperor announced on the radio Japan's total defeat, Prince Higashikuni became the first (and most probably the last) prime minister chosen from the imperial house. It was up to him to disarm the nation, hand over the country to the Allied occupation forces, sign the document accepting Japan's unconditional surrender, and, most critically, raise the morale of the thoroughly devastated nation.

The prince was a good orator who spoke simply and convincingly. On September 5, addressing a parliamentary session that included American GIs in the audience, Higashikuni insisted that the Japanese not dwell on the question of how the war was started and instead look forward. He proposed that the whole nation of one hundred million was to blame and so the whole nation had to repent. This was the same nation that had been told, until very recently, to fight until the bitter end, armed only with spears and helmets of bamboo. Higashikuni's argument had some merit, especially in the late summer of 1945, when so much work lay in front of the Japanese people. But his words set the tone for Japanese leaders as well as those who followed them to overlook the most basic question of responsibility: Who was responsible for starting the war? The suggestion that the war might have been unnecessary was too difficult for any Japanese to accept, having lost so much and so many in the war. But this neglect, legitimized as a matter of official policy, in turn encouraged the general temptation to do away with various other kinds of responsibility, such as coming to terms with its war crimes and remembering the war after it was over.

This, of course, does not mean that people could forget what they had lived through. Contrary to received opinion, some serious attempts have been made in Japan to examine aspects of the country's wartime past. Soldier U, who lived to be eighty-four, had enough time to reflect, discreetly and quietly, on his experiences. Though he never discussed any of them in his lifetime, he cared enough to leave a written record, unbeknownst even to his family.

Yet by claiming that every Japanese was to blame for the war, Higashikuni implied that nobody was to blame, fudging and diluting the real responsibility of the leaders who brought Japan to that momentous decision. Prince Konoe, who resurfaced as a public figure in Higashikuni's cabinet, was doubtless the first to support this line of argument. Conservative politicians, in power for most of the postwar period, were only too happy to inherit such a partial and incomplete rendering of Japan's past. Despite the efforts of some individual citizens, academics, and journalists to have a more honest debate, it is difficult to deny that Japan's official impulse has been to look away from what is undesirable and unpleasant in its history. And this pattern was perpetuated as much, if not more, by what Kafu had so astutely noted on the eve of Pearl Harbor as the fundamental indifference to politics among many Japanese, absorbed as they were by their "primary pursuit . . . to pass one day at a time without encountering too much trouble," as by the misplaced desire of some politicized right to impart glory to Japan's lost war.

In 1952, *Gone with the Wind* was finally released to general audiences in Japan, and it became a huge box-office hit. Many Japanese identified with the spirited, impetuous, and indomitable southern belle Scarlett O'Hara, who remained determined to rise above any obstacles, even after having lost almost everything that mattered to her. Her celebrated last words, "After all, tomorrow is another day," resonated with the generation of postwar Japanese trying to glimpse a better future through the wreckage of war. That was exactly what Japan opted to do—and that is why the past, with its improbable story of how the war came to pass, became another country.

Acknowledgments

Why did Japan attack the United States at Pearl Harbor? In trying to answer this seemingly simple question, I felt at times as if I had unwisely taken that blind plunge off the platform of Kiyomizu Temple myself. That I survived the jump is undoubtedly because of all the inspiration and help I have received along the way. Kazuo Osugi was always generous with his time and advice, while his books served as remarkable models of disciplined scholarship for me to aspire to. Naoki Inose kindly helped to clarify some questions concerning his pioneering work on the Total War Research Institute. Tali Kfir gave me the opportunity to read her father Yaoki Iijima's excellent memoir, cowritten by her mother, Geneva Cobb Iijima.

An invitation from Takashi Shiraishi in 2009 to conduct research at the National Graduate Institute for Policy Studies in Tokyo came as a welcome relief as I was struggling to cope with the demands of starting a new book. The institute's generous resources allowed me to get the project off the ground. A visiting professorship in 2010 at the Hebrew University of Jerusalem gave me a chance to test my work in progress. I am especially thankful to Yuri Pines for reading my manuscript with his ever-vigilant eyes and to the students who attended my graduate seminar for their positive feedback, which gave me an added incentive to finish the first draft of the book.

I cannot thank Christopher Szpilman enough for his friendship, generosity, and incisive comments at various stages of the writing. Edward Chancellor gave me enormously thoughtful comments and pointers, which guided me throughout the rewriting of the manuscript.

The idea for this book was first suggested seven years ago by Jin Auh, my agent and greatest supporter throughout the process. I thank her for her unwavering faith in my ability to take on the challenge and for her sense of humor, which sustained me. Special thanks are due to Scott Moyers for taking me on board at the Wylie Agency. I am grateful to Steve Wasserman for bringing my work under the consummate editorship of Jonathan Segal at Knopf. Without Jon's painstaking edits and comments, this book simply could not have been finished. Joey McGarvey and Meghan Houser were always receptive to my questions while Maria Massey, Cassandra Pappas, Lorraine Hyland, and Jason Booher on the production team contributed enormously to finalizing the book. I owe debts of gratitude to them all.

Last thanks are due to friends and family. Hiroko Wakunaga, Ikumi Okamoto, Nina Khrushcheva, Betsy Opio, and Laura Bresler all gave me tremendous moral and practical support. Antonia Phillips went out of her way to help with the illustrations. Brigitte Lacombe generously provided an author portrait. Gwen Robinson and Willem Diepraam were the first to read the finished manuscript. I am thankful for their helpful comments and great enthusiasm. My aunt Hiroko Anzai and my cousin Miki Anzai Kawakatsu were especially helpful and encouraging. My parents, Kimiko and Kensuke Hotta, were unconditionally encouraging of my project and helped in every way imaginable. My biggest thanks go to my husband, Ian, and daughter, Josephine, without whom my life would be woefully lacking in love, laughter, and a proper sense of perspective.

Notes

PROLOGUE · WHAT A DIFFERENCE A DAY MAKES

3   It was announced: "Daihon'ei Kaigun bu Happyo," December 8, 1941, http://cgi2
    .nhk.or.jp/shogenarchives/sp/movie.cgi?das_id=D0001400296_00000.
4   Life was becoming monochromatic: Masaki Hiroshi, *Chikakiyori*, in *Showa
    Nimannichi no Zenkiroku (5) Ichioku no "Shintaisei,"* ed. Harada Katsumasa, Ozaki
    Hotsumi, Matsushita Keiichi, and Mikuni Ichiro (Kodansha, 1989), 277.
5   In the autumn of 1940, the sixty-year-old complained: Nagai Kafu, *Kafu Zenshu
    (24)* (Iwanami Shoten, 1994), 89.
5   These righteous women admonished: *Showa Nimannichi no Zenkiroku (5)*,
    276–77.
6   A man who was a second grader: Tomaru Shigeru, "Rajioten no Mae wa Hitoda-
    kari," in "Watashi no Junigatsu Yoka," ed. Nishiha Kiyoshi, http://www.rose.san-
    net.ne.jp/nishiha/senso/19411208.htm#tomaru.
7   Aboard an overcrowded train: Nagai Kafu, *Tekiroku Danchotei Nichijo (2)* (Iwa-
    nami Bunko, 1987), 159.
7   One of the most distinguished poets: Kato Yoshiko, *Saito Mokichi no Jugonen
    Senso* (Misuzu Shobo, 1990), 124.
7   The thirty-six-year-old novelist: Yomiuri Shimbun, *Kensho Senso Sekinin (1)*
    (Chuo Koron Shinsha, 2006), 55.
7   Indeed, that war started: Note, however, that Japan had informed Russia of the
    termination of its diplomatic relations, and warned that it retained the freedom to
    act independently, four days prior to the actual attack.
7   Takeuchi Yoshimi, a thirty-one-year-old Sinologist: Takeuchi Yoshimi, *"Daitoa
    Senso to Warera no Ketsui (Sengen),"* *Chugoku Bungaku* 82 (1942): 482–84.
7   A nine-year-old in a rice-growing village: Yaoki Iijima, as told to Geneva Cobb
    Iijima "Growing Up in Old Japan" (self-published memoir, 2010), 19.
8   A young man working for Mitsubishi: Suzuki Shun, "Fuan to Yatta to iu Kimo-
    chi," in "Watashi no Junigatsu Yoka," http://www.rose.sannet.ne.jp/nishiha/
    senso/19411208.htm#suzuki.
9   The isolationist opposition with which: Robert Dallek, *Franklin D. Roosevelt and
    American Foreign Policy, 1932–1945* (New York: Oxford University Press, 1995), 312.
9   Hawaii must have seemed almost like: This point is emphasized in *December 7th*,
    the United States Navy propaganda film from 1943 directed by John Ford and
    Gregg Toland.

9   That night, Churchill: Winston S. Churchill, *The Grand Alliance*, vol. 3 of *The Second World War* (London: Cassell, 1950), 540.

10 "Our elite Imperial Army and Navy": Tojo Hideki, "Oomikotonori wo Haishi Tatematsurite," http://cgi2.nhk.or.jp/shogenarchives/jpnews/movie.cgi?das_id= D0001300464_00000&seg_number=001.

10 True, Tojo is famous: Konoe Fumimaro, *Heiwa e no Doryoku* (Nihon Denpo Tsushinsha, 1946), 94.

11 According to his aide and son-in-law: Hosokawa Morisada, "Konoeko no Shogai," in *Konoe Nikki* (Kyodo Tsushinsha, 1968), 150.

11 On December 22, just two weeks after: Yomiuri Shimbun, *Kensho Senso Sekinin, (1)*, 56.

12 One doctor's wife in her forties: Takahashi Aiko, quoted in *Showa Nimannichi no Zenkiroku (6) Taiheiyo Senso,* ed. Harada Katsumasa, Ozaki Hotsumi, Matsushita Keiichi, and Mikuni Ichiro (Kodansha, 1990), 54.

13 Kafu, awakened by the neighbors' shouting: Nagai, *Tekiroku Danchotei Nichijo (2)*, 253–54.

13 Kafu, who claimed: Ibid., 255.

18 After the victory: Marius B. Jansen, "Monarchy and Modernization in Japan," *Journal of Asian Studies* 36, no. 4 (August 1977): 617.

18 One of postwar Japan's leading political scientists: Masao Maruyama, *Thought and Behaviour in Modern Japanese Politics,* ed. and trans. Ivan Morris (Oxford: Oxford University Press, 1979), 88–89.

20 As a coolheaded political analyst: Yamamoto to Navy Chief Nagano, September 29, 1941, quoted in Gomikawa Junpei, *Gozen Kaigi* (Bunshun Bunko, 1984), 9.

CHAPTER 1 · **RUMORS OF WAR**

24 It immediately boosted its support: "Informal Conversations Between the Governments of the United States and Japan, 1941," May 19, 1942, in U.S. Department of State, *Papers Relating to the Foreign Relations of the United States and Japan, 1931–1941* (Washington, D.C.: Government Printing Office, 1943), 2:326.

26 "Compared to half a year ago": Nagai, *Tekiroku Danchotei Nichijo* (2), 140.

26 Within a few months, he would write: Ibid., 146.

26 In a letter addressed: Joseph C. Grew, *Turbulent Era: A Diplomatic Record of Forty Years, 1904–1945* (Cambridge, Mass.: Riverside Press, 1952), 2:1258.

27 In Grew's analysis: Ibid., 1257.

29 "One should be greatly alarmed": "Konoe Naikaku no Dekibae," *Osaka Mainichi Shimbun,* June 3, 1937.

31 Konoe took it upon himself: Fujiwara Akira, *Showa no Rekishi (5)* (Shogakukan, 1994), 91–92.

31 But Konoe was, in the words: Ashida Hitoshi, falsely attributed to "Hitoshi Asa," quoted in Otto D. Tolischus, "Synthesis of Japan," *New York Times,* August 3, 1941.

31 In the summer of 1937: Ikeda Sumihisa, quoted in Fujiwara, *Taiheiyo Senso (5),* 108.

32 Konoe charged that the Guomindang's: Konoe Fumimaro, "Kokuminseifu wo Aite to sezu" (January 16, 1938), Gaimusho, *Nihon Gaiko Nenpyo narabi ni Shuyomonjo (2)* (Hara Shobo, 1966), 386.

33 "I have neither obvious enemies": Yamaura Kan'ichi, "Konoe Shuhen no Hensen," *Kaizo* (November 1938), 120.

33 It was Marquis Saionji Kinmochi: Saionji Kinkazu, *Kizoku no Taijo* (Chikuma Gakugei Bunko, 1995), 153.

34 Saionji, a practical man: Ibid., 135–37.

35 He said that those countries: Konoe Fumimaro, "Eibei Hon'i no Heiwa Shugi wo Haisu," reprinted in *Sengo Nihon Gaikoronshu* (Chuo Koronsha, 1995), 52.

36 Saionji also reproached him: Hosokawa, "Konoeko no Shogai," 122.

36 Commenting on the rising anti-Japanese sentiments: Konoe Fumimaro, *Sengo Obei Kenbunroku* (Chuko Bunko, 1981), 138.

38 As Saionji remarked to his grandson: Saionji Kinkazu, *Saionji Kinkazu Kaikoroku "Sugisarishi Showa"* (Ipec Press, 1991), 160.

39 "Why should anyone be punished": Nagai, *Tekiroku Danchotei Nichijo* (2), 145.

45 Correspondents were sent to war zones: *Osaka Asahi*, September 22, 1941; *Osaka Mainichi*, November 22, 1931.

48 The number of men qualified for military service: *Showa Nimannichi no Zenkiroku (4) Nicchusenso e no Michi*, ed. Harada Katsumasa, Ozaki Hotsumi, Matsushita Keiichi, and Mikuni Ichiro (Kodansha, 1989), 237.

48 One soldier, Ushiotsu Kichijiro: All accounts related to Soldier U are from Ushiotsu Kichijiro, "Jibunshi," http://www.rose.sannet.ne.jp/nishiha/taikenki/ushiotsu/.

51 "How dreamy they are": Quoted in Fukada Yusuke, *Bibonare Showa: Suwa Nejiko to Kamikazego no Otokotachi* (Bunshunbunko, 1985), 124.

53 Shortly after its formation, the association convoked a conference: *Showa Nimannichi no Zenkiroku (6)*, 39.

53 Whenever a notice from the distribution center: David J. Lu, *Japan: A Documentary History* (London: M. E. Sharpe, 1997), 448.

54 In a meeting the day before the pact was signed: "Sumitsuin Honkaigi Giji Gaiyo" (September 26, 1940), B1-176 (KK24-5), 2-3, at http://d-arch.ide.go.jp/kishi_collection/b1.html.

54 But Ishii could not dissuade Konoe: "Matsumoto Joyaku Kyokucho 'Nichidokui Sangokujoyaku ni kansuru Sumitsuin Shinsaiinkai Giji Gaiyo'" (September 26, 1940), B1-173 (KK24-5), 38, at ibid.

54 Konoe followed up on his swaggering posture: Toyoda Jo, *Matsuoka Yosuke: Higeki no Gaikokan* (2) (Shincho Bunko, 1983), 362.

56 Apparently flustered upon reading the telegram: Gomikawa, *Gozen Kaigi*, 53.

56 According to Kido's journal entry: Kido Koichi, *Kido Koichi Nikki* (2) (Tokyo Daigaku Shuppan, 1980), 870.

57 Resources in the Dutch East Indies had to be gained: Boeicho Boeikenshusho Senshishitsu, *Senshi Sosho: Daihon'ei Rikugunbu, Daitoa Senso Kaisen Keii (4)* (Asagumo Shimbunsha, 1974), 110; Osugi Kazuo, *Shinjuwan e no Michi: Kaisen, Hisen Kokonotsu no Sentakushi* (Kodansha, 2003), 221.

CHAPTER 2 · THE RETURN OF DON QUIXOTE

58 Courtesy of Joseph Stalin: Saionji, *Saionji Kinkazu Kaikoroku*, 190–91.

58 All railway stations in Berlin had been adorned: Saionji, *Kizoku no Taijo*, 82.

59 "To shake hands with Germany is": Kase Toshikazu, *Senso to Gaiko* (2) (Yomiuri Shimbunsha, 1975), 104.

59 He was one of the rare people: Hitler's translator Paul Schmidt to Matsuoka's secretary, quoted in Toyoda, *Matsuoka Yosuke* (2), 433.

60 His Oregon classmates were impressed: Toyoda Jo, *Matsuoka Yosuke: Higeki no Gaikokan (1)* (Shincho Bunko, 1983), 106.

61 In his fifties, he would revisit the place of his adolescence: James L. McClain, *Japan: A Modern History* (New York: W. W. Norton, 2002), 419.

62 On the podium, Matsuoka abandoned his prepared text: Stewart Brown, "Japan Stuns World, Withdraws from League," United Press, February 24, 1933.

62 Reporting from Geneva, the United Press correspondent described: Ibid.

63 "Currently, no one sees the significance of it": Toyoda, *Matsuoka Yosuke (1)*, 538–49.

64 The same assistant also revealed: Ibid., 24–25.

64 On that fateful day when Matsuoka announced: Brown, "Japan Stuns World."

64 For about a year afterward, he traveled: Toyoda, *Matsuoka Yosuke (2)*, 181.

65   "I don't think that party politics is the only way": Ibid., 182–183.

65   **As the president of the South Manchurian Railway:** Hayasaka Takashi, *Shikikan no Ketsudan: Manshu to Attsu no Shogun Higuchi Kiichiro* (Bungei Shinsho, 2010), 131–49.

65   "Diplomacy is power, my dear young man": Saionji, *Saionji Kinkazu Kaikoroku*, 190–91.

66   "You must really support Prince Konoe": Saionji, *Kizoku no Taijo*, 70–71.

66   "You see, I am an Asian": Ibid., 197.

66   When Japanese and Soviet delegates took turns: Kase, *Senso to Gaiko* (2), 35.

67   "Matsuoka is an able man!": Osugi, *Shinjuwan e no Michi*, 234.

67   According to a journalist who accompanied Matsuoka: Ibid., 236.

68   When he first heard about the Draft Understanding: Kase, *Senso to Gaiko* (2), 105.

68   He was convinced that the proposal: Konoe, *Heiwa e no Doryoku*, 46.

68   But most of those in the room: "Dai 21-kai Renraku Kondankai," April 22, 1941, in *Taiheiyo Senso e no Michi (Bekkan)*, ed. Inaba Masao, Kobayashi Tatsuo, Shimada Toshihiko, and Tsunoda Jun (Asahi Shimbunsha, 1988), 410–11.

68   Nomura kept apologizing: "Memorandum by the Secretary of State," May 2, 1941, in U.S. Department of State, *Papers*, 2:411.

71   On April 16, Hull asked Nomura: "Memorandum by the Secretary of State," April 16, 1941, in U.S. Department of State, *Papers*, 2:407.

71   In early May, he complained to a Foreign Ministry official: Tajiri Akiyoshi, quoted in Toyoda, *Matsuoka Yosuke* (2), 514.

72   One of the more conspicuous changes involved: "Draft Proposal Handed by the Japanese Ambassador (Nomura) to the Secretary of State," May 12, 1941, in U.S. Department of State, *Papers*, 2:420–25.

73   When he had just returned from the United States: Toyoda, *Matsuoka Yosuke* (1), 107–8.

73   When Hull complained to Nomura: "Memorandum by the Secretary of State," May 11, 1941, in U.S. Department of State, *Papers*, 2:416.

73   Hull murmured to himself: Osugi, *Shinjuwan e no Michi*, 257.

73   For instance, Hull had said he could negotiate: "Memorandum by the Secretary of State," April 16, 1941, in U.S. Department of State, *Papers*, 2:407.

74   But in a personal exchange with Nomura: Ibid., 409.

74   Konoe said he had gone: Konoe, *Heiwa e no Doryoku*, 46.

74   As one army officer on the general staff: Toyoda, *Matsuoka Yosuke* (2), 400.

CHAPTER 3 · THE BEGINNING OF IT ALL

77   His lesser-known *Un Bal à Yeddo:* Julia Meech-Pekarik, *The World of the Meiji Print: Impressions of a New Civilization* (New York: Weatherhill, 1986), 149.

78   Okura Kihachiro, an eccentric: Ibid., 154.

78   "We are your Supreme Commander-in-Chief": Ryusaku Tsunoda, Wm. Theodore de Bary, and Donald Keene, *Sources of Japanese Tradition* (New York: Columbia University Press, 1958), 705–6.

81   Erwin von Bälz, a German physician: Jansen, "Monarchy and Modernization in Japan," 614.

85   In the words of one historian: Geoffrey Best, "Peace Conferences and the Century of Total War: The 1899 Hague Conference and What Came After," *International Affairs* 75, no. 3 (1999): 619–20.

CHAPTER 4 · THE SOLDIER'S DILEMMAS

94   This was true even in an all-boys preparatory school: Masuda Masao, "Senjika no Morioka Chugaku," http://morioka-times.com/topics/bungei/senjika/senji2.html.

96 Fuchida Mitsuo, a bomber pilot: Fuchida Mitsuo, *Shinjuwan Kogeki Sotaicho no Kaiso: Fuchida Mitsuo Jijoden* (Kodansha, 2007), 20–22.

96 "Japanese victories stirred up my enthusiasm": Jawaharlal Nehru, *An Autobiography: With Musings on Recent Events in India* (London: John Lane, 1939), 16.

97 "I entered the navy with the great ambition": Yamamoto Yoshimasa, *Chichi, Yamamoto Isoroku* (Kobunsha, 2001), 21.

97 When he first started playing catch: Ibid., 22–23.

99 In the black leather-bound pocket agenda: Ibid., 125–30.

99 Whenever young Japanese asked him: Ibid., 25.

100 Knowing that the supreme commander: Sheldon Garon, *State and Labor in Modern Japan* (Berkeley: University of California Press, 1987), 158.

102 "Had the government resigned": Hayashi Kyujiro, *Manshujihen to Hoten Soryoji* (Hara Shobo, 1978), 145–46.

103 Yonai kept Japan from the unseemly alliance: Osugi, *Shinjuwan e no Michi*, 162.

103 "The historically isolationist United States": Hando Kazutoshi, *Shikikan to Sanbo* (Bunshun Bunko, 1992), 109.

105 When Yamamoto heard the news: Ibid., 131.

105 When Grew wrote to Hull: "The Ambassador in Japan (Grew) to the Secretary of State," January 27, 1941, 711.94, in U.S. Department of State, *Papers*, 2:133.

106 In early February 1941: Genda Minoru, *Shinjuwansakusen Kaikoroku* (Bunshun Bunko, 1998), 11–23.

CHAPTER 5 · GOOD RIDDANCE, GOOD FRIENDS

109 Throughout the performance, Kase Toshikazu: Kase, *Senso to Gaiko* (2), 45.

110 When news of the German offensive: Ibid., 44.

110 "Do you really think we can": Inose Naoki, *Showa Jurokunen Natsu no Haisen* (Bunshun Bunko, 1986), 181.

111 "Matsuoka has been likely bribed by Hitler": *Showa Tenno Dokuhakuroku*, ed. Terasaki Hidenari and Mariko Terasaki Miller (Bunshun Bunko, 2010), 67.

111 "I would if I were": Gomikawa, *Gozen Kaigi*, 34.

111 "Germany and Italy have been preparing": "Dai 21-kai Renraku Kondankai," May 3, 1941, *Taiheiyo Senso e no Michi (Bekkan)*, 412.

111 "Roosevelt is keen to go to war": "Dai 22-kai Renraku Kondankai," May 8, 1941, *Taiheiyo Senso e no Michi (Bekkan)*, 415; emphasis added.

112 Hull summarily dismissed it: "Memorandum by the Secretary of State," May 7, 1941, in U.S. Department of State, *Papers*, 2:412.

112 On April 16, the day Washington decided: "Memorandum by the Secretary of State," April 16, 1941, in U.S. Department of State, *Papers*, 2:406.

113 The Roosevelt administration had predicated: "Informal Conversations Between the Governments of the United States and Japan, 1941," May 19, 1942, in U.S. Department of State, *Papers*, 2:328.

113 While commending the earnest efforts: "Oral Statement Handed by the Secretary of State to the Japanese Ambassador (Nomura)," June 21, 1941, in U.S. Department of State, *Papers*, 2:485–86.

114 "Heroes change their minds decisively": "Dai 36-kai Renraku Kondankai," June 30, 1941, in *Taiheiyo Senso e no Michi (Bekkan)*, 460.

114 Then, in a meeting with the Soviet ambassador: *Kase Toshikazu Kaisoroku (1)* (Yamate Shobo, 1986), 179.

115 The next day, June 15, 1941: Nagai, *Tekiroku Danchotei Nichijo (2)*, 142–43.

116 "People these days": Ibid., 145.

116 "I have taken occasion to speak to you": Winston S. Churchill, "The Fourth Climacteric," June 22, 1941, http://www.winstonchurchill.org/learn/speeches/speeches-of-winston-churchill/809-the-fourth-climacteric.

117 **Roosevelt felt the same:** Ian Kershaw, *Fateful Choices: Ten Decisions That Changed the World, 1940–1941* (New York: Penguin, 2008), 302–4.

118 **When Nomura called on Hull:** "Memorandum of a Conversation," June 22, 1941, in U.S. Department of State, *Papers*, 2:493.

CHAPTER 6 · JAPAN'S NORTH-SOUTH PROBLEM

119 **On June 23, 1941, the day after Germany attacked:** "Doitsu no tai Sobieto Senso ni kakawaru Nihonseifu no Tachiba ni tsuiteno Joho wo Hokoku seyo," June 23, 1941, no. 6058/6897, in Shimotomai Nobuo and NHK Shuzaihan, *Kokusai Supai Zoruge no Shinjitsu* (Kadokawa Shoten, 1992), 321.

119 **His mission, as he once summed it up:** Richard Sorge, "*Zoruge no Shuki* (2)," October 1941, in *Gendaishishiryo (1)* (Misuzu Shobo, 1962), 180.

120 **Sorge efficiently recruited members:** "Zoruge wo Chushin toseru Kokusaichobodan Jiken," in *Gendaishishiryo (1)*, 4–21.

120 **He recalled that his close contact:** Ozaki Hotsumi, "*Ozaki Hotsumi no Shuki (1),*" June 1943, in *Gendaishishiryo (2)* (Misuzu Shobo, 1962), 5.

120 **He said that Shanghai:** Ibid., 8.

121 **Sorge described their relationship:** Sorge, "*Zoruge no Shuki* (2)," 160.

121 **"Those people [Smedley and Sorge] were":** Ozaki, "*Ozaki Hotsumi no Shuki (1),*" 8.

121 **When Guillain caught sight:** Shimotomai and NHK Shuzaihan, *Kokusai Supai Zoruge no Shinjitsu,* 162–63.

123 **Ozaki later said that he had associated:** Ozaki, "*Shuki (1)*," 12–13.

124 **If, for example, one division or section:** Hatano Sumio, *Bakuryotachi no Shinjuwan* (Asahi Shimbunsha, 1991), 24.

126 **The navy, too, had its middle-ranking hawks:** Hando, *Shikikan to Sanbo*, 101.

127 **Ishikawa would later boast:** Yoshida Toshio, *Kaigun Sanbo* (Bunshun Bunko, 1993), 293.

127 **The navy's chief of staff, Nagano Osami, summarized:** *The Final Confrontation: Japan's Negotiations with the United States,* ed. James William Morley, trans. David A. Titus (New York: Columbia University Press, 1994), 109.

127 **Five decades later, Ishii Akiho, a *bakuryo* officer:** Ishii Akiho, television interview, *NHK Supesharu: Gozen Kaigi,* August 15, 1991.

128 **"This matter requires speedy action":** "Dai 32-kai Renraku Kondankai," June 25, 1941, in *Taiheiyo Senso e no Michi (Bekkan),* 445–46.

129 **Vice Army Chief Tsukada became adamant:** "Dai 33-kai Renraku Kondankai," June 26, 1941, in *Taiheiyo Senso e no Michi (Bekkan),* 456.

129 **"You are telling me that we ought to":** Inose, *Showa Jurokunen Natsu no Haisen,* 157–59.

129 **He became uncharacteristically inarticulate:** "Dai 33-kai Renraku Kondankai," June 26, 1941, in *Taiheiyo Senso e no Michi (Bekkan),* 456.

129 **He said he understood the *broad* strategic logic:** "Dai 34-kai Renraku Kondankai," June 27, 1941, in *Taiheiyo Senso e no Michi (Bekkan),* 457.

130 **"My foretelling for the near future":** "Dai 36-kai Renraku Kondankai," June 30, 1941, in *Taiheiyo Senso e no Michi (Bekkan),* 460.

130 **"Why not postpone [the southern Indochinese takeover]":** Ibid.

131 **"Imperial conferences," Hirohito once said:** *Showa Tenno Dokuhakuroku,* 56.

131 **On July 2, the greatest concern for Hara:** *The Final Confrontation,* ed. Morley, 128.

131 **"Going to [occupy] Thailand or Indochina requires":** "Dai 25-kai Renraku Kondankai," May 22, 1941, in *Taiheiyo Senso e no Michi (Bekkan),* 418.

132 **Sawamoto Yorio, the vice navy minister:** Gomikawa, *Gozen Kaigi,* 101.

132 **He said to the leaders:** "Gozen Kaigi," July 2, 1941, in *Taiheiyo Senso e no Michi*

(*Bekkan*), 464–66. All the following quotations from this conference are from the same source.

134 **When the proposal was introduced:** Osugi, *Shinjuwan e no Michi*, 277.

134 **He later recalled:** "Dai 43-kai Jinmon Chosho," March 17, 1942, in *Gendaishishiryo* (1), 287.

134 **Sorge noted:** "Dai 41-kai Jinmon Chosho," March 11, 1942, in *Gendaishishiryo* (1), 275.

135 **Sorge knew which one to trust:** Communication Nos. 163, 165, 166, and 167, July 10, 1941, in Shimotomai and NHK Shuzaihan, *Kokusai Supai Zoruge no Shinjitsu,* 322; emphasis in the original.

135 **"Are we really ready":** Gomikawa, *Gozen Kaigi,* 102.

CHAPTER 7 · A QUIET CRISIS IN JULY

136 **The nation was informed:** *Showa Nimannichi no Zenkiroku* (6), 73.

136 **He remarked to Secretary of the Interior:** Kershaw, *Fateful Choices,* 300.

137 **Matsuoka, understandably, was upset:** "Dai 38-kai Renraku Kondankai," July 10, 1941, in *Taiheiyo Senso e no Michi* (*Bekkan*), 471.

137 **"Hull's oral statement should in fact":** "Dai 39-kai Renraku Kondankai," July 12, 1941, in *Taiheiyo Senso e no Michi* (*Bekkan*), 472–74. All the following quotes from this conference are taken from this source, unless indicated otherwise.

139 **"Why are you military men":** Toyoda, *Matsuoka Yosuke* (2), 538.

141 **The novelist Nogami Yaeko speculated:** *Showa Nimannichi no Zenkiroku* (6), 76.

141 **As usual, Kafu was more perspicacious:** Nagai, *Tekiroku Danchotei Nichijo* (2), 147.

143 **Visiting Toyoda before Japan's formal announcement:** "Joho Kokan Yoshi," July 26, 1940, in *Taiheiyo Senso e no Michi* (*Bekkan*), 484.

143 **In a liaison meeting on July 24:** "Dai 41-kai Renraku Kaigi," July 24, 1941, in *Taiheiyo Senso e no Michi* (*Bekkan*), 483.

144 **The next day's log definitively repeated:** Hatano, *Bakuryotachi no Shinjuwan,* 117.

144 **"We had no inkling that the United States would":** Takada Toshitane, television interview, *NHK Supesharu: Gozen Kaigi,* August 15, 1991.

144 **According to Welles, he then made:** "Memorandum by the Acting Secretary of State," July 24, 1941, in U.S. Department of State, *Papers,* 2:529.

146 **He immediately went to see Toyoda:** "Memorandum by the Ambassador in Japan (Grew)," July 27, 1941, in U.S. Department of State, *Papers,* 2:535.

147 **He "fully recognized":** Ibid., 536.

147 **As far as the existing records show:** Osugi, *Shinjuwan e no Michi*, 315.

147 **He said he tried:** Konoe, *Heiwa e no Doryoku,* 71.

148 **But rather than suggesting a Japanese withdrawal:** Kido, *Kido Koichi Nikki* (2), 895–96.

CHAPTER 8 · "MEET ME IN JUNEAU"

149 **Ishii Hanako, a woman with luminous, feline eyes:** Shimotomai and NHK Shuzaihan, *Kokusai Supai Zoruge no Shinjitsu,* 166–67.

150 **On the day Germany opened fire on the Soviet Union:** Ibid., 159–60.

150 **But doubt persisted among some observers:** "Josei no Suii ni tomonau Teikoku Kokusaku Yoko," July 2, 1941, *Taiheiyo Senso e no Michi* (*Bekkan*), 467.

152 **Konoe responded to Arita on August 3:** Correspondence, August 3, 1941, *Kensei Shiryoshitsu Shushu Monjo,* no. 1159, National Diet Library.

152 **The Republican administration, maintaining that:** Kate Zernike, "Senators Begin Debate on Iraq, Visions in Sharp Contrast," *New York Times,* June 22, 2006.

153 **"The 'war' that's mentioned in the July 2 policy":** Hatano, *Bakuryotachi no Shinjuwan,* 118.

154　A collector of rumors: Nagai, *Tekiroku Danchotei Nichijo* (2), 144.

154　On July 26, he wrote to one of his most trusted advisers: Roosevelt to Harry Hopkins, July 26, 1941, http://docs.fdrlibrary.marist.edu/PSF/BOX3/T32D01 .HTML.

156　Army Minister Tojo's support was more qualified: Osugi, *Shinjuwan e no Michi*, 320.

157　Foreign Minister Toyoda, without referring to the specifics: Toyoda to Nomura, telegram 162, August 12, 1941, in Gaimusho, *Nichibei Kosho Shiryo*, part 1, 162.

157　From August 9 to 12, the U.S. cruiser *Augusta*: Kershaw, *Fateful Choices*, 315–17.

158　They were greatly influenced by the positive view: Ibid., 308.

158　Chief of Naval Operations Harold Stark: Ibid., 304.

158　Hull reported that Nomura: "Memorandum by the Secretary of State," August 17, 1941, in U.S. Department of State, *Papers*, 2:554–55.

159　The president responded in even broader terms: "Oral Statement Handed by President Roosevelt to the Japanese Ambassador (Nomura)," August 17, 1941, in U.S. Department of State, *Papers*, 2:556–57.

160　Over the meal, Ozaki asked: Saionji, *Saionji Kinkazu Kaikoroku*, 231.

160　"I have made a big mistake": Ibid., 208.

161　The original English text: "The Japanese Prime Minister (Prince Konoye) to President Roosevelt," August 27, 1941, in U.S. Department of State, *Papers*, 2:573.

161　Roosevelt complimented: "Memorandum by the Secretary of State," August 28, 1941, in U.S. Department of State, *Papers*, 2:571.

161　The ambassador was encouraged because: Ibid., 572.

161　He described the likely composition: "Memorandum of a Conversation," August 28, 1941, in U.S. Department of State, *Papers*, 2:576–78. All the following quotations from the meeting are from this source.

CHAPTER 9 · AN UNWINNABLE, INEVITABLE WAR

164　The institute was opened in April 1941: Inose, *Showa Jurokunen Natsu no Haisen*, 45. Originally published in 1983, this book includes interviews conducted with surviving members of the institute.

165　He responded with due deference: Ibid., 76–78.

166　The guidelines presented to the researchers: Ibid., 119.

167　His own ministry's War Economy Research Office: Akimaru Jiro, television interview, *NHK Supesharu: Gozen Kaigi*, August 15, 1991.

167　"This is, after all, a desktop exercise": Inose, *Showa Jurokunen Natsu no Haisen*, 193–94.

168　The instructor Horiba Kazuo, an army man: Ibid., 122.

169　Kafu noted that Okubo was rumored: Nagai, *Tekiroku Danchotei Nichijo* (2), 118.

169　The president, now echoing Hull: "Memorandum by the Secretary of State," September 3, 1941, in U.S. Department of State, *Papers*, 2:588–89.

169　But Konoe took heart: "President Roosevelt's Reply to the Japanese Prime Minister (Prince Konoye), Handed to the Japanese Ambassador (Nomura)," September 3, 1941, in U.S. Department of State, *Papers*, 2:592.

169　Though the countries they led: The characterizations of Roosevelt are from Steven Casey, "Franklin D. Roosevelt," in *Mental Maps in the Era of Two World Wars*, ed. Steven Casey and Jonathan Wright (London: Palgrave Macmillan, 2008), 217–18.

170　An August 29 journal entry by an officer: Gomikawa, *Gozen Kaigi*, 145–46.

170　"What idiots they are in Washington!": Osugi, *Shinjuwan e no Michi*, 331.

170　Ishii believed the likely sequence: Ibid., 331–32.

171　"The empire is getting skinnier": "Dai 50-kai Renraku Kaigi," September 3, 1941, in *Taiheiyo Senso e no Michi (Bekkan)*, 507-8. All quotations from this conference are from this source.

172   "Tomita [the chief cabinet secretary] should have coordinated": Saionji, *Saionji Kinkazu Kaikoroku,* 212.

173   "That would be impossible": *Showa Tenno Dokuhakuroku,* ed. Terasaki Hidenari and Mariko Terasaki Miller (Bunshun Bunko, 2010), 74.

174   Displaying the incisiveness: Konoe, *Heiwa e no Doryoku,* 86–87.

174   "I speak broadly on behalf": Ibid., 87.

175   He asked Nagano the same question: Hando, *Shikikan to Sanbo,* 122.

176   The emperor recited: Konoe, *Heiwa e no Doryoku,* 87.

177   Afterward, Grew wrote a lengthy report: "Memorandum by the Ambassador in Japan (Grew)," September 6, 1941, in U.S. Department of State, *Papers,* 2:604–6.

CHAPTER 10 · ONE LAST OPPORTUNITY

178   "The United States in the end demands": Quoted in Osugi, *Shinjuwan e no Michi,* 346–47.

180   But instead, he told Sugiyama: Gomikawa, *Gozen Kaigi,* 170.

180   The navy also intensified its preparations: Ibid., 170–71.

181   When Germany invaded Denmark: Kershaw, *Fateful Choices,* 312.

181   By sending professional soldiers: Ibid., 313.

181   The *Greer,* a U.S. destroyer: Ibid., 319.

182   "This was piracy": Franklin D. Roosevelt, "Fireside Chat 18: On the *Greer* Incident," September 11, 1941, http://millercenter.org/scripps/archive/speeches/detail /3323.

183   Roosevelt had confirmed his oratorical genius: Kershaw, *Fateful Choices,* 322–24.

183   After hearing from Sorge: Shimotomai and NHK Shuzaihan, *Kokusai Supai Zoruge no Shinjitsu,* 220.

184   Hull replied that this proposal: "Memorandum of a Conversation," September 10, 1941, in U.S. Department of State, *Papers,* 2:613–14.

184   The banker and amateur diplomat: Osugi, *Shinjuwan e no Michi,* 349.

185   Negotiating a U.S.-Japanese understanding without settling: "Memorandum by the Under Secretary of State (Welles)," October 13, 1941, in U.S. Department of State, *Papers,* 2:685.

185   If Konoe had proposed: Matsumoto Shigeharu, *Konoe Jidai: Janarisuto no Kaiso* (2) (Chuko Bunko, 1987), 200; emphasis added.

185   He sent a telegram to Tokyo: Nomura to Toyoda, telegram 865, September 28, 1941, in Gaimusho, *Nichibei Kosho Shiryo* (Hara Shobo, 1978), part 1, 320.

185   "The general staff is an organ": Osugi, *Shinjuwan e no Michi,* 351.

186   That evening, Saionji and Ozaki dined: Saionji, *Saionji Kinkazu Kaikoroku,* 236.

186   Unlike most others, they could still: *Showa Nimannichi no Zenkiroku* (6), 55.

187   "The timing of the opening of war": "Dai 55-kai Renraku Kaigi," September 25, 1941, in *Taiheiyo Senso e no Michi (Bekkan),* 528–29.

187   A *bakuryo* officer in the War Guidance Office: Gomikawa, *Gozen Kaigi,* 172–73.

188   "If the military insists on the October 15 deadline": Kido, *Kido Koichi Nikki* (2), 909.

188   "You are the one who called": Gomikawa, *Gozen Kaigi,* 174.

188   In a lengthy eleven-point communication: "The Ambassador in Japan (Grew) to the Secretary of State," September 29, 1941, in U.S. Department of State, *Papers,* 2:649.

189   He suggested as much in a carefully cushioned double-negative supposition: Ibid., 650.

190   Grew, aware of this, insisted: Ibid., 647.

190   "If the United States continues to deliberately misread": Toyoda, *Matsuoka Yosuke* (2), 362.

190   True, in trying to oust Matsuoka: "Dai 32-kai Renraku Kondankai," June 25, 1941, in *Taiheiyo Senso e no Michi (Bekkan),* 446.

191   A fanatical believer in Japan's inherent greatness: "Dai 66-kai Renraku Kaigi,"
        November 1, 1941, in *Taiheiyo Senso e no Michi (Bekkan)*, 553.
191   "The likely prospect might be war": Gomikawa, *Gozen Kaigi*, 177.
191   Hence his assessment to Nagano: Ibid., 187.
192   Oikawa responded: Ibid., 182.
193   He was handed a statement urging Japan: "Oral Statement Handed by the Sec-
        retary of State to the Japanese Ambassador (Nomura)," October 2, 1941, in U.S.
        Department of State, *Papers*, 2:658.
193   Hull then asked Japan to present: Ibid., 660.
193   Most emphatically, there would be no summit: "Memorandum of a Conversa-
        tion," October 2, 1941, in U.S. Department of State, *Papers*, 2:655.
193   Nomura was repeatedly: Ibid.
193   Nomura was also told: Ibid., 656.
194   Army Chief of Staff Sugiyama warned: "Dai 57-kai Renraku Kaigi," October 4,
        1941, in *Taiheiyo Senso e no Michi (Bekkan)*, 530.
195   In January 1946, in a roundtable discussion: Excerpts of the conference are
        quoted in Gomikawa, *Gozen Kaigi*, 183–86.
196   On October 5, the navy held a top-level meeting: Ibid., 190.
196   The October 5 entry of the War Guidance Office journal: Ibid., 188.
197   "The United States demands us to leave": Ibid., 189.
197   They agreed that the Army General Staff should: Ibid., 191–92.
197   According to Vice Minister Sawamoto, Oikawa was: Ibid.
198   The army's War Guidance Office log: Ibid., 190–91.
198   The navy's unusually frank admission: *The Final Confrontation*, ed. Morley, 213.
199   In a cabinet meeting, Tojo announced: Osugi, *Shinjuwan e no Michi*, 360.
199   Oikawa replied: Gomikawa, *Gozen Kaigi*, 197.
200   But even he could not help occasionally: Ibid., 193–94.
200   "We absolutely cannot do that": Ibid., 198–200. All the following quotes from this
        meeting are taken from this source, unless otherwise indicated.
201   Jumping into the abyss was: Konoe, *Heiwa e no Doryoku*, 94.
201   "We've lost tens of thousands of lives": Osugi, *Shinjuwan e no Michi*, 365.
202   In early October, the commander in chief of Japanese forces: Ibid., 367.
202   Hull's damning postwar assessment: Cordell Hull, *The Memoirs of Cordell Hull*
        (New York: Macmillan, 1948), 2:1054.
202   "We must continue to seek a diplomatic settlement": "Gosho Kaigi," October 12,
        1941, in *Taiheiyo Senso e no Michi (Bekkan)*, 531–33.
203   "It's not up to the military to say": Gomikawa, *Gozen Kaigi*, 203–4.
204   "If I am allowed to be brutally frank": "Gosho Kaigi," 532.

CHAPTER 11 · A SOLDIER TAKES OVER

206   "The fall of Xuzhou! The fall of Xuzhou!": rebroadcast in a television documen-
        tary, *NHK Supesharu "Nihonjin wa Naze Senso e to Mukattanoka"* (3), February 27,
        2011.
206   "How utterly bizarre": Nagai, *Tekiroku Danchotei Nichijo* (2), 146.
207   "But Ambassador Nomura is an able man": Shimotomai and NHK Shuzaihan,
        Kokusai Supai Zoruge no Shinjitsu, 223–24.
208   Now, for a change, Konoe spoke: Gomikawa, *Gozen Kaigi*, 212.
208   "I believe the prime minister's argument": Konoe, *Heiwa e no Doryoku*, 95–96.
209   The speech went as follows: "Kakugi ni okeru Rikugun Daijin Setsumei no Yoshi,"
        October 14, 1941, in *Taiheiyo Senso e no Michi (Bekkan)*, 533–34.
209   Tojo, going right against the theatrical, hard-hitting prowar tone: "Rikugun
        Daijin Setsumeigo Kyuchu ni Okeru Kido, Tojo Kaidan Yoshi," October 14, 1941, in
        Taiheiyo Senso e no Michi (Bekkan), 535.
210   "The navy minister doesn't say": Ibid.

211 "I've got some awful news!": Saionji, *Saionji Kinkazu Kaikoroku*, 220.

213 One day in early October, Kafu chatted: Nagai, *Tekiroku Danchotei Nichijo* (2), 153–54.

214 "Minister, you cornered Prince Konoe": Inose, *Showa Jurokunen Natsu no Haisen*, 85–87.

214 Hirohito covered for his subject's embarrassing silence: Ibid., 87.

215 "No pain, no gain, wouldn't you say?": Kido, *Kido Koichi Nikki* (2), 918.

215 "I gather that you [Tojo] have now received": Ibid., 917.

216 "I do not have any problem reexamining the issue": Osugi, *Shinjuwan e no Michi*, 388.

217 "Mr. Sorge! It's Saito from the police": Shomitomai and NHK Shuzaihan, *Kokusai Supai Zoruge no Shinjitsu*, 232.

217 "I have three things to say to you": Saionji, *Saionji Kinkazu Kaikoroku*, 217.

CHAPTER 12 · WINDING BACK THE CLOCK

219 He did not mince his words: Gomikawa, *Gozen Kaigi*, 233–34.

220 Nagano, who had commented earlier: "Dai 59-kai Renraku Kaigi," October 23, 1941, in *Taiheiyo Senso e no Michi (Bekkan)*, 537–38. All of the quotes from this conference are taken from this source.

222 In preparing new data to be presented: Nakahara Shigetoshi, television interview, *NHK Supesharu: Gozen Kaigi*, August 15, 1991.

223 Nagano declared: Gomikawa, *Gozen Kaigi*, 246–47.

223 When Suzuki was invited to share his views: "Dai 62-kai Renraku Kaigi," October 27, 1941, in *Taiheiyo Senso e no Michi (Bekkan)*, 539.

224 According to its research: Gomikawa, *Gozen Kaigi*, 249.

224 These overwhelming figures were: Ibid., 421.

224 Later, when he was ninety-three: Inose, *Showa Jurokunen Natsu no Haisen*, 184.

224 So Suzuki simply skated over: "Dai 62-kai Renraku Kaigi," 539.

225 The Army General Staff record of October 27: Ibid., 540.

225 "Unless we decide quickly": Osugi, *Shinjuwan e no Michi*, 402.

225 The War Guidance Office of the Army General Staff noted: Gomikawa, *Gozen Kaigi*, 256.

226 They declared at the meeting: "Dai 63-kai Renraku Kaigi," October 28, 1941, in *Taiheiyo Senso e no Michi (Bekkan)*, 541.

226 On the material front: Ibid.

227 "Our economy would survive": "Dai 65-kai Renraku Kaigi," October 30, 1941, in *Taiheiyo Senso e no Michi (Bekkan)*, 541–48. All of the other quotes from this conference are taken from this source.

228 He was also surprised that the navy had not come: Togo Shigenori, *Jidai no Ichimen: Taisen Gaiko no Shuki* (Chuko Bunko, 1989), 318–19.

228 Shimada confided in Vice Navy Minister: Osugi, *Shinjuwan e no Michi*, 402.

CHAPTER 13 · ON THE BRINK

230 "I intend to take the third route": "Tojo Rikusho to Sugiyama Socho tono Kaidan Yoshi," November 11, 1941, in *Taiheiyo Senso e no Michi (Bekkan)*, 548–49. All of the quotes from this meeting are taken from this source.

231 Humiliated, Sugiyama asked Shimada: Gomikawa, *Gozen Kaigi*, 284.

231 He asked the navy leaders impatiently: "Dai 66-kai Renraku Kaigi," November 1, 1941, in *Taiheiyo Senso e no Michi (Bekkan)*, 550–51.

234 "Well, my dear Yamamoto": Osugi, *Shinjuwan e no Michi*, 407.

235 Pilots had been superbly trained: Fuchida, *Shinjuwan Kogeki Sotaicho no Kaiso*, 104–8.

236 "Couldn't the deadline be extended": "Dai 66-kai Renraku Kaigi," 551–52.

240 He also questioned the chiefs of staff on some technical issues: *The Final Confrontation,* ed. Morley, 264.

240 "If we just stand by with our arms folded": Osugi, *Shinjuwan e no Michi,* 413.

241 "President Roosevelt is taking advantage": "Gozen Kaigi," November 5, 1941, in *Taiheiyo Senso e no Michi (Bekkan),* 573.

CHAPTER 14 · "NO LAST WORD BETWEEN FRIENDS"

242 "There is no last word between friends": Kurusu Saburo, *Homatsu no Sanjugonen* (Chuko Bunko, 2007), 88.

243 "In this dangerous emergency": Togo, *Jidai no Ichimen,* 331.

244 He went on to say that in his estimation: Kurusu, *Homatsu no Sanjugonen,* 26–27. All of the following quotes from this meeting are taken from this source.

245 The escalation, in his words, came about: Ibid., 221–22.

247 "The negotiations at hand represent": Togo to Nomura, telegram 725, November 4, 1941, in Gaimusho, *Nichibei Kosho Shiryo,* part 1, 385.

247 The president made no specific references: "Memorandum by the Secretary of State," November 10, 1941, in U.S. Department of State, *Papers,* 2:718.

247 When Wakasugi Kaname, the minister-counselor, visited: "Memorandum of a Conversation," November 13, 1941, in U.S. Department of State, *Papers,* 2:730–31.

248 "If the situation allows": Nomura to Togo, telegram 1090, November 14, 1941, in Gaimusho, *Nichibei Kosho Shiryo,* part 1, 428.

248 Hull had not accepted: "Oral Statement Handed by the Secretary of State to the Japanese Ambassador (Nomura) on November 15, 1941," in U.S. Department of State, *Papers,* 2:734.

248 "If we are to work out a peaceful settlement": "Memorandum of a Conversation," November 15, 1941, in U.S. Department of State, *Papers,* 2:732–34.

249 "Regrettably," wrote Togo: Togo to Nomura, telegram 781, November 16, 1941, in Gaimusho, *Nichibei Kosho Shiryo,* part 1, 444.

249 In Tokyo, Togo had given him: Sato Motoei, "Togo Gaisho wa Nichibei Kaisen wo Soshi Dekita," *Bungei Shunju* (March 2009): 313.

250 "Are you bringing a new proposal?": Kurusu, *Homatsu no Sanjugonen,* 28.

252 He was dismissive of Kurusu's: "Memorandum by the Secretary of State," November 17, 1941, in U.S. Department of State, *Papers,* 2:740.

252 Hull had said in a previous meeting: "Memorandum of a Conversation," November 14, 1941, in U.S. Department of State, *Papers,* 2:733.

252 Whatever the reason, Hull's opinion of Kurusu: "Memorandum by the Secretary of State," November 17, 1941, in U.S. Department of State, *Papers,* 2:742–43.

253 Looking back in 1948: Hull, *The Memoirs of Cordell Hull,* 2:1062.

253 Tojo's policy speech in the Diet: See http://cgi2.nhk.or.jp/shogenarchives/jpnews/movie.cgi?das_id=D0001300461_00000&seg_number=002.

255 Despite U.S.-German hostilities: Kershaw, *Fateful Choices,* 326.

257 Hull impressed on the Japanese envoys: "Memorandum of a Conversation," November 18, 1941, in U.S. Department of State, *Papers,* 2:745–50. All of the other quotes from the meeting are taken from this source.

258 Kurusu sent a message to Tokyo: Kurusu, *Homatsu no Sanjugonen,* 96–97.

259 Walsh congratulated Kurusu on the near completion: Ibid., 98.

259 He expressed his view that an agreement: "Memorandum of a Conversation," November 19, 1941, in U.S. Department of State, *Papers,* 2:751.

259 In Togo's mind, Nomura's action was a typical case: Togo, *Jidai no Ichimen,* 338.

260 "There is absolutely no room for such maneuver": Togo to Nomura, telegram 798, November 20, 1941, in Gaimusho, *Nichibei Kosho Shiryo,* part 1, 467.

CHAPTER 15 · THE HULL NOTE

261 **Togo had prohibited its immediate use:** Kurusu, *Homatsu no Sanjugonen,* 105.
262 **Thus he presented Hull with his personal note:** "Draft Letter Handed by Mr. Saburo Kurusu to the Secretary of State," November 21, 1941, in U.S. Department of State, *Papers,* 2:756–57.
262 **"You came all this way, Ambassador":** Kurusu, *Homatsu no Sanjugonen,* 106.
263 **"Please, do take care of yourself":** Ibid.
263 **Hull's memorandum of his tête-à-tête:** "Memorandum by the Secretary of State," November 21, 1941, in U.S. Department of State, *Papers,* 2:756.
264 **He said that oil purchased by Japan:** "Memorandum of a Conversation," November 22, 1941, in U.S. Department of State, *Papers,* 2:757.
264 **Hull wondered why there was:** Ibid., 758.
264 **Why had Japan "pushed everything":** Ibid., 761.
265 **But there were to be:** Togo to Nomura, telegram 812, November 22, 1941, in Gaimusho, *Nichibei Kosho Shiryo,* part 1, 478–79.
265 **On the evening of November 25:** Kershaw, *Fateful Choices,* 368–70.
265 **Hull's own postwar explanation:** Hull, *The Memoirs of Cordell Hull,* 2:1081.
266 **Based on this intercepted communication:** Henry Stimson, quoted in notes, Kershaw, *Fateful Choices,* 558.
266 **Roosevelt's secretary of war:** Ibid.
267 **These were crystallized in the third, fourth, and fifth points:** "Outline of Proposed Basis for Agreement Between the United States and Japan," November 26, 1941, in U.S. Department of State, *Papers,* 2:769.
267 **Even though the outline was marked:** *The Final Confrontation,* ed. Morley, 313.
268 **Kurusu expressed his grave fear:** "Memorandum of a Conversation," November 26, 1941, in U.S. Department of State, *Papers,* 2:766.

CHAPTER 16 · JUMPING OFF THE HIGH PLATFORM

269 **"I was struck by despair":** Togo, *Jidai no Ichimen,* 375.
269 **For those restlessly itching:** Osugi, *Shinjuwan e no Michi,* 463.
270 **Until the arrival of the note:** Togo Shigehiko, *Sofu Togo Shigenori no Shogai* (Bungei Shunju, 1993), 278.
270 **"This is terribly written indeed!":** Osugi, *Shinjuwan e no Michi,* 464.
270 **Yoshida told Togo that whatever the true intentions:** Ibid.
271 **Despite having warned his closest advisers:** Kurusu, *Homatsu no Sanjugonen,* 111–12.
271 **He and his government were grateful:** "Memorandum by the Secretary of State," November 27, 1941, in U.S. Department of State, *Papers,* 2:770–72. All of the quotes from this meeting are taken from this source.
273 **"They would be ground to powder":** Churchill, *The Grand Alliance,* 539.
274 **"If Japan is to join the war":** "Gozen Kaigi," November 5, 1941, 569–570.
275 **"Excuse me for speaking my mind":** Osugi, *Shinjuwan e no Michi,* 481.
275 **"Is there any time left for diplomacy?":** "Dai 74-kai Renraku Kaigi," November 29, 1941, in *Taiheiyo Senso e no Michi (Bekkan),* 592.
276 **He concluded his message with a plea that:** Kurusu, *Homatsu no Sanjugonen,* 121.
276 **The lord keeper of the privy seal would have none of it:** Ibid., 122.
276 **"The navy cannot afford to fight":** Kido, *Kido Koichi Nikki (2),* 928.
276 **"If I did not approve of war, Tojo would resign":** *Showa Tenno Dokuhakuroku,* 89–90.
277 **"Naval strategies are everything":** Osugi, *Shinjuwan e no Michi,* 483.
277 **Shimada, in order to:** Ibid.

277 "We aim to demolish the Far Eastern bases": "Dai 69-kai Renraku Kaigi," November 15, 1941, in *Taiheiyo Senso e no Michi (Bekkan)*, 585.

278 Finally, Hirohito gave his approval: "Gozen Kaigi," December 1, 1941, in *Taiheiyo Senso e no Michi (Bekkan)*, 596.

EPILOGUE · THE NEW BEGINNING

280 After he had finished reading: "Memorandum of a Conversation," December 7, 1941, in U.S. Department of State, *Papers*, 2:787.

280 Before his departure for Washington: *The Final Confrontation*, ed. Morley, 19.

281 In a communication from Tokyo on November 28: Togo to Nomura, telegram 844, November 28, 1941, in Gaimusho, *Nichibei Kosho Shiryo*, part 1, 505–6.

281 Togo's exact words read: Togo to Nomura, telegram 878, December 3, 1941, in Gaimusho, *Nichibei Kosho Shiryo*, part 1, 530.

282 That Kurusu and Nomura delivered the message: For a critical exploration of the debate, see Takeo Iguchi, *Demystifying Pearl Harbor: A New Japanese Perspective*, trans. David Noble (International House of Japan, 2010).

284 Kurusu immediately recalled his interview: Kurusu, *Homatsu no Sanjugonen*, 164.

284 "Which one's Kurusu?": Ibid., 139.

284 "I want to leave something more tangible": Ibid., 211.

285 Prince Takamatsu, more straightforward: Ibid., 167.

285 At the prime minister's luncheon: Ibid.

289 "Sponge cakes, dumplings, pastries": *Showa Nimannichi no Zenkiroku* (6), 336.

291 "We must be losing the war": Iijima, "Growing Up in Old Japan," 20.

292 And this pattern was perpetuated: Nagai, *Tekiroku Danchotei Nichijo* (2), 143.

Index

"ABCD encirclement," 146, 153, 179, 269
Acheson, Dean, 151
Act of Union, 181
Afrika Korps, 108
Aizawa Saburo, 91
Aizu domain, 84
Akagi, 268
Alien Land Law, U.S., 250
aluminum, 224
American Affairs Bureau, 244
American-British Conversations, 27
Anglo-Satsuma War, 83
Anti-Comintern Pact, 25, 65
Araki Sadao, 90, 91
Arita-Craigie Agreement, 26
Arita Hachiro, 26, 151–2
Arizona, 12
Army General Staff, 39, 45, 124, 125, 126,
      128, 130, 143–4, 159, 167, 170, 184, 196,
      197, 210, 225–6, 227, 229, 234, 246,
      269, 285
   see also War Guidance Office
Army Ministry, 91, 124, 125, 127, 153, 156,
      163, 186, 191, 222
Art of War, The (Sun Tzu), 232
Asahi, 6, 50, 51, 67, 120, 122, 213
Asamu Maru, 279, 283
Asian Exclusion Act, U.S., 251
Atholl, Duke of, 87

Atlantic Charter, 158
Atlantic Conference, 157–8, 159, 181
Augusta, 157
Australia, 35, 153
Austria, 16

Bacon, Alice Mabel, 84
Bacon, Leonard, 84
Baden-Baden, 89, 90, 91
bakuryo, 124–7, 131, 170, 185, 187, 196, 269,
      282, 286
Bal à Yeddo, Un (Loti), 77
Ballantine, Joseph, 247–8
Bälz, Erwin von, 81
Batavia (Jakarta), 27–8
Binyon, Laurence, 87
Bloy, Léon, 142
Bolshevism, 17, 26, 44, 194
Boshin War, 82, 217
Boxer Protocol, 267
Boxer Rebellion, 30
Breakfast Club, 122, 155, 177, 211,
      218
Britain, Battle of, 24, 108, 117
Bryan, William Jennings, 250
Buddhism, 41
Burma, 11, 143, 153, 173
Burma Road, 26

Cabinet Planning Board, 39, 110, 130, 175, 202, 210, 219, 224, 226, 230, 231
Cambodia, 12
Canada, 35, 143, 157
cancer, 277–8
Carinhall, 111
charcoal, 26
Chiang Kai-shek, 49, 55, 185, 246, 253
  British and U.S. aid to, 24, 26, 173, 237, 269, 282
  Communists fought by, 46
  jubilant at news of Pearl Harbor, 9
  Konoe's impatience with, 38–9
  truce with Japan and, 31
  in war with Japan, 4, 24, 26, 30, 32, 52, 55, 56, 67–8, 70, 72, 102, 140
  as willing to negotiate with Japan, 33
Chichibu Yasuhito, Imperial Prince, 92
China, 10, 17, 40, 47, 80, 143, 144, 248, 265, 266
  Japanese importing of culture from, 40–1
  Japan's 1931 truce with, 30–1
  nationalism in, 17
  Open Door policy on, 43, 70
  see also Sino-Japanese War
China Incident, *see* China War
China War, 10, 18, 24, 27, 39, 48, 49, 50, 52, 54, 55, 56, 68, 69, 71, 72, 94, 96, 103, 108, 110, 122–3, 148, 174, 179, 184, 208, 212, 237, 253, 255, 260, 277
  austerity prompted by, 4–5, 6, 168, 218
  casualties of, 201–2
  Ishiwara's opposition to, 44
  Japanese atrocities in, 32, 48–9, 154
  Japanese belief in swift victory in, 4, 8, 32
  Japanese withdrawal from, 152, 193–4, 200–2, 217, 227, 244, 251
  outbreak of, 29–30, 116, 190, 245
  Tutuila bombing in, 155
  wartime care packages in, 6, 213
Chinda Sutemi, 250–1
Chongqing, 40, 155, 267
Choshu domain, 82, 90
Chuo Koron, 169
Churchill, Winston, 116–17, 169, 273, 282
  alleged conniving to get U.S. into war, 266

FDR's meeting in Newfoundland with, 157–8, 159, 181
  jubilant at news of Pearl Harbor, 9
Clausen, Max, 120, 217
Clemenceau, Georges, 34, 36, 179
coal, 26, 224
Combined Fleet, 104, 198–9
Comintern, 150
Communist Party, U.S., 211
Communists, Chinese, 32, 44, 46, 47
Communists, in Japan, 168–9
Conder, Josiah, 78
Confucianism, 41
Congress of Vienna, 66
Conscription Ordinance (1873), 48
constitution, Japanese, 19, 203
Constitutional Democratic Party, 99
Conte Verde, 283
Control faction, 90–1, 92
copper, 224
Craigie, Robert, 26, 143
Czechoslovakia, 16, 185

Dalian, 41, 256
Denmark, 181
department stores, 6, 213
Diet, *see* Parliament, Japan
DNB, 121
Dooman, Eugene, 177
Draft Understanding, 56–7, 68, 71, 73, 111, 112
Drought, James M., 57, 162
Dunkirk, 52
Dutch East Indies (Indonesia), 11, 24, 57, 123–4, 143, 144, 153, 166, 237, 249, 260, 276

East Asian Coprosperity Sphere, *see* Greater East Asia Coprosperity Sphere
Edo Castle, 81
education, 213
Egypt, 108
"Essentials for Carrying Out the Empire's Policies," 171, 172–3, 204, 278
Eternal March Forward, 40

Index · 313

Ethiopia, 62
Export-Import Bank, 24

Final Proposal, 260
Finland, 117, 130
Foreign Ministry, 55, 56, 58, 61, 69, 109, 125, 144, 189, 226, 234, 236–7, 244, 282
Foreign Office, 161
  see also Foreign Ministry
Formosa, see Taiwan
49th Parallel, 157
"Four Freedoms" speech, 93–4
Four Principles, 73–4, 147, 193, 197, 199, 201, 202, 227–8, 263
"Fourth Climacteric" speech, 116–17
France, 16, 26, 42, 63, 103, 123–4, 274
  German invasion and occupation of, 23, 52, 115, 117
  war declared on Germany by, 121
Franco-Prussian War, 83, 121
free trade, 113, 179, 228, 267
French Indochina
  FDR's proposal on, 154–5, 156–7, 185, 269
  Japan in, 4, 12, 23–4, 26, 123, 126, 128–30, 131–5, 136, 139–40, 144–5, 146, 151–3, 162, 166, 171, 173, 185, 227, 237, 244, 249, 253, 255, 258, 260, 265, 266, 267, 269, 273, 276
Friends of Constitutional Government, 61, 64, 100
Friends of Italy, 116
Fuchida Mitsuo, 96, 287
Fujiwara family, 28, 33
Fukudome Shigeru, 198–9, 234
Fushimi Hiroyasu, Imperial Prince, 105, 225, 228

Genda Minoru, 106, 107, 234, 235
George II, King of Greece, 108
George V, King of England, 86–7
George VI, King of England, 50
Germany, 17, 20, 23, 37, 42, 52, 63, 65, 72, 133, 139, 141, 145, 162, 219–20, 258, 274, 275, 277
  British and French declarations of war against, 121

Denmark invaded by, 181
France invaded by, 23, 115, 117
Japanese alliance with, 4, 10, 24–5, 40, 56, 58, 59, 65, 66, 67, 70, 110, 114, 118, 135, 140, 190, 246, 251, 273
Soviet Union invaded by, 109–10, 113, 114, 115, 116, 117, 118, 119, 120, 123, 127, 143, 149, 150, 151, 185, 219, 266, 270
Ginza district, 26, 109, 149, 207
Goebbels, Joseph, 285
Gone with the Wind, 291, 292–3
Göring, Hermann, 111
Great Britain, 10, 16, 25, 42, 67, 103, 111, 131, 132, 133, 136, 138, 143, 144, 173, 193, 219–20, 222, 248, 255–6, 258, 265, 266
  and Anti-Comintern Pact, 25, 65
  forces dispatched to Iceland by, 181
  in Japanese war game, 166
  Japan's deteriorating relationship with, 26
  Japan's entering war with, 3
  racial prejudice in, 37
  U.S. aid to, 17, 117–18, 145, 155
  war declared on Germany by, 121
Great Depression, 16, 17, 29, 46, 100, 113
Greater East Asia Coprosperity Sphere, 11, 153, 263
Great Kanto Earthquake, 13
Greece, 108
Greer, 181–2, 255
Grew, Joseph, 26–7, 105–6, 145–8, 177, 186, 188–90, 250, 252, 270–1, 283–4, 285
Grew, Mrs., 250
Gripsholm, 279, 281, 283
Guam, 97, 153, 289
Guillain, Robert, 121
Guomindang, 4, 26, 32, 38, 40, 46, 49

Hague Convention, 96, 282
Hainan, 152, 184, 227
Halifax, Lord, 183
Hamaguchi Osachi, 99–100, 101, 156
Hangzhou, 31
Hara Yoshimichi, 131–4, 175, 273–4, 277, 278
Harbin, 256

Harriman, Averell, 9
Hata Shunroku, 104
Hatoyama Ichiro, 100–1
Havas, 121
Hawaii, 3, 9, 68, 106, 153, 159, 170, 180, 235, 236, 240, 257, 279, 287
Heilongjiang, 45
Higashikuni Naruhiko, Imperial Prince, 178, 179, 210, 211, 215, 291–2
Higasa Hiroo, 165
Higuchi Kiichiro, 65
Hiranuma Kiichiro, 25, 137–8, 139, 177
Hirohito, Emperor Showa, 55, 56, 86–8, 92, 103, 105, 111, 112, 131, 148, 178, 180, 197, 225, 273–4, 276–7, 282, 285, 286
alliance with Germany explained to, 118
diplomacy desired by, 173–6, 178, 179, 240
European tour of, 86–7
made emperor, 88
Nagano desired replaced by, 173–4
and occupation of French Indochina, 134
Tojo made prime minister by, 214
as worried about "Essentials," 172–3
Hiroshima, 288
Hirota Koki, 47, 239
Hitler, Adolf, 4, 16, 18, 19, 24, 38, 108, 111, 114, 118, 121, 130, 144, 145, 157, 182, 226, 245, 246, 258
assassination attempt on, 290
Matsuoka's visit to, 58–9
Stalin's nonaggression pact with, 150
suicide of, 290
war declared on U.S. by, 9
Hitokappu Bay, 257
Hochi, 277–8
Hokkaido, 84
Holocaust, 65
Home Ministry, 53
Hong Kong, 3
Hopkins, Harry, 155, 158
Horiba Kazuo, 168
Hornbeck, Stanley, 252
Hosokawa Morisada, 11
House of Peers, 36, 42
House of Representatives, U.S., 64, 255

Hull, Cordell, 8, 66, 69, 71, 72, 73, 74, 105, 112, 113–14, 118, 137, 138, 140, 141, 156, 161, 162, 179, 184, 185, 282–3
Four Principles of, 73–4, 147, 193, 197, 199, 201, 202, 227–8, 263
Kurusu's meeting with, 250, 251–3, 257–8, 259, 261–4, 266–8, 271–3, 275, 279–80
Nomura's meetings with, 193–4, 247, 248–9, 250, 251–3, 259, 263–4, 266–8, 271–3, 275, 279–80
Hull Note, 266–7, 269, 272, 273, 274, 275, 278, 281
Hyuga, 165

"I Call to Reject the Anglo-American Peace" (Konoe), 35–6
Iceland, 180–2, 255
Ickes, Harold, 136
Iimura Jo, 165
Iinuma Masaaki, 50, 285
Ikawa Tadao, 69, 162, 184
Ikeda Sumihisa, 31–2
Immigration Act of 1924, U.S., 251
Imperial Defence College, 164
Imperial General Headquarters, 124–5
Imperial Hotel, 78
Imperial Japanese Army, 55, 83, 87, 95, 128, 161, 195, 210, 231, 259–60
reform of, 89
Imperial Japanese Navy, 3, 55, 87, 95, 96–7, 126, 128, 161, 195–6, 210, 226, 231, 284, 287
as confident of war with west, 190–3
Midway defeat of, 12, 284
Tripartite Pact approved by, 25
Imperial Palace, 7, 19, 39, 55, 76, 143, 213
Imperial Rescript on Education, 78, 94
Imperial Rescript to Soldiers and Sailors, 77–9, 80, 81, 83, 85, 87, 93
Imperial Rule Assistance Association (IRAA), 138, 253
Imperial Way faction, 90, 91–3
India, 52, 96
Indonesia, 11
see also Dutch East Indies
Information Division, 206

Inner Mongolia, 40, 46, 162, 194, 227
Inoue Shigeyoshi, 103, 105, 195, 196
"Instructions for the Battlefield," 93
Inukai Takeru, 122
Inukai Tsuyoshi, 45, 122
Iraq War, 152
Ishii Akiho, 127, 153, 170, 185–6
Ishii Hanako, 149, 150, 207
Ishikawa Shingo, 126–7
Ishiwara Kanji, 30, 43, 44–5, 126
isolationists, 117
Italy, 62, 108, 275, 277
    Japanese alliance with, 4, 10, 24–5, 40,
        56, 58, 59, 65, 66, 67, 140, 190, 273
Ito Hirobumi, 274
Ito Sei, 7, 11, 12
Ito Seiichi, 233
Iwakuro Hideo, 69

Jakarta, 28
Japan
    as ambivalent about preemptive actions
        in Pacific and Asia, 10–11
    austerity in, 4–6, 168, 218
    Britain's deteriorating relationship with,
        26
    China's truce with, 1931, 30–1
    Chinese culture imported to, 40–1
    conception of marriage in, immediately
        before Pearl Harbor, 212–13
    consensus preferred in, 19
    destruction of cities in, 290–1
    and Draft Understanding, 56–7, 68, 71,
        73, 111, 112
    end of parliamentary politics in, 19, 29
    fashion in, 4–5, 6
    food shortages in, 4, 12–13, 26, 288–9,
        291
    in French Indochina, 4, 12, 23–4, 26,
        123, 126, 128–30, 131–5, 136, 139–40,
        144–5, 146, 151–3, 162, 166, 171, 173,
        185, 227, 237, 244, 249, 253, 255, 258,
        260, 265, 266, 267, 269, 273, 276
    in Great Depression, 16, 29, 46, 100
    Hitler's desire to see attack Britain, 111
    imperial conferences in, 130–4, 138, 172,
        175–6, 197, 273, 278

    industrialization of, 85–6, 224
    liaison conferences in, 71–2, 111–12,
        128–30, 136–9, 138–40, 143, 163, 166,
        171, 187, 194, 195, 196, 222, 230, 231–4,
        239, 240, 275, 277
    Manchuria invaded and occupied by, 18,
        30, 45–6, 151, 159, 160, 171
    mid-nineteenth century opening of, 17
    military budget of, 132, 142
    mobilization plan in, 256–7
    nationalism of, 16–17
    neighborhood associations in, 53–4, 213
    North Pacific Fur Seal Convention
        signed by, 222
    patriotic women's association in, 5–6
    plans to invade Soviet Union, 114–15,
        127, 128–9, 132, 134, 150–1, 183, 190
    primary schooler evacuation program
        in, 288–9
    rationing in, 12–13, 218
    rumors of war with U.S., 25–6, 105–7,
        108
    scarcity of conference records on, 14–15
    self-imposed isolation of, 17
    Soviet neutrality pact with, 58, 59, 65–7,
        112–13, 115
    Soviet Union's battles with, 74
    trade by, 41
    in Tripartite Pact, 4, 10, 24–5, 40, 56, 58,
        59, 65, 66, 67, 70, 103, 110, 112, 114, 118,
        135, 142, 143, 148, 163, 173, 178, 190,
        201, 227, 228, 245, 246, 248, 249, 250,
        251, 252, 261–2, 263, 273
    U.S. carpet bombing of, 13, 290
    U.S. embargo on scrap metal to, 24
    U.S. "moral embargo" on aircrafts to, 23
    U.S. oil embargo on, 151–3, 257
    U.S.'s informal talks with, 69–74, 96,
        259
    voting rights in, 101
    war game played by, 166–8, 191–2
    wartime censorship of, 12
    war with U.S. seen as inevitable by, 20
    in withdrawal from League of Nations,
        46, 61–4
    women in, pre–Pearl Harbor, 5–6, 53,
        213–14
    in World War I, 16

Japan (*continued*)
  World War II surrender of, 291
  writing system of, 41, 42
Japan, war plans against U.S., 171
  delay until 1942 considered by, 226
  Final Proposal and, 260
  Ishikawa's plan, 126–7
  Japan's material shortages and, 226–7,
    237–8
  Navy General Staff's ambivalence
    about, 222
  Plan A and, 228, 236, 238, 239, 243, 244,
    246–7, 248, 249, 259
  Plan B and, 236–7, 238, 239, 243, 244,
    246–7, 249, 250, 259, 260, 263, 264,
    265, 267, 281
  securing goods for, 224–5
  September 6 resolution and, 175–6, 201,
    204, 210, 212, 214–15, 219, 224
  Tojo's ambivalence on, 230, 231–3
  see also Pearl Harbor, Japanese attack on
Japanese Americans, in internment
    camps, 280
Japanese language, 19
Japan's Crisis (Ishikawa), 126
Japan Youth Center, 64–5
Jiangsu, 206
Jilin, 45
Julius Caesar (Shakespeare), vii
Justice Department, U.S., 151

Kabukiza, 109
Kaga, 106
Kagoshima, 106, 235, 290
Kamensky, Boris, 285
Kamikaze aviators, 50–2, 246, 284–5
Karachi, 51
Kase Toshikazu, 109
Katori, 86
Kaya Okinori, 217, 219, 220–1, 223, 225,
    226, 229, 230, 231, 232–3, 238–9
Kazami Akira, 122
Kearny, 255
Kellogg-Briand Pact, 15
Kicho, 115
Kido Koichi, 56, 118, 175, 176, 187–8,
    209–11, 214, 215, 273–4, 276, 286

Kido Takayoshi, 211
Kinko Bay, 166, 235
Kishi Dozo, 211
Knappertsbusch, Hans, 285
Knox, Frank, 117
Kobe, 13
Koga Mineichi, 135
Kokumin Shimbun, 168
Konoe Atsumaro, 33, 42
Konoe Fumimaro, 23–42, 57, 59, 60, 66,
    68, 85, 93, 102, 104, 110, 111, 120, 121,
    174, 175, 177, 178, 190, 196, 218, 243,
    275, 292
  as ambivalent about China, 38
  attack on Singapore opposed by, 112
  attempts to dissuade Tojo from war,
    196–7, 200–1
  at commemoration ceremony of
    Japanese imperial house, 55
  confidence of, 32
  declined to be in cabinet, 47
  end of China War desired by, 32–3, 185
  "Essentials" plan and, 172, 173
  and FDR's neutrality proposal, 147–8, 156
  as impatient with Chiang, 38–9
  influenced by fascism, 34, 137–8
  influenced by Marxism, 33, 34
  Japan's diplomatic policy with U.S.
    discussed by, 136–7
  Marco Polo Bridge Incident and, 29–30,
    47
  military government maximized by, 11
  occupation of French Indochina
    approved of by, 128, 130, 134, 140,
    151–2
  at Paris Peace Conference, 34–6, 61
  as picky about food, 28–9
  popularity of, 28, 29
  proposed summit with, 155–7, 159,
    160–3, 169–70, 171, 179, 180, 186, 187,
    188, 189–90
  resignation considered by (first), 52
  resignation of first cabinet of, 52
  resignation of second cabinet of, 141
  resignation of third cabinet of, 214
  at Tekigaiso Conference, 202–4
  in tension with Matsuoka, 67, 72, 74–5,
    111, 239

Tojo's desire to remove from office,
208–9, 210
Tojo's meeting with Higashikuni
arranged by, 178
travel book published by, 36–7
troops sent to northern China by, 30–1
upbringing of, 33, 34
war with Soviet Union opposed by, 115,
134
war with West opposed by, 11, 187–8,
192, 196–7
Konoe Fumitaka, 37–8
Korea, 18, 40, 41, 42, 48, 80, 95, 159, 289
Kuomintang, see Guomindang
Kuroda Kiyotaka, 84
Kuroshima Kameto, 234, 235, 236
Kurusu Saburo, 51, 242–6, 249–53, 255,
258–9, 275–6, 284
deadline for diplomacy given to, 265, 281
exchange of peace messages desired by,
285–6
expulsion from U.S., 279, 281, 283–4
Hull's meetings with, 250, 251–3, 257–8,
259, 261–4, 266–8, 271–3, 275, 279–80
as ignorant of Pearl Harbor, 279–82
in meeting with FDR, 250, 251
withdrawal from French Indochina
desired by, 258
Kwantung Army, 43–4, 46, 101
Kyoto, 81

Laos, 12
lead, 224
League for the Elimination of Political
Parties, 64
League of Nations, 15, 16, 36, 46, 61–4, 99,
130, 289
Le Corbusier, 50
Lend-Lease Act, 27, 117, 155
Liaodong Peninsula, 41, 42, 45
Libya, 108
Lincoln, Abraham, 99
Lohmeyer, August, 207
London Economic Conference, 263
London Naval Conference, 99–100, 126,
156, 221
Loti, Pierre, 77

Luftwaffe, 24, 108
Lytton Commission, 62, 63–4

MacArthur, Douglas, 143
Madama Butterfly (Puccini), 77
Madame Chrysanthème (Loti), 77
Makino Nobuaki, 270
Malaya, 3, 11, 52, 123, 127, 133, 143, 153,
208, 256, 279, 287
Malaysia, 11
Manchukuo, 40, 46, 56, 63, 65, 113, 186,
278
Manchuria, 25, 41–2, 62, 135, 151, 159, 209
Japanese invasion and occupation of, 18,
30, 45–6, 151, 159, 160, 171
Jews in, 65
Manchurian Incident, 43–4, 45, 61
Marco Polo Bridge Incident, 29–30, 47
Marshall, George, 183
Maruyama Masao, 18–19
Masaki Jinzaburo, 90
Matsukata Masayoshi, 122
Matsukata Saburo, 122
Matsumoto Shigeharu, 122, 155, 160, 218
Matsuoka Plan, see May 12 Plan
Matsuoka Yosuke, 24, 57, 58–69, 95–6,
104, 109, 147, 166, 179, 189–90
attack on Singapore desired by, 111–12,
114
on blitzkrieg diplomacy, 108
dismissal of, 141, 143, 152
Draft Understanding discarded by, 71
Hitler visited by, 58–9
Hull's criticism of, 113–14, 137, 138, 140,
141
and Japanese withdrawal from League
of Nations, 61–4
May 12 Plan of, 71–3, 112–13, 140–1
neutrality pact with Soviet Union signed
by, 58, 59, 65–7
neutrality pact with U.S. desired by, 112
obliviousness of, 114
and occupation of French Indochina,
128, 129, 130, 131–4, 136
at Paris Peace Conference, 61
poker skills of, 60, 98
response to U.S. drafted by, 140–1

Matsuoka Yosuke (*continued*)
  in tension with Konoe, 67, 72, 74–5, 111,
    239
  on Tripartite Pact, 112, 115, 246
  in U.S., 60–1
  war with Soviet Union desired by, 114,
    115, 127, 128–9, 132, 134
  as worried about Anglo-American
    retaliation against Japan, 124
May 12 Plan, 71–3, 112–13, 140–1
May Fourth Movement, 43
Meiji Constitution, 79, 81–2, 141, 176, 239
Meiji Palace, 131, 240, 291
Meiji Restoration and new regime, 34, 41,
    76–88, 90, 99, 116, 211, 214, 270, 274,
    286
Meiji Shrine, 215
Mein Kampf (Hitler), 103
mercury, 224
Metternich, Klemens von, 65–6
Midway, Battle of, 12, 284
Military Affairs Bureau, 126, 130, 175
Military Service Law, 48
Mill, John Stuart, 80
Millard's Review of the Far East, 36
Ministry of Health and Welfare, 212
Mitsubishi, 50
Mitsubishi Heavy Industries, 8
Miyagi Yotoku, 120, 211–12
Molotov, Vyacheslav, 66–7
Molotov-Ribbentrop Pact, 25
Mongolia, 25, 123
Mongols, 168
Monroe Doctrine, 43
Morgenthau, Henry, Jr., 151
Mothers of the Big Sky, 206–7
Mr. Smith Goes to Washington, 9
Munich Conference, 189
Mussolini, Benito, 4, 24, 38, 59, 118
Muto Akira, 125, 126, 130, 191
Mutsuhito, Emperor Meiji, 76–88
  meat-based diet endorsed by, 81
  peace poem read by, 176
Mutsu Munemitsu, 274
Myanmar, 11

Nagai Kafu, 5, 7, 13, 26, 39, 115–16, 141–2,
    154, 169, 206, 213–14, 290, 292

Nagano Osami, 102, 105, 127, 135, 140, 148,
    171, 173–5, 187, 191–2, 194–5, 198,
    199–200, 215, 220, 222, 223, 225, 229,
    232, 233, 234, 236, 239
Nagasaki, 97
Nagata Tetsuzan, 89, 90–1, 92, 93, 101
Nagato, 165, 278
Nagoya, 13
Nagumo Chuichi, 12, 268, 278, 287, 289
Nakahara Shigetoshi, 222
Nanjing, 31, 32, 33, 49, 190
Napoleonic Wars, 66
National Budget Bureau, 220
National Mobilization Law, 39, 126, 205
National Socialism, 16, 65, 137
Naturalization Act, U.S., 250–1
Naval Academy, 234
Naval Affairs Bureau, 126, 175
Naval Battle from Hawaii to Malaya, The,
    287
Naval Defense Policy Committee, 126
Naval War College, 168, 180, 234, 236
Navy General Staff, 39, 105, 124, 128, 130,
    180, 219–20, 222, 225, 236, 256, 276
Navy Ministry, 102, 103, 104, 124, 126,
    130–1, 156, 163, 197, 203, 229, 287
Nehru, Jawaharlal, 96
Netherlands, 10, 144, 173, 209, 248, 258,
    265, 266
Neutrality Acts, U.S., 27, 255
New Bureaucrats, 91
New East Asian Order, 38, 94
New European Order, 38
New Imperialism, 17
New Order Movement, 27, 52, 91, 211
New York Times, 110, 143, 169–70, 254,
    272
New Zealand, 143
NHK, 3, 31, 205–6, 253
nickel, 70
1940 Olympic Games, 49–50
1937 Paris Exposition, 50
Nixon, Richard, 55
Nogami Yaeko, 141
Nomonhan, battles in, 74, 123
Nomura Kichisaburo, 4, 28, 56, 67, 68–9,
    70, 71, 72, 73, 112, 118, 137, 143, 161,
    162, 177, 184, 187, 207, 242, 246, 250,
    258–9, 280

deadline for diplomacy given to, 247, 265, 281

desire to return to Japan, 243

détente with U.S. sought by, 258

expulsion from U.S., 279, 283–4

and FDR's neutrality proposal, 144–5, 146, 147, 157, 185

FDR's talks with, 247–8

Hull's meetings with, 193–4, 247, 248–9, 250, 251–2, 259, 263–4, 266–8, 271–3, 275, 279–80

as ignorant of Pearl Harbor attack, 279–82

in meeting with FDR, 250

withdrawal from Indochina desired by, 258

Northern Expedition, 44

North Pacific Fur Seal Convention, 221–2

Obata Toshiro, 89, 90

Ohashi Chuichi, 56, 57, 68, 71

Oikawa Koshiro, 104, 105, 130, 132, 138, 142, 147, 174, 190–3, 194–5, 197–8, 199–200, 201, 202–4, 209, 215, 225

oil, see petroleum

Okamura Yasuji, 89

Oka Takazumi, 103, 125, 126, 140, 203

Okinawa, 289, 290

Oklahoma, 12

Okubo Tomejiro, 168, 169

Okura Kihachiro, 78

Onishi Takijiro, 106, 107, 234, 235, 285

Open Door policy, 43, 70

Operation Barbarossa, 109–10, 113, 115, 116, 118, 120, 123, 270

Operation Changsha, 180

Operation Valkyrie, 290

opium, 41

Osaka, 13, 159

Oshima Hiroshi, 25, 109

Ott, Eugen, 120, 134

Ottoman Empire, 17

"Outline of National Policies in View of the Changing Situation," 171

"Outline of Proposed Basis for Agreement Between the United States and Japan," see Hull Note

Oyama Iwao, 76–7, 82–3, 84, 85

Oyama Sutematsu, see Yamakawa Sutematsu

Ozaki Hotsumi, 52, 120–1, 122, 135, 150, 151, 160, 165, 186–7, 211–12, 217, 218

Ozu Yasujiro, 40

Panama, 182

Paris Commune, 34

Paris Peace Conference, 34–6, 43, 61, 190

Parliament (Diet), Japan, 29, 61, 253–4

end of, 19

Pearl Harbor, Japanese attack on, 3–4, 12, 79, 105, 126, 127, 279

damage to U.S. ships in, 12

decision to attack, 13–14

diplomatic alternative to, 240–1

FDR's congressional speech on, 8–9

final decision on, 281

final preparation for, 278

Japanese planes lost in, 287

Japanese public celebration of, 3, 6–7, 8, 11, 13, 18, 286–7

Japanese public fear after, 8

midget submarine pilots chosen for, 256–7

Naval General Staff's opposition to, 236

Yamamoto's plan for, 21, 106–7, 234, 235, 236, 240

Peers Academy, 188

Perry, Matthew, 145

Pétain, Marshal, 179

petroleum, 26, 27, 28, 70, 129, 143, 144, 148, 166, 177, 224, 237–8

Philippines, 11, 12, 70, 97, 143, 153–4, 166, 243, 256, 265

Pius XII, Pope, 114

Plan A, 228, 236, 238, 239, 243, 244, 246–7, 248, 249, 259

Plan B, 236–7, 238, 239, 243, 244, 246–7, 249, 250, 259, 260, 263, 264, 265, 267, 281

"Plan for the Facilitation of the Conclusion of War with the United States, Britain, and the Netherlands," 277

Poland, 25, 130

Port Arthur, 7, 41
Porte des Humbles, La (Bloy), 142
Powell, Michael, 157
Pressburger, Emeric, 157
Prince of Wales, 157
Privy Council, 100, 130, 131, 132, 273–4
protectionism, 113
Puccini, Giacomo, 77
Pushkin, Aleksandr, 20

Qing China, 18, 43, 86
Qingdao, Battle of, 207
"Queen of Spades, The" (Pushkin), 20

Rankin, Jeannette, 9
Red Arrow, 58, 65, 122
Rehe (Jehol), 46
"Remember Pearl Harbor," 9
Reuben James, 255
Rhineland, 16
Ribbentrop, Joachim von, 216
rice, 4, 123
Rockwell, Norman, 94
Rokumeikan, 77–8, 109
Rommel, Erwin, 108
Roosevelt, Franklin D., 26, 57, 66, 67–8,
    69, 99, 138, 241, 247, 262, 265, 275–6
  and aid to Britain, 145, 241
  and aid to Soviet Union, 117–18, 145
  alleged conniving to get U.S. into war,
    266
  alleged foreknowledge of Pearl Harbor
    attack of, 282
  Churchill's Newfoundland meeting
    with, 157–8, 159, 181
  congressional speech on Pearl Harbor
    by, 8–9, 282, 283
  "Four Freedoms" speech of, 93–4
  isolationist opposition to, 27
  Konoe's proposed summit with, 155–7,
    159, 160–3, 169–70, 171, 179, 180, 186,
    187, 188, 189–90
  Nomura's talks with, 247–8, 271–3
  peace message of, 285, 286
  proposal for neutrality with Japan,
    144–5, 146–8, 154–5, 156–7, 185, 269

  radio talk on fight against Hitler by,
    182–3
Roosevelt, Theodore, 41, 95
Roosevelt administration, 23, 72, 113, 118,
    143, 281
Rousseau, Jean-Jacques, 80
rubber, 70, 123–4, 145
Russia, 41, 42, 43, 62, 95, 96, 148, 222, 274
Russo-Japanese War, 7, 11, 20, 61, 83, 96,
    97, 105, 148, 176, 213, 215, 225, 235

Saigo Takamori, 82–3
Saionji Kinkazu, 122, 142, 155, 160, 163,
    172, 186–7, 206, 210, 217
Saionji Kinmochi, 28, 33–4, 36, 38, 47, 52,
    65, 66, 122
Saipan, 289
Saito Mokichi, 7
Sakakura Junzo, 50
Sakhalin, 42
Same Character Society, 42
Samoa, 153
Sandburg, Carl, 99
Sato Kenryo, 126, 170
Sato Naotake, 270
Satsuma, 82, 83, 90
Saturday Evening Post, 94
Sawamoto Yorio, 132, 192, 195, 196, 229
Selective Training and Service Act, U.S.,
    157, 181
Senate, U.S., 152, 182, 255
Sendai, 13
September 6 resolution, 175–6, 201, 204,
    210, 212, 214–15, 219, 224
Shakespeare, William, vii
Shandong, 43
Shanghai, 31, 42, 95, 120
Shibushi Bay, 166
Shidehara Kijuro, 45, 237
Shimada Shigetaro, 217, 225, 228–9, 230,
    231, 235, 236, 277
Shimada Toshio, 254
Shimonoseki, Treaty of, 41, 274
Shintoism, 80–1, 82
Shiratori Toshio, 55
Shiseido, 6
Siberia, 123

Singapore, 11, 57, 111–12, 114, 139, 143, 148, 153, 208, 281, 287

Sino-Japanese agreements, 46

Sino-Japanese War, 18, 20, 38, 41, 42, 83, 274

Smedley, Agnes, 120–1

Smetanin, Constantin, 115

Snow White and the Seven Dwarfs, 291

Social Darwinism, 17

Soldier U (Ushiotsu Kichijiro), 48–9, 151, 159–60, 256, 287–8, 292

Sorge, Richard, 119–22, 134–5, 149–51, 159, 165, 183, 187, 207–8, 211–12, 217

"Soul of Man Under Socialism, The" (Wilde), 23

Southeast Asia, 10–11, 18, 24, 27, 127

South Manchurian Railway, 43, 61, 65, 122

South Seas, 265–6

Soviet Union, 26, 30, 47, 74, 103, 116–18, 141, 158, 166, 171, 180, 184, 266
    Finland attacked by, 117, 130
    Five-Year Plans of, 44–5
    German invasion of, 109–10, 113, 114, 115, 116, 117, 118, 119, 120, 123, 127, 143, 149, 150, 151, 185, 219, 266, 270
    Japanese neutrality pact with, 58, 59, 65–7, 108, 112, 115, 150–1
    Matsuoka's desire for war with, 114, 115, 127, 128–9, 132, 134
    rise of Bolshevism in, 17
    Sorge's spying for, *see* Sorge, Richard
    U.S. aid to, 117–18, 145

Spain, 16

Spanish-American War, 97

Spanish Empire, 17

Special Higher Police, 53–4, 168

Squadron Group, 105

Stalin, Joseph, 30, 58, 59, 66–7, 109–10, 117, 119, 130, 141, 150, 151, 155, 158, 160, 183
    as paranoid about Japanese invasion, 160

Stark, Harold, 144

State Department, U.S., 151, 186, 266–8, 272, 280

steel, 231

steel ingot, 224

Steel Control Association, 109

Steinhardt, Laurence, 67

Stimson, Henry, 66, 117

Sugiyama Hajime, 14, 111, 128–9, 130, 133, 137, 139–40, 171–2, 173, 174, 180, 187, 194, 199–200, 210, 215, 220, 230, 231, 232, 237, 239

Sugiyama Memo, 14–15

Sumatra, 180, 208, 287

Sun Tzu, 232

Sun Yat-sen, 36, 40, 42

Supreme War Council, 240

Suwa Nejiko, 51, 285

Suzuki Teiichi, 110, 118, 202, 210, 219, 223–4, 226–7, 230, 233

Taisho Democracy, 86

Taiwan, 18, 40, 41, 265, 289

Takamatsu Nobuhito, Imperial Prince, 276, 277, 285

Takarazuka, 206–7

Takeuchi Shigeyo, 213

Takeuchi Yoshimi, 7

Tanaka Shin'ichi, 125–6, 127, 234

tariffs, 17, 41

Tekigaiso Conference, 202–4, 208

Thailand, 123, 131, 171, 266, 272, 276, 288

"Three Are Good Friends, The" postcard, 24–5

Time, 102

Times (London), 51

tin, 70, 123, 145

Tinian, 289

Togo Heihachiro, 215, 216

Togo Ise, 270

Togo Shigenori, 216, 219, 225, 227, 228, 230, 233, 237, 238, 240–1, 243, 247, 248, 249–50, 258, 259, 260, 261, 264–5, 269, 270, 275, 276, 281, 282, 286

Togo Shrine, 215

Tojo Hideki, 9–10, 89, 90, 92, 93, 97, 98, 110, 118, 138, 139, 147, 171, 191, 217–18, 219, 222, 229, 239, 243, 260, 266, 276, 286
    as ambivalent about Japanese aggression, 10–11, 220, 221, 230–3, 244–5, 285
    attack on Soviet Union opposed by, 129

Tojo Hideki (*continued*)
  as delighted by Draft Understanding, 56
  desire to remove Konoe from office,
    208–9, 210
  Diet speech on peace by, 253–4
  free trade desired by, 228
  Konoe's attempts to dissuade from war,
    196–7, 200–1
  made prime minister, 214–17
  occupation of French Indochina
    approved by, 129, 130, 133
  Pearl Harbor attack defended by, 9, 10,
    15, 285–6
  resignation of, 289–90
  synthetic oil desired by, 167
  war game and, 167–8
  war preparations desired by, 178–80,
    187, 196–7, 199, 200–2, 204, 208–9
Tokugawa shogunate, 17, 41, 80, 81, 82,
  84, 145
Tokyo, 13, 25, 30
  air raid on, 290
  Americans in, 255
  nearly successful military coup in, 29,
    47, 91–2
  sewage problem of, 168–9
Tokyo Foreign Office, *see* Foreign
  Ministry
Tolischus, Otto D., 110, 170, 254
Tomita Kenji, 203, 204
Total War Research Institute, 164–8, 177
Toyoda Teijiro, 132, 142, 143, 146–7, 157,
  186, 188, 189, 190, 193, 204, 216
Trans-Siberian Railway, 58
Treasury Department, U.S., 151
Tripartite Pact, 4, 10, 24–5, 40, 56, 58, 59,
  65, 66, 67, 70, 103, 106, 110, 112, 115,
  118, 135, 142, 143, 148, 163, 173, 178,
  190, 201, 227, 228, 245, 246, 248, 249,
  250, 251, 252, 261–2, 263, 273
Triple Intervention, 42, 274
Tsukada Osamu, 128, 129, 130, 190–1,
  233–4, 236, 237
Tsukagoshi Kenji, 50, 285
Tsushima, Battle of, 95, 97
Turkey, 165
Tutuila, 155
Twenty-One Demands, 43

Ugaki Kazushige, 215
Umeya Shokichi, 42
United Press, 62
United States, 16, 20, 26, 55, 67, 103, 129,
  131, 132, 133, 135, 136, 162, 173, 209,
  222, 255–6
  as assertive in Japanese affairs, 17
  Chiang aided by, 24, 26, 173, 237, 269,
    282
  and Draft Understanding, 56–7, 68, 71,
    73, 111, 112
  embargo on scrap metal to Japan, 24
  Hitler's declaration of war against, 9
  and Iceland, 180–2, 255
  industrial output of, 224
  Japanese meeting on policy with, 136–9
  and Japanese occupation of French
    Indochina, 139–40, 151, 269
  in Japanese war game, 166
  Japanese war plan against, *see* Japan,
    war plans against U.S.
  Japan's entering war with, 3
  Japan's informal talks with, 69–74, 96,
    259
  "moral embargo" on aircrafts to Japan
    by, 23
  and 1940 Olympics, 50
  oil embargo on Japan enforced by, 151–3,
    257
  as Open Door policy watchdog, 43
  post–Boxer Rebellion treaty and, 30
  racial prejudice in, 35, 37, 251
  rumors of war with Japan, 25–6, 105–7,
    108
Universal Declaration of Human Rights, 94
Ushiba Tomohiko, 122, 155, 177
Ushiotsu Kichijiro, *see* Soldier U

Vichy France, 139, 143
Victory Program, 183
Vietnam, 12
"Views of the Imperial Government," 281
Vukelic, Branko de, 120, 150, 217

Wakasugi Kaname, 71, 247–8
Wakatsuki Reijiro, 45, 101–2

Walker, Frank C., 57
Wallace, Henry, 281
Walsh, James, 57, 259
Wang Jingwei, 40, 44, 56, 70, 109, 185, 190, 246, 267
War Guidance Office, 187, 196, 198, 225–6, 230
Washington Conference, 15, 43, 100, 126
Welles, Sumner, 143, 144, 145–6, 185
white supremacy, 17
Wilde, Oscar, 23
Wilson, Woodrow, 35, 36, 99, 137, 251
Winant, John Gilbert, 9
World Federation of Education Association, 50
World War I, 15, 16, 87, 119, 184, 207, 271

Xuzhou, 206

Yamagata Aritomo, 79, 90
Yamaguchi, 60
Yamaguchi Yoshiko, 67
Yamakawa (Oyama) Sutematsu, 83–5
Yamamoto Isoroku, 20–1, 97, 98, 103, 104, 105, 135, 165, 195, 278, 282
    attitude toward death, 98–9
    early victories against U.S. deemed necessary by, 191–2
    gambling by, 98
    Pearl Harbor attack plan of, 21, 106–7, 234, 235, 236, 240, 257
    as worried about U.S. resolve, 222
Yamamoto Kumaichi, 234, 244, 281
Yamato spirit, 168
Yangtze River, 48
Yasukuni Shrine, 206, 216
Yijiang Gate, 49
Yokohama, 13, 279, 284
Yomiuri, 153
Yonai Mitsumasa, 52, 102–4, 105, 195, 274–5, 280
Yongding River, 30
Yoshida Shigeru, 237, 270–1
Yoshida Zengo, 25, 104, 198
Yoshihito, Emperor Taisho, 86, 88
Yoshizawa Kenkichi, 27–8
Yuan Shikai, 43
Yugoslavia, 108

Zero fighter plane, 8
Zhang Xuelliang, 47
Zhang Zuolin, 47
zinc, 224
Zionism, 65